Charles Pelham Villiers:
Aristocratic Victorian Radical

This book provides the first biographical study of Charles Pelham Villiers (1802–1898), whose long UK parliamentary career spanned numerous government administrations under twenty different prime ministers.

An aristocrat from a privileged background, Villiers was elected to Parliament as a Radical in 1835 and subsequently served the constituency of Wolverhampton for sixty-three years until his death in 1898. A staunch Liberal free trader throughout his life, Villiers played a pre-eminent role in the Anti-Corn Law League as its parliamentary champion, introduced an important series of Poor Law reforms and later split with William Gladstone over the issue of Irish Home Rule, turning thereafter to Liberal Unionism. Hence Villiers, who remains the longest-serving MP in British parliamentary history, was intimately involved with many of the great issues of the Victorian Age in Britain.

Roger Swift is Emeritus Professor of Victorian Studies at the University of Chester, United Kingdom.

Routledge Studies in Modern British History

For a full list of titles in this series, please visit www.routledge.com.

8 **Disability in Eighteenth-Century England**
   Imagining Physical Impairment
   David M. Turner

9 **British Student Activism in the Long Sixties**
   Caroline M. Hoefferle

10 **Philanthropy and Voluntary Action in the First World War**
    Mobilizing Charity
    Peter Grant

11 **The British Army Regular Mounted Infantry 1880–1913**
    Andrew Winrow

12 **The Chartist General**
    Charles James Napier, The Conquest of Sind, and Imperial Liberalism
    Edward Beasley

13 **The Great Church Crisis and the End of English Erastianism, 1898–1906**
    Bethany Kilcrease

14 **Opening Schools and Closing Prisons**
    Caring for Destitute and Delinquent Children in Scotland 1812–1872
    Andrew Ralston

15 **Charles Pelham Villiers: Aristocratic Victorian Radical**
    Roger Swift

16 **Women, Mission and Church in Uganda**
    Ethnographic Encounters in an Age of Imperialism, 1895–1960s
    Elizabeth Dimock

Charles Pelham Villiers: Aristocratic Victorian Radical

The Member for Wolverhampton, 1835–1898, and Father of the House of Commons

Roger Swift

LONDON AND NEW YORK

First published 2017
by Routledge
2 Park Square, Milton Park, Abingdon, Oxon OX14 4RN

and by Routledge
711 Third Avenue, New York, NY 10017

First issued in paperback 2018

Routledge is an imprint of the Taylor & Francis Group, an informa business

© 2017 Roger Swift

The right of Roger Swift to be identified as author of this work has been asserted by him in accordance with sections 77 and 78 of the Copyright, Designs and Patents Act 1988.

All rights reserved. No part of this book may be reprinted or reproduced or utilised in any form or by any electronic, mechanical, or other means, now known or hereafter invented, including photocopying and recording, or in any information storage or retrieval system, without permission in writing from the publishers.

Trademark notice: Product or corporate names may be trademarks or registered trademarks, and are used only for identification and explanation without intent to infringe.

British Library Cataloguing-in-Publication Data
A catalogue record for this book is available from the British Library

Library of Congress Cataloging-in-Publication Data
CIP data has been applied for.

ISBN 13: 978-1-138-33189-1 (pbk)
ISBN 13: 978-1-138-28835-5 (hbk)

Typeset in Bembo
by codeMantra

In memory of Dorothy Thompson

Contents

	List of figures	ix
	Foreword	xi
	Acknowledgements	xiii
	Introduction	1
1	The making of a Radical	8
2	The Member for Wolverhampton	31
3	The young Parliamentarian	51
4	The campaign against the Corn Laws	79
5	Interlude	115
6	The Cabinet Minister	158
7	The view from the backbenches	191
8	Gladstone and the Home Rule crisis	229
9	The Father of the House	263
	Epilogue	294
	Bibliography	303
	Index	319

List of figures

Frontispiece: 'Charles Pelham Villiers', Portrait by Sir Arthur Cope, colour, 1885, first exhibited at the Royal Academy and then placed in the Reform Club, Pall Mall, reproduced by kind permission of the Reform Club, London. xiv
1 'The Hon. Mr Villiers', Pen and ink drawing by A. Bickell, 1840, reproduced by kind permission of ©Wolverhampton Archives and Local Studies. 155
2 'Charles Pelham Villiers', Mezzotint steel engraving by J. Cochran, after Charles Allen Du Val, 28 February 1840, reproduced by kind permission of ©National Portrait Gallery, London. 155
3 'Charles Pelham Villiers', c. 1846. Oil on canvas. Anon, reproduced by kind permission of Charles N. Villiers, from his private collection. 156
4 'Charles Pelham Villiers', Photograph by W. & D. Downey, albumen carte-de-visite, mid-1860s, reproduced by kind permission of ©National Portrait Gallery, London. 156
5 'Caricature of the Right Hon. C.P. Villiers, MP', Lithographic print, colour, by James Tissot ['Spy'], in Statesmen Series, No. 123, *Vanity Fair*, 31 August 1872. 156
6 'The Late Right Hon. C.P. Villiers, Father of the House of Commons', black and white photograph by Whitlock Bros, Wolverhampton, c.1896, published in *The Graphic*, 22 January 1898. 157
7 Statue of Charles Pelham Villiers, by William Theed, in Snow Hill, Wolverhampton, 1879, reproduced by kind permission of ©Wolverhampton Archives and Local Studies. 157

Foreword

Charles Pelham Villiers was a leading radical Liberal in the Victorian era. For sixty-three years – from 1835 until 1898 – he was continuously an MP for the Borough of Wolverhampton. That was the longest span of uninterrupted parliamentary representation in British history. In the early Victorian period Villiers persistently campaigned for the repeal of the Corn Laws and he played an important, though under-appreciated, role in the triumph of Free Trade. Throughout his career he showed a sincere concern for the welfare of the working classes and, as a minister, he secured significant reform of the Poor Law. In the late nineteenth century his opposition to Irish home rule led him to break with Gladstone and become one of the pillars of Liberal Unionism in the West Midlands. Yet, despite the political influence that Villiers wielded throughout his long career, his role and achievements are virtually unknown today. His name is absent from the general histories of the Victorian era and he figures little more than incidentally in monographs that deal with issues with which he was closely involved.

There are various reasons why Villiers has been neglected. As an aristocratic cadet, he was somewhat overshadowed, in wealth, status and ministerial office, by his older brother, the Earl of Clarendon, who was Foreign Secretary in the 1860s. Yet as an aristocrat, Villiers seemed, in retrospect, a less-representative leader of radical Liberalism than middle-class mill owners, such as Cobden and Bright. Villiers, however, held views as advanced as theirs and his stance secured the loyalty of a constituency that was as industrial and as working class as any in the country. He was, moreover, a Cabinet minister – unlike Cobden – and a much more effective one than Bright.

There is another reason why Villiers has been largely ignored by historians: the lack of a comprehensive collection of his correspondence and papers. But Roger Swift, in this pioneering study of Villiers, has unearthed many hitherto unknown or un-consulted sources about many aspects of his career. They provide rich detail about the activities of Villiers in Parliament, in the Cabinet and in his constituency. This study is characterized by exemplary research and a thorough knowledge of the wider Victorian context. It not only restores Villiers to his rightful place in the pantheon of Victorian radicals but also throws new light on Victorian politics and society both in London and in the West Midlands.

Roland Quinault
Institute of Historical Research

Acknowledgements

This political biography of Charles Pelham Villiers has evolved from an occasional lecture delivered at the Centre for Victorian Studies at the University of Chester in 2007, from papers presented subsequently at the Gladstone Umbrella colloquium at Gladstone's Library, Hawarden, and from research conducted during an honorary visiting professorship at the Research Institute for Humanities at the University of Keele. A study of this kind inevitably draws upon the work of other scholars, to whom I owe a debt of gratitude and I trust that this is fully acknowledged in the notes and bibliography. It has also benefited from the support provided by various archive repositories, and I wish to thank, in particular, Alf Russell, Lisa Hale and the staff of Wolverhampton Archives and Local Studies; the Reverend Dr. Peter Francis, Warden and Chief Librarian, of Gladstone's Library, Hawarden; Jo Taplin-Green and the staff of the Archives and Special Collections Team at the London School of Economic and Political Science; Helen Burton, at the Special Collections and Archives, University of Keele, and the British Newspaper Archive. I also wish to thank the National Portrait Gallery, London, the Reform Club, and Wolverhampton Archives and Local Studies for granting permission to reproduce illustrations. I am particularly grateful for the advice, encouragement, and support provided by many academic friends and colleagues, most notably David Amigoni, Owen Ashton, D. George Boyce, Anthony Howe, Deryck Schreuder, and Roland Quinault, all of whom perused various drafts of chapters and made extremely helpful and incisive suggestions. I am also indebted to Mr Charles N. Villiers, the great-great-grandson of C.P. Villiers' younger brother, Henry Montagu Villiers, Bishop of Durham, not only for his great kindness and enthusiastic support but also for providing illustrations from his private collection. Indeed, his knowledge of the Villiers' family history has been of invaluable assistance. My greatest debt, however, is to the late Dorothy Thompson, mentor and friend, who first suggested that I embark upon this project, and to whom this book is dedicated.

Roger Swift
University of Chester

'Charles Pelham Villiers', Portrait by Sir Arthur Cope, colour, 1885, first exhibited at the Royal Academy and then placed in the Reform Club, Pall Mall, reproduced by kind permission of the Reform Club, London.

Introduction

> When, in the fullness of time, history shall be so revealed to posterity, Charles Pelham Villiers will stand out from among his contemporaries with a clearness far greater than it does now as that of the farseeing statesman who, with rare singleness of purpose, forgot himself in his zeal for the welfare of the people. It would be well if the House of Commons possessed more members of the type of the venerable statesman who has now gone to his rest.[1]

Thus wrote *The Times*, in a lengthy obituary of over four thousand words, on 17 January 1898, following the death of Charles Pelham Villiers (1802–1898) on the previous evening. Indeed, as the newspaper observed, Villiers had been a rare parliamentarian, with a long and distinguished parliamentary career spanning the reigns of four monarchs – George III, George IV, William IV and Victoria – and encompassing numerous government administrations under no fewer than twenty different prime ministers.[2] An aristocrat from a privileged background, Villiers was first elected to Parliament as a Radical in 1835 and subsequently served the constituency of Wolverhampton for an unbroken period of sixty-three years, and he remains the longest-serving MP for the same constituency in British history, as well as the oldest candidate to be returned at a parliamentary election. A staunch Liberal free-trader, Villiers played a pre-eminent role in the Anti-Corn Law League as its parliamentary champion, long before Richard Cobden and John Bright were elected to Parliament. Later, between 1859 and 1866, Villiers was an innovative President of the Poor Law Board in the Liberal Ministries of Palmerston and Russell and introduced the most important series of Poor Law reforms since 1834, helping to establish the Board as a major government department. Excluded from office by Gladstone in 1868, Villiers spent the final thirty years of his parliamentary career on the backbenches, but in 1886, he split with Gladstone over Irish Home Rule and, thereafter, was returned as a Liberal Unionist, ending his career as 'Father of the House of Commons' from 1890 to 1898.

Yet Charles Villiers remains one of the forgotten men of the Victorian political world, for his distinguished career, for which he declined both a knighthood and a peerage, has been largely neglected by historians, despite the fact that during his lifetime he was widely revered within and without Parliament as a Radical reformer, as the erection of statues of Villiers, raised by public subscription in Manchester and Wolverhampton, and the numerous obituaries published in the national and provincial press following his death illustrate. Indeed, in South Lancashire, Villiers' contribution to the repeal of the Corn Laws and his indefatigable efforts to combat the Lancashire Cotton Famine remained long in the public memory and live on in the streets named after him in the cotton districts.

Villiers has, however, defied serious biographical study, apart from brief sketches of his career provided by W.O. Henderson in a short article published in *History* in 1952,[3] and, more recently, by Anthony Howe in a succinct seven-page entry in the *Oxford Dictionary of National Biography*.[4] This neglect may in part be explained by the fact that, at first sight, Villiers is not easily accessible to the historian, for he left few personal records, the huge collection of private papers and correspondence that he amassed during his lifetime (including all the letters which he had received from his numerous political associates) having been destroyed on his instructions by his housekeeper, Maria Walsh, after his death. Moreover, and unlike some of his contemporaries, Villiers did not produce either a diary or an autobiography, whilst his *Political Memoir*, which provided the introduction to his *Free Trade Speeches*, edited by Agnes Lambert, a member of the Cobden Club, and published in two volumes in 1883,[5] predated the last fifteen years of his parliamentary career.

As this study illustrates, however, there is a body of primary source material (much of which has been largely untapped hitherto), which can provide varied insights into Charles Villiers' contribution to Victorian political life. These include Villiers' numerous contributions to parliamentary debates on economic, social and political matters – he spoke on 504 occasions in the House of Commons during his long career – as recorded in *Hansard*; his contributions to various parliamentary select committees as recorded in parliamentary papers; his extensive correspondence with Thomas Thornely, his fellow Liberal MP for Wolverhampton, and his surviving correspondence with some of his political contemporaries, most notably, but not exclusively, Cobden, Bright, Palmerston, Disraeli and Gladstone. Then there are references to, and reminiscences of, Charles Villiers in an extensive body of contemporary memoirs, diaries, autobiographies and biographies as well as national, provincial and local newspapers, all of which present valuable external perceptions of Villiers' life and work. Finally, and most importantly, there is the voluminous and hitherto unpublished correspondence (comprising over 600 letters) from Villiers to William McIlwraith, the Secretary of the Villiers Reform Club in Wolverhampton, between 1884 and 1898, which sheds much light on Villiers' relationship with his Wolverhampton constituency during his later career as well as his private views on contemporary political issues, including the question of Irish Home Rule and its divisive impact on the Liberal Party.

A second reason for Villiers' neglect by historians arises from his exclusion from Gladstone's cabinet in 1868, despite the undoubted successes of his earlier career. This denied Villiers – a modest man who never sought public office for its own sake – the opportunity to attain higher ministerial rank on the political centre stage and, consigned to the backbenches, he played no part in the formulation and delivery of Liberal strategies and policies during the heyday of Gladstonian Liberalism, which he witnessed, albeit with an increasingly critical eye, from the galleries. He was not, in short, one of the 'big beasts' of late-Victorian politics and has not, therefore, been considered to be a sufficiently attractive or important subject for historical study, unlike many of the leading players of the age, including Hartington, Forster, Morley, Chamberlain, Dilke, Rosebery and, of course, Gladstone himself.

A final explanation for the image of Charles Villiers as a 'forgotten Victorian' lies in the fact that many of his achievements were themselves minimised by some of his contemporary political opponents and have, correspondingly, been understated by historians. For example, Villiers' key role in the repeal of the Corn Laws and in the movement for Free Trade has been largely underplayed by historians, who have overly (and, admittedly, understandably) concentrated on the important contributions of Richard Cobden and John Bright as the leaders of the Anti-Corn Law League. Similarly, Villiers' role as a reforming Poor Law administrator has been largely ignored by historians of the English Poor Law who, whilst describing the important legislation passed during his tenure, have failed to consider – and in many cases to even mention – the man behind the legislation. Moreover, whilst Villiers served his Wolverhampton constituency faithfully throughout his parliamentary career, and was honoured by the borough accordingly, local historians – perhaps influenced unduly by his absence from Wolverhampton after 1875 (which was due largely to ill-health) – have understated and, in some instances, wholly misrepresented the true nature of his relationship with his constituency. Indeed, few people in Wolverhampton today are aware of the significance of the life and work of the politician whose statue still stands in the city's West Park.

It is for these reasons, perhaps, that the prognosis of *The Times* in 1898 has yet to be achieved. This study, the first comprehensive political biography of Charles Pelham Villiers, seeks to redress this anomaly by showing that his contribution to Victorian public life was greater than historians have been willing to concede hitherto. In essence, it adopts a narrative approach towards its subject, largely in order to illustrate both the continuities and discontinuities in Charles Villiers' lengthy political career, although discrete themes are also examined within this framework. Moreover, the deliberate focus throughout lies primarily on domestic politics, both local and national (and the interplay between them), due largely to the fact that although Villiers was not entirely uninterested in foreign affairs (where his elder brother George, Lord Clarendon, a Foreign Secretary of renown, was an undoubted authority), he rarely spoke in Parliament or wrote on foreign matters, unless these impinged on Free Trade issues. As a political biography, this study invariably concentrates on Villiers' *public* life; however, *inter alia*, it also sheds some light on the *private* man – of his family relationships, his social life, and his relationships with women, notably Catherine Mellish, but also Queen Victoria and London's society hostesses.

Thus, the first chapter examines, in the context of the contemporary political world in the aftermath of the Napoleonic Wars, the various influences which shaped the development of Villiers' emerging radicalism and reforming political agenda, which included Catholic emancipation, the repeal of the Corn Laws and Parliamentary reform, during his youth. Here, particular reference is made to his aristocratic and Liberal Tory upbringing; the privileged social and political circles in which he moved; his education at Cambridge; his affiliation, as a young lawyer, with Benthamite Radical groups in the Metropolis; his unsuccessful candidacy at the Kingston-on-Hull election in 1826; his courtship of Catherine Mellish, and his formative and influential experiences as an Assistant Poor Law Commissioner, which are placed in the broader context of the great Poor Law Inquiry of 1832–4.

The following chapter explores, in the context of local politics during a period of rapid urbanisation, the circumstances surrounding Villiers' election in 1835 as Radical MP for the recently formed, urban–industrial constituency of Wolverhampton, which became a Liberal stronghold during the Victorian period. It also examines his attitude towards his constituents and his radical electoral pledges, and explains why he, as an aristocratic outsider, was able not only to acquire the public confidence, achieving considerable popularity in the process, but also to consolidate his position in the constituency between 1835 and 1841.

Chapters 3 and 4, which complement each other, focus on Villiers' growing national reputation as a Radical reformer during the early Victorian period. Chapter 3 examines, in the context of the recent historiography of early Victorian Liberalism, the ways in which Villiers established a reputation as a leading Radical within Whig/Liberal circles in the House of Commons during the late 1830s and early 1840s. Particular reference is made to his role within the group of Philosophical Radicals with whom he initially identified, his relationships with his peers, and the significance of his contributions to parliamentary debates on a range of contemporary issues, including parliamentary reform, municipal reform, social policy, the New Poor Law, factory reform, education reform, and to the anti-slavery movement. By contrast, the fourth chapter provides a detailed analysis and re-assessment of Villiers' specific contribution to the movement for the repeal of the Corn Laws between 1837 and 1846, for which he acquired a national reputation as a champion of Free Trade. Placed firmly within the context of the historiography of the Anti-Corn Law League, this chapter examines Villiers' arguments in favour of repeal by reference to his speeches in both Parliament and the provinces, the difficulties and the opposition that he faced in the House of Commons from Tory and Whig Protectionists, his relationship with Richard Cobden and John Bright, and the significance of his contribution to both Corn Law repeal in 1846 and the wider free-trade movement.

Chapter 5 examines and assesses Villiers' fluctuating political fortunes in the years between 1846 and 1859, which for Villiers marked a somewhat frustrating period. Particular reference is made to the lack of recognition he received in the immediate aftermath of Corn Law repeal, to the efforts made by Cobden and Bright (which were blocked by Lord John Russell) to secure Villiers, first, a cabinet position and, second, the great county seat of South Lancashire (which he declined in favour of Wolverhampton, where he was pressured to stay), and Villiers' role in the final settlement of the Free Trade question in 1852. Other themes which are examined include Villiers' attitude to further parliamentary reform; his important role as chair of the Select Committee on Public Houses, in regard to the Licensing Question; his promotion to Judge Advocate General by Aberdeen (but without a seat in the Cabinet) and his role, in the broader context of the Crimean War, in the parliamentary furore surrounding Lord Lucan's demands for a court-martial; and his relationship with his Wolverhampton constituency. In so doing, this chapter sheds further light on Villiers' relationships not only with leading politicians such as Cobden, Bright, Russell, Palmerston, Disraeli and Gladstone, but also with Queen Victoria.

This is followed by a detailed examination and re-assessment of Villiers' contribution, as President of the Poor Law Board, with a seat in the Cabinet, to the Liberal Ministries of Palmerston and Russell between 1859 and 1866. By reference to the historiography of the English Poor Law, particular emphasis is placed on the important and successful series of Poor Law reforms which Villiers introduced – much admired by contemporaries, although much neglected by historians – in response to several crises, notably the American Civil War (which cut off supplies of raw cotton to the textile districts), the Lancashire Cotton Famine, and the problem of Metropolitan poverty (which he addressed with the assistance and support of Florence Nightingale). These reforms not only modernised the New Poor Law but also witnessed the acceptance of the Poor Law Board as a permanent part of the machinery of government (subsequently reshaped as the Local Government Board in 1871). The chapter also explores Villiers' contribution to the contemporary debate within the Liberal Party on parliamentary reform up to, and including, the Reform Bill of 1866, and his response to the changing face of Wolverhampton Liberalism. In so doing, this chapter sheds further light on Villiers' relationships with his ministerial colleagues, especially Palmerston (of whom he became less critical) and Gladstone, whose presence loom large in this study and with whom Villiers shared an increasingly mutual distrust.

By contrast, Chapter 7 explores and examines Villiers' political career as a Liberal backbencher between 1866 and 1885, by reference to a variety of themes. These include his stance on parliamentary reform during the debates of 1867; the reasons for, and his response to, his exclusion from Gladstone's cabinet in 1868; his opposition to some Liberal reforms during Gladstone's first and second ministries; his chairmanship of the Select Committee on Conventual and Monastic Institutions; and his support for women's suffrage. Villiers' iconic status in his Wolverhampton constituency, despite his absenteeism after 1874, is also examined, as well as his involvement in the social, cultural and political milieu of life at Westminster, where he was an immensely popular socialite, and the renewal of his relationship with Catherine Mellish. Paradoxically, these were the years when Villiers, although in the political wilderness, received numerous public accolades, both locally and nationally, yet also rejected Gladstone's offers of a knighthood and a peerage.

Chapter 8, which is placed firmly within the historiography of Irish Home Rule, provides a detailed examination and analysis of the causes, features and consequences of the split between Villiers and Gladstone in 1886 over the Home Rule question, as a result of which Villiers joined the Liberal Unionists. It explores, with particular reference to Villiers' extensive private correspondence with William McIlwraith, the Secretary of the Villiers Reform Club in Wolverhampton, several inter-related issues. These include the relationship between Villiers and Gladstone, Villiers' attitude towards Ireland and the Home Rule question, his arguments against Gladstone's Irish policy in the context of the debates of 1886–93, and the implications of his 'desertion' of the Liberal Party for his constituency, where he faced an unsuccessful press campaign mounted by local 'Gladstonites' to oust him as an MP.

The final chapter examines the twilight of Villiers' political career when, in declining health and increasingly reclusive, he was a much-revered 'Father of the House of Commons'. As such, it draws especially upon his letters to William McIlwraith, to a rare interview he granted the *Northern Echo* in 1895, and to his insightful address to the Cobden Club in 1896. These, and other sources, provide unique insights into his views on *fin de siècle* politics, both domestic and foreign, including Free Trade, 'Advanced Liberalism', Socialism and Imperialism. Reference is also made, through the *Gladstone Papers*, to the final correspondence between Villiers and Gladstone, which suggests that, at the end of their careers, they had at least accepted a grudging tolerance of one another. The circumstances leading up to Villiers' death in January 1898 and public responses to his passing are also examined, with particular reference to the numerous obituaries in the international, national and provincial press which, collectively, provide significant observations and assessments of his political career. Finally, the chapter also explores the furore surrounding the publication of his will, which showed Villiers, who had never married, to have been an extremely wealthy man, due largely to his relationship with, and inheritance from, Catherine Mellish, and which subsequently prompted questions in Parliament.

The concluding section provides a re-assessment of Villiers' parliamentary career, with particular reference to the light it sheds on the changing fortunes of the Liberal Party (and, indeed, on the personality and policies of William Gladstone) during the Victorian period. Consideration is also given to the value Villiers placed on his 'independence' as a Member of Parliament (which constrained his appointment to cabinet office); to his contribution to social and economic reform; to his role as a Black Country MP; to his essential paternalism and his emphasis on constitutionalism and gradualism in achieving reform; and to his principled and consistent support for radical causes which, though much admired by his contemporaries, was in many respects out of step with a changing political landscape during his later years.

Notes

1 *The Times*, 17 Jan. 1898.
2 These were Henry Addington (1801–4); William Pitt the Younger (1804–6); Lord Grenville (1806–7); Duke of Portland (1807–9); Spencer Percival (1809–12); Lord Liverpool (1812–27); George Canning (1827); Lord Goderich (1827–8); Duke of Wellington (1828–30); Lord Grey (1830–34); Lord Melbourne (1834, 1835–41); Sir Robert Peel (1834, 1841–46); Lord John Russell (1846–52, 1865–6); Earl of Derby (1852, 1858–9, 1866–8); Lord Aberdeen (1852–55); Lord Palmerston (1855–8, 1859–65); Benjamin Disraeli (1868, 1874–80); William Gladstone (1868–74, 1880–5, 1886, 1892–4); Lord Salisbury (1885–6, 1886–92, 1895–1902); Lord Rosebery (1894–5).
3 W.O. Henderson, 'Charles Pelham Villiers', *History*, 37 (1952), 25–39.
4 A.C. Howe, 'Villiers, Charles Pelham (1802–1898), Politician', *O[xford] D[ictionary] of N[ational] B[iography]*, online, 42282 (Oct. 2009).
5 C.P. Villiers, *The Free Trade Speeches of the Right Hon. Charles Pelham Villiers, M.P., with a Political Memoir*. Edited by a Member of the Cobden Club (London, 1883).

1   The making of a Radical

Charles Pelham Villiers was born on 3 January 1802 in Upper Grosvenor Street, London, during the reign of King George III and the premiership of Henry Addington, the first of the twenty prime ministers to hold office during Villiers' long life. His was an aristocratic background and upbringing, as the third son of the Hon. George Villiers and his wife, the Hon. Theresa Parker, who were married in 1798. Thomas Villiers, second Earl of Clarendon, was his uncle, whilst his mother was the only daughter of John Parker, first Baron Boringdon, and the sister of John Parker, second Lord Boringdon and first Earl of Morley. George and Theresa Villiers had ten children, three of whom died in infancy, and the surviving children, in addition to Charles, were his elder brothers, George William Frederick[1] and Thomas Hyde,[2] his younger sister, Maria Theresa,[3] and his three younger brothers, Edward Ernest,[4] Henry Montagu,[5] and Augustus Algernon.[6]

Charles Villiers' father, George Villiers, referred to by the family as 'The Governor', was a royal courtier and a great favourite of George III, and had been appointed Groom of the Bedchamber in 1784 and Paymaster of Marines in 1792. The King had also indulged Villiers, providing him with a private bounty of £400 per annum and accommodation for his family in Windsor Old Lodge and, from 1805, Cranborne Lodge. However, by 1810, and largely through incompetence, he had amassed debts in the Paymaster's Office amounting to £220,000 and resigned, whereupon his royal duties were transferred to the Prince Regent (later George IV), who nevertheless continued to have a soft spot for Villiers and his family. In 1812, supported by an allowance from his brother Thomas, George and his large family moved from Cranborne Lodge to Old Kent House, Knightsbridge, which they shared with the family of his wife's brother, Lord Morley.[7]

Charles Pelham and his elder brothers, George and Hyde, were educated initially in their convivial but frenetic home environment before attending a private day school in Kensington kept by the pioneering educationist and mathematician, Thomas Wright Hill (the father of the postal reformer, Rowland Hill), where Charles showed great ability in mathematics.[8] In 1818, at the age of sixteen, with civil service in India as a possible career, and supported financially by his uncle Thomas, the Second Earl of Clarendon, of

The Grove, Watford,[9] Charles Villiers was sent to the East India College at Haileybury. Here he attended lectures given by Sir James Mackintosh, the Scottish jurist, politician and historian,[10] and the Revd. Thomas Malthus,[11] passing his examinations 'with great credit' in May 1820,[12] although his health was subsequently considered too delicate for a career abroad. Charles was widely held to be the most brilliant of the Villiers brothers, but it was observed that he 'had a vein of hardness in his nature which made him the only "difficult" member of a singularly harmonious family'.[13] Whilst George and Hyde were very close, Charles, as the third child, often felt left out, and his mother, Theresa Villiers (known as 'Mrs George' within the family), a strong-minded and intelligent woman who, in view of her husband's financial difficulties and declining health, was largely responsible for bringing up the family, was once moved to express her wish 'with all my heart Charles was to take Orders. I cannot help thinking it would do him so much good'.[14] Later, his sister, Maria Theresa, observed that

> C [Charles] is one of those who one must love in spite of his faults and not on account of his virtues. He has many merits and great cleverness, and mixed up with merits and talent is a singular wrong-headedness and puzzle-headedness.[15]

Charles Villiers' childhood and youth coincided with a turbulent period in British history when, as J.L. Hammond once observed, 'The French Revolution had transformed the minds of the ruling classes, and the Industrial Revolution had convulsed the world of the working classes'.[16] When Charles Villiers was born, Britain and her allies were at war with Revolutionary France and Villiers was already thirteen years old when Napoleon was finally defeated at Waterloo in 1815, and he witnessed the celebrations in London on the Duke of Wellington's return from Belgium. Meanwhile, at home, Britain was struggling to come to terms with the profound social, economic and political consequences of industrialisation and increasing urbanisation, a situation exacerbated by wartime shortages and post-war dearth, distress and discontent. These were the years that witnessed the development of working-class consciousness, manifested in various forms of popular protest, including Luddism in South Lancashire, the West Riding and North Midlands in 1811–12, the Spa Fields Riots in London and the East Anglian Rising in 1816, and the Pentrich Rising in Nottinghamshire and Derbyshire in 1817.[17] 'Alarm' became the watchword of Lord Liverpool's Tory government, formed in 1812, which responded to what were perceived to be revolutionary threats with a range of reactionary measures,[18] using the military to suppress not only the Luddites but also erstwhile peaceful radical meetings, most infamously at St. Peter's Fields in Manchester in 1819 ('the Peterloo massacre'), suspending the Habeus Corpus in 1817, introducing the 'Six Acts' in 1820,[19] and, aided by the evidence of spies and informers, invoking the full penalties of the law against convicted ringleaders. These tumultuous years culminated in the Cato Street Conspiracy of 1820, an abortive attempt to assassinate the Cabinet, which Charles Villiers frequently recalled in his later years.

It was in the context of events such as these that, in July 1820, Charles Villiers followed his brothers George and Hyde to St John's College, Cambridge,[20] where his closest friends included Lord Howick (the son of the future Prime Minister, the third Earl Grey),[21] and Thomas Babington (later Lord) Macaulay,[22] with whom, amongst others, Villiers engaged in earnest conversations on the issues of the day,[23] despite the fact that he and his brothers were sometimes the butt of light-hearted jokes from Macaulay, an undergraduate at Trinity College, about the Johnonians.[24] Life at Cambridge also enabled Villiers to develop his debating skills and, alongside Macaulay, he contributed to the Union debates, which were then held in the back room of a coaching inn, the Red Lion, in Petty Cury, and which were often followed by dinner in various Cambridge hotels.[25] In 1822, Villiers was elected President of the Cambridge Union Society, becoming one of the first of many future Cabinet Ministers to attain this particular honour,[26] and graduated BA in 1823 and MA in 1827.[27] Of greater significance, however, was the fact that although the Clarendons were by tradition Tory, whilst at Cambridge the three Villiers brothers were converted to liberal causes, adopting the cry of 'Reform' – of the electorate, of civil and legal institutions, and of the social condition of the poor, whose distress was attributed in part to the Corn Laws of 1815, which had protected landlords and farmers (and their profits) from foreign competition by restricting imports of foreign corn. Charles Villiers, once described as 'a passionate radical, an ardent reformer, but cross-grained, malicious, with a sarcastic tongue that was to gain him many enemies in the course of his long parliamentary history',[28] was reputed to be the most radical of all three. Indeed, during the Queen Caroline affair of 1820, when George IV sought to attempt to divorce his wife, Caroline of Brunswick, and strip her of the title of Queen Consort through the Pains and Penalties Bill, Charles Villiers attended the proceedings in the House of Lords. The Queen had become something of a rallying point for many Radicals, who demanded parliamentary reform and disliked an unpopular Monarch, and Villiers returned to Kent House, apparently 'holding, of course, quite the wrong views', and praising the efforts of Henry Brougham in defending the Queen, whom he declared to be wholly innocent of the allegations against her, much to the consternation of 'Mrs George', an ardent supporter of the King.[29] Ironically, in the aftermath of the affair, Charles Villiers served as a royal page at the coronation of George IV in July 1821.

In May 1823, Villiers entered Lincoln's Inn, where he attended lectures by, and received private tuition in political economy from, the economist J.R. McCulloch.[30] John Stuart Mill later recalled in his *Autobiography* that, at the suggestion of McCulloch, Charles Villiers and his brothers George and Hyde were among former members of the Oxford and Cambridge debating societies and members of the Inns of Court who contributed to a weekly discussion forum in Chancery Lane, known as 'The Academics', which focused on contemporary political and economic issues, including the 'population question' debate between the political economists.[31] Sir Henry Taylor,[32] the dramatist and poet, who was an intimate friend and colleague of Hyde Villiers at the Colonial Office, provides an interesting description of Charles Villiers at this time:

> Charles, with still more wit than George (who however had not a little) was sarcastic and unpopular, but amongst friends very agreeable ... He was handsome, but in a feminine way; and in order to indicate the small value that he set upon such beauty he affected slovenliness in dress and respect of his person. He generally appeared in a threadbare coat which had lost one or more of its buttons, and Hyde said of him that he was a very good-looking fellow 'when he was picked and washed'. He was idle ... but he was shrewd and acute, and by living with instructed men he got the knowledge that can be so acquired; and pretending to nothing, paid for what he got by the interest he took in what others possessed, and by the keenness and brightness of his wit; in so much that he would have been as much missed in our circle as any other of us ... It was a mischievous wit, and made him many enemies. But on the other hand, I do not believe that it proceeded from any practical ill-nature. On the contrary, I have reason to know that there was in him no little kindness of disposition, carefully concealed.[33]

According to Taylor, Villiers and his circle were 'radical Benthamite doctrinaires; and were regarded by prudent people as very clever young men who were thwarting the gifts of Providence and throwing away their prospects of worldly advancement by audaciously avowing extreme and extravagant ideas'.[34] Villiers subsequently became personally acquainted with Jeremy Bentham, the founder of the creed of utilitarianism,[35] and the political economist James Mill,[36] and was thereafter associated with the Benthamite school of philosophic radicals, whose members included Sir William Molesworth,[37] George Grote,[38] Joseph Hume,[39] Thomas Perronet Thompson,[40] Charles Buller,[41] Edward Bulwer Lytton,[42] John Arthur Roebuck[43] and John Temple Leader.[44] Villiers was subsequently elected to the two key Benthamite societies, the Political Economy Club (founded by James Mill in 1821) and the London Statistical Society (established in 1824), and Finer has suggested that his aristocratic contacts made him doubly attractive to the radicals.[45] Thereafter, Villiers was to retain a lifelong association with the Political Economy Club, attending meetings regularly and occasionally chairing the proceedings, as both Frederick Harrison[46] and Lord Courtney[47] later recalled.

Encouraged by this Radical elite, Charles Villiers attempted to enter Parliament in the summer of 1826 when he accompanied his brother, Hyde, into Yorkshire, and whilst his elder brother successfully contested the venal borough of Hedon, Charles Villiers plunged at the last moment into a desperate contest as the 'third man' for the representation of Kingston-upon-Hull, a two-member constituency. This was a close-run election characterised by bribery, corruption and some disorder. Christopher O'Neill, an Irish landowner, stood for the Tories on a platform of Free Trade plus some modification of the Corn Laws but was against Catholic emancipation. It was claimed after the election that his campaign had cost him £12,000. Mr D. Sykes, the Whig candidate, was a local man, and was strongly supported by local subscription but also enlisted the help of out-voters from York. These were in fact 'proxies' voted in place of the fishermen who were away in the North Sea and who claimed monetary payments of between one and two pounds for their votes. Charles Villiers stood as a Liberal Tory under the banner of Canning and Huskisson on a Free Trade, anti-Corn Law, anti-Slavery and pro-Catholic emancipation platform.

The candidates attended the hustings on Friday 9 June. Villiers stated that he had long wished to fulfil the duties of a member of Parliament and had studied the law and the history of the country for three years in order to prepare himself for the task. He explained that he supported the changes in the Navigation Laws and Catholic Emancipation but, in a telling comment which he was to reiterate many times in his later political career, he emphasised that 'He was independent of government and should vote as his reason dictated on issues', showing in principle a dislike of 'party' labels.[48] The poll was taken on Saturday 10 June. The popular candidate, O'Neill, received 1,537 votes, whilst the Whig candidate, Sykes, came next with 1,138. Villiers was 'a good third' with 1,055 votes and claimed that his narrow defeat was due to his late start, the impact of out-voters, and other unspecified 'means of influence'.[49]

Despite his defeat, a dinner was held in Villiers' honour on Thursday 3 August in the Dog and Duck Tavern, Scales Lane, Hull, attended by fifty people and chaired by the Mayor, George Coulson, who, in regretting Villiers' defeat, paid tribute 'to the handsome manner in which he had come forward as a candidate'. In his reply, Villiers stated his dedication to the present Administration, 'which combines the rare qualities of talent, integrity, and a zealous wish to promote the welfare of the country'. In particular, he paid tribute to Canning, 'the most able diplomatist this country has ever produced', for amending Britain's relations with her European neighbours and for acknowledging the independence of the South American states; to Mr Robinson, the Chancellor of the Exchequer, for remitting many taxes; to Peel, for his reform of the criminal law; to Lord Bathurst, for his colonial reforms; and especially to Huskisson, for his economic and commercial policies. He then dwelt at some length on the evils of the Corn Laws and their contribution to popular distress, stating his confidence in the government to repeal them. He concluded by emphasising his willingness to stand again as a candidate for Hull if invited to do so.[50]

But Villiers had cut a very good impression in Hull, returning to the city for several weeks before departing on 13 October. During his stay, he was invited to the Mayor's Dinner on 30 September, where it was reported that the

Rev. J. Bromby, in an elegant speech, had praised the talents of Mr Villiers and, in raising a toast, had pledged himself to support Villiers at any future election. The *Hull Packet* observed:

> We do not ever remember to have met so young a man as Mr Villiers, with so many qualifications to represent a great commercial community, and indeed so popular has he become amongst all classes, and so high an opinion have all parties of his talents, that we doubt not at any future election he will be returned by acclamation.[51]

Like his elder brothers, Charles Villiers was extremely well-connected socially and politically, which was to his advantage in his subsequent career. George Canning, Liberal Tory Foreign Secretary from 1822 and short-lived Prime Minister in 1828, then at the height of his fame, and a close friend of Lord Morley, was a frequent visitor to Kent House and his influence helped to secure posts for both George and Hyde Villiers on their leaving university (in the diplomatic and colonial services respectively). Moreover, Canning's conversations helped to foster Charles Villiers' interest in politics and he often frequented the galleries of the houses of parliament to witness the proceedings. Born of a family which combined high rank and royal patronage with intellectual distinction, Villiers' parentage alone was a passport to all that was best in contemporary political and social circles, where he soon became a great favourite for his conversation and conviviality. He was a frequent and welcome guest at Holland House, the London residence of Lord and Lady Holland, which was then in its ascendancy, according to Benjamin Weinstein, 'as an epicentre of political Whiggery and English cosmopolitanism, where politics and society were inseparable';[52] at Lord Cowper's residence at Panshanger House in Hertfordshire; and at Lord Lansdowne's Wiltshire home at Bowood. The charmed circles there were essentially but not absolutely aristocratic and the society of Holland House, in particular, included distinguished figures such as Henry Brougham, Sir Walter Scott, Lord Byron, Sydney Smith and, later, Charles Dickens. As G.W. Russell later observed, such an environment 'presented every variety of accomplishment and experience and social charm, and offered to a man beginning life the best conceivable education in the art of making oneself agreeable', adding that 'for that art Mr. Villiers had a natural genius'.[53]

Indeed, Charles Villiers quickly established a reputation in social circles not only for his intellect and conversation but also as a popular 'man about town' and Regency 'Dandy', the outward manifestations of which, given his penchant for wearing tail-coats with high collars and shirts with frills, Villiers was to maintain for much of his life.[54] He also fell in love. The object of his affection was Catherine Mellish, a beautiful and rich heiress, and an acquaintance of Theresa Villiers,[55] who lived at Hammels Park, Hertfordshire, close to the Clarendon estate at Watford. Catherine's father, the late John Mellish, Esq., MP for Great Grimsby, had belonged to a wealthy family of landowners, bankers and politicians of Nottinghamshire,[56] and had been murdered by highwaymen on Hounslow Heath in April 1798.[57] John Mellish had bequeathed his entire estate – valued in 1798 at £120,000 – to Catherine, his only child, then two years old, and this legacy was confirmed by the Court of King's Bench in 1824, following a family dispute.[58] Charles and Catherine embarked upon a passionate affair, the nature of which only fully came to public light after Charles Villiers' death in 1898, when the *Evening Telegraph* published an article entitled 'The Romance of Mr Villiers: A remarkable and delightful story'.[59] This carried an interview with an old (and unnamed) lady friend of both Catherine and Charles, who recalled that they were once engaged to be married but that Catherine was very wealthy whilst Charles was then relatively poor, and when Catherine joked that he only wanted her money, which he refuted, a lover's tiff ensued and they called off the marriage. They both subsequently resolved never to marry and remained single, but were, in private, both still passionately attached to one another. The break-up of this relationship appears to have had a profound effect on Villiers, who remained a bachelor for the rest of his life,[60] although, as we shall see, there was to be a remarkable twist in this particular tale in later years.

In May 1827 Villiers was admitted to the Bar by Lincoln's Inn, and went on the Western Circuit (including Wales), and in 1830 he was appointed Secretary to Sir John Leach, the Master of the Rolls and a friend and confidant of George IV.[61] Two years later, through the influence of Leach, he was appointed an Examiner of Witnesses in the Court of Chancery. This post, which he retained until 1852, provided him with sufficient financial security to support his subsequent political career, although his brother George had also provided him with an annual allowance after their father's death in 1827. This allowance was the source of some temporary friction within the Villiers family,[62] although in 1838, when George (who was now forging a distinguished diplomatic career and reputation as Minister to Spain during the Carlist Wars) succeeded to the title of fourth Earl of Clarendon, he granted Charles (now designated 'the Honourable Mr. Villiers'), and who had always worried about money, a voluntary annual allowance of £300 for life.[63] Nevertheless, life for Villiers as an Examiner of Witnesses was hardly ideal, as the journalist and rural commentator Alexander Somerville, a fellow Free-Trader, later recalled in 1846:

> In an apartment sombre and far from healthful, in the Old Buildings, Lincoln's-inn, sits a barrister every day, save for about six weeks in the year, during most hours of the day, devoting himself to the dull drudgery of an examinership in the Court of Chancery ... Why, burrowing in that dark place, in that office of drudgery, do we find one of a noble family, the bearer of an aristocratic name, the possessor of talents higher in order than any entered by nature save on nature's own nobility? We may only answer this by saying that the Hon. Mr. Villiers has no more honourable

part in name or nature than that desire for independence which, in the absence of an independent fortune, has led him to work for his subsistence, while political subservience might have procured for him, as for many others with less family influence and far less ability than his, higher honours and greater wealth.[64]

In the meantime, whilst Villiers was ensconced in Chancery Lane, two of the causes for which he had earlier campaigned at York were realised. First, in 1828, Lord John Russell's Bill for the repeal of the Test and Corporation Acts, which discriminated against Protestant Dissenters, was passed by Parliament and, in 1829, after a six-year campaign by Daniel O'Connell and the Catholic Association, Catholic emancipation was secured by the Catholic Relief Act. Then, with the fall of Wellington's administration in November 1830 and the advent of Lord Grey's Whig Ministry, and against the background of extensive extra-parliamentary agitation by middle- and working-class Radicals, supported by the provincial press, parliamentary reform was eventually realised when Russell's Reform Bill, first introduced in March 1831, was passed – at the third attempt – by the House of Lords in June 1832.[65] The Great Reform Act essentially extended the franchise to the middle classes, virtually doubling the size of the electorate to just over 800,000 in a population of 24 millions. Moreover, the redistribution of seats swept away many (but not all) rotten and pocket boroughs and provided forty-two new towns and cities in the industrial and manufacturing districts with parliamentary representation for the first time.[66] Ironically, one of the corrupt pocket boroughs to be disenfranchised was the two-member constituency of Wootton Bassett, which had long been jointly controlled by the Clarendon (Tory) and Bolingbroke (Whig) families, and which had briefly provided Hyde Villiers with a seat in 1830–1.[67] For the Whigs, the Reform Act was a triumph, having preserved landed influence by admitting the middle classes into the political establishment, but for the Radicals, and particularly for working-class Radicals (who regarded the Act as a sell-out), it was merely a starting point, a means to further electoral reform, for as Charles Villiers duly observed, the distribution of seats remained unrepresentative of the populace, voting remained open, bribery and corruption still existed, and working people were still disenfranchised.[68]

However, in August 1832, Villiers was offered an interesting, if temporary, distraction from his labours at the Court of Chancery when, through the influence of Hyde Villiers and Nassau Senior, he was appointed as an Assistant Commissioner (for the Midland and Western counties) for the Poor Law Inquiry promoted by Lord Grey's Ministry. This appointment suited Villiers' intellectual interests and brought him for the first time into contact with the agricultural labourer and his condition, as well as with urban poverty, issues that he was to confront in his later career.[69]

By 1830 there had been mounting concern with the ability of the Old Poor Law to address the age-old problem of poverty, which had been exacerbated during the late-eighteenth and early-nineteenth centuries by the socio-economic dislocations arising from the agricultural and industrial revolutions. Moreover, rapid population growth and increasing urbanisation, coupled with cyclical fluctuations in trade and commerce which depressed working-class living standards, had made poverty more visible and the total cost of poor relief soared from £4 millions to £7 millions between 1800 and 1830.[70] This was a matter of particular concern in the southern agrarian counties of England, where the Speenhamland System of subsidising labourers' wages out of the poor rates had been widely practised since 1795, and it was perceived that whilst the Laws of Settlement served to immobilise surplus labour, the Old Poor Law in general encouraged pauperism, idleness, unemployment and discontent among rural labourers, of which the widespread Swing Riots of 1830–1, which frightened landowners and farmers, appeared an outward manifestation.[71]

The initial proposal for the Poor Law Inquiry originated with Charles Pelham's brother, Hyde Villiers, an influential Benthamite, who had established a respected reputation in Parliament as a reforming MP and had, in 1831, been promoted by Lord Grey from the Colonial Office to the position of Secretary to the Board of Control (the future India Office).[72] In January 1832, and encouraged by Nassau Senior, he wrote to his Under-Secretary (and friend) Lord Howick (the Prime Minister's son) suggesting the appointment of a Royal Commission to inquire into the operation of the Poor Laws.[73] Two months later, the government initiated the inquiry. Hyde Villiers and Senior subsequently influenced the membership of the Royal Commission, which co-ordinated the Inquiry, largely under the direction of Senior. Twenty-six Assistant Commissioners were also appointed, with a subsistence allowance of £1 per day plus travelling expenses, to gather the evidence upon which the Commission's final report and recommendations would be based. They were instructed to ask specific questions of magistrates, poor-law overseers, clergymen and employers within a standardised blueprint designed to both expose the deficiencies of the existing system and shape the final recommendations of the Royal Commission.[74] In this sense, as Boyd Hilton has observed, the New Poor Law was a preconceived measure, for, once in action, the commissioners clearly knew what conclusions they would reach.[75]

Charles Villiers was appointed on 8 August 1832 and duly visited parts of Warwickshire, Worcestershire, Gloucestershire and the Northern Division of Devonshire, conversing personally not only with overseers and other parochial officials but also with employers and labourers. These districts were partly agricultural and partly manufacturing and brought Villiers face-to-face with a world beyond the select confines of Knightsbridge, for he was to witness not only the realities of urban and rural poverty but also the weaknesses of the Old Poor Law in addressing this.

In general, in a lengthy, detailed and insightful report, Villiers observed that poor relief in each of these counties was regulated on the same general principle – to relieve all claimants according to their alleged actual necessities.

In each district, a separate table of relief had been drawn up by JPs for the guidance of overseers, although this varied according to the condition of the pauper and the price of bread. However, the variety of forms in which indoor relief was given varied from place to place. These included Poorhouses, which simply provided lodging for paupers settled in the parish or for the casual poor who were disabled, and which 'appear calculated to extend and confirm every bad habit among the poor',[76] and Workhouses, which were administered by a master or matron, provided a regular dietary need and subjected the inmates to some form of control. Of these, few (with the exception of those at Birmingham and Kenilworth) appeared to be well-run – 'the separation of the sexes and the prohibition of luxuries, such as snuff and tobacco, was a principle of management that appeared not to be understood, or indeed recommended' and 'whenever paupers become familiar with a workhouse life, it is with difficulty that they are induced to quit them'.[77] Nevertheless, Villiers observed that

> A very general desire was expressed amongst all classes with whom I conversed, that workhouses should be more generally used and more economically managed, and little doubt was entertained that a vast saving might be effected, not only by deterring men from applying for relief who will only receive it when awarded in money, but also by shortening the duration of their dependence, in many who would be unwilling to submit to the discipline which ought to be established ... To rescue individuals from the extreme consequence of want is perhaps all that the law can wisely undertake, and by establishments of this kind it appears possible to effect this with great economy.[78]

Some workhouses provided schools for the instruction of pauper children but these were largely inadequate, often consisting of

> a small outhouse attached to the workhouse, where a certain number of children of both sexes, from the ages of three to twelve, might be seen sitting on a bench, attended by an old male or female pauper who, having the reputation of being able to read, is expected to instruct the children.[79]

Villiers was, however, impressed by the establishment of an Asylum in Birmingham for the education of the infant poor, whose parents were unable to support them, and who were taught to read and write and then apprenticed to various masters, maintained by the parish at 2s.6d per head. Such initiatives, Villiers argued, 'raised the moral feeling of the working classes [and] affords the best check to pauperism and crime'.[80] Equally inadequate was the medical relief afforded to the poor, with doctors paid at the poorest rates and the poor badly attended, although there were some efficient local dispensaries at Coventry and Birmingham, a more general establishment of which Villiers regarded as 'most desirable' on the grounds that 'they appear to be admirably adapted and immediately applicable to large cities and their neighbourhoods and as being well calculated to check a fruitful source of pauperism'.[81]

Villiers also noted the existence of a variety of forms of out-relief for the able-bodied poor. These included monetary payments without labour, according to the single or married status of the pauper, or money with labour, where paupers were paid by the parish for work done, usually on the roads. Earnings were regulated so as to be lower than normal wage-rates for independent workers, which either de-motivated men from seeking independent employment and/or encouraged idleness and dependence.[82] There were also great variations and a lack of consistency, even within the same county, in the nature and scale of allowances provided by the parishes to pauper families. In Warwickshire, the printed scale allowed a man, wife and three children 8s.6d. per week, without work, yet at Leamington the allowance was 9s.6d. and at Stratford, 2s. per head. In some places, allowances were given for the first and subsequent children, in others, from the third child onwards. This was a general source of criticism from ratepayers, who held that monetary payments induced dependence on the parish and disincentivised labourers from seeking employment.[83] Drawing an implicit distinction between the honest and dishonest poor, Villiers, citing examples from Kenilworth, Pershore, Stow-on-the-Wold, Cubbington, Bedworth and Stratford, also noted that whilst some labourers supported themselves independently of the parish, others, not worse off, claimed relief.[84] However, where the Allowance system had been discontinued, 'the pauperism of the able-bodied has been prevented', as at Rugby, where a workhouse had been established and all paupers obtaining orders from JPs had been ensconced therein: 'restraint was imposed upon their liberty, regular work in the manufacture of sacking was exacted and the children of those who were unable to maintain them were also placed there' and, as a result, the annual poor rate had been considerably reduced from over £1,290 in 1819 to £343 in 1832,[85] and Villiers cited further examples from Warwickshire and Gloucestershire in order to illustrate the financial advantages of this system.

In the agricultural districts, Villiers was well positioned to observe and record the plight of the rural labourer in the aftermath of the Swing Riots. In Warwickshire he noted that there had been disturbances in 1830 and that 'the labourers are much demoralised, and the mode in which the Poor Laws are administered is notoriously bad'.[86] In Gloucestershire, Villiers acquired evidence from the labourers themselves. One pointed out that he had never claimed parish relief but knew many who, though not less well-off, were getting pay from the parish. Another labourer, thirty years old and unmarried, complained of his low wages, claiming that if he was married with a parcel of children he would be better off with either work or allowances for the children provided by the parish. Villiers provided some evidence to suggest that when farmers paid fair wages to their labourers, the men were more content and less inclined to disturbance, noting that one farmer, who paid his men £36.8s. per annum, had claimed that during the Swing riots over one hundred of his labourers offered to protect his property.[87] Villiers concluded that 'When the poor are not degraded by the Poor Laws ... they are well-disposed to rely on their own exertions', pointing out that some labourers at Kenilworth, Bedford and Stow had contributed to various friendly, benefit and provident societies designed to provide mutual assurance against sickness and old age, although it was noted that the parochial system was a disincentive for the poor to take advantage of such initiatives.[88]

A similar picture emerged in the Northern Division of Devonshire, a region largely dependent on agriculture, where Villiers observed that 'the more objectionable modes of applying the law are perhaps more uniformly adopted'.[89] Indoor relief was provided in parochial houses 'in a far worse condition than those in other counties', whilst out-relief payments were given to pauper children, who were then frequently apprenticed and billeted with a master at the age of nine. Villiers noted that wherever the poor rates had been misapplied, as at Tiverton, Crediton, Barnstable and South Molton, the influence on the poor was the same as elsewhere and illustrated 'the danger of entrusting to local arrangement the important and difficult business of providing for the unemployed poor', adding that every witness that he had examined 'was agreed upon the point of the enormous magnitude and extent of the evils arising out of the present system of maintaining the poor'.[90] Villiers also observed that in Devonshire, in particular, there was a 'very strong disposition' among some farmers and labourers to emigrate, especially to Canada and the United States, some succeeding and others failing, although, in general, he met with few people who considered pauper emigration to be a remedy for the problem of rural poverty and he doubted the value of schemes to encourage the poor to emigrate; these, he held, were counterproductive in that they were expensive and would potentially deprive this country of its best and most industrious labourers among the honest and able-bodied.[91]

Emphasising the importance of the Poor Law Inquiry to the agricultural interest, 'both as regards its present condition and its prospects', Villiers, in an analysis that provides insights into his developing critique of the agricultural economy which underpinned his later campaign for the repeal of the Corn Laws, observed:

> The increased demand for agricultural produce by an increasing population has long since rendered a resort to soils other than those of England a matter of necessity, and the English producer is exposed to a double disadvantage in having to compete with soils less exhausted than his own, and with fewer burdens to bear; prohibitive duties [Corn Laws] are imposed to protect the agriculturist from the produce of the continent, but the same protection is not afforded to Ireland, and that country is now the great source of agricultural depression; the population, however, of this country continues to increase; the necessity, for further importation will each year become more imperative, and agriculture consequently more depressed; and though the positive wealth of this country

> may be increased by this circumstance, since what is lost by agriculture will be more than recovered by commerce, manufacture and the general consumer, yet it is highly important, if possible, to prevent a sudden destruction of capital, and to preserve the labouring population from any unnecessary hardships.[92]

Villiers also noted that upon any failure in trade, the rural parishes were threatened with a return to the settlements of unemployed persons, whose recent occupations rendered them wholly unfit for agricultural service, and the congregation of masses of people, as in the manufacturing districts, by its tendency to promote vice and crime, added considerably to the rate upon the county, whilst adding that, from his inquiries in the rural districts, he believed that

> there is no redundancy of able and willing labourers, that the means for their employment exist, and if the present operation of the Poor Laws did not prevent the legitimate contact between employer and labour, that the latter would have ample means of maintaining himself, independently of all public support.[93]

In regard to the manufacturing districts of Warwickshire, Worcestershire and Gloucestershire, Villiers provided detailed reports on the operation of the Poor Law in each town that he visited,[94] noting that poverty was a particular problem in urban areas,[95] although his general conclusion in regard to the operation of the Poor Law in these districts was that

> In every division of these counties ... there may be found as many different systems as there are Acts of Parliament ... with little reference to the circumstances for which they are suited, and may succeed or fail, according to the character of the individual who may happen for the time being to administer them.[96]

Villiers duly painted a portrait of the nature of poverty and Poor Law provision in manufacturing towns of varying sizes and with different economic infrastructures. For example, in Coventry, the causes of distress were explained variously by unemployment, the reluctance of silk weavers to embrace mechanisation, competition from French weavers, and 'past improvidence and injudicious conduct at present'[97]; in Bedworth, poor trade contributed to the increase in the poor rate, coupled with 'improvidence among the people'[98]; at Nuneaton it was noted that there were many instances of men receiving more money in out-relief allowances from the parish than they were paid when in work[99]; at Atherstone, a felt-hat manufacturing town, poverty was attributed to drunkenness and the improvidence of workers.[100] At Birmingham, with a broad range of manufactures, low wages were in many cases subsidised by parish relief. This, according to Villiers, may degrade the mechanic, as it does the labourer; it may render him equally improvident and reckless in his habits, it may therefore give a stimulus to population and ultimately reduce the rate of wages in all employments where particular skill is required.

Pauperism here was 'very extensive', with between 6,000 and 7,000 persons 'in a state of great debasement, perfectly uninstructed and reckless and dissolute in their habits, and this must account for a great portion of the misery and pauperism in the town'.[101] At Stourbridge, a nail-making centre where production was based on the domestic system, the character of the people was said to be 'reckless and dissolute beyond belief, some ... living almost promiscuously, with large families' and workers and their children were frequently subsidised with parish allowances when in work, provided gross family income did not exceed 25s. per week. The workhouse was 'in a state of great filth and confusion'.[102] Villiers also noted that in these districts the truck system had been practised, 'and doubtless continues to be so, and the owners of the tommy shops, being the manufacturers, are frequently the persons who are expected to regulate the distribution of relief to their own men'.[103] At Worcester, a glove-making centre, the workhouse was well-run and much outdoor relief in kind (food and clothing) was provided. Here, poverty was variously attributed to the improvidence of the poor, early marriages, large families, low wages, and the reluctance of the poor, when employed, to save, thereby becoming dependent on relief.[104] Finally, at Tewkesbury, a lace-making and stocking-weaving town, distress was explained in terms of competition from other districts coupled with a surplus of apprentices, which overstocked the labour market and reduced wages, which were often subsidised by the parish.[105]

Villiers was also critical of the various persons and agencies delivering relief in these districts. Overseers, usually chosen annually, and of whom one-quarter were unable to write, were 'totally disqualified for the duty' and Villiers recommended the appointment of permanent paid overseers, as at Banbury. Select Vestries, whose members rarely possessed suitable qualities for the office, were 'unable to exercise a wise or an honest discretion ... in their distribution of relief they were partial or injudicious, in their attendance they were irregular, and in their system of management they were uncertain and inconsistent'. Open Vestries, where the ratepayers at large could attend, were described as 'more objectionable than select vestries'.[106] Villiers was also critical of the Magistracy, whose control over the distribution of relief had 'occasioned great discontent' because 'from their station and habits in life they are said to be generally unacquainted with the real condition of the poor' and were often irregular in their attendance and incompetent, especially in the boroughs, as at Kidderminster.[107] Moreover, Villiers acknowledged that the appointment of magistrates were so numerous and indiscriminate that 'all uniformity in practice or permanent improvement is rendered hopeless' and demanded that only competent and responsible persons should be invested with a jurisdiction for administering the laws affecting the poor.[108]

In particular, Villiers was highly critical of the Laws of Settlement, noting the arbitrary operation of these laws, the abuse of the system by some parishes in removing the poor, and the enormous expense which it occasioned. In recommending the repeal of the Laws of Settlement, he pointed to two major consequences of the present law: first, its partial and injudicious operation upon individual property; second, the impediment it presented to the poor man seeking the best market for his labour. Of equal concern were the variety of means of acquiring settlement, which also contributed to abuses and inconsistencies, and which included settlement by birth, by marriage, by apprenticeship if resident for forty or more days under the terms of an indenture, by hiring and service for twelve months, and by occupation for twelve months of a tenement valued at £10 annually.[109]

In concluding his report, Villiers stated,

> though I found in every place which I visited a deep sympathy with the interests and distress of the poor, I met with no dissentient voice on the expediency of immediately effecting an extensive change in the administration of the Poor Laws.

He accordingly recommended: first, the framing of regulations for a revised system which would be 'permanent and uniform throughout the country'; second, the establishment of a Central Board, 'with complete control in the general execution of the Poor Laws'; third, district establishments to implement and co-ordinate poor relief, including a workhouse for the reception of the poor, with inmates classified according to age, sex and occupation, the means of providing employment to able-bodied applicants as a condition of relief, and the establishment of an office for the registry of all matters connected with public relief, including accounts; and finally, the appointment of a paid and permanent officer to superintend each district, receiving his instructions from the Central Board and having authority over all subordinates.[110] Villiers submitted his report in March 1833 and the final report of the Royal Commission was completed in March 1834, largely under the auspices of Senior and Edwin Chadwick, and was duly presented to the House of Commons. However, Hyde Villiers, so influential in Charles' appointment, and for whom a bright political future had been predicted, never lived to read this. In November, he had travelled to Cornwall with a view to canvassing the constituency of Penryn but, having suffered greatly, died from an abscess on the brain at Carclew, the seat of Sir Charles Lemon, in December 1832.[111]

The Poor Law Amendment Act, passed in August 1834, implemented the recommendations of the Royal Commission. The Act abolished the distinction between outdoor and indoor relief, providing that relief to all able-bodied persons should be given in well-regulated workhouses instead of outdoor relief doles and allowances. The key principle was one of 'less eligibility', whereby the condition of a worker would be far worse on relief than when in employment, the idea being that conditions in workhouses would be so harsh that only the genuinely destitute would apply for relief. Thus the workhouse was regarded as a deterrent, striking fear into the hearts of the honest poor, who would do anything to avoid entry into what became known as 'Poor Law Bastilles'. It also endorsed Chadwick's belief in the virtues of 'the Preventive Principle', which was, in part, designed to reduce poor law expenditure.

On the local level, the Act provided for the establishment of Poor Law Unions, whereby local parishes, which had previously administered the Old Poor Law in various ways, were merged into one union, each with its own workhouse. The administration of the new unions was vested in Boards of Guardians, elected annually, who were responsible for the appointment of salaried officers, including the relieving officer, the workhouse master or mistress, and workhouse staff; settling applications for relief; the supervision of the workhouse; and the collection and expenditure of the poor rate. The Act also provided for national uniformity in the administration of poor relief by establishing the Poor Law Commission, based in London, which, in theory at least, could issue rules, orders and regulations, and held wide, if permissive, powers over the local authorities, and its establishment not only illustrated the practical application of the Benthamite procedural blueprint for reform[112] but also represented a significant departure from laissez-faire principles in social policy.[113]

With his duties as an Assistant Poor Law Commissioner successfully concluded, Villiers returned to the Court of Chancery. Yet his political apprenticeship was now almost complete. The scion of an aristocratic Tory family, he had moved through Liberal Toryism to Benthamite Radicalism and had become a convinced Reformer, committed to a wide-ranging Radical agenda. Yet, as with many aspiring politicians who were to achieve eminence during the Victorian period, Charles Villiers' political convictions and principles, to which he was to cling resolutely throughout his career, had been shaped largely by pre-Victorian influences. In seeking to improve the social and material condition of the people, which he had witnessed at first hand as a Poor Law Commissioner, Villiers had been influenced in part by the lessons of the French Revolution, for he both abhorred and feared class-conflict, which he regarded as the precursor to revolution, and he believed that the politics of reform in an increasingly industrialised and urbanised society should be essentially inclusive rather than divisive, setting class against class. Indeed, he even disliked the tribalism of party politics, which he regarded as an impediment to good government, frequently asserting the rights of the 'independent' member of parliament to vote on issues according to their good judgement rather than by party dictat. Moreover, for Villiers, the question of the condition of the people was largely, though not exclusively, an economic question, and one which only Free Trade could resolve by enhancing the material prosperity of the nation and assisting in achieving the Benthamite goal of 'the greatest happiness of the greatest number', hence his vehement opposition to the Corn Laws of 1815, which impeded this. Yet, whilst his political interests lay primarily in the sphere of domestic politics, Villiers' subsequent views on British foreign policy and international relations were also shaped by his upbringing during the Napoleonic Wars, not least in regard to France and French nationalist intentions, which he consistently viewed with suspicion, but also in regard to War, which he regarded as the *great curse* of mankind and something to be avoided, if at all possible, by arbitration and negotiation between nations, although he was never to become a complete pacifist.[114]

Charles Villiers now sought to realise his ambition of obtaining a seat in Parliament, and in December 1834, at the age of thirty-two, he was provided with the opportunity to do so when he was invited to stand as a candidate for the newly created parliamentary borough of Wolverhampton. This was to prove the first step on the road to a long and distinguished parliamentary career, but one within which Villiers never quite succeeded in escaping from the pre-Victorian world that had moulded him.

Notes

1 George William Frederick Villiers (1800–1870), later 4th Earl of Clarendon, diplomat and statesman, educated at St John's College, Cambridge, Chancellor of the Duchy of Lancaster (1840–1, 1864–5), President of Board of Trade (1846–7), Lord Lieutenant of Ireland (1847–52), and Foreign Secretary (1853–8, 1865–6, 1868–70). George married Katherine Barham in 1839 and they raised six children: Constance (1840–1922), who married Frederick Stanley, 16th Earl of Derby, in 1864; Alice (1841–97), who married Lord Skelmersdale (later Earl of Lathom) in 1860; Emily (1843–1927), who married Odo Russell (later Lord Ampthill) in 1868; Edward (1846–1914), 5th Earl Clarendon; George (1847–91); and Francis (1852–1925). For further details, see George Villiers, *A Vanished Victorian: Being the Life of George Villiers, Fourth Earl of Clarendon, 1800–1870* (London, 1938); Sir H. Maxwell, *The Life and Letters of George William Frederick, Fourth Earl of Clarendon* (2 vols, London, 1913).
2 Thomas Hyde Villiers (1801–1832), politician, educated at St. John's College, Cambridge, MP for Hedon (1826–30), Wootton Bassett (a family 'pocket' borough, 1830–1) and Bletchingley (1831–2), Secretary to the Board of Control (1831–2). For further details, see David R. Fisher, 'Villiers, Thomas Hyde (1801–1832)', in D.R. Fisher (ed.), *The History of Parliament: the House of Commons, 1820–1832* (Cambridge, 2009).
3 Maria Theresa Villiers (1803–1865), writer, married the novelist Thomas Lister in 1830 and, following his death in 1842, she married Sir George Cornewall Lewis, lawyer and politician, in 1844.
  She had three children by Lister: Thomas, who married Florence Hamilton; Maria Theresa, who married William Harcourt in 1863; and Alice Beatrice (1844–98), who married Algernon Borthwick (later Baron Glenesk). For further details, see D.A. Smith, 'Lewis, Lady (Maria) Theresa (1803–1865)', *ODNB*, 16595 (Oct. 2006).
4 Edward Ernest Villiers (1806–1843), married Elizabeth Liddell, daughter of Lord Ravenscroft, in 1835 and served as a Commissioner of the Colonial Land and Emigration Board. They had four children: Edward (1838–1921); Edith (1841–1936), who married Robert Bulwer-Lytton, first Earl of Lytton and

was Lady of the Bedchamber to both Queen Victoria and Her Majesty Queen Alexandra; Elizabeth, Lady Locke (1841–1938); and Maria Theresa (1836–1925).
5 Henry Montagu Villiers (1813–1861), Anglican clergyman, educated at Christ Church, Oxford, Vicar of Kenilworth (1837–56), Bishop of Carlisle (1856–60) and Bishop of Durham (1860–1). He married Amelia Hulton in 1837. Their eight children included the Revd. Henry Montagu Villiers (1837–1908). Prebendary of St Paul's Cathedral, who married, first, Lady Victoria Russell and, later, Charlotte Cadogan, granddaughter of the 3rd Earl Cadogan and the Marquis of Anglesey. For further details, see A.F. Munden, 'Villiers, Henry Montagu (1813–1861)', ODNB, 28298 (2004).
6 Augustus Algernon Villiers (1817–1843), Lieutenant in the Royal Navy and Knight of the Royal Order of Isabella the Catholic of Spain (awarded for his role as Mate on HMS Ringdove during the siege of Bilbao).
7 For further details, see R.G. Thorne, 'Villiers, Hon. George (1759–1827)', in R.G. Thorne (ed.), *The History of Parliament: The House of Commons, 1790–1820* (London, 1986).
8 Villiers, *A Vanished Victorian*, 35.
9 On the death of the 2nd Earl in 1824, the estate passed to his brother John Charles, the 3rd Earl Clarendon, and on his death in 1838 was inherited by Charles Villiers' eldest brother, George Villiers, as 4th Earl Clarendon. Thereafter The Grove became the hub of domesticity for the wider Villiers family.
10 Sir James Mackintosh (1765–1832): Jurist, historian, Whig politician; Professor of Law and Politics at Haileybury, 1818–24; supporter of Catholic emancipation, legal and penal reform, and parliamentary reform.
11 Thomas Malthus (1766–1834): Cleric, scholar and political economist; educated at Jesus College, Cambridge; Professor of History and Political Economy at Haileybury from 1805; most famous for his influential yet controversial *An Essay on the Principle of Population* (1798) and outspoken critic of the Old Poor Law. See J.M. Pullen, 'Malthus, (Thomas) Robert (1766–1834)', ODNB, 17902 (May 2008).
12 *The Asiatic Journal*, 10 (July–December 1850), 51: East India College at Haileybury Examination Results, 26 May 1820.
13 Maxwell, *The Life and Letters of George William Frederick*, I, 136.
14 Ibid., I, 38: Theresa Villiers to George Frederick Villiers, 12 Jan. 1823. For further details of family affairs at Old Kent House, see also Villiers, *A Vanished Victorian*, 17–52.
15 Maria Theresa Lister (Villiers' sister) to George Villiers, nd. late 1837, in Maxwell, I, 136–7.
16 J.L. and B. Hammond, *The Town Labourer* (London, 1917), 101.
17 The outstanding study of this subject remains E.P. Thompson, *The Making of the English Working Class* (London, 1963), especially chapters 14 and 15, 515–76.
18 See, for example, R.J. White, *Waterloo to Peterloo* (London, 1957), 110–200.
19 These variously prohibited drilling, restricted the right to bear arms, regulated the right and size of public meetings, and punished libels.
20 George Villiers was admitted to St John's College at the early age of 16 in 1816, graduating MA in 1820, whilst Thomas entered St John's in 1819, graduating BA in 1822 and MA in 1825.
21 Viscount Howick, Henry George, later 3rd Earl Grey (1802–94): Whig politician; son of Charles, 2nd Earl Grey, Prime Minister 1830–4; educated at Trinity College, Cambridge; staunch free trader; Under Secretary of State for the Colonies, 1830–3; Secretary for War, 1835–9; Secretary of State for the Colonies, 1846–52. MP 1826–45 and Leader of the Whigs in the House of Lords thereafter.
22 Thomas Babington Macaulay, 1st Baron Macaulay (1800–59): Writer, historian and Whig politician; educated at Trinity College, Cambridge; variously MP for

Calne, Leeds and Edinburgh; Secretary of the Board of Control (India), 1834–8; Secretary of War, 1839–41; Paymaster General, 1846–8.
23 Sir George Trevelyan, in his *Life and Letters of Lord Macaulay* (2 vols, London, 1876), I, Ch. 2, recalled that 'Charles Villiers still delights our generation by showing us how they talked'. See also J. Cotter Morrison, *Macaulay* (London, 1882), 9.
24 Trevelyan, *Life and Letters*, I, Ch. 2, for details about life at Cambridge in the early 1820s.
25 P. Linehan, *St. John's College, Cambridge: A History* (Woodbridge, 2011), 226–7.
26 See, especially, Ged Martin, *The Cambridge Union and Ireland, 1815–1914* (Cambridge, 2000), chapter 1.
27 For further details of Villiers' early life, see also *A Political Memoir* (1883), ix–xiv; Obituaries, *The Times*, 17 Jan. 1898; *Wolverhampton Chronicle*, 19 Jan. 1898; L.S. Stephen and S. Lee (eds), *Dictionary of National Biography*, LVIII (1899), 'Villiers, Charles Pelham', 318–323; A.C. Howe, 'Villiers, Charles Pelham (1802–1898), Politician', ODNB, 42282 (Oct. 2009).
28 Villiers, *A Vanished Victorian*, 41–2.
29 Ibid., 46.
30 John Ramsay McCulloch (1789–1864): political economist and statistician; author of *Principles of Political Economy* (1825) and of articles for the *Edinburgh Review*; edited 1828 edition of Adam Smith's *Wealth of Nations*; appointed Professor of Political Economy at London University, 1828; Originally influenced by the ideas of Thomas Malthus, he later rejected the,'Malthusian trap' theory.
31 John Stuart Mill, *Autobiography* (London, 1873), 123–6.
32 Sir Henry Taylor (1800–1886): dramatist, poet, man of letters; anti-slavery campaigner; clerk in the Colonial Office, 1824–72; wide circle of literary friends, including Robert Southey, William Wordsworth and Thomas Carlyle.
33 Sir Henry Taylor, *Autobiography* (London, 1865), 81–2.
34 Taylor, *Autobiography*, 77.
35 Jeremy Bentham (1748–1832): philosopher, social reformer, founder of the creed of utilitarianism.
36 James Mill (1773–1836): historian, political economist, philosopher, Bentham's chief ally and father of John Stuart Mill (1806–1875): philosopher, political economist, civil servant and Liberal MP for Westminster 1865–8. See J. Harris, 'Mill, John Stuart (1806–1873)', ODNB, 18711 (Jan. 2012).
37 Sir William Molesworth (1810–55): Radical MP for East Cornwall (1832–7), Leeds (1837–41) and Southwark (1845–55); educated at St John's College, Cambridge; editor of the *London Review* and the *Westminster Review* from 1835 as the main organ of the Philosophic Radicals. See P. Burroughs, 'Molesworth, Sir William, eighth baronet (1810–1855)', ODNB, 18902 (Jan. 2008). His wife, Andalusia Grant, Lady Molesworth (1809–1888) became a noted society hostess after Sir William's death in 1855 and Charles Villiers remained one of her intimate friends until her death in 1888: K.D. Reynolds, 'Molesworth, Andalusia Grant, Lady Molesworth (c.1809–1888)', ODNB, 47908 (2004).
38 George Grote (1794–1871): political radical and classical historian, Liberal MP for the City of London 1832–41, and co-founder of University College, London: J. Hamburger, 'Grote, George (1794–1871)', ODNB, 11677 (May 2008).
39 Joseph Hume (1777–1855): Scottish doctor and radical politician, MP for Middlesex (1830–37), Kilkenny (1837–41) and Montrose (1841–55): J. Potter, 'Hume, Joseph (1767–1844)', ODNB, 14147 (Jan. 2008).
40 Thomas Perronet Thompson (1783–1869): Radical reformer, a leading figure in the Anti-Slavery Society, and MP for Hull (1835–7) and Bradford

(1837–69): M. Turner, 'Thompson, Thomas Perronet (1783–1869), *ODNB*, 27280 (May 2009).

41 Charles Buller (1806–1848): Educated at Trinity College, Cambridge; barrister and radical MP for Liskeard (1832–48): H.J. Spencer, 'Buller, Charles (1806–1848)', *ODNB*, 3913 (Jan. 2008).

42 Edward Bulwer Lytton (1803–1873): Educated at Trinity College, Cambridge; Novelist and Radical reformer; MP for St Ives (1831–2), Lincoln (1832–41) and Hertfordshire (as a Conservative, 1852–66); raised to the peerage as Baron Lytton of Knebworth, 1866: A. Brown, 'Lytton, Edward George Earle Lytton Bulwer, first Baron Lytton (1803–1873), *ODNB*, 17314 (2004).

43 John Arthur Roebuck (1802–1879): Radical reformer and MP for Bath (1832–47) and Sheffield (1847–68, 1874–79): S.A. Beaver, 'Roebuck, John Arthur (1802–1864)', *ODNB*, 23945 (2004).

44 John Temple Leader (1810–1903): Educated at Christ Church, Oxford; Radical politician and connoisseur; MP for Bridgwater (1835–7) and Westminster (1837–47); spent his later life in Italy: S. Lee, 'Leader, John Temple (1810–1903)', rev. H.C.G. Matthew, *ODNB*, 34453 (Jan. 2009).

45 S.E. Finer, 'The transmission of Benthamite ideas, 1820–50', in Gillian Sutherland (ed.), *Studies in the Growth of Nineteenth Century Government* (1972), 11–32. Finer argued that there were three key stages in the transmission of Benthamite ideas during the period. First, the process of irradiation, by which small knots of Benthamites attracted into their salons and committees a wider circle of men who they infused with their ideas (making friends and influencing people); second, the process of suscitation, the process of arranging public inquiries and the press in order to create a favourable public opinion; third, the process of permeation, that of securing official positions and influencing the appointment of others. Villiers' early career well illustrates this.

46 Frederick Harrison, *Autobiographical Memoirs* (2 vols, London, 1911), II, 92–3:

> In 1876 I was proposed by John Morley as a member of the Political Economy Club, of which the great lights then were the Hon. C.P. Villiers, the earnest champion of Free Trade in Parliament, who lived to the age of ninety-six and was as stout a Free Trader as ever, and a champion long after the death of Bright and Cobden.

47 *Political Economy Club Minutes of Proceedings, Roll of Members and Questions Discussed, 1821–1920* (London 1921), vi, 330: Courtney stated that 'Mr Charles Villiers was fairly constant in attendance and debate and kept up his service to an advanced period of his prolonged life'.

48 For further details see *Yorkshire Gazette*, 17 June 1826; *Hull Packet*, 13 June 1826; K.J. Alison (ed.), *Victoria County History, A History of the County of York East Riding*, vol. 1., *The City of Kingston-upon-Hull* (1969), pp. 202–7; *The Times*, 10 Jan. 1895: 'The Father of the House of Commons: A Political Record'.

49 *Hull Packet*, 13 June 1826; *Yorkshire Gazette*, 17 June 1826.

50 *Hull Packet*, 8 Aug. 1826.

51 Ibid., 17 Oct. 1826.

52 B. Weinstein, *Liberalism and English Government in Early Victorian London* (Woodbridge 2011), 20–1; see also L. Kelly, *Holland House: A History of London's Most Celebrated Salon* (London, 2015).

53 G.W.E. Russell, *Collections and Recollections* (London, 1903), 66.

54 *Sunday Times*, 3 Jan. 1898.

55 See letter from Theresa Villiers to George Villiers, 6 Jan. 1823, in Maxwell, I, 38. This mentions a Miss Mellish being pursued by a Colonel Stewart, who

wished to marry her, 'she snubbing him quite brutally' and that 'the other night she was obliged to get Edward [Villiers] to protect her from him'.

56 University of Nottingham, Manuscripts and Special Collections: *Mellish Family Biographies: William Mellish (1764–1838)*.
57 For further details of this case, see *The New Annual Register* (April 1798), 38. The Mellish home at 21 Albemarle Street, London, was subsequently purchased by the Royal Institution of Great Britain for £4,850 and thereafter became its headquarters: Frank James, 'Founders of the Royal Institution of Great Britain', *ODNB*, 59214 (May 2013).
58 The case was brought by Catherine Mellish against her three uncles – and joint guardians – William, Edward and Thomas Mellish on the grounds of their improvidence and mismanagement of her estate both prior to, and immediately after she came of age. For further details, see *Reports of Cases Argued and Determined in the Court of King's Bench* (London, 1824), Mellish v Mellish, 520–34; see also Sir John Leach, *Reports of Cases decided in the High Court of Chancery*, Vol. 1 (London, 1843), Mellish v Mellish, 138–47.
59 *Evening Telegraph*, 5 Feb. 1898.
60 For example, during a debate in the House of Commons in May 1836 in regard to a proposal that Ladies be admitted to the Stranger's Gallery, Villiers, who supported the proposal, stated that as he was not 'blest with daughters', he might be considered an impartial judge on the matter: *Parl. Debs*, 3rd ser., vol. 33, cc.527–31, 3 May 1836.
61 For further details see B. Murphy and D. Fisher, 'Leach, Sir John', in R. Thorne (ed.) *History of Parliament, 1790–1820* (Cambridge, 1996).
62 Maria Theresa Lister to George Villiers, nd. late 1837, in Maxwell, I, 136–7, which refers to a disagreement between Charles and George over money matters. Maria Theresa observed that

> He has vexed us all and angered us rather, but he is not much lowered in my estimation by what has passed, for I cannot honestly say that I should have expected much better of him, and it does not efface from my mind the sense of much kindness and many hours of pleasure and mirth which he has contributed to the family circle ... He is beyond my powers of description or comprehending, for with all his unmeasured and abusive language, and his want of integrity and straightforwardness in money matters, I do not believe he is devoid of affection, nor is he miserly or extravagant. He seems to like the by-way better than the highway, and he would rather do an honest thing in a dishonest manner than not. I am sure there is no mending him.

Maxwell concluded that in this matter Charles Villiers showed 'a keener regard for his own interest rather than for the feelings of others'.
63 Maxwell, I, 138.
64 *The Times*, 10 Jan. 1895. For Alexander Somerville, see J. Hamburger, 'Alexander Somerville (1811–1885)', *ONDB*, 26016 (Sept. 2004); see also K.D.M. Snell's introduction to Alexander Somerville, *The Whistler at the Plough: Containing Travels, Statistics and Descriptions of Scenery & Agricultural Customs in most Parts of England* (1852, reprinted London, 1989), i–xxxi.
65 See, for example, D. Fraser, 'The Agitation for Parliamentary Reform', in J.T. Ward (ed.), *Popular Movements c.1830–1850* (London, 1970), 31–53.
66 For the 1832 Reform Act, see especially M. Brock, *The Great Reform Act* (London, 1973); E. Evans, *The Great Reform Act of 1832* (London, 1983); E. Pearce, *Reform!: The Fight for the 1832 Reform Act* (London, 2010).
67 Stephen Farrell, 'Wootton Basset', in D.R. Fisher (ed.), *The History of Parliament: The House of Commons, 1820–1832* (Cambridge, 2009).

68 *Staffs Advertiser*, 3 Jan. 1835; *Speech of C.P. Villiers, Esq. M.P. at a Dinner given by the Constituency of Wolverhampton to the Representatives of that Borough, 26 January 1836* (Printed by J. Bridgen, Darlington Street, Wolverhampton).
69 For further details, see *The Report from His Majesty's Commissioners for Inquiring into the Administration and Practical Operation of the Poor Laws: Appendix (A), Reports of Assistant Commissioners, Part II, P[arliamentary] P[apers]* (1834), No. 23, Report from C.P. Villiers, Esq, 1–82.
70 There is an extensive historiography on the Old Poor Law and the work of the Royal Commission of 1832–4. See especially the relevant sections in M. Rose, *The English Poor Law, 1780–1930* (Newton Abbot, 1971); P. Dunkley, *The Crisis of the Old Poor Law in England, 1795–1834* (London, 1982); P. Wood, *Poverty and the Workhouse in Victorian Britain* (Stroud, 1991); A. Brundage, *The Making of the New Poor Law: The Politics of Inquiry, Enactment and Implementation, 1832–39* (London, 1978); Peter Mandler, 'The Making of the New Poor Law *Redivivus*', *Past and Present*, 117 (1987); A. Brundage, *The English Poor Laws, 1700–1930* (Basingstoke, 2002); A. Kidd, *State, Society and the Poor in Nineteenth-Century England* (Basingstoke, 1999).
71 The classic study of these popular disturbances is E.J. Hobsbawm and G. Rude, *Captain Swing* (London, 1969), but see also Carl J. Griffin, *The Rural War: Captain Swing and the Politics of Protest* (Manchester, 2012).
72 Fisher, 'Villiers, Thomas Hyde (1801–1832)': Hyde Villiers had supported a number of reformist campaigns and had voted for Catholic Emancipation in 1829 and for Parliamentary Reform in 1832.
73 Ibid. See also Hyde Villiers to Howick, 19 Jan. 1832, in P. Mandler, *Aristocratic Government in the Age of Reform* (Oxford, 1990), 135.
74 The members of the Royal Commission appointed in 1832 were Bishop Blomfield of London; Bishop Sumner of Chester; William Sturges Bourne; Walter Coulson; Nassau Senior; Henry Bishop of Oriel College, Oxford; Henry Gawler; J. Traill. Edwin Chadwick, who was initially appointed as an Assistant Commissioner in July 1832, replaced the Commission's first Secretary, J. Taylor, in April 1833 in order to assist with the preparation of the final report. For further details, see List of Commissions and Officials, 1830–1839, Poor Laws 1832–4, http://www.british-history.ac.uk/office-holders/vol9/pp16–28.
75 Boyd Hilton, *The Age of Atonement: The Influence of Evangelicalism on Social and Economic Thought, 1785–1865* (Oxford, 1988), 244–5.
76 *The Report from His Majesty's Commissioners for Inquiring into the Administration and Practical Operation of the Poor Laws: Appendix (A), Reports of Assistant Commissioners, Part II, PP* (1834), No. 23, Report from C.P. Villiers Esq, 1.
77 Ibid., 3.
78 Ibid., 4.
79 Ibid., 7.
80 Ibid.
81 Ibid., 11.
82 Ibid., 12.
83 Ibid., 13.
84 Ibid., 15–17.
85 Ibid., 17–18.
86 Ibid., 18.
87 Ibid.
88 Ibid., 20.
89 Ibid., 43.
90 Ibid., 49.

91 Ibid., 68–70.
92 Ibid., 21.
93 Ibid.
94 Coventry, Bedworth, Nuneaton, Atherstone, Birmingham, Warwick and Alcester in Warwickshire; Bromsgrove, Stourbridge, Kidderminster, Worcester, Evesham, and Pershore in Worcestershire; and Tewkesbury in Gloucestershire.
95 Ibid., 22.
96 Ibid., 42.
97 Ibid., 24.
98 Ibid., 26.
99 Ibid., 29.
100 Ibid., 30.
101 Ibid., 32.
102 Ibid., 34–5.
103 Ibid., 35.
104 Ibid., 38.
105 Ibid., 40.
106 Ibid., 50–1.
107 Ibid., 52–3.
108 Ibid., 54.
109 Ibid., 61–4.
110 Ibid., 65–73.
111 Fisher, 'Villiers, Thomas Hyde (1801–1832)'.
112 Finer, 'The Transmission of Benthamite Ideas, 1820–50', 29. The Secretary of the Commission was Edwin Chadwick and its three Commissioners – popularly referred to as 'The Bagshaws of Somerset House' – were Sir George Nicholls, Sir Thomas Frankland Lewis and J.G. Shaw Lefevre.
113 W.E. Rubenstein, *The Politics of Government Growth: Early Victorian Attitudes Toward State Intervention, 1833–1848* (Newton Abbot, 1971), 34–5.
114 For further discussion of this subject, see S. Conway, 'Bentham, the Benthamites, and the Nineteenth-Century British Peace Movement', *Utilitas: The Journal of Utilitarian Studies*, 2 (1990), 221–43.

2 The Member for Wolverhampton

For the young Charles Villiers, the town of Wolverhampton must have seemed a world away from London society and his comfortable surroundings at 11 Wilton Street, Belgravia, in the City of Westminster. During the early nineteenth century, the town had emerged as a commercial and manufacturing centre second only to Birmingham within the West Midlands,[1] and its economic development was closely associated with the progress of the Industrial Revolution in the Black Country.[2] White's *Directory* of 1851 depicts a town whose bounds contained mills, foundries, mines and manufactories, where specialist local trades such as sheet-tin and japanned ironwares, papier-mache trays, steel toys and locks co-existed with secondary manufactures connected with finished iron, steel and brass, whilst the commercial importance of the town was reflected in the profusion of professional persons, merchants, brokers, shopkeepers and coal, iron and metal dealers.[3] Yet the town also retained its pre-industrial role as a market centre for the neighbouring agricultural hinterland of South Staffordshire. During the same period, the population of Wolverhampton increased rapidly, rising from 12,565 in 1801 to 49,985 in 1851 and 94,187 by 1901, a process which was accompanied not only by urban expansion but also by overcrowding and urban squalor in working-class districts, where contemporary parliamentary reports testified to the prevalence of acute social problems in regard to poverty, crime, dirt and disease.[4] Prior to 1848, when Wolverhampton achieved borough status, the responsibility for dealing with these and other local issues rested with the town's Improvement Commission, established in 1777, an oligarchy of professional, commercial, and manufacturing men, whose meagre efforts at 'improvement' were largely confined to enhancing the town's central business district.[5]

The Parliamentary Borough of Wolverhampton was a two-member constituency created by the First Reform Act of 1832, when Wolverhampton became one of many industrial towns to be granted the right to parliamentary representation under the redistribution of seats sanctioned by the Act. The parliamentary constituency, which included the township of Wolverhampton and the adjacent townships of Wednesfield and Willenhall in the east, and Bilston, Coseley and Sedgley to the south, comprised a population of almost

60,000.[6] The town had a reputation for supporting liberal causes and, prior to the passing of the Reform Act, John Barker, the Liberal election agent in Wolverhampton had observed that

> any individual who is not an advocate of liberal measures, who would not strive to remove monopolies of every description, would have but little chance of being returned for this place – the slave trade, the East India trade, and the Corn Laws will be used as tests.[7]

However, there were divisions within the reform movement in Wolverhampton between the 'Moderates' and their Whig allies and the Radicals. In 1832, William Whitmore,[8] a Shropshire landowner who supported the reform of the Corn Laws, represented the former and Richard Fryer,[9] a local ironmaster and banker, the latter. Both were returned in 1832 by some 1,749 electors following a fiery campaign during which the Riot Act was twice read, and there followed a political truce between the Moderates and the Radicals. This was threatened subsequently when first, Whitmore, and then Fryer decided to stand down on the eve of the 1835 Election, and Jon Lawrence has suggested that a deal was hatched between these two sitting MPs to bring in two new candidates from outside the borough who were acceptable to both groups.[10] Accordingly, it was agreed to approach Thomas Thornely, a Liverpool merchant and Unitarian, to represent the 'moderates'. Thornely possessed extensive experience in the American trade, having once been employed by the Rathbone family of Liverpool merchants, shipowners and philanthropists, and had acquired a reputation in the city for supporting Radical causes, including the abolition of the Corn Laws, Free Trade, and Catholic Emancipation. He had also played a significant role in the agitation in Liverpool for parliamentary reform and had stood unsuccessfully in 1831 and 1832 as a Liberal candidate at elections in the borough, which were characterised by gross bribery, treating and corruption.[11] Richard Fryer also despatched his son, Richard Fryer Jnr., to London to secure a suitable Radical candidate and Charles Villiers made known his willingness to stand. Nicholas Throckmorton, an elderly Liverpool merchant and free-trader, who was on friendly terms with Villiers, and who had also emerged as a prospective candidate for the seat, agreed to support Villiers' nomination. On 15 December 1834, at a meeting at the Swan Hotel in Wolverhampton, Charles Villiers, supported by the Fryers and Throckmorton, was chosen as the Radical candidate.[12] On the following day, Villiers issued his electoral address, which reflected his Benthamite principles, stating:

> Anxiously desiring to see the Laws and Institutions of this Country accomplish the effects for which they ought to exist, – namely 'THE HAPPINESS OF THE GREATEST NUMBER', I shall be ever found a warm supporter of such reforms and changes as may conduce to this end.

With this view, I shall ever oppose myself to all restrictions upon Trade and Monopolies of every kind. I hold most sacred the cause of CIVIL AND RELIGIOUS LIBERTY. As a member and friend of the Church of England, I wish to see a Distribution of its Property better suited to the MORAL AND RELIGIOUS WANTS OF THE PEOPLE, and this particularly in Ireland. Believing that all measures of National importance will only be accomplished by Electors having an effective control over their REPRESENTATIVES, and being also protected in the exercise of their privileges, I am a decided advocate for Triennial Parliaments and for Vote by Ballot.[13]

Subsequently, in what proved to be a lively campaign, Thornely and Villiers were opposed by Dudley Fereday, for the Tories, and John Nicholson, for the ultra-Radicals, and Charles Villiers, in particular, was the recipient of rough treatment by both parties. The local Tories condemned him for his aristocratic background and questioned his reforming credentials, falsely claiming that he had opposed Catholic Emancipation and Free Trade at the Hull election in 1826, and depicting him as an unprincipled adventurer. By contrast, Nicholson's supporters, who described Villiers as 'the rejected of Hull', pointed to his previous flirtation with Liberal Toryism, and alleged that he was 'a wolf in sheep's clothing', and little more than a government placeman seeking a safe seat, who had been imposed on the constituency due to the influence of Richard Fryer and others of the local Liberal elite.[14] Indeed, Nicholson went further, stating:

Of Mr VILLIERS' name and pretensions, not one of you, I dare say, ever heard until a week ago; his pedigree has been blazoned forth with no little vaunting, and his friends seem to think that the stock of a peer must be peerless ... In fact, you will find him to be a *Tory dressed-up Whig fashion! A piece of ministerial, musical clockwork* sent down to be set a going for the first time by the Electors of Wolverhampton. He may perhaps play *one* or *two* good tunes to you during his contest, just to gull you into a belief of his pretty mechanism, but you will find that they are all set to *variations* when performed in Parliament. Mr Villiers has confessed that he is engaged six hours a day in an office at a salary of £1,000 a year; and he is now attempting to do what has been declared to be impossible, viz. to serve *two* masters. He would fain have you believe that when he leaves his desk and stool at 3 o'clock, nothing is easier for him than to *run* down to the House of Commons to attend to your interests! – that is, no *Club House* yawns open to tempt his allegiance from St. Stephens ... Place no reliance on this flimsy and shallow assertion: he cannot *honestly* serve you.[15]

In successfully countering these, and other allegations, Villiers published a collection of private letters affirming his reforming credentials, which he had received from his Radical friends John Romilly, Edward Strutt, and Charles Poulett Thompson.[16] Romilly, the MP for Bridport, observed

> We have for so many years speculated upon the reforms necessary to be carried into effect in Church and State that it would be a great gratification if it were possible that we might, side by side, contribute to the success of some of the measures in the House of Commons, as we used to discuss them at Cambridge, and since,

adding that allegations that Villiers was a sinecurist were absurd since he would relinquish his present office if elected to Parliament.[17] Strutt, the MP for Derby, stated

> If I had any friends in that town [Wolverhampton], I should have had great pleasure in assuring them that I have been intimately acquainted with you ever since we were at college together; that I believe your political opinion upon all leading points to agree with my own; that I have no doubt you would, in the House of Commons, prove yourself a steady reformer; and that, in my opinion, your principles and your talents equally qualify you for being a most useful representative of a large town.[18]

Poulett Thompson, the MP for Manchester, stated

> I am told that the Tories are circulating all kinds of lies about you ... You will have no difficulty in giving the lie to their rascally falsehoods ... you can tell them, what we all know, that eight years ago you stood upon liberal principles for Hull – principles from which, to my knowledge, you have not varied ... Their malice will recoil upon themselves.[19]

These weighty testimonials were further endorsed by a letter, which Villiers received from his friend George Grote, now MP for the City of London (and described by Villiers' committee as an 'unflinching, consistent and uncompromising reformer'), who stated

> In all the acquaintance which I have had the pleasure of enjoying with you, I have never known you as entertaining any other sentiments than those of a *Sincere* and *Reflecting Reformer*; nor do I understand on what grounds the absurd imputation of your being a disguised Tory has been advanced ... you have uniformly advanced *Most Liberal Political Principles*. I should certainly be very sorry if any thing should happen to defeat your success at Wolverhampton, for I feel a very strong confidence that your *Votes* would be constantly on the side of *Reform* and of *Good Measures*, and that your Abilities would assist those Objects materially and effectually.[20]

As the *Staffordshire Advertiser*, a Radical newspaper published in Wolverhampton, observed, these and other testimonials assisted Charles Villiers in refuting the false allegations made against him, adding that Villiers was 'a good orator and has secured golden opinions from many electors',[21] and on Tuesday 6 January 1835 the four candidates – Thornely, Villiers, Fereday and Nicholson – appeared at the hustings in St James Square, Wolverhampton, where it was observed that

> the partisans of the different candidates expressed their feeling of approbation and contempt in the usual manner, and in some instances with a degree of violence, but the whole passed off much better than many expected from the party feeling known to exist.[22]

Richard Fryer proposed Villiers, who was seconded by the Rev. Mr Leigh. Mr Garwood seconded Nicholson and said of Villiers:

> till lately he was unknown in this place and since his arrival he had acquired no enviable notoriety. He could not but suspect the sincerity of a candidate who appeared among them, professing to be a Whig, who recently appeared at Hull as a Tory!, adding that 'Mr Villiers had not sufficiently expiated his political offences'.[23]

When Villiers attempted to address the meeting, he was almost drowned out 'by manifestations of impatience on the part of many, which hardly subsided throughout the delivery of his speech', but he emphasised that he was no Tory, but a Reformer of liberal principles and always would be, adding that Laws were made for the people, and the happiness of the greatest number ought to be uniformly promoted.[24] By contrast, Nicholson was received with popular applause and a show of hands declared in favour of Thornely and Nicholson, whereupon Villiers and Fereday immediately demanded a poll, which was set for Thursday 8 January, and it was noted that on the return of Villiers and his committee to their hotel, 'they were saluted with a few stones, which continued in the vicinity of the Lion Inn'.[25] In the event, the poll was adjourned until Friday, when the final result was Villiers, 773; Thornely, 772; Fereday, 650; Nicholson, 370, and Villiers and Thornely were returned for the parliamentary borough of Wolverhampton. Thornely duly observed that 'My honourable colleague, Mr. Villiers, is a most thorough Reformer', adding that 'we shall always be found at our posts, ready and willing to promote the cause of Reform and the general interests of the country'.[26] Later, Charles Villiers wrote to his brother George, informing him of his success:

> I leave you to judge what sort of a Christmas I passed in canvassing the freeborn of Wolverhampton, population 60,000, unknown before to any of them myself. However, as my difficulties were great, so is my victory glorious. The respectable people rather took a fancy to me, and

> I had the extreme good fortune to have opposed to me one of the greatest ruffians and blackguards that ever existed, named Nicholson, and he did me the good turn of charging me with everything in the world; which, of course, not being able to prove, I became a sort of victim ... I ended at the head of the poll. It is one of the new boroughs and, as yet, uncorrupted.[27]

Villiers, who in later life earned a somewhat unenviable reputation in Parliament for being parsimonious, then went on to explain that he had announced to the electors when he first went to Wolverhampton that he would be very happy to be returned, but that they must understand that he would not be prepared to spend one 6d. more than legal expenses, therefore there would be no treating, with the result that 'I did not give a glass of brandy and water to a human being, would not retain any agent, or treat, or allow any ribbons, flags, or music'.[28] Villiers' expenses were therefore limited to 'the polling booths, a few cars used for my own canvassing and dining out ... and a dinner which I foolishly gave three nights ago to my own committee'.[29] Despite this frugality, Villiers expenses came to £250 rather than the £200 he had initially hoped for. Nevertheless, he told George, 'I think you will say that this is doing pretty well.' Moreover, and again pre-empting the perennial concern about his own health which he expressed to his friends and Parliamentary colleagues throughout his life, Villiers stated that 'The only drawback to it is that, now I am in, I don't care a damn about it and I am afraid my health will not stand it. This contest has been too much for me and my health does not improve'.[30] In lighter vein, however, he reported to George that his younger brother, Henry Montagu (later Bishop of Durham) had been with him throughout the campaign, adding that 'He is a d..n good speaker, and the women were so gone upon him that he was quite a host for me'.[31] Indeed, following his election victory, Charles Villiers was required to return immediately to London in order to sign papers in the Court of Chancery, and it was Montagu Villiers who delivered the vote of thanks to the Electors on his brother's behalf.[32]

On Friday 24 April, a public dinner was held at the Kings Arms, Bilston, in celebration of the return of Thornely and Villiers, 'who made a speech of great length and power' and referred to 'the noble struggle they had made for their principles, and the manner in which they had resisted the evil reports which were circulated to prejudice him in their eyes', adding that 'the motive which actuated him was to give all support in his power to a liberal policy, the end of which was the attainment of cheap and good government'. After a few other observations, Villiers concluded 'a long and brilliant speech amid loud and oft repeated cheers'.[33] On the following day, a further dinner was given at the Swan Hotel in Wolverhampton for those supporters of Thornely and Villiers who had been unable to attend at Bilston, and when the party adjourned to the Peacock Inn it was reported that Villiers gave 'a humorous and sarcastic speech which kept the room in a roar of laughter during its delivery', after which several electors who had previously supported Nicholson pledged their future support to Villiers in light of 'his worthy conduct in the House of Commons'.[34]

Charles Villiers and Thomas Thornely duly established not only a close working relationship which was to last until Thornely's retirement in 1859 but also developed an enduring friendship, as their mutual correspondence illustrates.[35] In many respects, they complemented one another, for the elderly Thornely was a wise yet sometimes cautious politician, experienced in municipal politics, whilst his younger colleague, who was still learning the politician's craft, had many gifts but could be impetuous on occasion. But both were committed Reformers and Free Traders and both valued their independence as MPs. Whenever possible, they subsequently arranged joint meetings in Wolverhampton in advance of elections in order to co-ordinate their political strategies whilst also working closely together at Westminster.

However, Villiers' radical credentials were soon to be tested by the serious disorders which attended a Staffordshire County by-election held in Wolverhampton on 26 May 1835. The election was contested by Colonel George Anson, brother of the Earl of Lichfield, for the Whigs, and Sir Francis Goodriche, for the Tories. On polling day, scuffles between their respective supporters escalated into more general violence, with electors assailed by sticks and stones at the hustings. Wolverhampton's two parish constables, watchmen, and a body of special constables found it impossible to contain the disorders, and military assistance was requested by the Rev. John Clare, J.P. On 27 May a troop of the King's 1st Dragoons duly arrived in the town, and Clare read the Riot Act and directed the mounted troops to disperse the crowds, now numbering some 3,000 people, but when the soldiers were greeted by volleys of stones in St Peter's Churchyard they were ordered to open fire, injuring several of the rioters. This served only to inflame the situation, and during the evening the Riot Act was read once again. The troops eventually restored order, fifteen arrests being made in the process (of whom ten men were charged with riot and disorderly behaviour), and Goodriche was duly elected MP for Staffordshire by 1,773 votes to Anson's 1,559.[36]

The events in Wolverhampton acquired national publicity and Lord John Russell, the Leader of the House of Commons, instituted a Parliamentary Inquiry, chaired by Sir Frederick Roe, Chief Magistrate of Bow Street, into the disturbances.[37] Roe's enquiry was held over seven days in Wolverhampton, commencing on 5 June, and reported back to Parliament on 1 July. In essence, Roe's report completely exonerated the military of any culpability for the disorders, and Lord John Russell informed the Commons that the evidence indicated that

> The conduct of the military at Wolverhampton was marked by a most commendable forbearance and a most correct judgement ... being called upon to perform a most painful and difficult duty ... they did perform that duty in such a manner as at once to obtain the result of preventing

the peace of the town from being seriously disturbed, and of preventing the occurrence of injury to both property and life.[38]

This assertion provided the occasion for Charles Villiers' maiden speech in the House of Commons on 1 July 1835, when, encouraged by Thomas Thornely,[39] he stated:

> He could not help thinking that it would have been more satisfactory to the House if time had been allowed for Members to have read the evidence themselves. He (Mr Villiers) was not in a situation now to say whether the noble Lord was justified in the opinion that he had expressed respecting the conduct of the soldiers, and therefore he could merely say that, judging from the only evidence that had as yet been before the public, he did not think the terms 'commendable forbearance' did entirely apply to the conduct of the soldiers during the late disturbance.[40]

Indeed, Villiers held not only that the actions of the military had been both premature and unwarranted but that the magistrates' decision to deploy them reflected the inadequacies of local governmental arrangements, including policing, in Wolverhampton.[41] These, he later argued, were rooted in the fact that Wolverhampton had not yet been incorporated under the terms of the Municipal Corporations Act of 1835, whereas borough status would have enabled the townsfolk to take responsibility for their own affairs:

> Had this town been incorporated in May last, I verily believe that the misfortunes of that day would not have occurred ... with what effect might authorities have acted who, chosen by the people, had the confidence of the people, in advising them to retire to their homes, and not give pretext of alarm for the peace of the town; they would have regarded them as friendly, and they would have felt that they stultified themselves in resisting men whom they had chosen themselves; – and does any man believe that the poorer householders of any town have not a common interest with the richer ones in preventing confusion? It is my honest belief, Gentlemen, that these odious collisions of the military with the people will be prevented in future in all corporate towns.[42]

In the aftermath of the disorders, however, Henry Hill, a Wolverhampton magistrate and Tory banker, misinterpreted Villiers' comments in Parliament as reported in *The Times* and accused him of seeking to impugn the conduct of the magistracy during the riots. This assertion initiated a heated exchange of private letters between the two men, which were subsequently published in the Tory *Wolverhampton Chronicle* on 8 July.[43] Writing from New Palace Yard, Villiers informed Hill that he was 'not disposed to impugn the conduct of the magistrates at the expense of truth', adding that Hill's comments were of 'so offensive a character that until some explanation of what it is meant to convey is afforded me by you, I must decline any further correspondence'.[44] Moreover, writing from Brooke's Club, Nicholas Throckmorton, acting on Villiers' behalf, called for Hill to retract his allegations, which impugned the honour of Mr Villiers, 'or appoint some friend of your own, with whom I may confer, as to that satisfaction which Mr Villiers has a right to demand at your hands'.[45] The intimation that the dispute might be settled by a duel had the desired effect, for on 3 July Hill retracted, stating that 'he had no intention of impugning the honour of Mr Villiers', and on the following day the matter was closed when Throckmorton accepted the retraction, stating 'Mr Villiers is satisfied with such a disavowal on your part'.[46] Subsequently, William Mannix, M.D., of Mosely Hall, who had supported Hill during the dispute, duly informed the *Wolverhampton Chronicle* that

> this was a most extraordinary correspondence to drag before the public – A Member of Parliament publicly insults magistrates by charging them with partiality, which instead of producing an apology that would have been decorous leads to a hostile message and a demand of satisfaction.[47]

In the event, however, the dispute with Hill did little damage to Villiers' reputation among Wolverhampton's Liberals, who were themselves largely excluded from the Staffordshire Magistracy.[48] On 26 January 1836, both Villiers and Thornely were invited to a public dinner given in their honour by the constituency of Wolverhampton. During the proceedings, Villiers thanked his constituents for their cordial recognition of his services during the previous year and then embarked upon a wide-ranging speech which is of broader significance, since it embodied the liberal principles upon which his future political career was to rest and from which he never once subsequently departed. In what effectively amounted to a personal pledge to work for reform in the future, Villiers focused on the advantages of the 1832 political settlement, the need for justice for Ireland, the removal of the civil disabilities on Dissenters, the removal of restrictions on trade, including the repeal of the Corn Laws, the reform of the mal-administration of the law, the need for educational reform for the poor, and support for Liberalism.

On the reform settlement of 1832, Villiers stated that the House of Commons was 'no longer a retreat for the idle and corrupt, or a place of exchange, where principles can be bartered for places without shame and disgrace', adding that 'the people have been roused into vigilance, new blood, by means of the new constituency', as a result of which 'it has pleased Providence to effect a moral revolution in this country; we have passed from a state of darkness to one of comparative light'. Indeed, Villiers believed that the settlement was now

> teaching the people to distinguish between their real and pretended friends; between those who honestly base their views on general good and would strike corruption at the root, and those who would grudgingly,

and upon no principle, consistently here and there dole out a change, ever hoping and ever expecting to retain the abuse.[49]

On Ireland, Villiers asked his audience what they would feel if they had belonged to four-fifths of a population honestly differing in religion from the remainder, yet bound to contribute the property bequeathed for the support of their own religion to that of the minority. Ireland, he claimed, provided

> the only instance in Christendom where religion has been so administered as to bring Protestantism into discredit, for the Protestants cannot deny the evidence of their own witnesses, that after the experiment of a hundred years under the influence of that vast and wealthy Establishment, Protestantism has diminished and Catholicism increased!

This, he argued, was, in the first place, 'an insult to the name of justice, in one breath to reproach the Irish with the attempt to separate themselves from us, and to deny to them the advantages which we extend to the other members of the union'. Moreover, he argued that the regeneration of Ireland depended upon the respect that Britain could inspire in the people for the law, yet Britain, he held, charged the Irish with being lawless whilst administering the law to them unfairly, with 'Orange judges, Orange magistrates, or Orange sheriffs, who empanel Orange juries – in a word, for Orange justice', and called for the extension of municipal reform to Ireland in order to 'heal that wound which civil inequality, grounded on religious difference, has inflicted upon her'.[50]

On trade, Villiers referred to the need for freedom in commerce, which,

> like freedom in thought, all say they approve, but when asked to give effect to the principle some obstacle is sure to be found; the landowner, the shipowner, the West Indian, and others, all approve of free trade in what they consume, but in the sources of their income and profit there are no such supporters of prohibitive law.

Delineating the advantages of free trade to the poor man, Villiers then outlined the effects of fettering British commerce:

> We impose high duties upon timber and corn, which articles we might get cheaper and better from countries in Europe than anywhere else. By these duties we have given to those countries a pretext for excluding our goods, and within two years a union in Germany has been formed of twenty-five millions of souls to resist the import of our manufactures, and let me observe, that these countries, with all the natural advantages of England, have not every disadvantage with which we are encumbered. They have no debt in proportion to ours; their habits are as peaceful and

industrious as ours; their living cheaper than ours; and their chief manufactures are those which your customers chiefly demand ... Let not, then, I say, any present improvements in trade induce you to lose sight of that great principle of policy 'FREE TRADE,' but rather, in these days, when monopolists are uniting to promote their own ends, let districts like these associate together to secure for the people the more benevolent system which may give them cheap food, good trade, and a friendly intercourse with all the nations of the globe.[51]

On Law reform, Villiers claimed that Britain should be reproached for the reason that her laws lacked 'those essentials which have from all time been named by every speaker, writer, or thinker upon the subject, as belonging to any good system, namely – cheapness, certainty, and expedition'. Above all, in a further attack on the magistracy, he argued for the establishment of local courts, 'presided over by responsible and removeable men', as indispensable to the wants and business of the country. To such qualified men, he held, should be transferred much of the business of the magistracy,

> for if we complain of the administration of justice in civil matters, what are we to think of the administration of the criminal law, the greater part of which in the counties is in the hands of men for whose appointment no-one is practically responsible.

Indeed, he argued that many magistrates were 'men who are selected for no rational qualification whatever; their property and their title are alone considered, unless the minister is a Tory, and then his politics are never overlooked', adding:

> Can we wonder then, when the Tory party held office for nearly thirty years together, that complaint should go up from every village that the magistrates are of the politics of the Lord Lieutenants, actively engaged in opposing the liberal cause, and proclaiming by their appointment, that any man to enjoy the power or the distinction of being a magistrate must first announce himself a Tory partisan.[52]

On the question of Municipal Reform, Villiers welcomed the recent legislation of 1835 and stated that he looked to the incorporation of large towns with interest and hope,

> as offering one great means of working out the public weal ... they add greatly, and usefully in my judgment, both to the power and responsibility of the people; and every new incorporation will be an accession to the means of good government.

Moreover, he argued for the extension of municipal powers to Wolverhampton, claiming:

> though necessarily less acquainted with the circumstances of this borough than yourselves, I should say that a community such as that of Wolverhampton, improving in character, increasing in wealth, and extending in population, should not be behind districts of lesser importance in the good management of its affairs. Gentlemen, if I thought the Municipal Bill would lead to confusion, God knows I would have been the last man, either to have supported it or to prescribe its adoption.[53]

Finally, Villiers made some general observations on contemporary politics and the need to sustain the reform agenda. He stated that he did not wish to set one class of the community against the other, because his intention was to do all to promote mutual goodwill amongst all, and reaffirmed his Radical credentials by stating that

> I will not, to please any class, not those with whom I am nearest connected in blood, or in social intercourse, be guilty either of an injustice to the people or shut my eyes to all that I see passing around me.

The aristocracy, he held, had nothing to fear from trusting the people, 'but they will provoke the dangers they apprehend by irritating and misrepresenting the people, and by resisting their just and reasonable demands'.[54]

In the following year, both Thornely and Villiers were again returned at the General Election of 1837 in a straight two-party fight with the Tory candidates, John Benbow and Captain J.R. Burton. During the campaign, on 13 July, Villiers, who was introduced by John Barker, addressed a large crowd outside the Plough Inn in Willenhall, where Nicholson had drawn much of his support from ultra-Radicals in 1835. Villiers, who had been aware of the need to strengthen his support in Willenhall since the previous election,[55] was praised by Thornely for 'the ability and eloquence which he had brought to their common cause',[56] and was received 'with great cheering'. Villiers observed that he was aware that the electors thought very little of him the last time he had appeared amongst them because they thought 'he had a speck of Toryism in him', and for that reason many had given their votes to John Nicholson (which aroused laughter among the audience). But on this occasion he was well received. He stated that, since his election in 1835, he had devoted all his time to his parliamentary duties, had been diligent in his attendance, and had never shrunk from voting on any question, and although he had been told to vote one way or another, he shrunk from none, 'for he had no favour to seek, and no frown to fear', adding that 'he was independent of any and every Minister and he had no selfish end to promote in soliciting to be their representative'.[57] Moreover, he reminded his audience that 'They had seen what his votes in Parliament had been:- that he had not given one vote which was not to throw the Tories out', and, to cheers, Villiers proceeded to give a lengthy speech on the need for Free Trade and the repeal of the Corn Laws.[58] On the eve of the election, Villiers reaffirmed his political principles, stating that these remained unchanged, namely 'to promote the welfare and the happiness of the Nation; to increase the happiness of the many, not to support the plunder of a few'.[59] Polling took place on Tuesday 25 July, with votes cast as follows: Villiers, 1067; Thornely, 1052; Burton, 613; Benbow, 605. Villiers and Thornely were duly elected, and in the aftermath of his victory, Villiers, who had returned to his London residence in Wilton Street, informed his brother George of his success. In his letter, Villiers stated:

> I certainly was lucky in having a constituency who could appreciate the very unscrupulous and incompetent blackguards who were opposed to me ... I was very desirous during the canvass to succeed, and I made great exertion, the effects of which I am feeling now, being not a little shaken by it ... I took fright, and was determined not to be beat, if possible ... I have had great satisfaction in beating all the fools and rogues who were opposed to me, and defeated some miserable scoundrels who, professing to be Liberal, were intriguing against me; so I don't complain.[60]

However, as in his letter of 1835, Villiers bemoaned the financial costs of the election campaign:

> I certainly incurred expenses which I shall also feel for some time, and which I now find in some degree unnecessary ... The principal expense I incurred for this purpose was in retaining agents. I had three at 5 guineas a day, which is no bargain! Also the entertainment of a large party of canvassers at dinner each day at an inn is very pleasant at the time; but, like other pleasures, not without the alloy of d ... d expense. However, I shall recover myself, I dare say, in a year ... I am (for the redemption of my sins) obliged to go back to Wolverhampton to act as a steward at the races, *which exactly suits me!!!* Three days of great general ordinaries and dances in the evening – if that is not paying dear for one's country! I accepted it to get votes; but having got them at no great bargain, this supplemental expense and bore is horrid.[61]

Nevertheless, Villiers was in an ebullient mood, claiming subsequently that the local Tories 'came by dozens to me at the races, assuring me that they would never oppose me again' and concluding, in a prophetic observation, 'so, if I manage well, I suppose I shall have the seat for life'.[62]

Following their defeat in 1837, the Tories did not contest another election in Wolverhampton until 1874. Villiers' victory was in part due to the fact that he had captured some of the ultra-Radical support given to Nicholson in 1835 and, thereafter, those plebian ultra-radicals, who continued to be suspicious of both the Whig Ministry and Wolverhampton's Liberal elite, established a new branch of the Wolverhampton Political Union in 1838 and subsequently supported Chartism,[63] leading Richard Fryer to demand that, if Villiers and Thornely wished to retain their seats, they should be more critical of Melbourne's government.[64] In this context, it is worth noting that both Villiers and Thornely were becoming increasingly annoyed by Fryer's persistent intrusions into their affairs. As early as November 1835, Thornely informed Villiers that

> Mr Fryer has given me today his latest Edition of Notions on the present state of things ... He says we must have a perfectly free trade in corn – no duty whatever, and he declares we must have a public meeting here which you and I must attend,[65]

adding 'I hope nothing of the sort will be done'.[66] In December 1836, following a meeting in Wolverhampton, Villiers confessed to Thornely,

> I don't know what to think of old Mr Fryer. If I did not believe that he was a perfectly honest man, I should suppose that he had had enough of the Liberals (but that is only between ourselves). He certainly held forth in the Reading Room yesterday in a strain by no means unpleasing to the Conservatives,[67]

to which Thornely replied 'Our friend Mr Fryer is so eccentric that one is seldom sure of the view he will take on anything'.[68] Fryer's intervention of May 1839 came to nothing for, as Thornely told Villiers,

> Whatever may be the intrigue against us in the Borough, depend upon it, it will utterly fail. It is the people who return us, and they will continue to do so – in fact, we have had very little influence exercised in our favour.[69]

Indeed, by August, Thornely was able to inform Villiers that 'Our friends say we are as safe as possible, we gain so much at Willenhall and elsewhere, that there is nothing to fear',[70] although he later noted

> Between ourselves, the only one among our friends that I think is unmanageable is Mr Fryer, who is rash in the extreme, and speaks of putting Ministers out, and putting them in again, as if it was merely shuffling a pack of cards.[71]

However, although Villiers had retained the confidence of the electors, he was yet to win over the Tory *Wolverhampton Chronicle* which, at least early in his political career, did not always regard him favourably. One illustration of this occurred in June 1840 when it was reported that, during a debate in the House of Commons on the feasibility of extending summary jurisdiction to magistrates when dealing with cases of seduction, Villiers had claimed that local magistrates would not always form competent tribunals in such cases, 'for their sons and servants might frequently be parties in those cases'.[72] There was, no doubt, a grain of truth in this generalisation, but it drew an angry response from the *Chronicle*, which, in a lengthy editorial, launched a withering attack on Villiers. Commencing with faint praise of its victim, the newspaper stated:

> We belong not to that class of individuals inclined to deny to one of our representatives, the Hon. C.P. Villiers, the possession of a certain degree of creditable reputation. He is, in point of ability, decidedly above many of his Radical associates. His manners have also been more elevated; though a democrat, he is not quite a demagogue; there still exist traces of that polish and refinement which constitute such a prominent and essential portion of the character of an English gentleman ... We have been thus careful to state our estimate of Mr Villiers, and we know that it concurs with that of several of his supporters, because, notwithstanding the debasing influence of his political associations, local and general, we have always conceived Mr Villiers to be as superior, generally speaking, in attainments as in rank and character to the political party here to which he has unfortunately attached himself. We always had hopes of him and still have. Wild oats are often dropped on political ground. Nothing short of experience will ever convince us that he can become a ruthless, vulgar demagogue.[73]

This said, the *Chronicle* then proceeded to accuse Villiers (as in 1835) of again insulting the British magistracy, with charges that were 'notoriously untrue', by branding every magistrate, county and corporate, 'not with the venal sin of incompetence, but with the broad and disgraceful mark of shameless partiality and corruption' and of committing 'general slander', when in reality the magistracy provided 'justice tempered with mercy and zealously endeavoured to assuage quarrels and little disputes, and to promote peace and goodwill'. In conclusion, the *Chronicle* opined,

> For the sake of the political party to which, we have no doubt, we shall at some time see Mr Villiers attached, we pray him to keep himself intact from the ungentlemanly contamination – foul and unfounded charges – on which we have, not in anger, but in sorrow, commented.[74]

For Villiers, however, this editorial must have appeared as little more than journalistic opportunism from the Tory press, which had made a mountain out of a molehill, fomented, no doubt, by the fact that his claim had been given credence by the Radical *Staffordshire Advertiser*, a newspaper which the *Chronicle* regarded as 'censurable, dangerous and inflammatory'.[75] As such, Charles Villiers did not dignify the editorial by according it a response.

Indeed, of greater importance to Villiers was the fact that he and Thomas Thornely were establishing a harmonious working relationship and were increasingly acquiring widespread public confidence and support in Wolverhampton, despite the fact that neither actually lived in the town, for Thornely also retained his Liverpool residence and a London home in Regent Square. In January 1841, the Wolverhampton Liberals gave a banquet, attended by five hundred people, in honour of their two members, at which John Barker proposed the health of Ministers and MPs, and Villiers returned thanks. *The Spectator* reported that:

> His speech ought to be read as a whole … Abstaining in general from the hackneyed commonplaces of party politics, he skilfully interwove passing hits, where party allusions were locally unavoidable, with statesmanlike remarks on the great leading questions of the day, forming the staple of a speech which might have been appropriately delivered by the first man in the House of Commons on a motion for inquiry into the state of the nation.[76]

At the subsequent General Election in July, which witnessed substantial Whig losses and the defeat of Melbourne's government, Villiers and Thornely were, for the first time, returned unopposed in Wolverhampton and jointly pledged 'to continue to support those principles of freedom of trade and those interests of labour which it has been our earnest and unceasing object to promote in the House of Commons'.[77] This feat was repeated in 1847, when, in recalling Charles Villiers' first appearance at the hustings twelve years earlier, John Barker was moved to comment:

> Though a stranger, they took him in … he had served them honestly, faithfully, and gallantly; the promises he then made he had fulfilled … every expectation he had held out he had more than realised; and he did not doubt they would send him again to the same place to carry out other reforms, to aid in removing every restriction which weighed on the manufacturers, industry, and commerce of the country; and he trusted his life might be long spared, that his talents might be consecrated to the emancipation of the country from every abuse.[78]

Indeed, as Jon Lawrence has observed, by this time Charles Villiers had emerged as the unlikely embodiment, because of his defiant 'outsider' status, of the town's political identity and civic pride, and his role in Wolverhampton was illustrative of the recurrent tradition in Victorian politics of the 'gentleman leader as a people's tribune'.[79] The question arises then, as to how and why Villiers was able to fulfil the promises he had made and, in so doing, realise the expectations of his constituents during these years? This is a subject to which we now turn, by reference to two concurrent and inter-related themes: first, Villiers' early parliamentary career as a Radical reformer and, second, his pre-eminent role in the fight against the Corn Laws, which was to accord him an iconic national and provincial status as a principled reformer.

Notes

1. For general histories of Wolverhampton, see G.P. Mander, *History of Wolverhampton* (Wolverhampton, 1960); J. Roper, *Wolverhampton: The Early Town and its History* (Wolverhampton, 1966); F. Mason, *The Book of Wolverhampton* (Wolverhampton, 1979); Chris Upton, *A History of Wolverhampton* (Wolverhampton, 2007).
2. D.B.M. Huffer, 'The Economic Development of Wolverhampton, 1750–1850', unpublished M.A. thesis (University of London, 1957).
3. W. White, *History, Gazetteer and Directory of Staffordshire* (Sheffield, 1851).
4. For further details, see D.B.M. Huffer, 'The Growth of the Township of Wolverhampton to 1850', *West Midlands Studies*, 7 (1974), 5–15; Roger Swift, 'Wolverhampton: Economy and Society, 1815–56' in R.E. Swift, 'Crime, Law and Order in two English Towns during the early Nineteenth Century: The Experience of Exeter and Wolverhampton, 1815–1856', PhD thesis, University of Birmingham (1981), 220–38; George J. Barnsby, *Social Conditions in the Black Country, 1800–1900* (Wolverhampton, 1980).
5. For further details, see F. Mason, *Wolverhampton: The Town Commissioners, 1777–1848* (Wolverhampton, 1976).
6. For the background to the political history of Wolverhampton during the period, see especially Jon Lawrence, 'Party Politics and the People: Continuity and Change in the Political History of Wolverhampton, 1815–1914', PhD thesis, University of Cambridge (1989); Jon Lawrence, *Speaking for the People: Party, Language and Popular Politics in England, 1867–1914* (Cambridge, 1998), Part II, 'A Local Study: Wolverhampton, c.1860–1914', 73–162.
7. John Barker to Thomas Spring-Rice, nd., 1832, cited in Joseph Coohill, *Ideas of the Liberal Party: Perceptions, Agendas and Liberal Politics in the House of Commons, 1832–52* (Chichester, 2011), 59. Spring-Rice was the Whig MP for Cambridge, and later Chancellor of the Exchequer, 1835–41.
8. William Whitmore (1787–1858): Shropshire landowner of the Dudmaston estate, Whig MP for Bridgnorth from 1820–32, and supporter of the parliamentary reform, catholic emancipation and anti-slavery movements.
9. Richard Fryer (1770–1846): Whig politician, Wolverhampton banker and landowner, founder of the Union Mill Flour Company and owner of the Hatherton colliery and ironworks at Bloxwich.
10. Lawrence, *Speaking for the People*, 74.
11. For Thomas Thornely (1781–1862), see obituary, *Wolverhampton Chronicle*, 7 May 1862. See also E.F. Rathbone, *William Rathbone: A Memoir* (London, 1905), 10–11; M. Escott, 'Liverpool Borough', in D.R. Fisher (ed.), *The History of Parliament: The House of Commons, 1820–1832* (Cambridge, 2009); D.W. Bebbington, *Unitarian Members of Parliament in the Nineteenth Century* (Stirling, 2009), 10; Thornely had also held a senior post (with responsibility for American affairs) in the Liverpool East Indies Association: see Y. Kumagi, 'The Lobbying Activities of Provincial Mercantile and Manufacturing Interests against the Renewal of the East India Company Charter, 1812–1813 and 1829–1833', PhD thesis, University of Glasgow (2008), ch. 5, 147–90.
12. *Wolverhampton Chronicle*, 19 Jan. 1898. See also Lawrence, *Speaking for the People*, 74; *The Times*, 10 June 1879, letter from Fryer's daughter on the origins of Villiers' candidacy. On Richard Fryer's death in 1846, Villiers acknowledged that

> He had introduced him, Mr Villiers, to the constituency, having objected to do so until he found they agreed in thinking the Corn Laws were oppressive to the people and injurious to the country; he then consented to nominate him on the hustings:
>
> *Staffs Advertiser*, 31 July 1847

13 *Wolverhampton Chronicle*, 7 Jan. 1835.
14 For further details, see the handbills circulated by Nicholson's committee during the election campaign: Wolverhampton Archives and Local Studies [hereafter WALS], DX-559/2/7, Handbill, 29 Dec. 1834, 'A Few Plain Words to the Electors of Wolverhampton', for Nicholson against Thornely and Villiers; DX-584/5/7, Dec. 1834, Address supporting Nicholson and Thornely, 'true friends of the people, against Villiers, a wolf in sheep's clothing'; DX-584/5/4, Dec. 1834, Address stating Nicholson was 'a more fit and proper person than Villiers to be an MP'. Nicholson's supporters claimed that Charles Villiers 'was originally a Tory and a Tory he would remain until the end of the chapter. He might put on the mask of Reform for a time, but they would find it all mummery': *Wolverhampton Chronicle*, 14 Jan. 1835.
15 WALS, DX-584/5/12: Address discussing the merits and pretensions of Thornely, Villiers and Nicholson, in support of Nicholson, Dec. 1834.
16 *Staffs Advertiser*, 3 Jan. 1835: These were influential referees. John Romilly (1802–74), a Cambridge contemporary of Villiers (albeit at Trinity College), lawyer and Liberal politician, was the son of the law reformer, Sir Samuel Romilly, and was elected MP for Bridport in 1832, appointed Attorney-General by Russell in 1850, and raised to the peerage as Lord Romilly in 1865: J.A. Hamilton, *DNB* 1885–1900, vol. 49, 186–7; Edward Strutt (1801–80), also a Cambridge contemporary (from Trinity), Liberal free trader and MP for Derby 1830–48, then Arundel 1851–2 and Nottingham 1852–6, Chancellor of the Duchy of Lancaster under Aberdeen 1852–4 and raised to peerage as Baron Belper in 1856; Charles Poulett Thompson (1799–1841), Liberal free trader, politician and diplomat, was MP for Dover 1826 and later Manchester 1832–9, Vice-President of the Board of Trade under Lord Grey in 1830, President of the Board of Trade under Melbourne, Governor of Canada 1839, and was created 1st Baron Sydenham in 1840: Charles Sutton, *DNB* 1885–1900, vol. 56, 236–8.
17 John Romilly to Villiers, 25 Dec. 1834: WALS, DX-584/5/10, Handbill, Address of Charles Villiers to the Electors of the Borough of Wolverhampton, 29 Dec. 1834.
18 Edward Strutt to Villiers, 27 Dec. 1834: WALS, DX-584/5/10, Address of Charles Villiers.
19 Poulett Thompson to Villiers, 22 Dec. 1834: WALS, DX-584/5/10, Address of Charles Villiers.
20 George Grote to Villiers, 30 Dec. 1834: WALS, DX-584/5/16, Handbill, Address supporting Charles Villiers.
21 *Staffs Advertiser*, 3 Jan. 1835. See also WALS, DX-584/5/17, Handbill, Dec. 1834, Address supporting Charles Villiers – 'a friend to all Liberal measures, an enemy to all sinecures and pensions'; DX-559/2/10, Handbill, 30 Dec. 1834. Address: 'Parliament is Dissolved – for Villiers (and the Laurel)'; DX-559/2/8, Handbill, 30 Dec. 1834, Address: 'Vilest and most malicious scandals', in support of Villiers; DX-584/5/24, Handbill, Jan. 1835, Address from the Committees of Thornely and Villiers, giving their support, 'as united they are invincible and must be victorious – they are the men!!'
22 *Staffs Advertiser*, 10 Jan. 1835.
23 Ibid.
24 Ibid.
25 Ibid.
26 *Wolverhampton Chronicle*, 21 Jan. 1835.
27 Charles Villiers to George Villiers, 20 January 1835, in Maxwell, I., 85–6.
28 Ibid.
29 Ibid.

30 Ibid.
31 Ibid.
32 *Wolverhampton Chronicle*, 14 Jan. 1835.
33 *Staffs Advertiser*, 3 May 1835.
34 *Birmingham Journal*, 2 May 1835.
35 British Library of Political and Economic Science [hereafter BLPES], GB0097R/SR1094, The Thornely–Villiers Correspondence, 2 vols (1835–61).
36 These disorders were covered extensively by the *Wolverhampton Chronicle*, 3 June 1835, 10 June 1835, 17 July 1835, 8 July 1835. For detailed analyses of these disorders, see Swift, *Thesis*, 'Election Riots', 432–41; David Cox, '"The Wolves let loose at Wolverhampton": A Study of the South Staffordshire Election Riots, May 1835', *Law, Crime and History*, 2 (2011), 1–31; Norman Gash, *Politics in the Age of Peel* (London, 1953), 150–3.
37 *The Wolverhampton Inquiry: Copy of the Minutes taken at Wolverhampton*, PP (1835), XLVI, 245, 343.
38 *Parl. Debs.*, 3rd Ser., vol. 29, cc.132–5, 1 July 1835.
39 BLPES/SR1094, Thornely to Villiers, 17 June 1835: 'Respecting the attack made by the military on the people at Wolverhampton … I think we must ask a question from Lord John Russell on the subject in the House on Monday'.
40 *Parl. Debs.*, 3rd Ser., vol. 29, cc.132–5, 1 July 1835.
41 *Wolverhampton Chronicle*, 8 July 1835; 15 July 1835. A borough police force was established when Wolverhampton achieved incorporation in 1848: for policing arrangements and their reform, see Swift, *Thesis*, 352–419.
42 *Speech of C.P. Villiers, Esq. M.P. at a Dinner given by the Constituency of Wolverhampton to the Representatives of that Borough, 26 January 1836* (Printed by J. Bridgen, Darlington Street, Wolverhampton).
43 *Wolverhampton Chronicle*, 8 July 1835.
44 Ibid.
45 Ibid.
46 Ibid.
47 Ibid., 15 July 1835.
48 For further details, see Roger Swift, 'The English Urban Magistracy and the Administration of Justice during the Early Nineteenth Century: Wolverhampton, 1815–1860', *Midland History*, XVII (1992), 75–92.
49 *Speech of C.P. Villiers*, 26 Jan. 1836, 5–8.
50 Ibid., 3–4.
51 Ibid., 9–10.
52 Ibid., 11–12.
53 Ibid., 12–13.
54 Ibid., 14–15.
55 BLPES/SR1094, Villiers to Thornely, 31 Dec. 1836.

> I do regret very much that you were unable to come [to Wolverhampton] and so for us both to have gone to Willenhall. Everybody seems to say that we have neglected that place. I do not like to have any meetings unless you are here, and many think I should do no good by calling upon a few. I do fear that we shall have to reproach ourselves at the Election for not going there. It would have been very important that we should know exactly how we stand there, for it is impossible to depend upon anything but one's own senses … Everybody that I see says, what they have said for three months past, that we are perfectly safe for the Borough.

56 *Wolverhampton Chronicle*, 19 July 1837.
57 Ibid.

58 *Staffs Advertiser*, 15 July 1837.
59 *Wolverhampton Chronicle*, 26 July 1837.
60 Charles Villiers to George Villiers, 22 Aug. 1837, in Maxwell, I. 134–5.
61 Ibid.
62 Ibid.
63 However, although Chartism was particularly strong in the mining districts of the Black Country it made relatively little headway in the township of Wolverhampton itself, which remained free from Chartist disturbances and became a major centre for policing arrangements in South Staffordshire between 1842 and 1848: Swift, *Thesis*, 442–3. Indeed, the most notable excitement engendered in the town occurred in March 1842, when Feargus O'Connor arrived at Wolverhampton station and was escorted by a Chartist procession, witnessed by vast crowds, from Horseley Fields to Bilston, where he addressed a Chartist meeting: *Northern Star*, 19 Mar. 1842.
64 Lawrence, *Speaking for the People*, 78–9. See also BLPES/SR1094, Thornely to Villiers, 20 May 1839.
65 BLPES/SR1094, Thornely to Villiers, 10 Nov. 1835.
66 Ibid.
67 Ibid., Villiers to Thornely, 31 Dec. 1836.
68 Ibid., Thornely to Villiers, 2 Jan. 1837.
69 Ibid., Thornely to Villiers, 30 May 1839.
70 Ibid., Thornely to Villiers, 25 Aug. 1839.
71 Ibid., Thornely to Villiers, 31 Dec. 1839.
72 *Wolverhampton Chronicle*, 17 June 1840.
73 Ibid.
74 Ibid.
75 Ibid., 24 June 1840; 12 Aug. 1840.
76 *The Spectator*, 4 Jan. 1840.
77 *Wolverhampton Chronicle*, 7 July 1841.
78 *Staffs Advertiser*, 31 July 1847.
79 Lawrence, *Speaking for the People*, 68.

3 The young Parliamentarian

When Charles Villiers entered Parliament in February 1835, sitting alongside the great Radical, William Cobbett,[1] where it was observed that he was 'a man of handsome appearance [whose] courteous manners and ready wit soon made him a great favourite',[2] the political world was changing, for the Reform Act of 1832 had altered the nature and organisation of British politics and power,[3] although the extent of that change continues to be a matter of dispute among historians. On the one hand, for example, Peter Mandler has argued that Whiggism and aristocratic styles of government were reasserted during the premierships of Grey (1830–34), Melbourne (1835–41) and Russell (1846–52) by governments representing well-connected elites with a sense of national responsibility who were willing to respond to demands for reform.[4] By contrast, Jon Parry has suggested that the following twenty years witnessed the gradual emergence of a relatively confident and cohesive 'Liberal' rather than 'Whig' Party with a liberal value-system focused largely on questions of morals, economy and efficiency,[5] so much so that 'Liberal' governments under Aberdeen (1852–5), Palmerston (1855–8 and 1859–65) and Russell (1865–6) were to dominate British politics during the mid-Victorian period. These were, however, essentially coalitions of Whigs, Peelites and Radicals and, as Eugenio Biagini has observed, it could be argued that it was not until the formation of Gladstone's first administration in 1868 that a truly Liberal Party, with a real sense of ideological cohesion, was returned by the electorate.[6]

During the 1830s, the Liberals were clearly not a 'Party' in the modern sense. 'Liberal' is a broad term and, initially, the 'Liberals' were not a unified and homogenous body with a coherent ideology; rather, they were a loose coalition of aristocratic Whigs, Liberals, Reformers, Radicals and Irish Repealers, although the distinction between 'Reformers' and 'Radicals' is somewhat arbitrary – Joseph Coohill, for example, describes Villiers as 'Reformer' MP for Wolverhampton, rather than 'Radical' (which is how Villiers saw himself).[7] Nevertheless, there is some evidence to suggest that, by mid-century, the Liberals were developing a sense of being a political 'Party' with its own conception of Liberal politics, and MPs, including Villiers, increasingly described themselves as 'Liberals' as the period progressed, and distinguished themselves as such in contradistinction to the 'Tories'.[8]

In particular, these men subscribed to a liberal politics emphasising social, economic and political improvement which, as Boyd Hilton has shown, was influenced in part by religion, notably liberal Anglicanism and nonconformism, through private reflections of salvation and atonement, with God's work on earth being exercised by political and social leaders.[9] The Liberal agenda, which was also informed in part by the Benthamite procedural blueprint for reform,[10] covered wide-ranging issues, including the governance of Ireland, the reform of the Church of England, institutional reform, the abolition of slavery, the New Poor Law, factory reform, educational reform and electoral reform, including the secret ballot and the further extension of the suffrage, and, most notably, free trade and the Corn Laws. Indeed, Free Trade, influenced by the idea of political economy, lay at the very heart of the rising tide of liberalism as a political ideology,[11] although 'Free Trade' itself reflected a broad and fluid spectrum of social, economic, fiscal and political ideas amongst Liberals, and 'Free Traders' included moderate tariff reformers, fixed duty men and strict free traders, of whom Charles Villiers was one. Nevertheless, most Liberal MPs were committed to Free Trade, which had virtually become a party article of faith by 1850.[12]

Among Liberal MPs, there was far from unanimity on this reform agenda, but despite differing opinions, ideas of co-operation between them were strong.[13] Moreover, as Miles Taylor has shown, there was a close connection between ideology and political action, whereby Radicals and Reformers provided a link between liberal and reform-minded electors in the country and MPs in Parliament, exerting pressure on Liberal ministers to address popular demands for reform which they articulated in various ways, including the presentation of petitions on issues such as electoral reform and free trade,[14] as Villiers' subsequent career was to illustrate.

As Harriet Martineau observed, the group of Philosophic Radicals with whom Charles Villiers was initially associated in Parliament, and who included Molesworth, Grote, Hume, Perronet Thompson, Buller, Bulwer Lytton, Roebuck and Leader, were remarkable for their individuality and were keen to prove that, far from being single-subject reformers, the Benthamite principles which prompted their pursuit of specific reforms were in fact applicable to a wider reform agenda based on utilitarianism and political economy.[15] They shared a common dislike of both Tories and Whigs, who they regarded as the enemies of progress and democracy, and believed that the tide of reform could not be checked.[16] Indeed, Charles Villiers held that the future of Liberalism lay with such men, claiming in February 1836 that, in the event of a dissolution of Parliament, whilst 'a great many timid, half-and-half, Glory-of-the-British-Constitution, rally-round-the-throne people would get returned ... there would also be a larger number than usual of independent, general-happiness, things-to-be-measured-by-their-utility people returned', adding that 'What would never appear again would be the good old Whig; come what will, the direction things are taking is onward and not backward'.[17] When George Villiers expressed a mild but friendly concern at his younger brother's extreme radicalism, Charles explained

> The history of my politics is shortly this. I am not the least ambitious of sharing either the honours or the emoluments of any government, and therefore I never speculate at all as to which party I will or will not belong; but as long as I am in Parliament, I just consider in any case what, according to the best of my judgment, will conduce the most to the advantage of the community at large, without reference to particular interest or the consequences to this or that class or privileged body; knowing well however that nothing can conduce less to the interests of the community than anything that at least shakes the great principles on which our social and political existence depends.[18]

These principles were, Villiers continued,

> security to life and property, but not in the narrow aristocratic sense of the word, which only contemplates keeping the masses down and quiet ... but that security which attends to every man the greatest possible protection in the free exercise of his industry and his intellect, and in the enjoyment of his property.[19]

He then proceeded to criticise the aristocracy who,

> while they have been trained to the expectation of political power, independently of any qualification of merit or fitness for its exercise, the circumstances of the country have so entirely changed with the progress of civilisation that they feel that their prospects are less and less bright ... and they can't understand or fathom the real causes of their position.[20]

Some Tories, he charged, were 'only rogues and have wit equal to the discernment of the senseless rant of their associates', and he was particularly critical of the Tory press in London who were 'predicting the end of all things from the advancement of liberal politics and the shocking march of radicalism', and calling for an end to Melbourne's ministry, when he had himself recently visited Scotland, Staffordshire and Lancashire and witnessed the great prosperity of trade and manufacture, 'unparalleled in the history of the country'.[21]

Indeed, Villiers regarded Liberalism as an unstoppable force. In a speech at Wolverhampton, Villiers told his constituents that resistance to the tide of Liberalism was 'as unwise as unjust – it is impossible', adding that 'For a century past there had been a party in this country denouncing all change, and resisting the party demanding reform', but history had witnessed that 'from that time to this hour, this conservative party has been in error and the liberal party right'.[22] Continuing in this vein, Villiers concluded his speech with a spirited call:

> To the liberal party then I would say – from all you remember, all you observe, and all you foresee, continue steady and firm in the course you have pursued hitherto; remember that all you enjoy has been gained by the party to which you belong; and that those who are now held most in regard are those who have been chiefly maligned; and, above all, forget not that the cause of justice, freedom, and benevolence can never give you cause to regret.[23]

However, the Philosophic Radicals, known as 'the violent party' at Westminster between 1835 and 1837, were disunited in that individual members were too independent and group unity was ultimately impeded by petty jealousies.[24] They also carried Benthamite ideas in different directions according to temperament and circumstances, developing loyalties to a range of specific reform causes. *The Britannia*, a Tory publication, described these men as 'Hammerers', observing

> There are agitators within the House of Commons as well as out of doors ... Where there is a demos, there will soon be a demagogue – and where there is a demagogue, the chances are too much in favour of there being ultimately a democracy. Now this defect, if it be a defect, has been of late years made a powerful lever by the party to which Mr Villiers may be said to belong. Among a multitude of these self-elected undergraduates of democracy, some will immediately strike the mind: – Mr Grote and his ballot; Mr Villiers and his repeal of the corn laws; Sir John Easthope and his Church Rates, and more, too many to enumerate; for every agitator is the patron of a specific 'grievance'. Their office is to hammer away at the same ideas without cessation ... and keep themselves and their subject continually in the mind's eye. It is the course, which conduced, with others, to the passing of Catholic Emancipation and Reform. One of the most persevering and pertinacious of these Hammerers is Mr Villiers.[25]

In February 1836, however, this Radical group was influential in the establishment of the Reform Club for the dual purpose of both bringing together Radical MPs and as a meeting place for provincial Liberals to use when visiting London, thereby rivalling the (Tory) Carlton Club,[26] although the Radicals also continued to meet privately at the home of Sir William Molesworth,[27] and, on occasion, at Temple Leader's home in Putney Hill.[28] Indeed, Molesworth hoped that the Reform Club would serve as a vehicle for enabling the Radicals to absorb the Whigs within parliamentary Liberalism, although these hopes were soon to be dashed when, as Millicent Fawcett observed, 'the philosophical Radicals especially quickly approached a vanishing point' following the General Election of 1837, occasioned by the death of William IV, when several Radicals, including Roebuck, lost their seats.[29] Moreover, Lord John Russell's assertion in the House of Commons of November 1837 (in response to proposals from Thomas Wakley, the MP for Finsbury, for a further extension of the franchise and the secret ballot) that the 1832 Reform Act represented a final and irrevocable political settlement,[30] (hence his nickname 'Finality Jack'), crushed the Radicals' assumption that the tide of reform could not be reversed. Mrs Grote duly informed Molesworth 'I don't see how we Radicals are to make head this coming Parliament ... the brunt of the battle will have to be sustained by Grote and you, aided by Buller, Leader, Charles Villiers and a few more'.[31] However, moderate Radicals were increasingly anxious to form an amicable arrangement with the government and, according to Charles Greville, became 'very angry' with Grote and his associates,[32] and the Philosophic Radicals – described by William Thomas as 'too public spirited to consider themselves an interest group and too divergent in opinion to form a party'[33] – were gradually assimilated into a larger Liberal party embracing different shades of reforming opinion, within which, as Angus Hawkins has recently shown, Philosophic Radicalism was peripheral to mainstream patriotic political debate.[34]

Nevertheless, Charles Villiers was widely regarded as 'one of the most accomplished, as well as one of the original members' of the Reform Club,[35] and when the Club held a banquet in celebration of the Princess Victoria's eighteenth birthday on 24 May 1837, Villiers proposed the health of her mother, the Duchess of Kent, and it was said that his eloquent speech was regarded as the best he had ever made. In the course of his address he refuted Tory allegations that the Reformers were enemies of the Throne and the Church, demonstrating how false and absurd such charges were and remarking that

> In those days when the old men were retrograding, it was perhaps not undesirable that the young should press forward; and that he did not scruple to express the joy he felt at the dawn of a bright day which that anniversary presented to those who desired by purifying and reforming to strengthen the institutions of the country.[36]

Subsequently, Charles Villiers welcomed the accession of Queen Victoria on 20 June 1837, a process which had provoked public controversy emanating from the counter-claims – advanced by some Ultra Tories and the Orange Lodges – of the unpopular Ernest Augustus, Duke of Cumberland (and later King of Hanover).[37] In a letter to George Villiers in August, Charles held that the support rendered by Lord Melbourne and the Whigs for the Queen, which was reciprocated, should be 'smiled at by everybody who heard it', although he added

> As everybody belonging to a Court is necessarily false, and as few have access there now but those who are interested in denying the truth if it

is otherwise than they wish, it is impossible to know what are the real sentiments of this little Queen; but what is most probable is that she likes popularity and, from what one hears, having good sense, besides that she sees the best prospect of having what she likes at an easy rate by retaining what is called a popular ministry. I dare say she would avoid, if possible, the hullabaloo there would be in the country if the Tories were to come in again.[38]

However, in a further letter to his brother in September, Charles Villiers, who supported the monarchy and later developed cordial relationships with both the Queen and Prince Albert, expressed some concern at Victoria's relative youth and inexperience and her dependence on Melbourne 'and those of her relations who now guide her' (and who included the Duchess of Kent, with whom Victoria had a difficult relationship). 'There are', he observed,

all sorts of stories afloat about her cleverness, goodness, & etc; but how can she really know anything? We all know what it costs us in experience to form any judgment about men and things; how can a girl of 18, without a miracle, be but very ignorant of all public matters?[39]

The so-called 'Bedchamber Crisis' of May 1839 perhaps confirmed Villiers' initial concerns. This arose from Lord Melbourne's decision to resign following a narrow government majority in the House of Commons. Melbourne advised the Queen to ask the Duke of Wellington to form a Tory ministry, but the Duke declined, suggesting that Victoria approach Sir Robert Peel instead. Peel accepted the invitation but insisted that the Queen replace some of her ladies of the bedchamber, who were close friends and largely represented Whig families, with Tories. The Queen, who was anxious to keep Melbourne at her side, refused, indicating that these were her personal appointments and not subject to political advice. Peel, who did not wish to lead a minority Tory ministry, and who also wished to avoid an open confrontation with the Queen, backed down and Melbourne resumed office, although the Queen was quick to learn from her misjudgement, for when Peel came to office in 1841 she replaced some of her Whig ladies in waiting with Tories.[40]

From the outset of his parliamentary career, Charles Villiers was committed to a broad reform agenda and contributed regularly to debates in the House of Commons on a range of contemporary issues. These included parliamentary reform, civil and religious liberty, the abolition of slavery, freedom of the press, the introduction of the penny post, and the need for social reform in the context of the 'Condition of England' Question. In so doing, Villiers more than honoured the electoral pledges he had made to his constituents in Wolverhampton.

In regard to parliamentary reform, Villiers regarded the 1832 Reform Act as a beginning rather than an end, but he was sceptical of the ability of Melbourne's Whigs to deliver further reform. As he informed George Villiers in February 1836:

> You ask me what I expect respecting the present Ministry. Why at first I should say, some d. ...d stupid blunder owing to their self-sufficiency and ignorance of what should be known to them ... The Whigs obtained and retained power by reforming the House of Commons. They are told that if they enfranchise populous and manufacturing districts they will be compelled to give the voters the protection of the ballot. They say when the time has come they will consider it. *The time is arrived!* There is not a large and independent boro' that cares much for any other question. They not only refuse it, but say we are so hostile to it that we won't do what the Tories did about the Catholic question, and leave it open.[41]

In June 1836, Villiers supported George Grote's motion for the introduction of the secret ballot to eliminate bribery, intimidation and other malpractices during elections. He noted that this issue was one of great interest to his own constituents in Wolverhampton, 'a great number of whom are operatives and mechanics', and stated that there were 'great moral advantages' which would result from the secret ballot, namely that

> It will teach the candidate that he must earn the good opinion of the constituency in order to obtain their votes ... And it will improve the constituency, for when they are secure in the discharge of their duty, they will be much more likely to discharge it than at present.[42]

In short, Villiers concluded that

> there is no danger in trusting the people in the free exercise of their elective franchise, because the protections at present to free exercise are not adequate, and because I believe the ballot to be the only effectual means for accomplishing that object.[43]

However, the motion was defeated by 139 votes to 88. Nevertheless, thereafter, Villiers continued to advocate the secret ballot, informing the House of Commons that 'The people of this country were now fully aware of the extent to which bribery and intimidation were carried on at the elections and they will endure it no longer', adding that

> what occurs now in the choice of Members is degrading to Parliament; and further, that those practices that had been so often pointed to as pernicious and objectionable, never were carried to a greater extent than they were at the last election.[44]

He also pointed out that the present expense of obtaining and maintaining a seat, consequent upon open voting, was such that no man of limited means could really aspire to a seat, and that, although he did not contend that the ballot was a perfect system, 'he knew of no other so likely to succeed in checking the vices and evils of the present system'.[45] In particular, Villiers regarded Russell as a major obstacle to further parliamentary reform, and in 1839 the diarist Charles Greville, in noting that Russell 'never would consent to begin again the work of disfranchisement nor to make the ballot an open question; that he *is alarmed* and determined to stop', stated that

> Lord Clarendon had told me much the same thing on the authority of his brother Charles, who is a very leading man and much looked to among them, probably (besides that he really is very clever) on account of that aristocratic origin and connexion which he himself affects to despise, and to consider prejudicial to him.[46]

In April 1842, William Sharman Crawford presented a motion in the House of Commons for a Parliamentary Commission to be established in order to discuss a petition from Joseph Sturge's Complete Suffrage Union which demanded further Parliamentary reform. Crawford highlighted the inadequacies of the 1832 Reform Act, noting that 107 MPs continued to be returned in boroughs where the influence of a patron was paramount, whilst 194 County MPs and 32 Irish County MPs were elected by the influence of the aristocracy.[47] The motion was overwhelmingly defeated by 226 votes to 67, but it was supported by Villiers, who stated that

> He intended to do on this occasion what he had done on every other since he had had a seat – namely to vote for an inquiry into a grievance alleged by the people to exist, and the existence of which, indeed, was not disputed by any body.[48]

Observing that the principle of the Reform Bill was that taxation and representation should go together, he then proceeded to attack the Tories for opposing the extension of the suffrage on the grounds that the people were wholly unfit to exercise their judgement on political matters. If this was so, asked Villiers, 'Why were they always appealing to the people's judgment? And why were they proud on the other side when they had it in their favour?', adding that he could 'not conceive that any intelligible ground could be assigned by any person in a free country, where people at least were allowed to consider their grievances'.[49]

Villiers responded in similar vein to Chartist demands for the famous 'Six Points' on parliamentary reform. Whilst he agreed in principle with elements of the Chartist programme, notably the secret ballot, universal suffrage, and redistribution, he held that the petitioners' belief that the whole programme could be implemented was 'a delusion', and he also deprecated Chartist violence. Moreover, he regarded the demands of some Radicals to link the campaign for free trade with the Chartist demand for universal suffrage as both diversionary and unhelpful.[50] Nevertheless, he was one of the 46 MPs who voted for Attwood's unsuccessful Chartist petition in July 1839,[51] and again, in May 1842, when the second Chartist petition was submitted to Parliament, he argued that the petitioners should be allowed to plead their case by counsel at the Bar of the House, stating that

> People were going to vote against this on account of the dangerous consequences of extending the suffrage suddenly, but who said that they were for its gradual extension. Why, if the petitioners were heard and treated fairly, they might see the importance of not claiming anything beyond the gradual extension, and many evils now complained of might be cured by thus giving the subject a patient consideration.[52]

However, the House refused to hear the petitioners.[53]

Villiers also supported local government reform, welcoming the Municipal Corporations Act of 1835, which he described as 'a noble work, passing power from the evil doer to the rightful owner',[54] and which he regarded as a logical corollary of the 1832 Reform Act, and the Municipal Corporations Act Amendment Bill of the following year,[55] which sought to terminate the power of the trustees of charities established under the old corporations who had continued to operate, paying the funds to particular individuals of one political party to the exclusion of others, notwithstanding other abuses. Villiers congratulated Russell on introducing this Bill, adding

> It was notorious that the administration of charitable trusts had been grossly abused by the old corporations, in whose hands it had hitherto been vested, and the noble Lord was therefore perfectly right in insisting that it should be removed from them.[56]

But Villiers was also particularly anxious that Wolverhampton should achieve municipal borough status under the terms of the 1835 Act and he lent his support to the lengthy campaign, spearheaded largely by local Liberals, as a result of which the town obtained a Charter of Incorporation in March 1848, when the powers of the Improvement Commissioners were transferred to the newly-elected Borough Council. Incorporation was to mark a watershed in the history of Wolverhampton and civic pride was reflected in subsequent attempts to combat some of the worst evils of the urban–industrial environment by facilitating public improvements during the second half of the century.[57]

In regard to civil and religious liberty, Villiers, although an Anglican (but not of the High Church variety), was an outspoken critic of the abuses in the civil and ecclesiastical institutions of both England and Ireland and campaigned for the lifting of civil disabilities on Dissenters.[58] In July 1836, during the debates on the Established Church Bill, Villiers welcomed the Report of the Ecclesiastical Commission, which had been appointed in 1835 to examine Anglican Church revenues and which recommended the creation of new sees and the redistribution of Church revenues, which the Bill of 1836 acknowledged. However, whilst accepting that the Bill 'was an improvement upon the present arrangements of the Church Establishment', he held that it did not go far enough, for it sought neither to disestablish the Church nor to advance the claims of Dissenters, especially in regard to the removal of financial levies by the Anglican Church such as church rates and tithes.[59] 'The evils and abuses connected with the Church were', he stated,

> well understood, and ... if people thought that much of the evil sprang from the capricious and irregular distribution of the property of the Church ... then he was afraid that this would not be regarded as a measure of that suitable or satisfactory character which he hoped His Majesty's Ministers would have proposed.[60]

Villiers added that

> People would judge of institutions in these days by their utility ... and it was natural in reason that people should require that the revenues of the Church should be distributed and allotted in a manner more likely to attain the end for which every Establishment existed.[61]

In supporting the measure, which was passed, Villiers declared that he expected further reforms, because public opinion would not be satisfied until the Establishment was rendered suitable to the wants of an intelligent and religious community.[62] In particular, he was critical of sinecures and venality within the Church of England (of which he was a member), informing his constituents in July 1837 that 'those in the Church who did the work should be paid for it; and those who were idle should be made to work', a statement that was greeted with loud cheers.[63] In May 1837, Villiers also supported two Bills relating to Sunday Observance; the first to restrain all open desecration of the Sabbath and to extend to all classes the opportunity of resting; the second, to give local authorities the discretion to move Saturday and Monday fairs to other days of the week. Nevertheless, Villiers pointed to the inconsistency, if not hypocrisy, of some MPs with industrial and commercial interests who, whilst encouraging their fellow Members to abide by the Sabbath, refused to close down their own enterprises on Sundays.[64]

However, in regard to the Church of Ireland, Villiers opposed Lord John Russell's Tithes (Ireland), Issue of Exchequer Bill of May 1838. This had arisen from a shortfall of £1 million in 1836–7 in the payment of tithes in Ireland to the Irish Church, due largely to the refusal of tenants to pay, and Russell had moved that the Treasury be allowed to remit such instalments from the public purse. Whilst acknowledging that 'a great debt was due to

Ireland for the manner in which we have long misgoverned her', Villiers stated that he would vote against 'this unjust appropriation of the public money', adding

> Was not every species of reform in England stopped for the want of money? Was not the education of the people – was not a better means of internal communication – was not an uniform rate of post – all stopped because they could not spare £100,000? And yet they were now called upon to vote away a larger amount of the public money for a useless purpose ... He was sure, that the English people would consider it a dangerous and serious violation of the security of property, and of the principles of justice, if they sanctioned this arbitrary resistance to the law.[65]

These comments annoyed Daniel O'Connell (with whom Villiers otherwise had a good working relationship) who retorted that 'The Church of the few in Ireland was an English luxury at the expense of Ireland, and it was only fair that a little of the expense should now be borne by England'.[66]

Villiers had long abhorred slavery and his support for Wilberforce's Anti-Slavery movement had in part underpinned his unsuccessful parliamentary campaign for the seat of Kingston-upon-Hull in 1826. The Slavery Abolition Act of 1833 had freed slaves below the age of six in the British colonies and re-designated former slaves in domestic and agricultural work as apprentices, whose servitude was to be abolished in two stages by August 1840, and the British government had raised £20 millions in compensation for slave owners.[67] However, the Act did not go as far as the anti-Slavery Society had hoped. In particular, it did not extend to territory possessed by the East India Company or to Ceylon and St. Helena, and Villiers continued to campaign in Parliament for the elimination of these last vestiges of slavery and the slave-trade in the British Empire.[68] In so doing, he was encouraged by his friend, and fellow free trader, Joseph Sturge, the Birmingham corn factor, Quaker, philanthropist, parliamentary reformer and a former leading light in the Anti-Slavery Society. Indeed, Henry Richard, one of Sturge's earliest biographers, claimed that Charles Villiers was one of Sturge's most faithful associates in his struggle for the liberation of the slave.[69] In November 1837 Villiers attended a large meeting of anti-slavery delegates at Exeter Hall to discuss the measures which should be adopted 'in consequence of the grievous oppressions practised on the negro apprentices of the British colonies', and seconded the resolutions of the meeting, whose speakers included Joseph Sturge and Daniel O'Connell.[70] In April 1838 Villiers voted for the Slavery Abolition Amendment Bill[71] and in May 1838 he seconded the motion by Sir Eardley Wilmot in the House of Commons 'that the system of negro apprenticeship in the British Colonies should immediately cease', with the result that Barbados, Granada, St. Vincent, St. Kitts, Nevis, Monserrat, the Virgin Islands and Jamaica duly passed Acts declaring apprenticeship at an end from 1 August 1838.[72]

In 1839, Sturge founded the British and Foreign Anti-Slavery Society and Villiers was elected an Honorary Corresponding Member of the Society at its inaugural meeting at Exeter Hall on 19 April 1839.[73] The Society sought to harry British governments over the anomalies in the 1833 Act, freedmen's rights in the West Indies, and the regulation of traffic in indentured labourers to the British colonies, as well as fostering anti-slavery movements abroad, and Villiers subsequently attended the BFASS annual conferences in London in 1840[74] and 1841.[75] In August 1842 Villiers put a question to the Government asking if any steps had been taken (as per the provisions of the East India Charter Act) to eliminate slavery and the slave-trade in India, and especially in the settlements of Penang, Province Wellesley and Singapore [Malaysia]. He was informed that the Governor-General in India and the Governors of Singapore and Penang were developing projects to this end.[76] He also raised a similar question in regard to slavery in Ceylon, where there were 'nearly 30,000 people in that condition'. Lord Stanley, the Secretary for the Colonies, stated that slavery there had been virtually extinguished but that he intended to introduce a new Registration Act, which would render the final abolition of slavery comparatively easy.[77] Slavery in India and Ceylon was duly abolished in 1843.

One issue which compromised the work of the BFASS was the question of sugar duties, for sugar, which became an increasingly popular commodity during the period, could be produced more cheaply in the slave plantations of Brazil and Spanish-controlled Cuba than in the slave-free West Indies. This posed something of a conundrum for the BFASS, many of whose supporters were free traders, for if British ports were opened up to Brazilian and Cuban sugar, which might make good commercial sense, this would serve only to perpetuate slavery in the South American plantations, which was morally wrong. Moreover, when demand for sugar rose, prices increased, the demand for labour grew, and the Brazilian and Cuban slave trade with Africa increased; whereas when demand fell, prices dropped, the demand for labour fell, and the slave trade lagged. This issue was further complicated by the fact that, as Charles Villiers observed in 1842, sugar could also be brought to European markets as cheaply and as good as that from Brazil from other parts of the world where labour was free, including Manila, Java, Siam and Cochin-China.[78] He rejected the view of many BFASS members that importing sugar from slave countries served only to encourage slavery, arguing that by opening up British ports to all sugar producers, plantation-owners in Brazil would lose the protection afforded to them by treaty, be forced to compete on the open market, and realise that it was in their best interests to discontinue slavery. However, as he pointed out to the House of Commons,

> if you succeed in making them [Brazil] abolish slavery you cannot let in their sugar unless you get the people of Cuba to do the same; of which, as you know, there is not the remotest chance.[79]

This latter observation was founded on good intelligence, for Charles Villiers' brother George, when British minister in Madrid, had informed him that

> All those Spaniards who are not absolutely indifferent to the abolition of the slave trade are positively averse to it. We think that an appeal to humanity must be conclusive. The word is not understood ... Cuba is the pride and hope and joy of Spain ... the place where revenue comes, and whither every bankrupt Spaniard goes to rob *ad libitum*.[80]

In the event, this issue effectively split the BFASS during the 1840s and lost it support. Villiers, Cobden, Bright and other free traders subsequently voted against the Sugar Duties Bill in June 1848,[81] and supported Hutt's motion against the use of the West Africa naval squadron to police slave ships off the coasts of Africa, the Americas and the Caribbean in March 1850.[82] On both occasions they were joined by William Gladstone, whose attitude towards both the sugar duties and the slave trade had hitherto been complex and at times ambivalent, as recent studies by Roland Quinault[83] and Richard Huzzey[84] have illustrated.

Opposition to the stamp duties had long been a key feature of the Radical campaign to secure a free press, for the 4d. duty on newspapers – which effectively created a monopoly – was widely regarded as a tax on knowledge which impeded the education of the working classes. Moreover, possession of an unstamped newspaper carried heavy penalties and impeded the development of working-class radicalism. When Lord John Russell's Stamp Duties and Excise Bill, which reduced the stamp duty on newspapers from 4d to 1d, secured a majority in the House of Commons in June 1836,[85] it was supported by some Radicals, including Roebuck and Villiers, as a step towards press freedom, although they held that the measure did not go far enough. As Villiers observed, any duty was 'opposed to the feeling of the country; it was considered that its object was rather to suppress intelligence than to facilitate the collection of the revenue', adding that the continued penalisation for possession of an unstamped newspaper still

> exposed the poor man to great hazard, inasmuch as he might be violating the law without knowing that he was doing so. Any one might go and place in the poor man's cottage an unstamped paper, and thus render him liable to a heavy penalty.[86]

The introduction of a postal duty was a logical corollary of the Stamp Duties Act of 1836, prior to which newspapers which carried a 4d stamp were permitted free use of the postal service, and Villiers gave considerable support to Rowland Hill's campaign to secure the Penny Post between 1837 and 1839. In January 1837, Hill, whose father had taught the young Charles Villiers, and who had family connections with Wolverhampton,[87] sought Villiers' help, as the MP for Wolverhampton, in gaining parliamentary support for his scheme, entitled 'Post Office Reform'. As Villiers later recalled, in a letter to Frederick Hill several days after Rowland Hill's death in 1879:

> I remember well, indeed, the frequent communications I had with your brother when he was first bringing his plan before the public, and also (to his honour) the great disinterestedness that he showed when he requested me to submit the scheme then in MS to the Government, offering to allow them to have the entire credit of its introduction, if they chose to undertake it, stipulating only that, if they should refuse, he should then refer it to the Press, and make it known to, and understood by, the country. The apprehensions that were then expressed at headquarters (when I executed his commission) are still fresh in my recollection, and most certainly was he left free to do what he liked about a measure that, in their view, would require such a sacrifice of revenue, and the success of which was so extremely problematical. I always considered it fortunate (with regard to its success) that the measure was thus left to the unbiased judgment of the public, and to the energetic support which such men as Grote, Warburton, and Hume, and the really intelligent reformers then in the House, gave to your brother.[88]

A motion for the establishment of a Select Committee to consider Hill's scheme was put forward on 23 November 1837 and the committee, which included Villiers, was formed on 27 November. The resulting inquiry, which heard evidence from Hill and Richard Cobden, amongst others, and which received many petitions from the provinces in support of reform, endorsed the need for and importance of an inexpensive and efficient system of postal communication and recommended the adoption of Hill's scheme.[89] Petitions supporting the scheme were also submitted to the House of Lords, where Lord Brougham was the leading advocate, and included one from 'a large number of merchants, bankers, and others, of Wolverhampton'.[90] The subsequent Bill, creating a uniform penny postage, and which Villiers supported, passed the House of Commons on 22 July 1839 and the House of Lords on 17 August.

With the passing of the Bill, Hill was presented with a silver candelabrum by the inhabitants of Wolverhampton, inscribed 'To Rowland Hill, Esq., presented by the Inhabitants of Wolverhampton in testimony of their high sense of his public services, as the Founder and Able Advocate of the Plan of Universal Penny Post. A.D. 1839',[91] The implementation of Hill's scheme in 1840 heralded a new age of postal communication in which the post and, later, the telegraph, were made state responsibilities, with obvious social, political, economic, and commercial benefits. Hill temporarily served thereafter as Secretary to the Postmaster General, although he was dismissed in August 1843, much to the disappointment of Brougham and Villiers, who, according to Rowland Hill's brother, Matthew Hill, 'express great anger and surprise'.[92]

In regard to social reform, Charles Villiers advanced the utilitarian argument that government should not enact legislation that protected one economic interest in the country at the expense of others, stressing the importance of commercial freedom and sound legislation in improving the welfare of the people and opposing restrictive legislation which impeded this.[93]

Villiers consistently supported the New Poor Law, a truly Benthamite-inspired measure (as indeed was much Whig social legislation during the 1830s), which was greeted by contemporaries with expressions of approbation and hostility in equal measure. For its detractors, including most Tories and many (but not all) Radicals and the Chartists, it was regarded as reactionary, despotic, misguided and malevolent, as an unwarranted and unconstitutional centralising measure which undermined traditional paternalistic approaches to the local control of welfare provision and threatened English liberty. For its supporters, by contrast, it represented progress, efficiency, the triumph of utility, the victory of common sense and uniformity over chaos, and financial responsibility. Indeed, these perceptions, and the extent to which the New Poor Law marked a radical break with the past, continue to inform the historiography of the subject.[94]

The system established in 1834 contained some inherent weaknesses. It was partly designed to save money by cutting the cost of pauperism rather than to alleviate poverty in the round and to address its root causes. It was also based on selective evidence drawn largely from the rural south rather than the industrial north and it later proved both impossible and impractical to enforce the proscription of outdoor relief in the industrial towns of the Midlands and the North during the economic slump of 1839–42.[95] Moreover, in practical terms, a great deal of power and discretion was vested in local Boards of Guardians, some of whom resented interference from the Poor Law Commission and disregarded its directives. Charles Villiers was not unaware of the anomalies that inhibited the new system, but consistently defended it, once reminding his constituents in Wolverhampton that the detractors of the New Poor Law 'should consider what was the iniquity, oppression and fraud practised under the old system'.[96] During a debate in the House of Commons in August 1836 on the implementation and operation of the new system, he observed that only two petitions had been received complaining of the working of the new law, whereas 277 unions, all voluntarily formed, had surrendered their former privileges and adopted the regulations of the Poor Law Commissioners.[97] Reminding the House that he was the only Member who had been one of the Commissioners of Inquiry into the Poor Laws, Villiers stated that

> What he had wished to see accomplished was, to put an end to parochial jobbing and to the fraudulent practice of degrading the labourer by keeping wages extremely low. Those who wished to raise the wages of the poor and maintain them in comfortable independence were better friends to them than those who consented to dole out to them a miserable

pittance in the shape of parochial relief. The English labourer, in his opinion, was far more likely to be honest and virtuous under the present system ... those who wished to revert to the old system wanted to make the labourer dependent and to lower his wages.[98]

Again, in 1844, during a debate on rural distress and discontent in Suffolk, which had resulted in the destruction by fire of ricks, stacks, hay and other farm products, Villiers refuted the claims of some Tories that the root of poverty in the district lay in the application of the New Poor Law. Noting that the district had suffered from great distress under the Old Poor Law and that then the evil had been traced to the maladministration of parochial relief, he ascribed the labourers' current plight to the continued existence of 'a law to impede trade and check the supply of food [Corn Laws] and thus lessen the demand for labour'.[99]

Villiers also defended the Poor Law Commissioners in the face of criticisms from the provinces and within Parliament. In 1842, when William Ferrand, the Tory MP for Knaresborough and a leading critic of the New Poor Law, engaged in a long-running and vitriolic dispute with the Commissioners in general, and George Cornewall Lewis in particular, over the Commissioners' assertion that Keighley Union was badly administered and that local magistrates had acted improperly in ignoring the Commission's directives,[100] Villiers defended the Commissioners in Parliament. Ferrand, however, persisted with his allegations of impropriety to the extent that, in 1846, Cornewall Lewis threatened to file a criminal investigation against him for conspiracy and falsehood. The matter was resolved in May 1847, due in part to Roebuck's intervention in the Commons in support of Villiers and Lewis. As Roebuck noted in his Diary:

> In the evening I went to the House and found Ferrand in full roar against the Poor Law. Charles Villiers was sitting behind me, and carried a message from me to George Grey, who was taking notes to answer Ferrand. My message was that if he would leave him to me I would give Ferrand a dressing. The answer came: 'Only too happy; pray proceed', and so indeed I did.[101]

Several days later, Roebuck noted

> Last night I repeated my infliction on Ferrand, carrying the House triumphantly with me, and obtained the warm cheers even of the Treasury Bench, with Lord John leading the band ... The sensation was great ... Charles Villiers felt himself personally indebted to me, as I defended Lewis against the atrocious charges brought by Ferrand against him.[102]

Similarly, when Sir George Nicholls expressed the Commissioners' growing concern that Edwin Chadwick was becoming dictatorial and was exceeding his authority as Secretary to the Commission, Charles Villiers supported him;[103] and when Mr Christie, the Member for Weymouth, alleged that the appointment of George Cornewall Lewis (who had married Villiers' widowed sister Theresa in 1844) as a Poor Law Commissioner had been fixed by his father, Sir Frankland Lewis, prior to his retirement, Villiers vehemently defended his brother-in-law in the Commons.[104] In the event, however, in light of continued criticisms from the provinces of the centralising tendencies of Chadwick and the Commission and, more especially, of the findings of the Parliamentary Select Committee into the Andover Union (where, in 1845, it had been discovered that workhouse inmates were eating decayed meat and bone marrow used in bone-breaking), the Poor Law Commission was dissolved in December 1847 and replaced by the Poor Law Board, whose President was thereafter a member of the Government with a seat in Parliament.[105]

Villiers was opposed to the exploitation of workers by their employers and was particularly critical of the prevalence of the 'truck' or 'tommy-shop' system in the manufacturing districts. This system, whereby workers were paid partly or wholly in kind by tokens or by being forced to purchase goods from their employer rather than in money, had long been prohibited by several Acts of Parliament, the most recent being in 1831, but was ignored by many masters, especially in the Black Country, including Wolverhampton.[106] However, on 4 March 1842, Mr Ferrand, in calling for the establishment of a Select Committee to investigate the prevalence of the truck system, alleged in the House of Commons that many manufacturers who belonged to the Anti Corn Law League paid their wages upon the truck system. This charge, which was refuted in numerous petitions submitted by manufacturers to Parliament, subsequently instigated a series of vitriolic debates in the House of Commons, and Charles Villiers called upon Ferrand to justify or retract what he had stated.[107] However, on 19 April, Ferrand not only repeated the charge but also attempted, albeit unsuccessfully, to implicate Charles Villiers in the whole issue by producing a letter from the Revd. Humphrey Poutney, an Anglican clergyman in Wolverhampton, and a Tory, which noted the existence of the truck system in the town and alleging that one of Villiers' leading supporters had an interest in a manufactory which practised the system. Poutney stated:

> Wolverhampton, April 2, 1842 – SIR ... I regret to say that I have too many opportunities of witnessing the working of this tyrannical system in my own parish, and Mr Villiers need go no further than the borough which he represents, for proof, that a great portion of the distress now existing amongst the poor, is caused by the payment of wages in provisions instead of money. I will mention one instance with which I think you should be made acquainted; others can be brought forward, if required: but this is a case which I have taken particular pains to investigate. One of the most active partisans of Mr Villiers, and a principal member of his

committee at the election, who was, by the late Administration, made a magistrate for the county of Stafford, is a chief partner in the – colliery, where the truck system is carried on more infamously than in any other works in the neighbourhood. The men are paid once in four and sometimes five weeks, when they may receive their wages in money if they demand it, but the man who made such demand would, in all probability, be dismissed; but as it is not possible for their families to wait till the expiration of the month for the means of subsistence, they are compelled to go to the 'Tommy shop', as it is called here, a ticket to which is given them for any goods they may require.[108]

The 'active partisan' of Charles Villiers to whom Poutney referred was none other than John Barker, one of Charles Villiers' chief supporters in Wolverhampton and now a Staffordshire County JP, who subsequently sought to defend and exonerate himself in a fiery exchange with Poutney in the columns of the *Wolverhampton Chronicle*. Barker denied Poutney's allegations, stating,

In this district it is well known that I am the managing partner in the Chillington ironworks, and anyone reading Mr Poutney's letter would conclude that a 'Tommy shop' was kept at the said works. No shop has been kept at the Chillington works for more than 10 years ... I have a completely trifling interest in another ironwork where a shop has been established for several years and long prior to my connection with it ... Mr Poutney has dragged into this case my late elevation to the Bench by the late administration. What has this to do with the matter? And why pass over my brother magistrate, Mr Hill, unless political or private feelings biased his pen?[109]

However, in seeking to exonerate himself, Barker exposed the true scale of the truck system in the district by implying that several local Tory coal and ironmasters also ignored truck legislation, stating

Has the Reverend gentleman, in his pastoral visits to Mr Sparrow and Mr Neve ever expostulated with them upon their vile practices or remonstrated with his neighbour Mr Ward on the iniquitous system pursued by him, or has he ever pleaded the cause of the miner with Mr Parsons?[110]

Following further exchanges between Barker and Poutney, the *Chronicle* claimed that Barker had been caught *in flagrante delicto*.[111]

In the Commons, Villiers, who had avoided becoming embroiled in the Barker-Poutney dispute, acknowledged the considerable existence of the truck system in the district, the circumstances under which it had arisen, and the great difficulties in preventing its continuance and supported the motion for a Select Committee to be established in order to ascertain the scale of the problem.[112] Appointed in May 1842, and chaired by Lord Ashley

[Shaftesbury], the Select Committee on the Payment of Wages, whose members included Ferrand, Charles Villiers, John Fielden, Richard Cobden, Thomas Duncombe and Sharman Crawford, completed its examination of witnesses in June and submitted its report in July.[113] It indicated that the 1831 Truck Act was frequently contravened in some of the Lancashire cotton towns, in the woollen districts of the West Riding, and in the coal and iron industries of South Wales and the Black Country. Charles Villiers attended all the sessions and was involved in the examination of the Revd. Poutney, who produced evidence of the scale of the truck system in Wolverhampton.[114] Poutney repeated his claim that truck had long existed in the town and was widespread among colliers and ironworkers. He added that the prices of goods issued by masters in lieu of cash were higher than normal retail prices; that truck was particularly prevalent when trade was bad, and that at such times workers were unable to contribute to the Wolverhampton Provident Society (an Anglican initiative) because they had no money. When asked by Villiers if the workers were decidedly against the system, Poutney stated that this was the case but added that there were no anti-truck societies in the district because many of the shopkeepers were connected in various ways to the ironmasters and were afraid of doing anything to offend them.[115] This, it seems, was a familiar story. However, although, the committee's final report, published in February 1843, was submitted to the House of Lords for further scrutiny, it was not until 1871 that further anti-truck legislation was passed by Parliament.

A further example of Villiers' opposition to measures which threatened to exploit workers arose in 1844 when a Bill for enlarging the powers of JPs in resolving disputes between masters, servants and artificers was presented before the Commons. This proposal, which allowed a magistrate to issue a warrant for the summary arrest of any workman complained of by his employer, or perceived to have misbehaved, on pain of two months' imprisonment with hard labour, resulted in numerous petitions from the provinces, and opposition in Parliament from Young England Tories, Liberals and Radicals, including Charles Villiers, duly forced the measure to be abandoned.[116]

Villiers also supported the removal of the abuses associated with the employment of women and children in the manufactories, mills and mines of the industrial districts, although he opposed excessive state intervention and regulation as proposed by the largely Tory-Anglican factory reform movement. In this, Villiers broadly followed the ideas of his mentor, Richard Fryer, who held that the evil of child labour was the result of necessity, which could only be removed by free trade in corn, which would both mitigate the difficulties faced by manufacturers, especially in times of economic hardship, and relieve the harsh conditions under which children were employed. For Villiers, as indeed for most laissez-faire Liberals and some (but not all) Radicals, the question of factory reform was fundamentally an economic question, despite moral and humanitarian considerations.[117] Hence Villiers accepted the system established by the Factory Act of 1833, which excluded children under the age of nine from all textile mills, set an eight-hour day for children aged between nine and thirteen, provided for part-time schooling, and established the Factory Commission, backed up by an Inspectorate.[118] However, he opposed the Factory Regulation Bill of 1836, introduced by Poulett Thompson, which proposed to limit the employment in textile mills of young persons aged between thirteen and eighteen to twelve hours a day. During the debate in the House of Commons, Villiers stated

> He could not admit that the present was a question between wealth and health. He thought that these factory regulations proceeded on the false principle that the poor were more indifferent to the welfare and happiness of their children than the rich, an assumption which his experience led him to deny. The promoters of this Bill were acting on a principle which must strike at the root of the domestic government of the poor, for the Bill deprived parents of the right to dispose of the time of their children to the best advantage. He was as anxious for the protection of the factory children as any other hon. Member of that House, but he thought, nevertheless, that there were many objectionable points in the proposition before the House. It went to the length of saying to the parents of children 'Your necessities drive you to send your children to work, yet we will deprive you of that power of augmenting the means of subsistence for your family, without, at the same time, providing you with a substitute' ... He was not for working the factory children too long; nothing could be more foreign to his views; but he thought that while there was a tax on the great necessary of life [Bread] which prevented the poor from feeding their families, a partial system of legislation such as this should not be adopted. Let hon. Members who wished well to the operatives consent to a repeal of the corn laws.[119]

The motion was passed by a narrow margin (178 votes to 176) and the Factory Regulation Act duly came into force, although it was widely circumvented by masters. Subsequently, Villiers advanced similar arguments against Graham's Factory Act of 1844 and Lord Ashley's 'Ten Hours' Act of 1847, believing that both the Corn Laws and Factory legislation were essentially protective, restrictive and regressive measures which impeded the progress of the nation and threatened to place English industry in an unfavourable competitive position. In this, Villiers was not alone for, as Anderson and Tollison have shown, Liberal free-traders shared similar views and the Anti-Corn Law League in particular devoted much time and money in its campaign against Tory Protectionist-inspired factory legislation, especially in the cotton textile districts where manufacturers (including members and financial backers of the League) feared that factory reform would be financially harmful.[120] Yet Villiers did support the Mines and Collieries Bill of 1842, which resulted from the findings of the Select Committee on the Employment of Children in Mines and Manufactories and which had exposed a litany of appalling abuses of women and children employed in the mines, stating in the Commons that

> They had never defended the employment of women and children in the manner described in the reports. Every one who had spoken had expressed an earnest wish to correct such evils as were really found to exist ... No time should be lost in legislating to prevent the continuance of those abuses which the coal-owners of the north had permitted, to their disgrace, to exist in their collieries.[121]

Whilst recommending that the good parts of the Bill be retained, he added, however, that he was at a loss to know how those boys, who had hitherto been employed six days a week, were hereafter to obtain the means of living when their employment was limited to three days a week.[122]

As Charles Villiers had observed, restrictions on the employment of children raised further the question of their education, a subject on which he had developed an initial interest as an Assistant Poor Law Commissioner. In 1833 the Whig government had introduced an Education Act which provided an annual government grant of £20,000 in support of the two societies – the National Society (Anglican) and the British and Foreign School's Society (Nonconformist) – who were largely responsible for elementary educational provision within the voluntary system. In August 1836, Villiers was one of a small group of Radicals, including George Grote and Sir William Molesworth, who met at the Thatched House Tavern, St James's, and formed a study group, the Central Society of Education, with the aim of promoting a national system of working-class education through the establishment of a Board of Education.[123] This Benthamite initiative subsequently attracted a wide range of supporters, including Leonard Horner (a factory inspector), Seymour Tremenhere (a mines and future school inspector), E. Carlton Tufnell (a poor law inspector), Thomas Spring Rice (Chancellor of the Exchequer) and Lord John Russell.[124] However, the Central Society faced opposition from the British and Foreign Schools Society, Whigs, and Tories and was discontinued in 1839, due largely to the establishment in 1839 of the Committee of the Privy Council on Education, which thereafter administered the government grant, backed up by an inspectorate. This in effect established a *de facto* Education Department in all but name and subsequently exerted an increasing influence on elementary educational provision prior to Forster's Education Act of 1870.[125]

By the early 1840s Charles Villiers had certainly acquired a notable reputation for his contribution to radical causes. Indeed, in February 1842, in an article entitled 'The Anatomy of Parliament: Mr Villiers', *The Britannia*, whilst acknowledging Villiers' undoubted sincerity, queried his motives in the course he was pursuing, stating that, as the brother of an Earl, and allied to the leading families of the aristocracy, one would not have expected him to have had a natural sympathy with 'the opposition, whose principles are avowedly democratic, if not revolutionary', and adding that Villiers could not pursue his present course with a view to the attainment of office, because his opinions were 'precisely those that would exclude him in the present state of the public mind, which tends to very slow and gradual change'.[126] Moreover, the article continued,

> Personally, Mr Villiers is as unlike a Radical or an agitator as one could possibly conceive. He is a mild, unassuming, gentlemanly man, with only just enough firmness and decision about him to make one distinguish him from the mere mob of noisy babblers. His manner of advocating his opinions is modest in the extreme. In fact, strange as it may appear, notwithstanding the subversive tendency of his opinions, he is universally liked and respected in the House; and this can only arise from the general impression entertained of his sincerity, and intimate conviction of the truth and practicability of his views, but as a politician he is looked upon as an absolute clog and obstruction.[127]

This said, *The Britannia* at least provided a rare, but interesting description of Charles Villiers at this time:

> In person he is somewhat above the middle height, and his figure, though not chargeable with any specific defect, is not remarkable for symmetry. He has a habit of stooping as he walks, which takes away from the dignity of his appearance. To look in his face, you would take him to be a hard close thinker, with certainly very little of the agitator about him. The general aspect of the countenance conveys the impression of constant, deep-rooted ill-health, from which I understand he suffers much and continually. The complexion is too pale for health. His hair and whiskers are a light sandy. Mr Villiers is very inattentive to the niceties of dress, so that many times he looks almost slovenly; but at all times the unobtrusive self respect and easy bearing of the gentleman are conspicuous, even under the disadvantage of unbrushed clothes and untidiness. This slovenliness is, however, only an occasional freak, not a constant practice.[128]

By contrast, the Liberal free-trader, Alexander Somerville, described both Villiers' appearance and politics in a more appealing light:

> Mr Villiers is a pleasant, fresh-complexioned gentleman, aged perhaps eight and thirty or forty. He possesses much of that aristocratic outline of countenance which indicates a consciousness of belonging to the exclusive classes; but his excellent sense and kindness of disposition keep whatever of him is aristocratic in the background, save that which is alike graceful and useful ... Much of his success in Parliament is, doubtless, to be attributed to his own talents and perseverance, though some of it is the result of family connection. It is no easy matter for a young member

to get a patient hearing in the House of Commons on an unwelcome subject unless he has a good cause, good talents, and a good connection. Mr Villiers has all these. He was thus spoken of in a newspaper two years ago:– 'Although one of the aristocracy, he is not one of the kid-glove and white-waistcoated gentlemen who stroll into the House of Commons to sleep off their claret, and then give a venal vote. He is a hard-working man of business, in and out of the House'.[129]

The 'unwelcome subject' to which Somerville referred was the campaign for the repeal of the Corn Laws, which was pre-eminent among the causes associated with Villiers' parliamentary career during the early Victorian period, and to which we now turn.

Notes

1 *Pall Mall Gazette*, 18 Jan. 1898.
2 *International Herald Tribune*, 17 Jan. 1898.
3 T.A. Jenkins, *Parliament, Party and Politics in Victorian Britain* (Manchester, 1996), 14; J.P. Parry, *The Rise and Fall of Liberal Government in Victorian Britain* (New Haven, CT, 1993), 14–20.
4 Mandler, *Aristocratic Government in the Age of Reform*, 1–4.
5 Parry, *The Rise and Fall of Liberal Government*, 14–20.
6 E.F. Biagini, *Liberty, Retrenchment and Reform: Popular Liberalism in the Age of Gladstone, 1860–1880* (Cambridge, 1992), 4.
7 Joseph Coohill, *Ideas of the Liberal Party: Perceptions, Agendas and Liberal Politics in the House of Commons, 1832–52* (Chichester, 2011), 172. Yet Coohill also states that most Radicals wanted the immediate abolition of the Corn Laws (as did Villiers) whereas most Reformers took a moderate free trade stance, advocating gradual reform towards eventual abolition (which Villiers did not), 53–4.
8 Ibid., 19–45.
9 Boyd Hilton, *The Age of Atonement: The Influence of Evangelicalism on Social and Economic Thought, 1785–1865* (Oxford, 1998), introduction.
10 Finer, 'The Transmission of Benthamite Ideas', 31–2.
11 A. Howe, *Free Trade and Liberal England* (Oxford, 1997) ch. 2.
12 Coohill, *Ideas of the Liberal Party*, 170.
13 Ibid., 46–76.
14 Miles Taylor, *The Decline of British Radicalism, 1847–1860* (Oxford, 1995), 6–10.
15 Harriet Martineau, *History of the Thirty Years Peace*, cited in Villiers, *Political Memoir*, xvi.
16 William Thomas, 'The Philosophic Radicals', in P. Hollis (ed.), *Pressure from Without in Early Victorian England* (London, 1974), 52–79.
17 Charles Villiers to George Villiers, nd., Feb. 1836, in Maxwell, I. 106–8.
18 Charles Villiers to George Villiers, 17 Nov. 1836, in Maxwell, I, 123–27.
19 Ibid.
20 Ibid.
21 Ibid. Villiers concluded his letter by saying

> I cannot of course expect you to assent to my views in all these matters; but I shall not impute either roguery or folly to you for not doing so, for that would be bad manners and worse folly. You are doubtless quite satisfied with your opinions and I am so with mine.

22 *Speech of C.P. Villiers, Esq., MP at a Dinner given by the Constituency of Wolverhampton to the Representatives of that Borough*, January 26, 1836 (J. Bridgen, Wolverhampton, 1836).
23 Ibid.
24 In 1838, for example, Charles Villiers was himself suspended by Mrs Harriet Grote from the Grote's Eccleston Street circle for one calendar month after having been found guilty of dining with Charles Pearson, the Radical Solicitor to the City of London, of whom Mrs Grote disapproved: Mrs Grote, *The Personal Life of George Grote* (London, 1878), 125–6. More famously, the friendship between George Grote and William Molesworth collapsed in 1844 following Molesworth's marriage to a widow, Mrs Andalusia Temple West, who was detested by Harriet Grote, who considered her to be of 'low birth': see Millicent Garret Fawcett, *The Life of the Right Hon. Sir William Molesworth* (London, 1901), 240–2.
25 *The Brittania*, 23 Feb. 1842.
26 Louis Fagan, *The Reform Club: Its Founders and Architect, 1836–1886* (London, 1887), 41. Fagan gave Edward Ellice, the Whig MP for Coventry, the credit for both the conception and foundation of the Reform Club, but it appears that the original idea was Molesworth's and that Ellice became associated with the project after it had been privately promoted by the Philosophic Radicals: see Alison Adburgham, *A Radical Aristocrat: Sir William Molesworth of Pencarrow and his Wife, Andalusia* (Padstow, 1990), 32–3.
27 For further details, see Adburgham, *A Radical Aristocrat*, 21–50.
28 In 1896 John Temple Leader recalled that

> Roebuck, Sir William Molesworth and Charles Pelham Villiers were, for many years, my colleagues in the House of Commons, of about the same political opinions, and my friends. In 1838, and for some years afterwards, I generally inhabited my villa on Putney Hill, where I received my friends, who came on Saturday afternoon and left on Monday morning.

Robert Eadon Leader (ed.), *The Life and Letters of John Arthur Roebuck* (London, 1897), 105.
29 Fawcett, *The Life of the Right Hon. Sir William Molesworth*, 78.
30 *Parl. Debs*, 3rd ser., 39, cc.68–71, 20 Nov. 1837. Later, in the aftermath of the French Revolution of 1848, Russell was to change his views and became amenable to the idea of further reform: see Roland Quinault, '1848 and Parliamentary Reform', *The Historical Journal*, 31/4 (1988), 831–51.
31 Fawcett, *The Life of the Right Hon. Sir William Molesworth*, 80.
32 *The Greville Memoirs* (Rev. edn., Cambridge, 2011), vol. 4, 198, 22 Apr. 1839.
33 Thomas, 'The Philosophic Radicals', 78.
34 A. Hawkins, *Victorian Political Culture: 'Habits of Heart and Mind'* (Oxford, 2015), 7.
35 Fagan, *The Reform Club*, 41. Significantly, at a meeting of Liberal Members on 12 February 1845, Villiers contributed to the work of a committee to organise the means by which the unity of the Liberal party might be strengthened, and the Reform Club duly established a permanent committee, to meet every Monday afternoon when Parliament was sitting, to receive notices from members, to secure the attendance of members at debates and divisions, and to consider the best means of promoting the objects and principles of the Liberal party. The Reform Club subsequently became the focus of liberal political life until additional clubs were formed in the 1870s, and Charles Villiers maintained a frequent and popular presence at the club throughout his parliamentary career. Coohill, *Ideas of the Liberal Party*, 97.
36 Fagan, 38–9.

37 For further details, see Dorothy Thompson, *Queen Victoria: The Woman, The Monarchy, and the People* (New York, 1990), 15–30.
38 Charles Villiers to George Villiers, 22 Aug. 1837, in Maxwell, I, 134–5.
39 Charles Villiers to George Villiers, 19 Sep. 1837.
40 Thompson, *Queen Victoria*, 29–30.
41 Charles Villiers to George Villiers, nd., Feb. 1836, in Maxwell, I. 106–8.
42 *Parl Debs*, 3rd ser., 34, cc.780–837, 23 Jun. 1836.
43 Ibid.
44 Ibid., 3rd ser., 100, cc.1225–68, 6 Aug. 1848.
45 Ibid.
46 *The Greville Memoirs*, vol. 4, 199, 22 Apr. 1839.
47 *Parl. Debs*, 3rd. ser., 62, cc.907–82, 21 Apr. 1842.
48 Ibid.
49 Ibid.
50 Lawrence, *Speaking for the People*, 78. Lawrence observes, for example, that in Wolverhampton the leaders of the town's Anti-Corn Law and Chartist movements briefly advocated a common programme of Corn Law repeal and universal suffrage but were opposed by the majority of Wolverhampton Liberals.
51 *Northern Star*, 20 Jul. 1839.
52 *Parl. Debs*, 3rd ser., 63, cc.25–88, 3 May 1842. See also *Wolverhampton Chronicle*, 11 May 1842.
53 Halevy noted that despite Macaulay's warning that universal suffrage meant the abolition of property and, in consequence, the end of civilization, and despite the fact that the Chartist petitioners also condemned the New Poor Law and demanded factory legislation restricting hours of work, Villiers was one of several free traders (including Bowring, Cobden, Fielden, Wakley and Duncombe) among the minority of 51 who voted in favour of taking the Petition into consideration. Elie Halevy, *A History of the English People in the Nineteenth Century*, 6 vols (London, 1927), IV, *Victorian Years 1841–1895*, 30.
54 Villiers, *Political Memoir*, xviii.
55 *Parl. Debs*, 3rd ser., 35, cc.1037–45, 9 Aug. 1836.
56 Ibid.
57 See especially W.H. Jones, *The Story of the Municipal Life of Wolverhampton* (London, 1903); J.B. Smith, 'The Governance of Wolverhampton, 1848–1888', PhD thesis, University of Leicester (2001), ch. 6, 'The Creation and Evolution of Civic Identity', 126–45.
58 Villiers, *Political Memoir*, xviii.
59 *Parl. Debs*, 3rd ser., 35, cc.203–18, 14 Jul. 1836.
60 Ibid.
61 Ibid.
62 Ibid., cc.523–51, 25 Jul. 1836.
63 *Wolverhampton Chronicle*, 19 Jul. 1837.
64 *Parl. Debs*, 3rd ser., 38, cc.539–45, 4 May 1837.
65 Ibid., 3rd ser., 44, cc.322–72, 19 Jul. 1838.
66 Ibid.
67 For further details of the anti-slavery movement, see Howard Temperley, 'Anti-Slavery' in Patricia Hollis (ed.), *Pressure from Without in Early Victorian England* (London, 1974), 27–51.
68 For a recent reassessment of relations between the free-trade and anti-slavery movements, including the role of Villiers, see especially Simon Morgan, 'The Anti-Corn Law League and British Anti-Slavery in Transatlantic Perspective, 1838–1846', *The Historical Journal*, 52 (2009), 87–107.
69 H. Richard, *Memoirs of Joseph Sturge*, 2 vols (London, 1865), II. 270.

70 *Morning Post*, 24 Nov. 1837.
71 *Parl. Debs*, 3rd ser., 42, cc.465–72, 6 Apr. 1838.
72 Richard Henry, *Memoirs of Joseph Sturge* (London, 1864), II, 169–70.
73 *The Spectator*, vol. 12 (1839), 401.
74 For a report of the proceedings, see, for example, *Birmingham Journal*, 27 Jun. 1840.
75 *Proceedings of the Anti-Slavery Convention* (London, 1841), 12–23 Jun. 1841. See also J.H. Grainger, *Character and Style in English Politics* (Cambridge, 1969), 73–107.
76 *Parl. Debs*, 3rd ser., 65, cc.1073–75, 5 Aug. 1842.
77 Ibid., 3rd ser., 65, cc.1227, 10 Aug. 1842.
78 Villiers, *Free Trade Speeches*, 326–7: House of Commons, 18 Apr. 1842.
79 Ibid.
80 Hugh Thomas, *The Slave Trade: The story of the Atlantic Slave Trade, 1440–1870* (London and New York, 1997), 649.
81 *Parl. Debs*, 3rd ser., 99, cc.1414–68, 30 Jun. 1848. Villiers had served on the Select Committee on Sugar and Coffee Planting, established to investigate the maintenance of preferential tariffs on sugar imports from the West Indian plantations. The committee, which sat for thirty-nine days, often beyond normal parliamentary hours, was balanced in its composition between protectionists and free-traders and equally divided in its opinion. The casting vote, however, lay with the Tory Protectionist chairman, Lord George Bentinck, and the committee duly passed resolutions favourable to the planters, although Villiers and his fellow free-traders on the committee at least achieved some success by limiting the continuation of tariffs to a period of five years only, as stipulated in the Sugar Bill, which passed its third reading in August 1848: *First Report of the Select Committee on Sugar and Coffee Planting, together with Minutes of Evidence and Appendix*, PP (1848); see also B. Disraeli, *Lord George Bentinck: A Political Biography* (London, 1852), ch. 26, 529–50.
82 *Parl. Debs*, 3rd ser., 109, cc.1093–4, 19 Mar. 1850.
83 Roland Quinault, 'Gladstone and Slavery', *The Historical Journal*, 52, 2 (2009), 363–83.
84 Richard Huzzey, 'Gladstone and the Suppression of the Slave Trade', in Roland Quinault, Roger Swift and Ruth Clayton Windscheffel (eds), *William Gladstone: New Studies and Perspectives* (Farnham, 2012), 253–66.
85 *Parl. Debs*, 3rd ser., 34, cc.612–63, 20 Jun. 1836.
86 Ibid., 3rd ser., 35, cc.110–32, 11 Jul. 1836. The Stamp Duty was finally removed in Jun. 1855.
87 Although born in Kidderminster, Hill had passed his childhood in a farmhouse on Compton Road in Wolverhampton and subsequently married his childhood sweetheart, Caroline Pearson, at St Peter's Church, Wolverhampton, in 1827, thereafter briefly living at Graisley House on Penn Road before moving to London.
88 R. Hill and G.B. Hill, *The Life of Sir Rowland Hill and the History of the Penny Postage*, 2 vols (London, 1880), II, 263; Eleanor C. Smyth, *Sir Rowland Hill: The Story of a Great Reform, told by his Daughter* (London, 1907), 110–11.
89 *First and Third Reports from the Select Committee on Postage, together with Minutes of Evidence, Appendix and Index*, PP (1837–8), 278, XX. Part I; see also *Second Report from the Select Committee on Postage, together with Minutes of Evidence, Appendix and Index*, PP (1837–8), 658, XX, part II.
90 John Henry Barrow (ed.), *The Mirror of Parliament, Second Series, Commencing with the Reign of Queen Victoria*, 2 vols (London, 1838), II, 835: House of Lords, 18 Dec. 1837.
91 This is commemorated in a Blue Plaque outside the current Post Office in Wolverhampton: openplaques.org/plaques/5166.

92 Hill and Hill, *The Life of Sir Rowland Hill*, II, 467.
93 *Parl. Debs*, xxxvii, 16 Mar. 1837.
94 See, for example, David Englander, *Poverty and Poor Law Reform in Nineteenth Century Britain, 1834–1914: From Chadwick to Booth* (Abingdon, 1998), 1–5; David. R. Green, *Pauper Capital: London and the Poor Law, 1790–1870* (Farnham, 2010), introduction, 1–16.
95 M.E. Rose, 'The Anti-Poor Law Agitation', in J.T. Ward (ed.), *Popular Movements, 1830–1850* (London, 1970), 78–94.
96 *Wolverhampton Chronicle*, 26 Jul. 1837.
97 *Parl. Debs*, 3rd ser., 35, cc.702–34, 1 Aug. 1836.
98 Ibid., 3rd ser., 35, cc.702–34, 1 Aug. 1836.
99 Ibid., 3rd ser., 76, cc.1084–120, 19 Jul. 1844.
100 Ibid., 3rd ser., 64, cc.233–71, 20 Jun. 1842; 64, cc.643–91, 27 Jun. 1842.
101 Leader, *The Life and Letters of John Arthur Roebuck*, 147. Extracts from Roebuck's parliamentary journal: 19 May 1847.
102 Ibid., 147: nd. May 1847.
103 *Parl. Debs*, 3rd ser., 93, cc.666–97, 17 Jun. 1847.
104 Ibid., 3rd ser., 93, cc.725–7, 18 Jun. 1847.
105 For further details, see M. Rose, *The English Poor Law, 1780–1930* (Newton Abbot, 1971), 121–34; P. Wood, *Poverty and the Workhouse in Victorian Britain* (Stroud, 1991), 78–84.
106 See, for example, J. Ginswick (ed.), *Labour and the Poor in England and Wales, 1849–1851* (5 vols, London, 1983), II, *Northumberland and Durham, Staffordshire, the Midlands*, 81–110. These letters to the *Morning Chronicle* from correspondents in the manufacturing districts testify to the widespread disregard by masters of the Truck Acts in the coal, iron and pottery industries.
107 *Parl. Debs*, 3rd ser., 61, cc.47–57, 4 Mar. 1842; 61, cc.140–51, 7 Mar. 1842; 61, cc.661–7, 16 Mar. 1842.
108 Ibid., 3rd ser., 62, cc.820–68, 19 Apr. 1842. Poutney's letter continued:

> The price of some few of the articles at this shop, compared with that asked by the shopkeepers in the town, I have ascertained, and it will show you at once the dishonest advantage taken by the oppressors of these poor men – At Tommy shop. Per lb. Sugar, 9d., Salt butter, 15d. & 16d., Bacon, 9d., Tea, 8s.; In the town. Per lb., Sugar, 7 1/2d., Salt butter, 10d. & 11d., Bacon, 7 1/2d., Tea, 5s. – there being a difference of more than 50 per cent, on the article of tea … During the severe weather in 1841, when soup was distributed to our poor at 1d. a-quart, it is a fact, which came to the knowledge of my curate, that some of the families, in receipt of nominally good wages, actually declined a ticket for the soup, on the plea that they had not the penny for it, as they received their wages in goods.

109 *Wolverhampton Chronicle*, 27 Apr. 1842.
110 Ibid.
111 Ibid., 4 May 1842; 11 May 1842.
112 *Parl. Debs*, 3rd ser., 62, cc.820–68, 19 Apr. 1842.
113 *Report from the Select Committee on Payment of Wages, together with Minutes of Evidence, Appendix and Index*, PP (1843), 38.
114 Ibid., 24 Jun. 1842: Evidence of Revd. H. Poutney, 124–32.
115 Ibid., 132.
116 S. and B. Webb, *The History of Trade Unionism, 1666–1920* (London, 1920), 186.
117 W.C. Lubenow, *The Politics of Government Growth: Early Victorian Attitudes Toward State Intervention, 1833–1848* (Newton Abbot, 1971), 154–5.
118 For further details, see Pamela Horn, *Children's Work and Welfare, 1780–1890* (Cambridge, 1994), 35–45; J.T. Ward, *The Factory System*, 2 vols (Newton

Abbot, 1970), II, 82–139; see also the relevant sections in C. Nardinelli, *Child Labor and the Industrial Revolution* (Bloomington, 1990).
119 *Parl. Debs*, 3rd ser., 33, cc.737–88, 9 May 1836.
120 G.M. Anderson and R.D. Collinson, 'Ideology, Interest Groups and the Repeal of the Corn Laws', in Cheryl Schonhardt-Bailey (ed.), *The Rise of Free Trade*, vol. 4, *Free Trade Reappraised: The New Secondary Literature* (4 vols, London, 1997), IV, 38–52.
121 *Parl. Debs*, 3rd ser., 64, 999–109, 5 Jul. 1842.
122 Ibid. Subsequently, the Mines Act of 1842 prohibited the employment of women and children underground.
123 D.G. Paz, The Politics of Working-Class Education in Britain, 1830–50 (Manchester, 1980), 69–72.
124 Ibid.
125 For further details, see M. Sanderson, *Education, Economic Change and Society in England, 1780–1870* (London, 1983). For the involvement of the Liberal Free Traders in education reform, see especially Richard F. Small, 'Free Trade Radicals, Education and Moral Improvement in Early Victorian England', in M. Shirley and T. Larson (eds), *Splendidly Victorian: Essays in Nineteenth and Twentieth Century British History* (London, 2001), 69–90.
126 *The Britannia*, 23 Feb. 1842.
127 Ibid.
128 Ibid.
129 Reuben [Alexander Somerville], *A Brief History of the Rise and Progress of the Anti-Corn Law League, with Personal Sketches of its Leading Members* (London, 1845), 48.

4 The campaign against the Corn Laws

The story of the successful campaign mounted by the Anti-Corn Law League which resulted in the Repeal of the Corn Laws in 1846 – an event which, according to Anthony Howe, launched Britain on a course seeking 'to lead the world towards a peaceful order based on free commercial exchange between nations'[1] – has been well charted by historians and has spawned an impressive historiography.[2] However, whilst these studies have, inevitably, and quite rightly, emphasised the critical roles played by the pre-eminent leaders of the League, Richard Cobden[3] and John Bright,[4] in its ultimate success, many of them have largely understated the significant contribution – widely acknowledged by his contemporaries – made by Charles Villiers as the spokesman for, and champion of, the repeal cause in Parliament, particularly, but not exclusively, in the years before Cobden and Bright were elected to the House of Commons. Indeed, with the exception of W.O. Henderson's short monograph of 1975, *Charles Pelham Villiers and the Repeal of the Corn Laws*,[5] and Anthony Howe's admirable study, *The Letters of Richard Cobden*,[6] which makes extensive use of the correspondence between Cobden and Villiers, it could be argued that studies of the Repeal movement have overly concentrated on the work, writings and speeches of Cobden and Bright at the expense of those of Charles Villiers.

Opposition to the Corn Laws, which were popularly regarded by their opponents as a 'bread tax', an example of aristocratic monopoly, and the last bastion of Protectionism, had been voiced since their inception in 1815, especially during periods of dearth and scarcity. During the 1820s, the Liberal Tories had moved towards freer trade through Huskisson's reforms (much admired by the young Charles Villiers) at the Board of Trade, including the Reciprocity of Duties Act of 1823 and the Corn Law Act of 1828, which introduced a sliding scale, and it has been suggested that this course may ultimately have led to the Repeal of the Corn Laws but for the return of the Whigs to office in 1830.[7] Moreover, as Cheryl Schonhardt-Bailey has shown, Liberal Tory legislation was paralleled by the rapid growth of the British population, the continued expansion of industry and manufacturing, especially of textiles, and the development of Britain's export trade, all of which cut against the fabric of protection for food and stimulated growing pressures from middle-class industrialists not only for greater political representation (which was achieved through the 1832 Reform Act) but also for the abandonment of Protectionism in favour of Free Trade.[8]

As we have seen, Charles Villiers had sought the repeal of the corn laws as early as 1826, during his unsuccessful candidacy at Kingston-upon-Hull, and he had been elected for Wolverhampton on a free trade/anti-corn law platform in 1835. In February 1836, when a fall in grain prices following the abundant harvest of 1835 prompted complaints from farmers that they faced ruin, the House of Commons ordered the appointment of a Committee on Agricultural Distress which sat for four months but rose without making a report. It was at this point that Charles Villiers forged links with the newly formed London Anti-Corn Law Association and, with the overt encouragement of Richard Fryer,[9] took the lead in representing the small group of free-trade members in the Commons, one of whom, William Clay, the MP for Tower Hamlets, was entrusted with presenting several petitions against the Corn Laws before the House on 16 March 1837. Villiers seconded the motion, arguing that whilst England's prosperity was due to the excess of production over consumption, the tendency of the Corn Laws was to limit production.[10] Although the motion was defeated, Villiers' speech was significant, not least for its timing. The Anti-Corn Law League had yet to be founded; four years were to pass before Richard Cobden entered parliament as MP for Stockport, and six years before John Bright took his seat for Durham. In July, at an election rally in Wolverhampton, Villiers informed his constituents that the time had now come for a crusade against the Corn Laws, stating

> The Tories, he was satisfied, did not understand the people of this country. The working classes did not want other men's property, but the just reward of their own industry; they wanted just wages and steady employment, not parish relief; they wanted good trade, and a steady trade; and when they called out for this, to give them a Corn Law was indeed to give them a stone instead of bread (cheers). They sought for what they ought to have, and what would make them happy from the fruits of their own industry (*Loud Cheers*). This, he declared, was the moment to make a struggle for the Repeal of the Corn Laws.[11]

On 22 January 1838 Villiers was invited to speak at a meeting of the newly formed Manchester Anti-Corn Law Association, whose leading lights were Archibald Prentice, a radical journalist, J.B. Smith, a Manchester Cotton merchant, George Wilson, a local starch manufacturer, Richard Cobden and John Bright. The meeting resolved that the mover and seconder of a motion for the repeal of the Corn Laws in the House of Commons would be Mr Villiers and Sir William Molesworth. As Archibald Prentice observed,

> Mr Villiers had entitled himself to the respect of Manchester before he had appeared in it, and now his appearance, at once intellectual and

gentlemanly, the tone of his address, the knowledge of his subject, the closeness of his argumentation, his obvious determination to persevere in the course he had undertaken, and the hopefulness of his expectation that the struggle would end in victory, confirmed his hearers in their belief that he possessed high qualifications to be the leader in the parliamentary contest.[12]

In February, Villiers sought the advice of Richard Cobden, asking for additional information, including statistical evidence, to strengthen his case in the forthcoming motion, and which Cobden duly provided, concluding 'I beg to tender the thanks of those interested for your philanthropic and statesmanlike efforts. If you should at any time desire any specific information which I can give, pray command me'.[13]

Subsequently, on 15 March, Charles Villiers began his long parliamentary campaign by calling for an inquiry into the working of the Corn Laws and, in delivering his motion in the House of Commons, he broadened the case against the Corn Laws beyond political economy to include social issues as well.[14] In his speech, Villiers argued that the Corn Laws should be examined because those enfranchised in 1832 demanded it, having deemed the Corn Laws as one of the greatest wrongs of the unreformed Parliament, adding that the newly enfranchised might turn to violence if the question was ignored; that many MPs stood as the champions of the poor, who now needed cheap bread, which repeal would satisfy; that the agricultural protectionists opposed any advance in technology and economic thinking; that the agricultural classes were already exempt from so many taxes that they no longer needed further government protection via the Corn Laws; that some foreign markets were closing themselves to British goods in retaliation against tariffs; and, finally, that the Corn Laws had done nothing to help the agriculturist or to ameliorate the plight of the agricultural labourer.[15] Villiers added

> I am told that it is of little use to raise the question of the Corn Laws in this House, and that I have no chance of success. I have not been blind to this consideration myself; but I have not on that account been discouraged; and I have recommended those whom I represent to persevere in seeking justice from the House as at present constituted.[16]

However, as Villiers anticipated, the House of Commons would not inquire and would scarcely even listen, rejecting the motion by 300 votes to 95. On the following day, Queen Victoria noted in her diary, 'Heard from Lord John [Russell] that a motion of Mr C. Villiers for the repeal of the Corn Laws was rejected yesterday ... No great interest was felt upon this topic'.[17]

Nevertheless, Villiers had articulated the essential case against the Corn Laws, tracing the depressed state of British manufactures to the loss of foreign markets in consequence of the negligence of commercial interests by ministers, who preferred to maintain the Corn Laws, and urging that commercial liberty was as essential to the well-being of the nation as civil and religious liberty. It has been suggested that at this time the free-trade cause was widely regarded in political circles as eccentric, and Villiers himself felt that his political associates regarded him with some suspicion because of his aristocratic origins.[18] Nevertheless, Villiers was undeterred by the defeat of his motion and, when the Commons adjourned for the summer recess, he informed Joseph Sturge, the Birmingham Radical Quaker:

> Before I left London I put a notice on the books to the effect that I would call the attention of the House to the taxes that raised the price of food, contracted the commerce of the country, limited the demand for labour, lowered the profit upon capital, and yielded nothing to the revenue. I will take the earliest opportunity in the next session to bring the matter on with a view to a motion for the total repeal of such taxes. I am determined to ask for nothing short of this, because they are *in principle* opposed to justice and sound policy and are really threatening this country with tremendous evils.[19]

Villiers spent the whole of the parliamentary recess travelling widely on the Continent, where he observed the current state of trade and manufacturing and acquired further evidence to support the case for Repeal. As he told Thornely upon his return:

> I never was so struck in my life as I have been with the progress making in Belgium and Rhenish Prussia in manufactures. I conversed with many intelligent people in the latter country, connected with trade, and they certainly seem thoroughly to appreciate the working of the Corn Laws. They one and all say there that manufactures owe their revival, if not their existence, to them, and they say they have nothing now to fear but the repeal of our Corn Laws ... our Consul [in Hamburg] told me that several men, in his hearing, had said that they would have given thousands out of their own pockets for the rejection of the Bill if that would have done it. Good people, as long as Lord John's preponderating influence rules this country, they may keep their money in their pockets and add to their stock at our expense.[20]

In January 1839 the Manchester Anti-Corn Law Association held a public dinner in honour of Villiers and the members who had supported his Commons motion, and Villiers was hailed as the parliamentary leader of the campaign.[21] In the following month, against the background of growing popular distress in the manufacturing districts, Villiers moved that a number of Anti-Corn Law petitions from Glasgow, Leeds, Liverpool, Manchester, Nottingham, Derby, Birmingham and Wolverhampton be referred to the House of Commons. Lord John Russell, for the government, declared that it would be his duty to oppose the motion, whilst Sir Robert Peel, for the opposition, stated that the repeal of the Corn Laws would be grossly unjust to the agriculturalists and that he too would oppose the motion, which was duly rejected by 361 votes to 172.[22] However, as one observer noted, 'Villiers's speech was not lost; the protectionist landlords began to believe in the possibility of their monopoly being endangered',[23] whilst the writer and reformer Harriet Martineau recalled 'Villiers's speech was a statement of singular force and clearness. On that night he assumed his post undisputed as the head authority in the legislature on the subject of the corn law.'[24] Even Lord John Russell, who had opposed the motion, and who was suspicious of Villiers' radicalism, was moved to report to Queen Victoria that the young MP had delivered 'a very able speech'.[25] Nevertheless, as Anthony Howe has observed, as the spokesman for a radical extra-parliamentary movement advocating total repeal, Villiers was placed in a difficult position in regard to the Whigs, who were generally in favour of freer rather than free trade.[26]

On 12 March 1839 Villiers again proposed that the House should examine the Corn Law question, emphasising the economic and commercial case for repeal, and pointing out that labourers of all classes had paid more for bread since 1828, which had a bad effect on wages, since manufacturers had to pay their employees more and this in turn impaired their ability to compete with other European nations. Hence, by affording exclusive protection (via the Corn Laws) to one class, 'we were ruining the manufactures and contracting the commerce of the country'. Moreover, Villiers broadened the case for Repeal by emphasising the deleterious effects of the Corn Laws on local and general taxation and illustrating how repeal would lift existing burdens on county and borough ratepayers.[27] On 19 March, after five sittings debating this proposal, the House defeated the motion by 342 votes to 195.[28] Far from being disheartened by this setback, Villiers suggested to Cobden that any future annual motion should be strengthened, emphasising that 'it is unjust & inexpedient to levy any tax whatever upon the bread-food of the people', which Cobden supported.[29] Meanwhile, in the House of Lords, a resolution by Lord Fitzwilliam condemning the Corn Laws was also massively defeated by 224 votes to 2, Lord Melbourne, the Prime Minister, declaring that 'To leave the whole agricultural interest without protection, I declare before God that I think it the wildest and maddest scheme that has ever entered into the imagination of man to conceive'.[30]

Paul Pickering and Alex Tyrrell have suggested that the failure of Villiers' resolution was the catalyst for the formation, a week later, of the Anti-Corn Law League in Manchester, with the specific aim of converting public opinion, both within and without Parliament, to the cause of repeal.[31] The League's executive committee in essence comprised that of the old Manchester Anti-Corn Law Association, with first J.B. Smith and (from 1841) George Wilson as President, although the key figures in the movement were clearly Cobden and Bright.[32] Thereafter, the ACLL provided a highly organised and centralised administration, funded by donations and subscriptions, with a formidable nationwide propaganda apparatus, comprising rallies, lectures, petitions and its own newspaper (the *Anti-Corn Law Circular*, later re-named as the *Anti-Bread Tax Circular*, and then *The League*). The League subsequently sought to register new voters and to organise electoral campaigns in order to attract free-trade electors and build up support in the Commons, thereby enabling middle-class manufacturers to gain momentum in the fight for free trade at the expense of the agricultural protectionists, who were to progressively lose ground. Moreover, as Schonhardt-Bailey has argued, this clash of class interests was complemented by growing public support for the ideas of the League, which linked Free Trade to national prosperity, to morality and Christianity, and to the injustice of aristocratic monopoly.[33] The League thus became, as Asa Briggs has observed, the second great extra-parliamentary pressure group to emerge from the severe economic crisis of 1838–9 and the radical impasse in the House of Commons (the first being the Chartist movement).[34]

From the outset, the League's leaders were impressed by Villiers' performances in advocating repeal in Parliament, so much so that an attempt was made by the Manchester free traders to prize him away from his Wolverhampton seat. Writing to Villiers on 25 August, Thomas Thornely, who had attended a meeting of leading Liberals in Wolverhampton on the previous afternoon, told Villiers that Richard Cobden and John Potter (the son of Sir Thomas Potter, Manchester's first mayor) had also attended the meeting and 'were discussing the expediency of your withdrawing from this Borough and offering for the representation of Manchester'.[35] This had taken Thornely by surprise, but he told the meeting that whilst he was 'very much gratified that such an invitation was sent to you – it was highly complimentary to you, complimentary also to Free Trade principles, and likewise to the Borough of Wolverhampton – that the decision ought to rest with yourself', adding that on the whole, he did not think that Villiers would accept, being so secure in his Wolverhampton seat, a view with which Villiers himself concurred.[36] Indeed, by December, and prior to meeting Villiers in Wolverhampton, Thornely was able to report that he had received letters from the Liberals in Wolverhampton which indicated that they were in excellent spirits and that there was unanimity on the Corn question, adding

> My opinion is that we shall find affairs are going on harmoniously. I beg you to fear nothing. You have done your duty to your constituents and you must be aware your exertions are appreciated by them and by others.[37]

On 13 January 1840 the ACLL held its first convention in a temporary pavilion – 'The Free Trade Hall' – in St Peter's Fields, Manchester (symbolically the site of the Peterloo Massacre of 1819), and called for 'the immediate and total repeal of the Corn and Provisional Laws'. Villiers attended the meeting and spoke on behalf of the twenty-six MPs present, declaring their intention 'to rescue the country from a law which makes them the scorn and mockery of their neighbours', adding 'Gentlemen, do fling away this badge of iniquity, English servility and ignorance'.[38] Thereafter, the League became the focal point of the movement for the repeal of the Corn Laws, albeit at a time when some leading Whigs were becoming increasingly convinced of the need for Corn Law reform, not just for economic reasons, but also for electoral and party purposes, since this offered Liberals the opportunity to strengthen their support in the boroughs and, with a free trade agenda, to present themselves as a disinterested party and government.[39]

Moreover, at a time of extensive Chartist agitation, the League was also anxious to attract working-class support in order to appeal to the fears of the landed aristocracy. Villiers observed that at a meeting of the working classes in Manchester, he had witnessed 'the most gratifying spectacle of upwards of 5,000 working men who had just quitted their daily avocations, assembled together at dinner to express their opinions upon this vital question', adding that 'A more orderly, respectful, or attentive meeting, and one where those most decent observances requisite in public assemblies were more regarded, I never witnessed'.[40] Accordingly, Villiers informed J.B. Smith of

> my thorough conviction that the working classes are really those most interested in the repeal of the Corn Laws ... My great object in getting them to speak out is that I am convinced that until they do the Aristocracy will never yield – I grieve to say that the brickbat argument is the only one that our nobles heed.[41]

Indeed, as Pickering and Tyrrell have noted, Cobden's letters to Villiers also show his strong support for 'elements of agitation', although he later modified his opinion,[42] and in February 1840 Cobden suggested to Villiers that he might delay his annual motion until March or later on the grounds that

> Every day we are gaining in strength, & our enemies are in proportion losing their confidence ... Let us have two or three months more to agitate in, & we will make the thieves tremble for even a fragment of their booty,

which Villers agreed to do in view of 'greater excitement' in the country.[43] However, both men were aware of the strength of the opposition they faced in Parliament, not only from Tory Protectionists but also from the Protectionist Whigs and, in particular, from the Prime Minister, Lord Melbourne, of whom Cobden remarked to Villiers '*He* is no better than a Tory in practice. In *feeling* he is *nothing* – he fills the office of premier as though such a thing could be done in *effigy*',[44] adding that 'I don't think they [the Whig Government] could do us any good with Melbourne at their head. His speech and his vote last year are still rankling in our memories'.[45] On 1 April 1840 Villiers duly called for a committee of the House of Commons to consider the Corn Laws. The House adjourned, but the motion was renewed and debated on

26 May 1840, when Villiers faced unabated hostility from Protectionist MPs. It was reported that

> It became manifest, the moment he began to speak, that there was a fixed determination to give neither him nor the petitioners a fair hearing. He was assailed from the outset with a volley of sounds, such as could have been heard in no other deliberative assembly in the world. The Speaker's calls to order were utterly disregarded, and it was not till, losing all patience, he commanded the bar to be cleared and members to take their seats, that the enlightened advocate of free trade could be heard in the gallery. Again did the Babel-like confusion arise, and again had the Speaker occasion, most peremptorily, to assert his authority; but even this would have availed nothing, had not the time arrived when the *fruges consumeri nati* [those born to consume the fruits of the earth] usually went to dine and then, with about a hundred auditors, Mr Villiers was allowed to proceed.[46]

Even then, the diners returned 'heated with wine' and a division was held, whereupon the motion was defeated by 300 votes to 177.[47]

However, in May 1840 Villiers had also pushed for the appointment of a Select Committee to inquire into Import Duties in order to confront the government with the facts supporting repeal.[48] As a member of the committee that was subsequently established (and which included his fellow Wolverhampton MP, Thomas Thornely), Villiers attended three-quarters of the meetings and largely conducted the examinations of key witnesses, including John MacGregor, Secretary of the Board of Trade, and George Richardson Porter, the famed economist and head of the statistical department at the Board of Trade. The report, which concluded that existing tariffs imposed a consumer tax which diminished the productive power of the country and limited trading relations, and which recommended further reduction and simplification,[49] was published on 6 August 1840 and was reprinted and circulated by the ACLL.[50] The council of the League declared that their entire case might be decided by the evidence in the report itself, for which Villiers was given great credit. Indeed, an article in the *Manchester Times* by 'Mask' (James Grant[51]) praised Villiers for his perseverance in the cause of repeal, describing him as 'not a dreamy theorist, not an ambitious or discontented crochet-monger, but a hearty, useful, practical reformer, pitting himself against some ever-acting abuse', and concluding

> Gallant, uncompromising and daring as is Villiers' conduct in the agitation with which he has so closely connected himself, he is nevertheless a man of highly cultivated intellect, of literary taste, and of aristocratic connections ... an energetic, an able, and an honest representative of a numerous and well-informed manufacturing constituency ... fighting heart and hand against the most monstrous curse that was ever endured by a free people.[52]

On 15 April 1841, the League held a public meeting at the Corn Exchange, Manchester, attended by nearly 2,000 members.[53] This meeting was convened in part to prepare for Villiers' annual motion in the House of Commons, and both Cobden and Bright, not yet in Parliament, were among the speakers, but the principal speech was given by Villiers,[54] who, in optimistic vein, claimed that the cause of repeal was making immense progress:

> The truth on this question is now penetrating the recesses of power, and the strongholds of Monopoly are beginning to be shaken. The appalling distress that for three years past has been bearing down the productive classes of the country has compelled public attention to the warnings and declarations of the opponents of the Corn Laws, and the Monopolists have at last been thrown on their defence ... I think that the present moment is most opportune for the display of our determination to procure justice for the country, and alleviation of the distress in the manufacturing districts which has so long been shocking the feelings of every well-disposed man.[55]

In particular, Villiers called upon the ministers of religion, who had hitherto held aloof, to give their support to the League, stating

> I cannot conceive anything more immediately within the province of the disciples of Him who said 'Feed my people' and 'the labourer is worthy of his hire' than to inculcate their Master's great lessons of charity by enabling the poor, through honest industry, to feed themselves.

Indeed, he added that it was a duty among those who held that no redress could be obtained for the poor 'until the suffrage was extended' to expose the frightful evils of the Corn Laws to the community at large 'under the present limited constituencies'.[56]

However, in April 1841, faced with a budget deficit of nearly £2 millions, Melbourne's Ministry made the surprising *volte face* of attacking the Corn, Sugar and Timber Monopolies and Russell declared that he would bring forward a motion for reconsidering the laws relating to the import of foreign corn, subsequently proposing a fixed duty of eight shillings. By contrast, Peel, still hostile to Repeal, revived the idea of a Sliding Scale in regard to corn imports. However, on 4 June, following the Government's defeat on the Sugar Bill, Peel carried a vote of no confidence by a majority of one and three days later Russell announced the intention of the Ministry to dissolve Parliament and go to the country.[57] These events preceded, and effectively undermined, Villiers' prospective annual motion on Repeal, which was scheduled for 7 June. As Cobden observed to Villiers,

> We are sold by the Whigs – *done* again! Let it be a first & final lesson to the Anti Corn Law League – never let us swerve again even in *appearance* from our principle or our way of working it out – Lord John took the

matter out of your hands & thus prevented our debate from coming on at the usual time.[58]

Villiers, however, was far from discouraged by these developments, informing the Commons in June that 'I see nothing in what is occurring at present that does not raise my most sanguine expectations of speedy success. The question must now exclusively engage the attention of the House till it is settled in some way'.[59] He also drew an analogy between the Slavery question in America and the Corn Law question in England, stating

> In America they refuse to discuss the Slave question in Congress. Two years ago it was mooted and the Members all rushed from the House as they rushed from this House to-night. The subject of slavery is offensive to the interests of the majority in Congress as the Corn Laws are offensive to both Houses here, and all refuse to discuss it. Does this discourage me? Far from it. Do I advise the country to be disheartened by it? Quite the contrary.[60]

The General Election of July 1841 witnessed the defeat of Melbourne's government and the return of Peel and the Tories, which Villiers actually welcomed as an indispensable preliminary to securing Free Trade, stating in the Commons that:

> We shall now have a large political party interested in converting the community on the subject. I am rejoiced that the dissolution has taken place, because it has produced discussion on the subject and invited the attention of the people to it; and I am happy to see with what result. If I stood here as a partisan I should regret the result; but the subject on which I am now speaking is the one that engrosses my attention. I am not here to promote any party whatever; it is this question which so largely affects the welfare of the country, that chiefly excites my interest in politics, and I am watching its progress.[61]

The election also witnessed the arrival of Richard Cobden in Parliament as the MP for Stockport. On taking his seat, Cobden was moved to thank 'the hon. Member for Wolverhampton, for whose great and incessant services I, in common with millions of my fellow-countrymen, feel grateful'.[62] As G.M. Trevelyan observed, 'Charles Villiers, who had hitherto borne the burden and heat of the day in Parliament with his annual motion for Repeal, now gave up without jealousy the place that worth and talent must yield to genius'.[63] Moreover, as Norman McCord noted, whilst the relationship between Cobden and Villiers subsequently remained perfectly friendly and open it was perhaps inevitable that Cobden should eventually lead the free trade campaign in Parliament, not only because he displayed real talent in the House of Commons as a representative of the manufacturing interest which drove the League (unlike Villiers, with his aristocratic background), but also because Charles Villiers' sincere co-operation with the League in the provinces was to some extent hindered by his dependence on an office in Chancery, which made it very difficult for him to leave London during the law terms.[64] Indeed, given this particular constraint, Villiers' great efforts in promoting the cause of repeal are all the more remarkable.

Charles Villiers welcomed Cobden's election, although he was initially sceptical in regard to Cobden's ability to move parliamentary opinion, informing Roebuck that

> There is a great deal of difference between talking to large public meetings composed of favourable auditors, who cheer every word you utter, and speaking to the fastidious audience found in the House of Commons, the greater part of whom are bitter opponents and all critical listeners. Cobden's success out-of-doors will excite attention for him in the House; but he will be required to reach a high standard to acquire the influence within the walls of Parliament which he has attained among the enemies of the Corn Laws.[65]

Thereafter, according to Cobden (who also held some reservations about Villiers' low-key, if sincere, style of leadership[66]), Villiers' main task was to rally the support of a corps of free-trade MPs in the House of Commons,[67] although Villiers (with the support of Lord Radnor, who had succeeded Henry Brougham as the chief spokesman for the repeal movement in the House of Lords[68]) remained the key link between Westminster and the League's heartland in Lancashire, and the League's London conferences were timed to coincide with his annual motions in the House of Commons,[69] thereby creating additional pressure from without in the capital.

In fulfilling this task, Villiers received constant advice, encouragement and support from Cobden. For example, writing to Villiers in July 1841, Cobden expressed his view that 'We must occupy the ground, & give notice that we will not give way for Toryism, Whiggism, Radicalism, or Chartism', stating that

> much will depend on *yourself* to give a right direction to our party at the outset – I hardly know two men in the present House on whose earnestness, tact, energy, & ability, I could depend for *spontaneously* working the Free trade question as it should be worked in Parlt.

He then observed that

> there are not a few on whom I have my eye, who, if led aright, & *whipped a little from without*, will do any thing that is necessary. The league will find the whip & spur – you must *lead* the pack – Count on my incessant aid – Out of the House I can do some service in keeping men up to

the mark, but within doors I shall use the privilege of a young member & learn my lesson instead of talking

adding 'I speak unreservedly to you, because your sincerity in a common cause inspires me with confidence'.[70] In September, Cobden expressed his hope that Villiers would draw Peel's attention to the state of the country and demand an instant repeal of laws which restrict food and diminish employment, citing the evidence of his previous motions and popular petitions for repeal, and encouraged Villiers to take a bold stand, 'you can do it, it is in you'.[71] Accordingly, Villiers complied.[72] Again, in November, Cobden praised Villiers' 'disinterested zeal', adding 'You & only you must have charge of our question, & when the time comes I know you will act judiciously yet boldly'.[73]

In February 1842 Sir Robert Peel bemoaned the continuing distress in the manufacturing districts but denied that this was attributable to the Corn Laws, citing a variety of other causal factors, including American trade, machinery, over-production and bad harvests, and introduced a new Sliding Scale, making 20s rather than 38s. 8d the highest duty on corn. He was supported by William Gladstone, a consistent opponent of Villiers' 'unsound' views, and soon to be advanced to the Presidency of the Board of Trade.[74] The League organised a rally of over 500 manufacturers in London to coincide with both the introduction of the Government's Bill dealing with the importation of corn and Villiers' annual motion. They marched to Westminster with cries of 'Down with tyranny', 'Down with the sliding scale', and 'Down with the Corn Laws'. In light of this agitation, Villiers declared, in moving for repeal in the Commons on 18 February, that

> The forced maintenance of the Corn Laws was making all men in the country politicians and driving the middle and working classes to think they were misrepresented … In his opinion, the people of this country – a sufficiently large number of persons of all classes to justify him in using that title – had determined that the 'Corn Law' should not continue. He believed that the mind of the great majority of the people was made up on the subject, and that they would use every means in their power to emancipate the industry and commerce of the country from this law.[75]

Villiers told the House that, notwithstanding the vast influence which the landed proprietary possessed and exercised, socially and politically, 'there was a power beyond them in the general opinion of the country, that they dared not resist', and he asked the Prime Minister, Sir Robert Peel, to consider 'whether the public mind had not now undergone a great change as to the principle or policy of imposing a tax at all on the food of the people', adding that during the last year, 'the folly, the cruelty – he could almost say the crime – of this law [Corn Law] had been generally detected and would not much longer be endured'.[76] In this, as in other motions, and given that there were strong feelings between 'town' and 'country' on the Repeal and

Free Trade issues, Villiers was clearly seeking to appeal to the whole national interest and not merely to the manufacturing interest. However, following five nights' debate, Villiers' motion was defeated by 393 votes to 90,[77] and he was described by one MP as 'the solitary Robinson Crusoe, standing on the barren rock of Corn Law Repeal'.[78] The Tory Protectionist *Wolverhampton Chronicle*, in a withering attack on Villiers' speech, went further:

> On Friday night the Hon. member literally vexed the House of Commons with a speech five columns long as given in the *Morning Chronicle*, and all this almost interminable outpouring of words was unrelieved by any originality of thought or novelty of expression. Brilliancy on such a trite and well-worn subject as the repeal of the corn laws was not to be expected; but downright tiresomeness might have been avoided. Such, as we have stated, except two or three epigrammatic sentences, was the general character of Mr Villliers' speech ... a tame and nerveless thing; scarcely a trace of earnestness or vigour was exhibited. The 'Hear, Hears' were few, and of cheering there was scarcely a sound: all was mediocrity and 'langour'. How is such an event to be accounted for? Has Mr Villiers, like other precocious children of 'vaulting ambition' thrust himself into a position which he cannot adequately fill? Or has he run the range of his mental tether on the subject on which he so languidly speaks?[79]

In the immediate aftermath of the defeat of the motion, Villiers suggested to Cobden that the League should produce a weekly newspaper to promote the free-trade cause, an idea which was accepted by the Council and resulted in the launch of *The Economist*, edited by James Wilson.[80] This proved ultimately to be a successful and significant initiative, so much so that even when repeal was eventually achieved in 1846, Cobden, Bright and Villiers agreed that the newspaper should continue to promote the free trade cause.[81]

However, it is important to note that these annual motions were not the only occasions when Villiers spoke at length in support of repeal. Between 1835 and 1852 (when the Free Trade question was finally settled), Charles Villiers made a total of 141 contributions to parliamentary debates, of which fifty-six focused on economic policy (including the Corn Laws), fifty-one on social issues, twenty-seven on political matters, and seven on foreign affairs. Indeed, all the ACLL MPs took well to Parliament and were far from being single-issue agitators, contributing conscientiously to debates,[82] and Villiers, as we have seen, was no exception. However, he took every advantage of parliamentary debates on other issues to illustrate the relevance of and need for the repeal of the Corn Laws, a fact largely ignored by historians of the anti-corn law agitation, including Chaloner, McCord and Pickering. Indeed, it was noted by one MP [Mr Darby] in July 1839, during the debate on the 'Penny Post' (when Villiers had stated that some of the post-horse masters had argued that they would be much more relieved by the repeal of the Corn Laws than by removing the tax on their business) that 'there was no question, whether one of education or post-horse duty, or be it what it might, which did not afford the hon. Member for Wolverhampton an opportunity to complain of the Corn-laws'.[83]

For example, in May 1842, during the debate on the introduction of Income Tax in Peel's budget, Villiers expressed his view that 'the measure was, financially speaking, wrong, that it was politically most unwise, and atrociously unjust', adding that 'a statesman in his [Peel's] position ought duly to have inquired, and fully to have explained the present anomalous and critical condition of this country'.[84] Linking the debate to the need for Corn Law repeal and the opening up of foreign trade, especially with the United States and Brazil, Villiers denounced the Bill, citing the evidence of a witness in a committee of the House that as

> bad as working people were off at present, they expected to be worse when the Income-tax came into operation, for the masters had declared that whatever they lost by the tax they must take out in the wages; that their profit was as low as would allow them to use their capital, and they must suspend their works if they did not reduce wages, and, as the man said, the Income-tax will be worse for the poor man than the truck system.[85]

The debates in the House of Commons on popular distress in the country in the summer of 1842 offer further examples of Villiers' opportunism. On 16 June 1842, Mr Ferrand, Tory MP for Knaresborough and a staunch protectionist, blamed the current distress in the manufacturing districts on the New Poor Law and proposed that the House should grant the sum of £1 million to afford temporary relief 'to the poor industrious classes in the manufacturing districts, and save them from starvation'. Only forty members were present and most opposed this suggestion, including Villiers, who pointed out that before the present Poor Law was passed, the agricultural labourers were much worse off than now, and treated worse than the people were in the collieries. For Villiers, as indeed for many other Repealers who wished for government to act in conformity with the requirements of laissez-faire political economy, there was no contradiction between support for the New Poor Law and support for the Repeal of the Corn Laws, for he regarded both as two sides of the same coin.[86] Mr Ferrand, Villiers observed,

> seemed to him to come into that House as the champion of restrictive laws [ie. the Corn Laws], and in order to be consistent with that character, he asked for a grant of money, to save the people from the consequences of those laws, or rather to save the landed proprietors,

adding that 'Anything that was not a permanent relief, was a mockery' and that the proposal 'was almost an insult to the people, and was making them paupers'.[87]

On 8 July, during a further debate on the subject, Villiers again took the opportunity to advance the cause of Corn Law repeal. Observing the 'deplorable distresses of the people', he asked the House to consider the real causes of the miseries to which the people were exposed, and how those miseries were to be removed. The wretchedness of the condition of the people was, he stated, broadly acknowledged, but instead of any remedy being applied, they had heard nothing other than 'lackadaisical phrases of sympathy, and vague generalities, and hopes for better times'.[88] Villiers stated that he had that day attended a meeting in London of delegates from the manufacturing districts who had declared that they viewed the Corn Laws as the cause of their poverty, and they asked for their repeal, adding that 'the people were starving. What was the remedy? It was food'.[89] To strengthen his argument, Villiers referred to a memorial he had received from the township of Bilston, within his Wolverhampton constituency, bemoaning the very great distress produced among the working classes of the district, by the unparalleled stagnation of trade, especially the coal and iron trades, and requesting the extension by the board of guardians of 'liberal out-door relief to the unemployed and their families'. Villiers observed that the people believed that their condition was solely attributable to the refusal of free-trade with America, where many southern and western States had called for English manufactures in exchange for their agricultural produce, but this was prevented by tariff barriers. Yet, he argued, 'if the trade with that country was opened, all the misery and wretchedness which now prevailed must cease'.[90] He also provided statistical evidence about American resources, as well as correspondence from Ohio and New Jersey, and asked the House on what grounds they sought to shut out the people of England from such resources:

> They knew it was true – they knew that abundance of food might come from America. They could not, dare not, deny this, yet they shrank from giving an answer when the people called up that House to do them justice.[91]

In concluding his remarks, Villiers stated:

> When the Corn-law was imposed, its advocates should have remembered that this country was limited, but that the population was fast increasing. There was a tendency in the people of all countries to increase beyond the means of sustenance, and it should have been the first care of the rulers of this country to be watchful that food should be commensurate with the extending wants of an increasing population. He believed that the history of human error and human selfishness showed no instance of greater folly and depravity than that of increasing the price of food by decreasing the quantity... He would not have troubled the House so long were he not impressed with a sincere conviction that the state of the country was such as to render some change absolutely necessary.[92]

On 22 July, in continuing to support the motion for 'an inquiry into the cause of the frightful distress prevailing in the country, with the view to its instant removal', Villiers attacked the Tory benches, who

> had refused every inquiry, assigned no intelligible reason for the distress, and had not proposed any remedy ... for the shocking stories brought from the great manufacturing towns, of the loss, misery and suffering, which is being endured by capitalists and labour.[93]

The remedy for distress, he argued, lay in the emancipation of trade and the repeal of the Corn Laws, adding that these laws had been maintained 'by appeals to the ignorance of the multitude ... and by bringing the social and pecuniary interest of the aristocracy to bear upon the selfishness, servility, and narrow-mindedness of the middle classes'.[94] Villiers stated that it was the duty of Government to actually and permanently improve the condition of the people, and he believed that the resources of the country, the skill and habits of the people, and the capital ready to give employment and development to both, could make this possible. The problem, he held, lay in 'inhuman, selfish, silly legislation'.[95] Broadening his argument, Villiers emphasised the moral and political benefits of repeal, 'for he felt satisfied that a people could never be morally improved, or rendered fit for political rights, unless they were first relieved from anxiety as to the mere means of supporting life',[96] adding that he wished to see the people well educated and in enjoyment of political rights. This, he firmly believed, was possible, 'in these two islands' (an acknowledgement of Ireland's problems) and that 'no trouble should be spared, or any opportunity lost to promote the first great object of emancipating trade'.[97]

In December 1842, Cobden praised Villiers for a speech he had made at Southampton Buildings which 'has vibrated through the Country as all London demonstrations do', adding that the line of argument taken by Villiers was 'well suited for the London public, & the middle class generally', and encouraging Villiers to 'put the screw upon any MPs who are in London or the neighbourhood to make them attend the meetings', concluding 'Every word you say is read by the whole country'.[98] Subsequently, Villiers not only rallied MPs in London but also sought to elicit the support of Thomas Carlyle, who had long opposed the Corn Laws, and who Villiers had first met in 1831,[99] to the cause. This approach proved unsuccessful, as Carlyle, with weightier matters on his mind, revealed in a letter to his brother Alexander:

> Yesterday, the Member *Villiers*, a very pitiful little person, whose name you may see in Corn-Law debates, had called here, and left his address, while I was out. My notion is he means to engage *me* too in the service of 'the league'; to 'lecture' for him, or the like. I am already engaged for a far bigger LEAGUE (that of the oppressed poor against the idle rich; that of God against the Devil); and will answer No to Villiers.[100]

Later, and somewhat ironically, Villiers was to develop a friendship with Carlyle,[101] who described him as a 'Hawk of Politics, and rather clever and consummately well-bred'.[102]

In January 1843 Villiers attended a meeting of the League in Manchester, where Cobden thanked him for his untiring exertions in the cause of Free Trade and Villiers, in reply, reminded the meeting of the justice of their cause. The League, he stated, was a justifiable institution, and for this reason:

> It was formed only after everything had been attempted in what might be called a constitutional way to induce Parliament and the public authorities to attend to the grievance, and had failed. The people petitioned; they asked to be heard at the Bar of the House; they asked for a Commission of Inquiry; they asked for a slight change of the Laws; and everything was refused, and with exactly the same stubbornness as the claim they now advance is refused. And though the Legislature tells the people when they agitate they will not yield to clamour, they have shown too plainly that they will not yield to anything else.[103]

At the same meeting, Mr Mark Philips, who had represented Manchester from the time of its enfranchisement in 1832, joined with Mr Cobden in thanking Mr Villiers. 'I am not accustomed to the words of flattery', he remarked,

> and I can say honestly that in his advocacy of the principles of Free Trade the hon. member has exhibited great talents; and I do not hesitate to affirm that he has shown a degree of zeal and industry in making himself acquainted with the practical details of the question which would do honour to any individual, and which no man in Parliament, to my knowledge, has ever before equalled.[104]

In the spring of 1843 the ACLL moved its headquarters to London and engaged Covent Garden Theatre for its weekly meetings, which Villiers frequently attended. As Greville observed,

> It is curious to look at the sort of subjects which now nearly monopolize general interest and attention. First and foremost there is the Corn Law and the League; the Corn Law, which Charles Villiers (I must do him the justice to say) long ago predicted to me would supersede every other topic of interest, and so it undoubtedly has.[105]

On 9 May 1843, Villiers again put forward his annual motion for repeal. The debate lasted for four days, amidst raucous scenes in the House reminiscent of 1840. According to *The Sun*,

> The wild beasts on both sides ... were all in the fiercest state of excitement – yelling, braying, roaring, each vying with the other in the

manifestation of impatience and irritability ... There was cock-crowing in the highest perfection, the bleat of the calf, the bray of the ass, the hiss of the goose, together with divers supplemental sounds ... the voice of the Speaker was little more regarded than a whisper amidst a storm.[106]

Following an adjournment, the motion was defeated in the Commons by 381 votes to 125.[107]

However, later in the year Villiers made one of his most significant speeches outside Parliament when he attended a meeting organised by the League in Colchester on 7 July. The town was a stronghold of Conservatism and, prior to the meeting, canvassing by local landowners, clergy and Agricultural Protectionist Associations had suggested that a majority in favour of maintaining the Corn Laws would be returned. In the event, thousands of people from all over the country descended on Colchester for the meeting and, anticipating trouble, the local authorities swore in a body of special constables. Richard Cobden duly spoke on behalf of the League, but was given short shrift by the farmers present, and was followed by Sir John Tyrrell, County MP for Essex, who, in defending the Corn Laws, took the opportunity to attack the League, describing Cobden's speech as 'the weakest and most impotent speech that he had ever heard'. Villiers then entered this maelstrom. He stated that he had initially intended to attend the meeting without making an address, but explained that he had since changed his mind:

> The thing that really determined me to come was an accidental meeting with Sir John Tyrrell yesterday. The first thing he asked me was whether I intended to show at Colchester. You all know that Sir John generally looks in pretty good humour with the world, not altogether forgetting himself; but there was something so very confident in his tone yesterday, something so like 'come if you dare', that I was almost afraid that if I did not come it would look like shrinking from the challenge. Moreover, I quite thought, from Sir John's manner, that if I came I should hear something new. I thought that there was to be a new set of arguments brought out in Colchester in favour of the Corn Laws.[108]

Villiers then proceeded not only to demolish Tyrrell's arguments but also to disabuse the farmers of the delusion under which they laboured — that the profit arising from the Corn Laws could belong to any but the owner of the land. In particular, Villiers negated the claim made by the Protectionists in Parliament that the Corn Laws should be maintained due to the heavy charges on land and also because they protected the interests of the labourers by providing employment and good wages. Pointing to the current scale of distress in the agricultural districts, Villiers observed that this impacted upon many farmers, who faced ruin because they had to pay wages from their capital rather than from profits, as well on the labourers, many of whom were earning less than eight shillings per week. In fact, he added, one-eighth of the rural population was in receipt of parish relief, numerous people wanted to leave their parish because they could not find employment and did not want to enter the workhouse, whilst in Ireland two million people were utterly destitute. He also articulated the case of the manufacturers, who argued that if their products could be exchanged abroad for foodstuffs, this would engender more employment, better wages, improved food supply and ameliorate distress. This being the case, he argued, the Corn Laws were a symbol of both injustice and cruelty, denying food to the people, and he asked his audience to deliver its verdict upon them:

> What do you say? Are the Corn Laws guilty or not guilty? [loud cries of 'Guilty!' and some cries of 'No!'] Well, then, you who think that they ought to be abolished speak out like men – in a manner no longer to be misunderstood; and never again allow yourselves to be misrepresented as wishing to perpetuate a system fraught with folly and injustice, and unattended with real benefit to any one.[109]

It was reported that Villiers, who had been received with great cheering,

> closed his speech amidst tumultuous applause. The victory of the Free Traders was unquestionable: the farmers' interest was carried, and Sir John Tyrrell had disappeared utterly discomfited,[110]

although this was not to be the only occasion on which Tyrrell was to suffer from Villiers' tongue.

Nevertheless, the Autumn of 1843 found Villiers not only unwell[111] but also depressed by the League's lack of progress, and he suggested to George Wilson that financial contributions to the League should be systematically called for.[112] Wendy Hinde, in her biography of Richard Cobden, has suggested that at this time Villiers was going through a crisis of confidence caused by Cobden's growing reputation in Parliament:

> Villiers was going through the unpleasant experience of being replaced by an abler man, and no one could shield him from it. But to his credit he did not withdraw from the very active role in the anti-Corn Law campaign that he had always played, both inside and outside Parliament.[113]

This may have been so, but Villiers' state of mind was also exacerbated by a double tragedy in his personal life during the year. On 13 July, his youngest brother, Augustus Algernon Villiers, who had been in delicate health for some time, had died from consumption at Kent House, aged twenty-seven, and it was discovered that his younger brother, Edward Ernest, was also suffering from the same affliction.[114] Cobden sought to lift Charles Villiers' spirits, urging him to 'draw freely upon the organs of cheerfulness & hope (if there be such bumps) & keep up your spirits', adding

> knowing that you are apt to take but a gloomy view of the state & prospects of the body-politic, I am inclined to think you are disposed to look despondingly upon your own health – more so I trust & believe than is warranted by the nature of your case.[115]

However, Edward Villiers' condition continued to deteriorate and, despite a short break on the French Riviera at Nice (to avoid the damps of an English winter), he passed away on 30 October, aged thirty-seven, and leaving a wife and four young children.[116]

These bereavements within a closely-knit family undoubtedly took a personal toll on Charles Villiers. Nevertheless, in January 1844, he visited his Wolverhampton constituency, informing Thomas Thornely that

> I found all things here just as you led me to expect them. Our friends all firm and only anxious to prove their steady zeal in the cause of Free Trade by a meeting to propose subscriptions to the League.[117]

However, he noted that although John Barker was disposed to take part in a League Contribution Meeting, many local ironmasters were not and there was 'some difficulty in getting the right people to take the lead', a situation for which he held Richard Fryer partly responsible:

> Fryer will not subscribe as he is expected to do from his position, and this throws a damper upon other people. If he would give £100 other people would give their £50 and £40 … £1000 could be raised here if he would do this. I expect his pounds would do more than his words nowadays.[118]

In London, where Villiers had been joined in Parliament by John Bright following his election as MP for Durham, the League's Covent Garden meetings were filled to overflowing and Villiers was one of the most popular speakers, alternating logical arguments in favour of repeal with humorous and mirthful descriptions of the fallacies advanced by the monopolists. As Andrew Bissett observed, Villiers' mind had been

> trained to that rigid analysis of the principles of economic science which enables it to detect a fallacy at a glance, and to set forth a truth with the simple force and clearness that are best fitted to give it a fair chance of success.[119]

When Villiers addressed the third metropolitan meeting of the League on 8 February, it was reported that every part of the building was filled to overflowing, hundreds failing to gain admittance due to lack of space, and that, at the conclusion of his speech, 'the whole assembly rose, and amidst the waving of hats and handkerchiefs, greeted the Parliamentary leader of Repeal with prolonged acclamations'.[120]

On 8 April 1844 an ACLL deputation, including Cobden and Bright, travelled to Wolverhampton, where they were met by Villiers and Thomas Thornely, and addressed a large meeting from a temporary pavilion, which had been erected in Horseley Fields. After describing his colleagues as 'The Apostles of Freedom of Commerce', Villiers reminded his audience that Wolverhampton had been 'early in the field on this question of the Corn Laws', adding 'it would indeed have been lucky for the country had other towns and other places acted and thought as Wolverhampton has done'.[121] In particular, he emphasised the effects that Monopoly was having on trade with Russia, Prussia and America, who had formerly been customers for goods manufactured in the district, with the result that 'the unfortunate people of this district are compelled to work longer and longer for less and less reward'.[122] Villiers added

> It is when I reflect on the privations of the working classes, knowing how much more than any other class they necessarily suffer from such cruel obstruction to their trade as the Corn Laws, that I am able to treat with contempt and indifference the reproach so often thrown at me, that I am eternally, and exclusively, on their account, demanding the repeal of those Laws.[123]

In June 1844 Villiers' introduced his annual motion in the Commons for the immediate and total repeal of the Corn Laws. In a lengthy speech, he reiterated the many familiar arguments in favour of Repeal, observing that the sufferings and misfortunes of the people resulted from a deficient supply of food and contributed to an increase in pauperism and the Poor Rates, and to increased crime and emigration. However, he also added a new ingredient into the discussion, namely expert medical evidence of the deleterious effects of the scarcity of food on the health and life of the people. Citing a substantial body of evidence from medical practitioners in Manchester, Blackburn, Stockport, the Potteries, Maidstone, London and Edinburgh, as well as in Ireland, Villiers illustrated that periods of scarcity were frequently accompanied by epidemic disease, especially typhus, and increased mortality rates. Villiers added that he possessed a great amount of evidence of the same kind relating to France, Belgium and Germany, all of which indicated that the health and well-being of the people varied according to the quantity of food with which they were supplied.[124] However, Peel was adamant that he did not intend to alter the Sliding Scale of 1842 or to reduce the degree of Protection afforded to agriculture, whilst Gladstone declared that it was his duty to respond to Villiers' motion with a direct negative.[125] After two nights' discussion, the debate closed with a division and Villiers' motion was defeated by 330 votes to 124.[126] However, the moral victory lay with the League since the size of the majority against repeal was declining and suggested that fewer MPs were now willing to stand up and defend the Corn Laws.

Later that year, Richard Cobden attempted to recruit Charles Villiers as the County MP for the great seat of South Lancashire at a time when the Anti-Corn Law League was seeking to secure County MPs in the north of England, and in a letter to Villiers he observed that 'South Lancashire is safe now – & we shall gain 1000 more (votes) next year I expect', adding 'We are unanimous at the League in wishing you to be our candidate. Will you stand, if it can be certified to you that you can win & *keep* the County?'[127] Villiers swiftly declined the invitation, explaining that if he accepted he would be criticised as 'a stranger and no proprietor in the county'.[128] Undaunted by Villiers' reply, Cobden continued to pursue the idea and in December he visited Wolverhampton and discussed the matter with William Walker, a leading local Anti-Corn Law campaigner and a Liberal. He reported the outcome of this meeting to Villiers in January 1845, observing that

> He [Walker] was of opinion that such a step, if sure, wd be highly politic, & however much they would regret at W'Hampton to lose you yet for the sake & for the causes they would be delighted to see you returned for the most important & populous district in the kingdom

adding 'There is perfect unanimity of opinion that you must be the man – Don't hesitate – Bright will stand for Wolverhampton if they want him shd he decide on not going to Durham'.[129]

Villiers, however, was somewhat perturbed by these overtures. Writing to Thornely in January 1845, he confided

> Do you know that I am beginning to be annoyed at the way in which the Leaguers are proclaiming me as the intended candidate ... I have objected to leave Wolverhampton under any circumstances but those of necessity, in the first place, and, in the next place, I have objected to anything being said on the matter at all now. But again Cobden asserts that I am to be the Candidate and misleads the people of our Borough and of the Country by doing so. I cannot contemplate the change of my circumstances that would make it short of insanity to engage in such a useless struggle.[130]

Villiers stated that he had always avoided having any open difference with the League, and did not wish to say or do anything to offend them, but that he would be extremely sorry to be supposed to be countenancing any deception upon any portion of the public in the matter. Moreover, Villiers added that he had written to William Walker to say that he would do nothing without the consent of the Wolverhampton Liberals, reminding him [Walker] that both he and Thornely had often agreed together that they would not change their seats with any one member in the House.[131] Nevertheless, the rumours that Villiers would stand for South Lancashire persisted and, in December, Villiers informed Thornely that

> I do not myself entertain any real doubt that the Electors of Wolverhampton will return me if I stand again, but I do believe there has been a little attempt on the part of our friend [Cobden] to induce some of our friends, though against their judgment, to recommend me to go to S. Lancashire ... I have had experience (and a great deal of it) of a great want of straightforwardness in a certain body [ACLL] and a disposition to serve and glorify themselves in the first place and then, etc., etc., and I am on my guard. I think your opinion and advice worth all theirs put together, but you, I dare say, see a difficulty that I should have if our Borough friends join with the others in making me abandon the bird in hand for the two in their bush. I want, at least to be free in that respect.[132]

Emphasising that he had 'no mind to be a martyr to the cause', Villiers expressed his hope that 'they will be quiet about it now', adding

> I had occasion to write to W. Walker, and I said that I took no notice of any idle reports about my change of seat, intending to do nothing without communicating with them, nor, I was sure, would they say or do anything without conferring with me.[133]

Nevertheless, Villiers continued to face the ire of the Protectionists in the House of Commons, and on 19 May 1845, during a debate on the Customs' Acts, he was the recipient of an unwarranted attack by his old foe, Sir John Tyrrell.[134] Tyrrell charged that

> The hon. Gentleman the Member for Wolverhampton, who deals so largely in abuse of the agriculturists, for participating, as he says, in the public plunder, is in possession of a seat in that sink of iniquity – the Court of Chancery, and I believe he is a pluralist, and in possession of a large salary.[135]

Villiers' response to this attack on his conduct and character was scathing, and he not only vehemently refuted the charge that he was a sinecurist,[136] but also took advantage of the opportunity to deliver a thinly-disguised and withering attack on the Protectionists and landed wealth in general:

> I tell you that I am paid for the work that I do; and tell you more, that you are not paid for the work you do. You come here to the House to get paid by the operation of iniquitous legislation. You come here to the House to pass laws to swell your own rents ... Your law is made – and you cannot deny it – for pecuniary objects; to support your younger children, and provide them with marriage portions. What do you do in return for all this? We pay your mortgages, and what do you give us in return? ... You work not for what you receive; you inherit your property like many other fortunate accidents of society, never having to work for

it in the least; and if you had the misfortune to lose it, your condition would be pitiable. The attack made upon me was no answer to the charge that we are aggrieved by the law to which I have alluded; and as between the hon. Baronet and myself tonight, I leave the House to decide which of us has made out the better defence.[137]

On 10 June 1845, Villiers presented his eighth annual motion for repeal and, in once again promoting Repeal as a national question, he pointed not only to the growing dissatisfaction of tenant farmers with the Corn Laws but also drew attention to the extreme destitution and distress existing in parts of Scotland (due to the Highland clearances[138]) and Ireland (due to the failure of the potato harvest), and the motion was defeated by only 254 votes to 122. Lord John Russell, who had hitherto maintained that it would be unwise to abolish all laws relating to the importation of corn, was moved to comment that he saw 'the fall of the corn law signified not only by the ability of the attacks made upon it, but also by the manner in which it is defended in this house'.[139] Despite this defeat, Villiers was praised for his efforts by W.J. Fox (later Liberal MP for Oldham) in one of his weekly letters to *The League* newspaper. Writing under his *nom de plume*, 'A Norwich Weaver Boy', Fox addressed Villiers in the following terms:

> Sir, The Free Traders of Great Britain ... notice with satisfaction how steadily you pursue the course you have marked out for yourself in Parliament, undiverted either by the right hand or the left by any personal or political inducement. Your public career is identified with this great cause. You adopted it in its feebleness, and you are one with it in its might. Your name is woven into the record of the struggle, and will be emblazoned in the glory of the triumph. Compared with the pure fame which you will achieve, how worthless is the transitory power of party leaders, pursuing crooked paths, surrounded by suspicions, guided by no principle, and, even when they are the inconsistent agents of benefit to a nation, conquered into the good they do by better men, whose perseverance has made the expediency to which they succumb![140]

During the Autumn of 1845 the Corn Law Question assumed increasing public importance in the light of a poor grain harvest in England, following several weeks of rain, and the failure of the potato crop in Ireland, and it was widely rumoured that the ports would have to be opened to foreign corn. In November, a grand banquet was given in honour of Charles Villiers in the Town Hall, Birmingham, chaired by the Mayor of Birmingham, Henry Smith, and attended by 700 guests, including Cobden, Bright and Fox, and many influential Birmingham Liberals.[141] According to *The Economist*, the Mayor stated that they were honouring Mr Villiers

> because they had seen in the conduct of that gentleman since the commencement of his political life everything to admire; that they had

witnessed his untiring advocacy of those principles in which they most concurred; and because they all admired the zeal and ability with which he had advocated the principles of commercial freedom.[142]

In reply, Villiers, in optimistic vein, stated that although it was now up to the Legislature to decide the question of Repeal, 'we who sit in the House of Commons have of late seen the most conclusive signs that those who will have to decide it feel that they are in error, and cannot much longer maintain their selfish position'.[143] Villiers was particularly critical of Peel's Sliding Scale, arguing that similar scales had been tried and abandoned in favour of Free Trade in Holland and Belgium, and that England should follow suit. There was, he said, a deficiency of food, whilst the price of the necessaries of life was rising everywhere, and it was likely that this would result in increased poverty, mortality and political discontent through the country unless the Corn Laws were repealed. Finally, in an implicit endorsement of the views of John Bright and, more especially, Richard Cobden on the wider benefits of Free Trade, Villiers adverted to the political implications of the Corn Laws:

> The Corn Laws are equally bad from a political point of view. They prevent that knitting together of nations in the bonds of mutual interest which tends to avert that great curse – War. And what is the further result of these restrictions as regards other nations? We are looked upon as a nuisance throughout Europe. We are looked upon as foes everywhere when we might be revered as friends by all.[144]

By the end of November 1845, against the background of the developing crisis in Ireland, Peel admitted that his opinions on the subject of Protection had undergone a change and on 27 January 1846 he unfolded his free-trade budget, reducing or repealing the duties on more than 150 articles, and proposing that from 1 February 1849 corn should be admitted duty free. This fell short of the repealers' demand for the immediate abolition of the Corn Laws and on the following day Villiers told Greville that there was a 'bad disposition among the Whigs, many indisposed to attend, and many only anxious to embarrass the Government', adding that Russell had asked him [Villiers] whether he intended to propose *immediate abolition*, should this not form part of Peel's plan.[145] That evening, Villiers, Cobden and Wilson dined at Ralph Ricardo's home, and were joined by Lord Grey. Villiers told Greville that Cobden was 'very bitter' against Peel and that Lord Grey was 'urgent for immediate repeal', which Villiers would propose and which would be supported by Lord John Russell.[146]

On 16 February 1846, Peel announced his intention to repeal the Corn Laws in the Commons. Bright wrote to his sister

> Peel delivered the best speech I ever heard in Parliament. It was a truly magnificent speech, sustained throughout, thoroughly with us, and

offering even to pass the immediate (repeal) if the House are willing. Villiers, Gibson and myself cheered continually, and I never listened to any human being with so much delight.[147]

During the debates, which lasted for twelve nights, Villiers, in moving for immediate repeal, reminded the House of the association between popular distress and revolution. Citing Thomas Carlyle's great work, *The French Revolution*, Villiers pointed to the state of France in 1789,

> when the people were threatened with famine; then came riot, disturbance, and speedily in their train a comprehensive change ... which struck deep into the roots of Society and effected vast changes in the relations of different classes.[148]

He then, with considerable foresight (for 1848 was to witness the rising of the Young Irelanders), linked this to the current state of Ireland, observing

> There is something like famine already existing in Ireland; and we are not sure that there may not be a bad harvest next year. What do Hon. Members mean to do? ... Hon. Members have undertaken to feed them, and the people are not fed. What answer will they give in 1846, and 1847, and 1848, if distress should ensue? ... They know that when men are driven desperate by distress, and driven to madness by suffering, and by the privations of those who are dear to them, they will accept only too readily any causes that are assigned for their misfortunes, they will only too easily grasp at any remedy that promises them relief.[149]

Villiers concluded his speech with an appeal to the landed aristocracy

> to consult their own true interests, and to sacrifice selfish prejudice to the cause of justice ... by the abolition *in toto* of Laws that, as long as a vestige of them remains, will be evidence against their wisdom and their honour.[150]

Although Villiers' motion was defeated by 267 votes to 78, Peel's Corn Bill was eventually carried on its third reading in the Commons in May,[151] with 329 votes for (112 Peelites, 217 Whigs and Irish MPs) and 231 (Tory Protectionists) against. The political controversy that followed was conducted with frightful acrimony between Tory Protectionists and Tory Free-Traders (Peelites) and ultimately split the Tory Party. Sir Robert Peel's Bill was passed in the Lords on 26 June 1846, and Peel resigned four days later. The ACLL had effectively achieved its aims, although it had been little more than a spectator in the final settlement of the Corn Law issue,[152] for the situation in Ireland,[153] and the attitude of Peel, who put the national interest above that of his party, had been the decisive factors in the League's victory. Indeed, as Howe has observed, the extent to which Peel was himself influenced by the League is debatable for, as a

Liberal Tory at the head of a Protectionist Party, his change of heart on the repeal question enabled him to complete the economic reforms begun during the 1820s and which he had himself extended by the introduction of Income Tax, a further Sliding Scale, and the reduction and abolition of many duties in the Budget of 1842. Hence Repeal in 1846 was the logical culmination of Liberal Tory economic reform, although it was also linked to the class politics of the 1840s and resulted in the separation of Peel from the bulk of the Tory party and its rural supporters.[154] Similarly, Schonhardt-Bailey, in arguing that Repeal should be understood as the product of interests, ideas and institutions and the interaction between them, also concedes that the attitude of Peel was critical in 1846,[155] although she suggests that Peel's politics were essentially pragmatic and concessionary, designed to effect a compromise between manufacturers and agriculturalists in order to maintain the 'territorial constitution', a key ingredient of Tory ideology.[156] For Disraeli and the Tory Protectionists, however, Peel's action marked his third 'Great Betrayal' of Tory principles (following his previous reversals on Catholic emancipation and parliamentary reform). By contrast, at an election rally in Wolverhampton in July 1847, Villiers praised Peel for conceding Repeal:

> He had acknowledged that he had been wrong about the Corn Laws, but had admitted his error. He had been forced to decide between his country and his constituency. I think that Sir Robert Peel acted patriotically in the course he took – he lost place, he lost power, he lost the attachment of old friends, but he saved the country from all the confusion which would have followed if, in the midst of dearth in Ireland, in the midst of scarcity in England, he had persevered in upholding a law, the object of which was to exclude the supply of the chief necessary of life to this country.[157]

Much of the public credit for this victory was directed towards Cobden and Bright, whose leadership of the extraordinary extra-parliamentary movement for repeal had been critical to the League's success. Indeed, the Tory *Fraser's Magazine*, a long-standing opponent of the League, sought to belittle Villiers' role in the League's victory. 'The advocacy of a repeal of the Corn-Laws', it observed,

> has been the one special hobby of the Hon. C.P. Villiers – a hobby he rode around the political arena with the flourish which usually attends hobby horsemanship, until the real men and horses of the Anti-Corn Law League came on the scene ... and even after the league had begun to make a figure in the House the annual motion of Mr Villiers was still regarded as an annual bore.[158]

Whilst grudgingly acknowledging Villiers' perseverance in the cause of Repeal, and the value of his arguments, noting that 'he argues rather than affirms, and appeals rather than denouncing' and that in his best speeches there had always been 'considerable logical force', the *Magazine* concluded, somewhat spitefully and unfairly, that

> These advantages are neutralised by his mode of delivery, which is neither stimulating nor dignified. A hard, grinding, plodding, though forcible monotony of voice, with a pronunciation the vulgarity of which strikes one the more as coming from a man of noble birth, are not helped by his action and delivery, both of which are commonplace in the extreme. He never was nor ever will be a favourite as a speaker, whether in the House or at public meetings.[159]

Yet, whilst perhaps lacking the fiery oratory of John Bright and the impassioned eloquence and strategic vision of Richard Cobden, Charles Villiers had played a crucial role in the success of the ACLL, for his annual motions set the agenda for a national debate, rehearsing, articulating and reiterating the case for repeal on commercial, economic, financial, social, political and moral grounds, and allowing the League to exert pressure on Parliament in such a way as to slowly erode the Protectionist majority.[160] Moreover, and particularly before Cobden and Bright entered Parliament, Villiers served as a vital link between Westminster, with its small group of Liberal free-traders, and the leaders of the ACLL in Manchester and the northern manufacturing districts. In this context, Villiers' many speeches on Free Trade, in both Parliament and the provinces, were not only critical to the whole debate, complementing the work of Cobden and Bright, but were also (and contrary to the opinions expressed by *Fraser's Magazine*) much admired, even by some of his opponents (even the arch Tory Colonel Sibthorpe was once moved to observe that Villiers had been 'bold, manly and independent').[161] As Alexander Somerville, writing under the pseudonym 'Reuben', noted in 1845, Charles Villiers had been distinguished as the parliamentary advocate of free trade before the League had any of its own members in the House of Commons and he had spoken with great effect in the debates raised by Mr Cobden, and by those raised by Sir Robert Peel by the alteration in the tariff, adding that

> Mild and unassuming in his manners, he has conciliated the respect of even his warmest opponents in the House. He has stated his case with the earnestness which the advocate of a good cause always exhibits, but he has not awakened anything like personal antagonism. His oratory is characterised by an ease of delivery and purity of expression more easily admired than commanded. He is fluent, without being hurried; and has the merit – which, if more general, would save much time – of not allowing his voice to be heard too frequently in the House. In reply, where the full mind is exhibited, Mr Villiers has always been particularly happy. Without once quitting the main argument, he oftentimes sends a wit-shaft home to his opponent's substitute for a heart, and the quiet

manner in which he thus cuts at 'gentle dullness' gives additional point to the sarcasm. The staple of Mr Villiers' speeches, however, is of better and more solid material ... Well acquainted with the statistics of the question, his arguments are all based upon facts; and, for this reason, the true bearing of the case can always be ascertained by reference to his speeches. So full is his information, and so exact his statements, that they have rarely been questioned in an assembly the most fault-finding, as well as the most absurdly fastidious, in the world.[162]

Similar observations were made by Cyrus Redding, the Liberal political journalist, who noted that Villiers had shown himself 'earnest, well read on the question, eloquent, and gentlemanly, never intrusive on the patience of the House, [he] obtained its ear before Cobden became the champion', adding that Cobden had 'obtained more praise than he merited through the desire of Sir Robert Peel to give to Manchester all praise in the way of conciliation, or rather so, I believe, than to a member of the aristocracy'.[163]

Lord Clarendon, in particular, was dismayed by the credit afforded by Peel to Cobden, which *The Times* had endorsed in a leading article. Writing to his friend, the journalist Henry Reeve, in January 1846, Clarendon observed:

> I don't think the 'Times' is quite fair in altogether omitting my brother Charles in its *resume* of the Corn Law battle. Charles, long before Cobden was heard of, persisted in bringing this question every year before the House, notwithstanding the sneers and opposition of the Liberals; and as Peel at the beginning of the session said he could no longer resist the arguments of the member for Wolverhampton, it is not just to say that 'Cobden was bearing the brunt of the battle in the H. of C., and unconsciously convincing the Prime Minister'. The subject will probably be reverted to in the 'Times', and if you will mention Charles to Delane, I have no doubt he will do him justice as a parliamentary leader, opponent of the Corn Laws; and Charles cannot, like the manufacturers, be supposed to have had the slightest interest in their abolition.[164]

In the event, Clarendon's plea was ignored. However, thirteen years later, on Charles Villiers' appointment as President of the Poor Law Board, *The Times* – albeit belatedly and retrospectively – finally provided a fulsome appreciation of Villiers' contribution to the repeal of the Corn Laws, stating:

> It was Mr. Charles Villiers who practically originated the Free Trade movement. For years before Messrs. Cobden and Bright were heard of as politicians, Mr. Villiers annually brought the subject before Parliament. He it was who had to contend with all the odium and all the ridicule of urging a proposition which in those days was looked upon much in the same light as a serious motion for realizing the ideas of St. Simon or Proudhon would be regarded in our time. Young politicians who are

just entering upon the arena of public life have no idea of the fierce animosities of twenty years ago. In those days a Radical was looked upon as a kind of monster, and a Free Trader was to a Radical what a Radical was to a truly respectable man. Still, even so, there were differences. Mr. Cobbett, or even the late Mr. Hume, might make proposals 'subversive of the throne and the altar', and it was taken that he was merely acting as a low vulgar fellow naturally would act. It was otherwise when a man connected by birth, education, and family with the territorial classes dared to raise the standard of rebellion against their views, and what they supposed to be their interests. Such a man was instantly 'Anathema' – a traitor to his order, as well as a disturber of the public peace. Now Mr. Villiers did this. As a youth he began the contest which he only saw ended when he had already attained middle life; he dissociated himself from the traditions of his class; he incurred their animosity; he sacrificed the ease and comfort of his own days, and all to fight a battle in which, as it turned out, he lost half the merit of success in the opinion of the vulgar.[165]

Villiers, the editorial continued, 'never got the credit of the philosopher who for practical purposes may be said to have originated the idea, or of the popular leader who manipulated the masses, and finally forced the Minister's hand,' yet his role in the repeal of the Corn Laws was just as important and it had been mainly due to him that the settlement of the question had been carried on in an orderly and Parliamentary way. Indeed, the article concluded,

One of the most ungenerous acts of the great Minister [Peel] who at last suffered himself to be convinced was that at the moment of surrender he did not give his fair share of praise to Mr. Villiers, who had so long brought the question before the House. His compliments were reserved for the 'unadorned eloquence' of the popular leader [Cobden] to whom he succumbed.[166]

Notes

1 Anthony Howe, *Free Trade and Liberal England, 1846–1946* (Oxford, 1997), 1; see also A. Howe, 'Free Trade and the Victorians', in A. Marrison (ed.), *Free Trade and its Reception, 1815–1960*, Vol. I, *Freedom and Trade* (London, 1998), 164–83.
2 See especially Reuben [Alexander Somerville], *A Brief History of the Rise and Progress of the Anti-Corn Law League, with Personal Sketches of its Leading Members* (London, 1845), 48–50; Archibald Prentice, *History of the Anti-Corn Law League* (2 vols, London, 1853); Norman McCord, *The Anti-Corn Law League 1838–1846* (London, 1958); W.H. Chaloner, 'The Agitation against the Corn Laws', in J.T. Ward (ed.), *Popular Movements, c.1830–1850* (London, 1970), 135–51; Norman Longmate, *The Breadstealers: The Fight against the Corn Laws, 1838–1846* (Hounslow, 1984); Paul A. Pickering and Alex Tyrell, *The People's Bread: A History of*

the Anti-Corn Law League (London, 2000); Cheryl Schonhardt-Bailey (ed.), *Free Trade: The Repeal of the Corn Laws* (Bristol, 1996); Cheryl Schonhardt-Bailey, *From the Corn Laws to Free Trade: Interests, Ideas, and Institutions in Historical Perspective* (Cambridge, MA, and London, 2006).

3 Richard Cobden (1804–1865): Anglican; Radical Liberal politician; commercial traveller and Manchester calico manufacturer; founder member of Anti-Corn Law League; MP for Stockport (1841–47), West Riding (1847–57) and Rochdale (1859–65); free trade and peace campaigner; negotiated Anglo-French (Cobden–Chevalier) Treaty in 1860. For further details, see J. Morley, *The Life of Richard Cobden* (London, 1879); M. Taylor, 'Cobden, Richard (1804–1864)', *ODNB*, 5741 (May 2009).

4 John Bright (1811–1889): Quaker; Radical and Liberal statesman; founder member of the Anti-Corn Law League; MP for Durham (1843–7), Manchester (1847–57) and Birmingham (1858–89); President of the Board of Trade (1868–71) and Chancellor of the Duchy of Lancaster (1873–4; 1880–2); split with Gladstone over Irish Home Rule in 1886. For further details, see William Robertson, *The Life and Times of John Bright* (London, 1912); M. Taylor, 'Bright, John (1811–1889)', *ODNB*, 3421 (Sept. 2013); Bill Cash, *John Bright: Statesman, Orator, Agitator* (London, 2012).

5 W.O. Henderson, *Charles Pelham Villiers and the Repeal of the Corn Laws* (Oxford, 1975). This eighty-one page booklet expands on the coverage of the subject outlined in Henderson's article in *History* (1952), together with a brief biography of Villiers.

6 A. Howe (ed.), *The Letters of Richard Cobden, Vol. I: 1815–1847* [hereafter *Cobden Letters*], (Oxford, 2007).

7 Howe, *Free Trade and Liberal England*, 3–4.

8 Schonhardt-Bailey, *From the Corn Laws to Free Trade*, 9–11.

9 Charles Pelham Villiers, *The Free Trade Speeches of Charles Pelham Villiers* [hereafter *Free Trade Speeches*], *With a Political Memoir* [hereafter *Political Memoir*], edited by a Member of the Cobden Club [Agnes Lambert], 2 vols (London, 1883), II, 92: Wolverhampton, 8 April 1844. Villiers stated that

> At the General Election of 1837 he requested me to bring forward total Repeal the following year. I assented but remarked that the harvests had been so good that it would deprive the subject of its usual interest. 'Good harvests, Sir,' he rejoined, 'what have they to do with it? A good harvest will not make a bad law a good one. The Corn Laws are bad Laws, and they will bear bad fruit as long as they last. They will do much more harm yet.' Mr. Fryer was a true prophet.

10 *Parl. Debs*, 3rd ser., 37, cc.562–615, 16 Mar. 1837.
11 *Wolverhampton Chronicle*, 26 July 1837.
12 Prentice, *History of the Anti-Corn Law League*, I, 97–8.
13 *Cobden Letters*, I, 128: Cobden to Villiers, 17 Feb. 1838.
14 Coohill, *Ideas of the Liberal Party*, 177.
15 *Parl. Debs*, 3rd ser., 41, 15 March 1838.
16 Villiers, *Free Trade Speeches*, 1, 3: House of Commons, 15 March 1838.
17 *Queen Victoria's Journals*, 4, 109, 16 Mar. 1838.
18 Henderson, *History* (1952), 26.
19 Villiers to Joseph Sturge, 15 Aug. 1838, cited in H. Richard, *Memoirs of Joseph Sturge* (London, 1864), 270–1. Sturge had previously played a prominent role within the anti-slavery movement (which Villiers had also supported) and opposed the Corn Laws on both moral (in that he held that trade restrictions encouraged war) and economic (in the belief that government interference in commerce was harmful) grounds, and he subsequently reciprocated Villiers' earlier support by joining

Villiers in his battle against the Corn Laws. By December 1843, however, Villiers had become sceptical in regard to Sturge's real commitment to Free Trade: BLPES/SR1094, Villiers to Thornely, 16 Dec. 1843. Villiers also subsequently enlisted the support of Francis Place, the great Radical and trades unionist (with whom he had previously worked in the campaign to secure the Penny Post) for the repeal cause: Longmate, *The Breadstealers*, 48–9.

20 BLPES/SR1094, Villiers to Thornely, 26 Oct. 1838.
21 For detailed reports of the proceedings, including Villiers' address, see especially *Manchester Courier*, 26 Jan. 1839; *Manchester Times*, 26 Jan. 1839; *Birmingham Journal*, 26 Jan. 1839.
22 *Parl. Debs*, 3rd ser., 45, cc.155–6, 7 Feb. 1839.
23 William Cooke Taylor, *Life and Times of Sir Robert Peel* (London, 1849), III, 82.
24 Harriet Martineau, *History of the Thirty Years Peace* (London, 1877), II, 405.
25 *The Letters of Queen Victoria*, A.C. Benson and Viscount Esher (eds), (3 vols, London, 1908), I, 148: Lord John Russell to Queen Victoria, 20 Feb. 1839: 'Mr Charles Villiers moved yesterday, after a very able speech, that the petitioners against the Corn Laws should be heard at the Bar of the House'.
26 A. Howe, 'The Anti-Corn Law League (1839–1846)', *ODNB*, 42282 (May 2011).
27 Villiers, *Free Trade Speeches*, I, 105–8: House of Commons, 12 Mar. 1839.
28 *Parl. Debs*, 3rd ser., 46, c.1118, 22 Mar. 1839.
29 *Cobden Letters*, I, 160: Cobden to Joseph Sturge, 30 Mar. 1839.
30 Villiers, *Free Trade Speeches*, I, 82.
31 Pickering and Tyrrell, *The People's Bread* (2000), 171.
32 Howe, 'The Anti-Corn Law League', *ODNB* (2011).
33 Schonhardt-Bailey, *From the Corn Laws to Free Trade*, 283–5.
34 A. Briggs, *The Age of Improvement* (London, 1959), 312.
35 BLPES/SR1094, Thornely to Villiers, 25 Aug. 1839.
36 Ibid.
37 Ibid., Thornely to Villiers, 31 Dec. 1839.
38 Longmate, *The Breadstealers* (1984), 48–9.
39 Coohill, *Ideas of the Liberal Party*, 182.
40 Villiers, *Free Trade Speeches*, 1, 196: House of Commons, 1 Apr. 1840.
41 Lucy Brown, 'The Chartists and the Anti-Corn Law League', in Asa Briggs (ed.), *Chartist Studies* (London, 1954), 342–71.
42 Pickering and Tyrrell, *The People's Bread* (2000). 93. By 1842 Cobden had become sceptical in regard to the 'brickbat' argument. Writing to Bright in June 1842, Cobden confided that

> Villiers, Hume, & others are constantly preaching, *in private*, the doctrine that the landlord will only yield to fear after the people have begun to burn & destroy again as they did in 1829. But this is a course which no Christian or good citizen can look at with hope of advantage – Is there not a still more effectual way of alarming them by the *moral* resistance so often put in force by the Quakers with such success?
>
> *Cobden Letters*, I, 278: Cobden to Bright, 21 June 1842

43 *Cobden Letters*, I, 179: Cobden to Villiers, 4 Feb. 1840.
44 Ibid., 210–11: Cobden to Villiers, nd. Jan. 1840.
45 Ibid., 181: Cobden to Villiers, 7 Feb. 1840.
46 Prentice, *History of the Anti-Corn Law League*, I, 160.
47 *Parl. Debs*, 3rd ser., 53, c.1091, 14 Apr. 1840.
48 Ibid., 54, cc.662–74, 28 May 1840.
49 *Report of the Select Committee on Import Duties*, 101–5, iii–vii, 6 August 1840; see also Coohill, *Ideas of the Liberal Party*, 183–4.

50 See also BLPES/SR1094, Thornely to Villiers, 12 Oct. 1840.
51 James Grant was the author of *St Stephens, or Pencillings of Politicians* (London, 1839).
52 *Manchester Times*, 20 March 1841; The same article was carried in the *Caledonian Mercury*, 19 Apr. 1841.
53 William Robertson, *The Life and Times of John Bright* (London, 1877), 57.
54 Prentice, *History of the Anti-Corn Law League*, I, 200.
55 *Free Trade Speeches*, I, 244–5, Manchester, 15 April 1841.
56 Ibid.
57 Ibid., 246.
58 *Cobden Letters*, I, 223–4: Cobden to Villiers, 6 June.
59 *Free Trade Speeches*, I, 249. House of Commons, 7 June 1841.
60 Ibid.
61 Ibid., 272. House of Commons, 27 Aug. 1841.
62 *Dictionary of National Biography*, lviii (1899), 321. For the relationship between Villiers and Cobden, see Howe, *The Letters of Richard Cobden*, I, and II, *1848–1853* (Oxford, 2010).
63 G.M. Trevelyan, *The Life of John Bright* (London, 1913), 65, nd., August 1841.
64 McCord, *The Anti-Corn Law League*, 95–6.
65 Leader, *The Life and Letters of John Arthur Roebuck*, 146–7. Extract from Roebuck's parliamentary journal, 2 Feb. 1843.
66 W. Hinde, *Richard Cobden: A Victorian Outsider* (New Haven and London, 1987), 95.
67 Pickering and Tyrrell, *The People's Bread*, 93.
68 Cobden told Villiers [himself an aristocrat] 'You have no idea (not being with the people) how much more respectable we shall become after being patronised by the Earl of Radnor'. Pickering and Tyrrell, *The People's Bread*, 181.
69 These continued to reflect the opinions of the League's Council, on Villiers' advice: see Villiers to George Wilson, 21 Sep. 1841, M[anchester] A[rchives] and L[ocal] S[tudies], George Wilson Papers, GB127. M20/3018.
70 *Cobden Letters*, I, 228–9: Cobden to Villiers, 11 July 1841.
71 Ibid., Cobden to Villiers, 13 Sept. 1841.
72 *Parl. Debs*, 3rd ser., 59, cc.567–74, 17 Sept. 1841.
73 *Cobden Letters*, I, 244–5: Cobden to Villiers, 19 Nov. 1841.
74 Gladstone had voted consistently against Villiers' motions for repeal on the grounds of the 'fundamental unsoundness' of Villiers' arguments: See, for example, *The Gladstone Diaries* [hereafter *GD*], 14 vols (Oxford, 1968–94), M.R.D. Foot (ed.) (vols 1–2); M.R.D. Foot and H.G.C. Matthew (eds) (vols 3–4); H.C.G. Matthew (ed.) (vols 5–14), vol. 2, 355: (Thursday) 15 Mar. 1838: 'Voted in 30:95 for Corn Laws' (against Villiers); vol. 3, p. 212; (Monday) 11 Jul. 1842: 'House 4½ – 2¾, Voted in 231 to 117 against Villiers on Corn Laws'. Gladstone later became converted to the Free Trade cause and supported Peel in cabinet on the Repeal question.
75 *Annual Register* (1842), 44; see also Elie Halevy, *A History of the English People in the Nineteenth Century* (6 vols, London, 1927), IV, *Victorian Years 1841–1895*, 29.
76 *Parl. Debs*, 3rd ser., 60, cc.40–69, 3 Feb. 1842.
77 Ibid., cc.814–81, 22 Feb. 1842; 60, cc.1018–82, 24 Feb. 1842.
78 Prentice, *History of the Anti-Corn Law League*, I. 324.
79 *Wolverhampton Chronicle*, 23 Feb. 1842.
80 *Cobden Letters*, I, 261: Cobden to Bright, 4 Mar. 1842. See also Mrs Russell Barrington, *The Works and Life of Walter Bagehot* (London, 1915) vol. 10, 399–400.
81 MCL. George Wilson Papers, GB127. M20/3027: ACLL circular.

82 Pickering and Tyrrell, *The People's Bread*, 172.
83 *Parl. Debs*, 3rd ser., 49, cc.642–56, 22 Jul. 1839.
84 Ibid., 63, cc.1024–48, 31 May 1842.
85 Ibid. Nevertheless, the Bill was passed 255–149, Villiers voting against.
86 Pickering and Tyrrell, *The People's Bread*, 142–3.
87 *Parl. Debs*, 3rd ser., 63, cc.1640–59, 16 Jun. 1842.
88 Ibid., 64, cc.1171–238, 8 Jul. 1842.
89 Ibid.
90 Ibid., For the local dimension, see also Andrew J. Hook, 'Charles Pelham Villiers and the Anti-Corn Law League in the Black Country, 1836–1846', unpublished MA dissertation (Wolverhampton Polytechnic, 1985), WALS, WM340.
91 *Parl. Debs*, 3rd ser., 64, cc.1171–238, 8 Jul. 1842.
92 Ibid.
93 Ibid., 65, cc.517–66, 22 Jul. 1842.
94 Ibid.
95 Ibid.
96 Ibid.
97 Ibid.
98 Ibid., 306: Cobden to Villiers, 4 Dec. 1842.
99 *The Carlyle Letters Online*, vol. 6, 45–53: Thomas Carlyle to John A. Carlyle, 13 Nov. 1831:

> Meanwhile I continue to look about me, and meet here and there with hopeful things. Chiefly among the young ... Mill (John Stuart) I continue to like: I met with a fresh lot of youths last week by his intervention; one Taylor (of the Colonial Office) is the centre of the group, and is to see me again; the rest were Hyde Villiers, his brother [Charles Pelham], and one Elliott, all Diplomatists; whole, pleasant young men, – by whom the world will not be made or unmade. We had a gay breakfast, however (from Taylor, in Grosvenor Street), and I did not regret my walk.

100 Ibid., 15, 252–54: Thomas Carlyle to Alexander Carlyle, 28 Dec. 1842.
101 Ibid., 26, 273–75: Thomas Carlyle to John A. Carlyle, 20 Dec. 1851: 'Villiers &c, and others have come and are coming: we are a fluctuating society here'.
102 Ibid., 30, 151–3: Thomas Carlyle to John A. Carlyle, 30 Dec. 1855.
103 Villiers, *Free Trade Speeches*, I, 345: Manchester, 3 Jan. 1843.
104 Ibid.; see also *Birmingham Journal*, 14 Jan. 1843.
105 Philip Whitwell Wilson (ed.), *The Greville Diary* (2 vols, London, 1927), II, 175, 16 Jan. 1843.
106 Longmate, *The Breadstealers*, 172–3.
107 *Parl. Debs*, 3rd ser., 69, c.1523, 14 June 1843. The Tory *Wolverhampton Chronicle* described Villiers' motion as follows:

> The debate consequent upon it has dragged its weary way through the rest of the week. Monotony, and a bold repetition of stale allegations, we were prepared to accept – but such a prolongation of the infliction, so little mercy for auditors, the public press, and the public itself, we must admit, did not enter into our calculations.
>
> *Wolverhampton Chronicle*, 17 May 1843

108 Villiers, *Free Trade Speeches*, II, 48–61, Colchester, 8 Jul. 1843.
109 Ibid.
110 Ibid., I, 48.

111 Villiers suffered perennially from gastric ailments, coughs and colds, a state of affairs which was hardly improved by his fondness for claret and cigarettes, and Richard Cobden once advised him to 'nurse your *physique* – keep your *stomach* in order ... by abstinence': Hinde, *Richard Cobden*, 95.
112 MALS. George Wilson Papers, GB127. M20/3021: Villiers to George Wilson, 6 Aug. 1843.
113 Ibid., 125.
114 G. Villiers, *A Vanished Victorian*, 149.
115 *Cobden Letters*, I, 336–7: Cobden to Villiers, 2 Sep. 1843.
116 Villiers, *A Vanished Victorian*, 150.
117 BLPES/SR1094, Villiers to Thornely, 11 Jan. 1844.
118 Ibid.
119 Andrew Bisset, *Notes on the Anti-Corn Law Struggle* (London, 1884), 140.
120 Villiers, *Free Trade Speeches*, II, 62: Covent Garden Theatre, 8 Feb. 1844.
121 Ibid., II, 83–4: Wolverhampton, 8 Apr. 1844.
122 Ibid., 87.
123 Ibid., 89–90.
124 Ibid., II, 99–169: House of Commons, 25 Jun. 1844.
125 Ibid., 99.
126 *Parl. Debs*, 3rd ser., 75, cc.1452–549, 26 Jun. 1844.
127 *Cobden Letters*, I, 374: Cobden to Villiers, 13 Nov. 1844.
128 Ibid., 375, n.5, Villiers to Cobden, 15 Nov. 1844.
129 Ibid., 379: Cobden to Villiers, 12 Jan. 1845.
130 BLPES/SR1094, Villiers to Thornely, 13 Jan. 1845.
131 Ibid.
132 Ibid., Villiers to Thornely, 31 Dec. 1845.
133 Ibid.
134 Ibid., 78, cc.1161–211, 19 May 1845. This arose from a resolution by Sir G. Clerk 'That the Duties of Customs charged upon the Goods, Wares, and Merchandize hereafter mentioned, imported into the United Kingdom, shall cease'. Mr Bramston, MP, objected to the inclusion of grease in the tariff and moved that it be omitted. He was seconded by Sir John Tyrrell. Charles Villiers pointed out that Mr Bramston was entitled to object to the repeal of the duty on grease, just as any other member had the right to object to the repeal of duties on other agricultural produce, but observed that Mr Bramston represented the grease interest, just as others represented the corn interest, adding that the agriculturalists were divided when they were robbing each other, and were united only when they were protected, 'or, to use a coarser expression, all robbing the public together'.
135 Ibid.
136 Ibid.:

> I state what I have before stated again, and the only answer I get from the hon. Baronet to my statement is, that he has poked about the Red Book to discover what place I held in the Court of Chancery. And that is your sole answer [addressing himself to the hon. Baronet] to the charge against you and your law. You must be reduced, indeed, to desperate shifts, if that is the only answer you have to give. Besides, in making your statement against me, you did not make it correctly. The place I hold is no sinecure. [Sir John Tyrrell did not call it a sinecure.] You did not say that it was a sinecure? Then if it is not a sinecure, why should I not hold it? If you say it is a sinecure, I tell you it is not.

137 Ibid.

138 For further details, see especially John Prebble, *The Highland Clearances* (London, 1969); Krisztina Fenyo, *Contempt, Sympathy and Romance: Lowland Perceptions of the Highlands and the Clearances during the Famine Years, 1845–55* (East Linton, 2000).
139 *Parl. Debs*, 3rd ser., 81, cc.285–381, 10 Jun. 1845.
140 *The League*, XXX, 17 May 1845.
141 *Birmingham Journal*, 15 Nov. 1845; *Wolverhampton Chronicle*, 19 Nov. 1845.
142 *The Economist*, 15 Nov. 1845; see also Robertson, *The Life and Times of John Bright*, 119–20.
143 Villiers, *Free Trade Speeches*, II, 266–7: Birmingham, 14 Nov. 1845.
144 Ibid., 287.
145 Charles C. Greville, *The Greville Memoirs: A Journal of the Reign of Queen Victoria* (3 vols, London, 1885), II, 8 Jan. 1846.
146 Ibid., 30 Jan. 1846.
147 R.A.J. Walling (ed.), *The Diaries of John Bright* (New York, 1931), 80, 16 Feb. 1846.
148 Villiers, *Free Trade Speeches*, II, 365–6: House of Commons, 26 Feb. 1846.
149 Ibid., 367–8.
150 Ibid., 368.
151 *Parl. Debs*, 3rd ser., 86, cc.616–727, 15 May 1846.
152 Howe, 'The Anti-Corn Law League', *ODNB*, 42282 (May 2011).
153 The extent to which Peel was influenced by famine in Ireland has been disputed by Christine Kinealy, who has argued that it was the 'Condition of England Question' rather than the Irish Famine that was the rationale for Corn Law repeal by 1846 and that although Peel 'occasionally and perhaps cynically referred to the Irish Famine' he did not believe that Repeal would be of immediate benefit to Ireland and in the long term Russell's subsequent Whig administration saw the Famine as an opportunity – much as Peel had seen – to end the dependence of the Irish on the potato and to restructure Irish agriculture: C. Kinealy, 'Peel, Rotten Potatoes and Providence: The Repeal of the Corn Laws and the Irish Famine', in Marrison, *Free Trade and its Reception*, I, 50–62.
154 Howe, *Free Trade and Liberal England, 1846–1946*, 3–4.
155 Schonhardt-Bailey, *From the Corn Laws to Free Trade*, 28–30.
156 Ibid., 285.
157 *Staffs Advertiser*, 31 Jul. 1847.
158 *Fraser's Magazine*, vol. 34 (July 1846), XI, 101.
159 Ibid., 102; see also M.M. Trumbull, *The Free Trade Struggle in England* (Chicago, 1892), 28–9.
160 Howe, 'Villiers, Charles Pelham', *ODNB*, 28286 (Oct. 2006).
161 Simon Heffer, *High Minds: The Victorians and the Birth of Modern Britain* (London, 2013), 107.
162 Reuben, *A Brief History of the Rise and Progress of the Anti-Corn Law League*, 48–50.
163 Cyrus Redding, *Fifty Years' Recollections, Literary and Personal, with Observations on Men and Things* (3 vols, London, 1858), vol. 3, 168. Redding (1785–1870) was co-editor of the *New Monthly Magazine* from 1821 to 1830, and editor of the *Staffordshire Examiner* from 1834 to 1840.
164 Lord Clarendon to Henry Reeve, 4 July 1846, cited in J.K. Laughton (ed.), *Memoirs of the Life and Correspondence of Henry Reeve* (2 vols, London, 1898), I, 178.
165 *The Times*, 1859, cited Villiers, *Political Memoir*, lxxxi.
166 Ibid.

5 Interlude

Yet in the aftermath of repeal, Villiers and his friends felt that his pioneering role had been undervalued, for the ACLL initially omitted to offer Villiers a testimonial for his services, whereas £10,000 was voted to George Wilson, a gift of £75,000 was given to Richard Cobden and a valuable library was presented to John Bright. As Agnes Lambert observed, 'what was strange with regard to the final proceedings of the League was their omission of all public recognition of their Parliamentary leader, and this was resented by Free Traders generally',[1] and Cobden himself admitted 'I have trod upon his heels, nay, almost trampled him down, in a race where he was once the sole man on the course'.[2] Indeed, the view that Villiers had been mistreated by Cobden and Bright, though unfounded, did acquire some currency and, many years later, in a speech at Woodstock on 31 January 1884, Lord Randolph Churchill went as far as to claim that 'the great battle of Free Trade ... was fought by Mr Charles Villiers long before Mr Bright made his appearance in public' and that 'Mr Charles Villiers bore the burden and heat of that protracted and lengthened contest', but

> when Mr Villiers had won the day, Mr Bright and his dear friend Mr Cobden stepped in and tried to rob him of all his glory ... and were nothing more nor less than two plundering cuckoos, who shamefully ejected Mr Charles Villiers from the nest which he had constructed, and who reared therein their own chattering and silly brood.[3]

In the event, a committee was organised in London to repair the League's neglect, but when Villiers heard of it he wrote to Ricardo, the chairman, and asked him to dissolve it, indicating that he would not accept any pecuniary gain for his service – stating 'the reward of public services is public confidence, and I will accept nothing else' – although he intimated that he desired a post in which he could better serve his country than the one he presently held (Examiner in the Court of Chancery).[4]

Subsequently, Richard Cobden made strenuous efforts to secure recognition for Villiers in Lord John Russell's Whig ministry and wrote to Joseph Parkes in July 1846 to this effect. Russell, then in a considerable minority in the House, had offered Villiers the Vice-Presidentship of the Board of Trade (Lord Clarendon, Villiers' brother, having accepted the Presidentship) but as Cobden noted, this was a post that Villiers could not with propriety take. 'If I were Lord John,' Cobden wrote,

> I would not sleep without having first found an appointment for Villiers, the higher the better – The Free Traders have felt confident that he would be rewarded at the hands of the next government for his services to the cause. To pass him over, under any plea, will give a colouring to the rumours that the Whigs are more disposed to conciliate the protectionists than to satisfy the Free Traders.

Cobden suggested to Parkes that 'an embassy, from which he would not be likely to be removed by any probable change of Government, would suit him and be most gratifying to the Free Traders', adding that

> if Villiers was appointed to any court where Protectionist principles are in the ascendant ... it would be most useful in influencing the Government, it would be a graceful way of promoting an honest man and pronouncing on the part of our rulers to a foreign nation.

Cobden added that

> He [Villiers] is not a party man, and therefore not likely to promote his own interests. But, as a man of the people myself, I do feel nettled that the only man of his class who from the first has been true to our cause should be neglected by the Government which has come into power upon the wreck of parties occasioned by our popular movement.[5]

Parkes subsequently wrote frankly to Lord John Russell, disclosing the contents of Cobden's letter and adding

> I write to you in justice more than friendship towards Villiers, although I have a great friendship for him. Also, I apprehend that if Villiers, the (and disinterested) leader of the Free Trade question in Parliament, is left where he is, it will be a scandal to your Administration.[6]

Russell replied that everything that could be done for Villiers ought to be done. On learning of this correspondence, Cobden again wrote to Parkes and his letter well illustrates the esteem with which Villiers was held by Cobden:

> Now for our friend Villiers, I agree with you that he will never make an administrator, if by that we mean a House of Commons partisan. He is too honest, too sensitive, too much like an unbroken high-spirited steed ... I know him well, have watched and probed him for eight years, and am ready

to swear by him as a true man. I love and venerate him more than he is aware of. I have felt for him what I could not express, because my esteem has grown out of his noble self-denial under trials to which I could not allude without touching a too secret chord ... When I came into the House ... I took THE position of the Free Trade. I watched him then; there was no rivalry, no jealousy, no repining; his sole object was to see his principles triumph. He was willing to stand aside and cheer me on to the winning goal; his conduct was not merely noble, it was godlike ... I wish he knew how long and anxiously the leading Leaguers discussed the subject of a testimonial to him and Bright jointly with myself.[7]

Villiers, as an essentially modest and unassuming man, was undoubtedly hurt by the lack of recognition for his contribution to the Repeal of the Corn Laws. As he told Thomas Thornely,

Utterly cast into the shade and neglected as I have been by the manufacturers and League people with whom I struggled at least (if they deny the service) there was perfect excuse for the Government to have done nothing. They have no reason to feel thankful to me for my services to them as a party seeking office, and their offers could only be in deference to what some people said in private of the singular injustice with which I have been treated ... However, I shall occupy myself no farther about them, and I only mention this privately to you. I have made no application to the Government for anything, and shall make none. I shall go on just as I have done. I have got that place for life, and I believe we both have our seats for life, if we chose it, and I shall take Parliament rather more quietly than I have done.[8]

In the event, both Villiers and Cobden – who had written to Villiers expressing his 'sincere regret at the apparent injustice, hitherto done him'[9] – were excluded from Russell's Cabinet of 1846.[10] Indeed, for Russell – and for many other Whigs – Villiers was never a true Whig, more an aristocrat who had betrayed his class through radical politics.[11] For his part, Villiers, whilst acknowledging that he 'thought well of that noble Lord [Russell] ... he did think him a very able man, and a very honourable man', declared that 'he was not going to sacrifice his principles in supporting him; he should act as he had hitherto done; he should vote independently'.[12] Lord Clarendon privately pressed his brother's case with Lord John Russell, who intimated that he was perfectly ready to recommend Villiers to go to Bombay as Governor if he so wished. As Villiers confided in Thornely,

Looking at the advantage of it as a means of saving some money and having an independence, if I survived the climate, I agreed to accept it. It was not a thing I desired, but feeling strongly the injustice with which I have been treated with regard to my past efforts in the cause that has lately triumphed, and feeling little encouragement to slave on here for another ten years as I have done for the last ten years, I felt that I should be unwise to refuse it.[13]

However, when Villiers heard that there had been some opposition from the East India Company to his appointment because he had been a prominent member of the League,[14] and that Sir Henry Pottinger had also expressed a strong desire to be appointed as Governor, Villiers had a change of heart and duly informed Lord Clarendon that the Government would best serve the interests of India by appointing Pottinger, adding that 'I am bound to say that Lord John has done all that he could be expected to do for me in making the different offers he has'.[15] Thereafter, with the exception of an invitation in February 1849, couched in the most flattering terms, to become Governor of the Ionian Islands at an annual salary of £7,000,[16] and an intimation by Lord Grey in 1851 that the Governorship of Mauritius was available to him — both of which were rejected — Villiers received no Ministerial recognition of his public services, and Anthony Howe has suggested that in the aftermath of repeal Villiers 'was never to recapture the political limelight that he had hitherto enjoyed'.[17] Indeed, many years later, the *London Standard* was moved to observe 'Why Mr Villiers was not invited to join the Russell Ministry of 1846 is one of those questions which nobody but a Whig could answer'.[18]

In the meantime, Cobden and Bright continued to promote Villiers' candidacy for the seat of South Lancashire. In May 1847, the *Manchester Times* reported that 8,340 Liberals in South Lancashire had signed a memorial in support of Villiers as their member.[19] Initially, Villiers told George Wilson that although he had some objections to standing, he was at least willing to discuss the matter,[20] but by the end of the month he declined the offer, owing to his commitments to Wolverhampton and its constituents.[21] Moreover, Villiers expected to be returned unopposed in Wolverhampton, where he had been astonished by the support he was receiving.[22] Nevertheless, in June, at a crowded meeting of Liberals at the Angel Inn, Oldham, it was resolved that Villiers was 'eminently qualified to represent the great commercial and industrial interests of this important district'.[23] On the eve of the General Election, Cobden duly wrote to George Wilson urging him to

> Make any use you can of my name for Villiers ... If he consents to stand you will carry him I am sure – the only difficulty I have felt about his leaving W'Hampton is for the *future* – But we must organize a nucleus of the *faithful* in each polling district to keep the enemy in check & secure the County for him – Villiers is sour with public matters, & has thought himself ill-used by the Free Traders & this Country – The return for the County may be useful to him in giving him a position with the government to secure him a reward for his political services – I have never felt satisfied with the present ministry for not having done something for him commensurate with his merits; & I think if he is returned for South

Lancashire it will appear something like a vote of censure upon those who have overlooked him.[24]

However, at an election rally in Wolverhampton in July, when pressed by the Chartist, Joseph Linney, about whether he would sit for Wolverhampton if elected for South Lancashire, Villiers replied that 'His inclination would lead him to stick to his old friends at Wolverhampton (cheers)'.[25] Nevertheless, on 7 August, the *Manchester Times* reported that Charles Villiers and Mr Brown had been returned without opposition for South Lancashire, adding that

> For ten years, Mr Villiers – allied by birth with the aristocracy, by sympathy and conviction with the people – has pursued an undeviating and uncompromising course in the advocacy of industrial freedom. His sacrifices in the cause have been proportionate to his devotion to it. No man has more systematically yielded himself to the unremitting prosecution of a great purpose than Mr Villiers to the constant and vigilant pursuit of free trade ... With powers of mind that would have realised any fair objects of political ambition – with position and connections that would have facilitated the attainment of such aims – Mr Villiers gave up all ... It was but fitting that homage should be rendered by the free traders of South Lancashire. They have honoured themselves in thus distinguishing their first and chosen champion.[26]

Villiers was clearly both annoyed and embarrassed by this continuing public speculation, informing Thornely that

> These Lancashire folks are beginning to put the screw on me. They are filling the papers again with their articles, and it is clear to me there is some dodge coming out of Lancashire and playing off at Wolverhampton to induce the Electors to release me!

adding that 'I dread their bullying the people in the Borough, and I really should be grieved to go'.[27] Caught between two stools, but not wishing to dishonour his previous pledges to represent Wolverhampton as long as the electors had confidence in him, Villiers duly requested that the Wolverhampton Liberals should meet and discuss the matter, although privately he had already decided to continue to stand for Wolverhampton.[28] In September, at a crowded meeting at the Star and Garter Hotel, chaired by John Barker, it was resolved unanimously that Villiers should stay.[29] Accordingly, Villiers despatched an open letter to the electors of Wolverhampton, published in the *Chronicle*, stating his intention to continue to represent Wolverhampton rather than to sit for South Lancashire, and recording his great pride in so doing.[30] Villiers also informed George Wilson of his decision, which was greeted with great disappointment at a meeting at the League's headquarters in Manchester. John Bright expressed his regret that they had been unable to get Villiers' committee in Wolverhampton to release him, stating that he had honestly believed that Villiers would sit for South Lancashire, and adding that 'He believed that Mr Villiers had made a sacrifice by the course he had taken'. Richard Cobden also regretted Villiers' decision, stating that 'He thought that the honour [of representing South Lancashire] was due to Mr Villiers, but he had been compelled, in fact, by his friends at Wolverhampton, to decline the honour which had most nobly been offered to him'.[31] The *Manchester Examiner*, however, went further, stating

> Mr Villiers has, we doubt not, been actuated by the purest motives; but we cannot disguise from ourselves that he has erred in judgment. He wisely discarded all private considerations; but, unwisely, he undervalued those of a public nature, or left them to be dealt with by his friends at Wolverhampton. He forgot that Wolverhampton has its petty jealousies, its local interests, and its narrow views. He lost sight of the fact that in that borough the convenience of certain parties might be made to weigh more than the wishes of a great county, or the interests of a great cause … Mr Villiers is possessed of a sense of honour refined above the measure of most men, and his friends at Wolverhampton have made this high quality the means of retaining him in their service. We deplore the course they have seen fit to take.[32]

By contrast, *The Economist* praised Villiers for the dignified and honourable stance he had taken over the whole matter, observing that, in deferring to the wishes of his constituents at Wolverhampton and electing to sit for that place, Villiers had put the connection between constituent and representative in a new and an amicable light:

> He is incorporated with them by perfect and reciprocal confidence, and justly does he say that this embodies the whole moral force of the representative system … How much more satisfying to the mind is that structure of the representation than the old practice of buying the electors to sell them again, or the still prevalent practice of sending a man to Parliament because he has large estates in the county, or because he happens on some one topic to have agreed with the multitude, and deluded them into the belief that he is on all points able and honest, and worthy of their confidence. Holding this office by such a moral incorporation, Mr Villiers rightly judged that he could not give it up, unless his partner thought it was for both desirable … Both to the Member and the constituency, this is highly honourable, and it is an example which other constituencies and other members would do well to follow.[33]

Villiers, the article continued, was not connected with Wolverhampton either by property or by birth, but his services had been marked and consistent, and he had, in doing his duty according to his own principles, done exactly what his electors would have done themselves. In particular, they devoted themselves heart and soul to removing the injustice of the Corn Law and Wolverhampton should pride itself on having its name imperishably associated with its abolition. Writing in similar vein, *The Examiner* observed that

> Mr Villiers, and Wolverhampton, are identified with each other to a degree that would have rendered it unwise and ungraceful to sever the tie which unites them; and Mr Villiers, as representative of Wolverhampton, is a more independent politician than he could have been as a member for South Lancashire. He is one of those clear-sighted, resolute, quiet members whose true position is to represent a constituency not too numerous.[34]

Yet, for Villiers, his decision had been a matter of principle and had not been intended as a snub to the efforts of either Cobden or Bright, both of whom Villiers held in the highest regard. As Anthony Howe has rightly observed, Cobden and Villiers were close political allies, despite the fact that their relationship was sometimes difficult, but they were never close friends and their letters dried up after 1846.[35] However, Charles Greville's claim that Villiers was 'not a little jealous' of Cobden[36] was largely unfounded, for Villiers did not bear grudges. Similarly, as G.M. Trevelyan, Bright's biographer, observed 'If Villiers had been a mean man, he might have been jealous of Bright as one who had entered into his Anti-Corn Law labours late in the day and reaped where he had sown',[37] yet this was not so, for a clear and intimate friendship existed between Villiers and Bright which continued until Bright's death in 1889 – a subject largely ignored by Bright's most recent biographer, Bill Cash.[38]

Villiers was also reticent in regard to overtures made to him by John Bright in December 1846 to capitalise on the success of the Anti-Corn Law League and to continue the battle against the landlord and the parson on a new front by embarking upon a further Radical reform programme. As Keith Robbins has observed, in essence, Bright hoped that this new crusade, which would be based in Manchester, would result in the creation of a 'middle-class party', a truly 'popular' party, distinct from Whig and Tory, with a common and distinct programme.[39] This programme, as Asa Briggs has shown, encompassed the extension of free trade, reduced taxation, a cheaper and more pacifist foreign policy and, above all, the extension of the franchise and the redistribution of seats in order that the inhabitants of the industrial districts would be more fairly represented.[40] Later, in 1848, at a time of revolutions in Europe and the revival of Chartism, when Bright claimed that 'Liberty is on the march and … we must have another league of some kind and our aristocracy must be made to submit again',[41] he approached Villiers again, stating that there was now 'a basis for a growing party and you and we and many others should go on together if possible'.[42] Bright added,

> Why not make one of the new popular party which must come out of present perplexities? We can have a party out of doors more formidable than we had in the League, and can *work the Constitution so as to reform it through itself*.[43]

Exactly how feasible the idea of a 'popular party' was remains a matter of conjecture,[44] but Villiers was, in any case, reluctant to embark on another reforming crusade. His passion had been for the Repeal of the Corn Laws and that great objective had been achieved in 1846. Moreover, he valued his independence as a Member of Parliament and did not wish to be constrained by considerations of party. Villiers was, after all, as Cobden had said, not 'a party man'. Indeed, on one occasion, Villiers was moved to comment in the House of Commons:

> I myself am not disposed to attach so much importance to the existence of any particular Ministry as some people are. I have seen four or five Ministries in office since I have been in Parliament, and, so far as I have been able to judge, there has been a strong family likeness between them all. The country never suffers much from any of them; those who accede to power generally do that which they resisted in opposition, which is pretty much what their predecessors did before them. My own impression is, that no great genius is required to administer a Government. I believe that all the real business in the public offices is done by a certain number of public servants – able and valuable men – of whom we hear very little; and that it must be owing to some lack of judgment or some want of capacity, whenever a Government becomes sufficiently unpopular to be displaced.[45]

Villiers did, however, attend a meeting of leading Radicals, including Roebuck, Hume, Milner Gibson, Cobden, Bright and W.J. Fox, at a dinner held at Sir Joshua Walmsley's house on 11 July 1849. According to Roebuck, the purpose of the meeting was to see if any combined system of action could be devised, but 'it soon became plain, amongst these men, a leader or a system was impossible'.[46] Indeed, Roebuck claimed that Charles Villiers was 'a fish out of water [and] came to prevent such a result',[47] as did Milner Gibson. He was equally scathing about Cobden, 'a poor creature, with one idea – the making of county voters. He is daunted by the County squires, and hopes to conquer them by means of these votes',[48] while Fox 'was about as much fit for a political chief as I am for a ballet dancer'.[49] As far as Roebuck was concerned, 'The only man of metal and pluck was Bright, the pugnacious Quaker'.[50] As Maccoby observed in his classic study, *English Radicalism, 1832–1852*, this meeting well illustrated the predicament of Radical Parliamentarians, for they were still a loose and disjointed section of the Whigs,[51] with diverse agendas and contrasting personalities. Although Bright and Cobden proceeded to establish the Parliamentary and Financial Reform Association to promote tax reduction and the extension of the franchise, and Bright worked with Hume and Roebuck in supporting the 'Little Charter', which supported household suffrage, the secret ballot, triennial Parliaments and the further redistribution of seats, these initiatives were short-lived.[52] Villiers eschewed involvement in both and, in the event, the idea of a Radical Parliamentary party came to nothing.

Nevertheless, Villiers continued to push for further parliamentary reform, with universal male suffrage as a long-term objective.[53] When asked by one of his constituents in Wolverhampton in 1847 if he would confer the vote on all adult males, Villiers stated that in principle he had no objection to the extension of the franchise 'upon every man of competent mind and unsustained by crime', adding that 'he trusted them; he had great confidence in them; and he certainly should do everything he though was wise or safe with a view to extend their power as soon as possible'.[54] This answer did not satisfy one local Chartist, Thomas Almond, who subsequently alleged, in an open letter to Villiers in the *Northern Star*, that Villiers' answer was 'a complete equivocation' because Villiers claimed the privilege of exercising his own judgement in opposition to the desires of the people if their opinions did not square with his own, and asking 'by what right you and your class deprive the working classes of the exercise of political rights'.[55] Nevertheless, in 1848, during the final phase of Chartism, Villiers submitted petitions in favour of the People's Charter to Parliament on behalf of some of his constituents in Wolverhampton, and in July he supported Hume's motion in the House of Commons in favour of parliamentary reform, stating that he thought it would be wise for the House to extend the suffrage. However, he added the caveat that this

> should be gradually and carefully done ... the great grievance he thought they had to complain of was to be found in the existence of bribery and corruption, which had prevailed to such an extent at the last election, and for this they ought to find a remedy. The extension of the franchise, without giving adequate protection for the exercise of it, would do no good whatever.[56]

Villiers made a similar observation during a debate on the Ballot in the House of Commons in August 1848, claiming that until the secret ballot was achieved, landlords in both rural and urban areas would continue to control the votes of their tenants.[57] This suggests that Villiers was beginning to entertain some doubts in regard to an immediate and radical reform of the franchise. Indeed, as Robert Saunders has observed, the rise in trade union militancy in the early 1850s, with strikes by railwaymen, colliers, dockers, seamstresses and cotton operatives in Lancashire (with the Preston lock-out from September 1853 to April 1854, which provided the background to Charles Dicken's celebrated novel, *Hard Times*), exacerbated tensions between the middle and working classes and 'cooled enthusiasm for reform among the very men who had formed the backbone of previous radical movements'.[58]

Writing to Cobden in 1853, Charles Villiers noted 'the apprehension on the part of our best friends ... at being swamped by the lowest description of workmen', and Robert Saunders suggests that Lord Hatherton, a Whig peer with property in Staffordshire, had told Lord John Russell that even Villiers doubted 'the prudence of doing anything more than improving the County Franchise, and perhaps correcting some defects in the Borough Franchise'.[59]

Charles Villiers also supported the campaign for the lifting of disabilities preventing Jews from sitting in Parliament, which was in keeping with his long-standing commitment to the removal of civil and religious disabilities. In so doing, Villiers was to develop a lifelong friendship with the banker Baron Lionel Nathan de Rothschild and the wider Rothschild family.[60] In 1847, Rothschild, a Liberal free-trader, was elected as Liberal MP for the City of London, but was barred from taking his seat by the Christian Parliamentary Oath. Accordingly, Lord John Russell introduced a Jewish Disabilities Bill in December 1847 which passed the House of Commons but was rejected by the Lords, and further Bills in 1848 and 1853 met with a similar fate, preventing Rothschild, who had since been re-elected, from taking his seat. Charles Villiers voted for all three measures,[61] and also spoke up in the Commons on behalf of David Salomons, who had been elected for Greenwich in 1851, but had, like Rothschild, been prevented from taking his seat.[62] Eventually, in 1858, Russell's Jewish Disabilities Bill, which Villiers had supported from its inception,[63] and which allowed Jews to omit the words 'and I make this Declaration upon the True faith of a Christian' from the Parliamentary Oath, was accepted by the Lords, and in July, Rothschild finally took his seat in the Commons (as did David Salomons, for Greenwich, in 1859). Thereafter, Charles Villiers and Lionel Rothschild remained firm friends,[64] and Villiers was a frequent dinner guest at Charlotte Rothschild's salon at 148 Piccadilly,[65] which was a select and intimate focus for the various social and political circles in which the Rothschild family moved, including the Jewish elite, Liberal politicians such as William Gladstone, and Benjamin Disraeli.

In this context, it is worth noting that despite their political differences, the private relationship between Charles Villiers and Benjamin Disraeli, who for obvious reasons supported the removal of Jewish disabilities, was friendly. Later, in 1865, Disraeli recalled that this friendship had commenced at a dinner party held at Bulwer Lytton's Hertford Street home in the Spring of 1830. Henry Bulwer, Alexander Cockburn and C.P. Villiers were also present. Disraeli recalled that these were 'men all full of energy and ambition, and all unknown to fame', adding that

> Writing this, nearly five and thirty years afterwards, it is curious to mark what has been the result of the careers of these five young men [of whom] ... Edward Bulwer has been Secretary of State, Henry Bulwer is at this moment HM Ambassador at Constantinople, Charles Villiers is at this moment a Cabinet Minister and Alexander Cockburn is Lord Chief Justice of England.[66]

Disraeli also spoke of Villiers in letters to his wife Sarah, describing in February 1832 'a very brilliant reunion at Bulwer's last night' attended by many notables of London society, including Charles Villiers;[67] noting in December 1848: 'we came from Erlestoke on Wednesday. It's a very fine place, belonging to Watson Taylor. I never saw a park so full of deer .... We caught a glimpse of the Van der Weyers, Bancrofts, and Charles Villiers';[68] reporting in April 1850 of a banquet at Anthony Rothschild's: 'The Hebrew aristocracy assembled in great force and numbers, mitigated by the Dowager of Morley, Charles Villiers, Abel Smith and Thackeray! I think he will sketch them in the last number of "Pendennis"';[69] and reporting in May 1850,

> On Sunday I dined with the Molesworths — a most agreeable party. The Lovelaces, the Rossis, Lady Morley, C. Villiers, Stafford, Milnes, Henry Hope, the Turkish Ambassador. I never saw a house better *monte* [stocked] or a dinner better served.[70]

Later, in a letter to his fellow-Tory, Lord John Manners (Duke of Rutland) in September 1850, Disraeli, who was then preparing a political biography of the Tory politician and famed racehorse owner, Lord George Bentinck, told Manners that 'Charles Villiers has been very kind' in recording some of his general impressions of Bentinck's character and career (and asked Manners to do the same).[71] Villiers also provided Disraeli with much of the material for the chapter on the Sugar Bill in his biography of Bentinck; as Disraeli duly acknowledged, he had been 'guided in his narrative by the impressions of Mr Charles Villiers'.[72]

In January 1850, in light of the continued reluctance of Tory Protectionists to accept the settlement of 1846 as final and irrevocable and, indeed, their avowed desire to re-impose protective tariffs on corn, Lord John Russell invited Charles Villiers to move the address in reply to the Queen's Speech in order to demonstrate that the Whig government had the full confidence of the Free-Traders. A correspondent to the Tory Protectionist *Bell's New Weekly Messenger* bemoaned Russell's decision, alleging that Charles Villiers was 'a sinecurist and a reformer', adding that

> to see this gentleman, however estimable in private life, to move the address at a time when agriculture is so deeply suffering, looks very like a disposition on the part of the government to add defiance and insult to injury.[73]

Villiers duly informed the House that 'not a single thing that was feared by the opponents of free Trade has come to pass, nor is there the slightest prospect that such will be the case', adding that 'the Home Trade has improved; the condition of the working classes has been ameliorated; not a sovereign has left the country; while ... the Revenue is improving'. Having provided detailed evidence to support this claim, Villiers concluded his address by stating that the Queen's Speech illustrated that the present Ministry was determined 'to continue the progressive course of later years, by reforming what is bad, supplying what is deficient, and showing confidence in the people'.[74]

However, with the defeat of the Whig Government on the Militia Bill on 20 February 1852 and the subsequent formation of Lord Derby's short-lived Tory Administration, the settlement of 1846 once again appeared under threat. The Peelites held the balance of power in the Commons and were prepared to sustain Derby's Ministry on the condition that there would be a dissolution of Parliament in the summer followed by a meeting of Parliament in November at which the new Ministry would clarify its position on the fiscal question.[75] However, on assuming office, Derby declared in favour of a duty on corn and, in a speech in Buckinghamshire, the new Chancellor of the Exchequer, Benjamin Disraeli, also promised the agricultural party, which included revived Protectionist societies, a fixed duty on corn. Fearing a complete reversal of the free-trade policies that had been successfully pursued since 1846, Villiers determined to move a motion in the House of Commons that the Government should provide an immediate and specific clarification of its commercial policy. In framing this motion, Villiers approached William Gladstone in private for further advice. In some respects this was a surprising move, for Gladstone, when a Tory, had once been one of Villiers' strongest critics during the early debates in the Commons on the repeal of the Corn Laws but, like Peel, Gladstone had, as President of the Board of Trade between 1843 and 1845, been gradually converted to the Free Trade cause and, now a Peelite, had accepted the settlement of 1846 as final.[76] Writing to Gladstone on 4 March, Villiers stated

> I am very anxious to communicate with you ... Should you not think this for any reason objectionable, will you be kind enough to name a time when it would be most convenient to yourself for me to call upon you.[77]

Gladstone's reply was encouraging:

> Dear Mr Villiers – I am aware of the motion which, although we are not united by any relations of party, should make it possible for us to communicate together upon a question of vast importance, now I trust approaching its final issue, upon which we have similar views and feel a common interest. In case it should be most convenient to you to call here today ... I shall expect you at half past eleven.[78]

Further to their meeting, Villiers delivered his motion in the Commons on 15 March 1852. Whilst declaring that he was not animated 'by factious motives, by no party object', Villiers proceeded to attack the Protectionists for seeking to reverse the policy of Free Trade and demanded of Disraeli that he should 'come forward in the face of this House – of the country, and make a candid, manly, and open avowal of the intentions of the Government on the subject of their policy with respect to our Foreign Commerce', adding that

The country wants no change of policy, it wants no Dissolution, no disturbance or struggle of any kind. People desire only to be allowed to remain in their present peaceful, prosperous condition; and for this nothing is necessary but a declaration on the part of the Government that they have not any intention of disturbing the policy of Free Trade.[79]

No such undertaking was, however, provided by Disraeli. Indeed, the Tory response was shrouded with ambiguity and Villiers was determined to pursue the matter by framing further resolutions whereby, as he explained to Gladstone, 'an opportunity would be given for clearly explaining to the country the results of Sir Robert Peel's policy and of securing from the Ministry upon what principles they intend to stand or fall', adding that 'it *now* seems uncertain where Lord John intends to take the opinion of the country'.[80] However, when the new Parliament met on 11 November and the Queen's Speech was read, Villiers gave immediate notice of forthcoming Resolutions that would pledge the Government to the acceptance of the 1846 settlement and to the maintenance of a Free Trade policy in future. The terms of the Resolutions were framed jointly by Villiers, Cobden, Bright and Milner Gibson at a meeting on 13 November,[81] and were then passed in private to Gladstone by Villiers, who asked 'Could you have the goodness just to consider how far such a Resolution would meet your views', adding 'it seems to me pretty much what the occasion requires'.[82] Gladstone thanked Villiers for making the Resolutions known to him, adding 'I was so entirely satisfied with the form of the draft ... there is nothing in the Resolutions as they now stand which is at variance with my opinions or will interfere with my giving them a zealous support'.[83] Villiers also sought the opinion of the Duke of Newcastle, Sir James Graham and Lord John Russell, all of whom, according to Villiers, 'said that they saw no serious objection to it and would offer none'.[84]

In the House of Commons on 23 November 1852, Villiers moved his Resolutions, which read:

> That it is the opinion of this House that the improved condition of the country, and particularly of the industrial classes, is mainly the result of recent Commercial Legislation, and especially of the Act of 1846, which established the free admission of Foreign Corn, and that that Act was a wise, just and beneficial measure;
>
> That it is the opinion of this House that the maintenance and further extension of the policy of Free Trade, as opposed to that of Protection, will best enable the property and industry of the nation to bear the burdens to which they are exposed, and will most contribute to the general prosperity, welfare, and contentment of the people;
>
> That this House is ready to take into its consideration any measures consistent with the principles of these resolutions which may be laid before it by Her Majesty's Ministers.[85]

128   *Interlude*

During his speech, Villiers stated:

> For what I believe to be great national reasons I want to have these Resolutions carried, and to have the views of the House of Commons on this question more distinctly, and most explicitly expressed; and most especially do I want these Resolutions to be placed on record, in order that we may at least during the existing Parliament have a settlement of a matter that, while unsettled, leaves men of business in the country uneasy, and the rest of the world in doubt as to what the permanent commercial policy of England is to be.[86]

During the debate, John Bright was moved to comment:

> My hon. friend [Villiers] could with perfect honesty say that he could not be actuated by factious motives in bringing this subject forward, and probably no public man suffered more in his political associations than my hon. friend suffered by his undeviating advocacy of what to him, at least, seemed a great and sacred question.[87]

However, prior to the debate, Bright had expressed the opinion that 'Villiers will win, unless there are more "shabbies" than we calculate on',[88] and this caveat proved correct during the debate itself, for Disraeli denounced the phrase 'wise, just and beneficial' as 'three odious epithets' and moved an Amendment to omit them, although he warmly complimented Villiers – who he had once described as 'the stormy petrel of Protection'[89] – for his consistent adherence to his principles.[90] Moreover, in order to avoid a defeat of the Ministry, Palmerston, who had previously expressed some doubts in private about the contents of Villiers' Resolutions,[91] stepped in – much to the dismay of the Free Traders – with the suggestion of a watered-down Amendment in favour of Free Trade, which was acceptable to the Protectionists, on condition that both Villiers' Resolutions and the Government Amendment were withdrawn. Villiers, however, persisted and his Motion went to a Division on 26 November, where it was rejected by 336 votes to 256, a majority of 80. To Villiers' surprise, Gladstone and other Peelites voted against the Resolutions, yet, as Villiers told the House, in what proved to be his last speech in the Commons on the subject of Free Trade, 'they had all approved of the terms of the Resolution, and most of them had been consulted before it was proposed, and some of them thought they were quite unexceptional'.[92] Gladstone expressed dissent, claiming that there had been some discrepancy between the precise wording of the original draft that Villiers had shown him and the Resolution now before them, but voted for Palmerston's Amendment, which was duly carried by 486 votes to 53, a majority of 415.[93] It read:

> That it is the opinion of this House, that the improved condition of the Country, and especially of the Industrious Classes, is mainly the result

of recent Legislation, which has established the principle of unrestricted competition, has abolished Taxes imposed for the purpose of Protection, and has thereby diminished the cost and increased the abundance of the principal articles of the Food of the People.[94]

Nevertheless, the Free Trade question was, in essence, effectively settled, although Bright observed that Charles Villiers 'has been treated very shabbily by the Peelites and Palmerston [who] is as dishonest as we have always described him'.[95] However, on 17 December, with the defeat of Disraeli's Budget – which had been majestically savaged by Gladstone – by 305 votes to 286, the Derby Ministry fell,[96] and was succeeded by a Coalition Ministry of Whigs, Peelites and Radicals – 'The Ministry of All the Talents' – headed by Lord Aberdeen.

Villiers' political fortunes now took a turn for the better. A memorandum by the Prince Albert on 22 December 1852 stated that he and the Queen had met Lord Aberdeen, who was forming his cabinet, and Aberdeen had stated that 'The Radicals might be conciliated in some of the lower Offices by the appointment of Mr Charles Villiers, Sir William Molesworth, and others'.[97] Accordingly, Villiers was offered, and accepted, the significant (and well-remunerated) post of Judge-Advocate-General, the legal advisor of the Sovereign and of the commander-in-chief of the British Army (a post he held until 1859), at an annual salary of £2,000, and was also appointed to the Privy Council. This was a prestigious position which brought Charles Villiers into direct contact with Queen Victoria, who was already well-acquainted with the Villiers family, largely through Lord Clarendon.[98] However, this post did not carry with it a place in the Whig-Peelite dominated Cabinet, a fact bemoaned by John Bright, who wrote to Lord John Russell that 'The man [Villiers] who Sir R. Peel followed is somewhat better, I think, than a man who merely followed Sir R. Peel',[99] whilst Stuart J. Reid observed that 'Charles Villiers, whose social claims could not be entirely overlooked, found his not inconsiderable services to the people rewarded by subordinate rank'.[100] Indeed, the Radical presence in the new Cabinet was minimal; neither Cobden nor Bright wished to serve, whilst Villiers' friend Sir William Molesworth was offered, and accepted, the minor post of First Commissioner of Works. The Duke of Argyll, who was Lord Privy Seal, duly noted that the cabinet was 'rather leaky', which he ascribed in part to Molesworth's habit of taking notes during cabinet meetings, adding that if their contents ever reached the ears of Charles Villiers 'they would have a wide circulation in the press and in the clubs of London', such was Villiers' reputation for gossip.[101] In February 1853 it was alleged in the House of Commons that since taking up his new post, Villiers had also continued to draw a retirement pension arising from his previous position as an Examiner in the Court of Chancery. This allegation, which implied that Villiers had acted dishonourably, and which was refuted by Villiers, was subsequently found to be wholly false and was retracted.[102]

130 *Interlude*

Villiers' attention now turned to other issues. In 1853, at the instigation of William Brown, Liberal MP for South Lancashire and former Anti-Corn Law Leaguer, Charles Villiers was elected chairman of the Select Committee of the House of Commons on Public Houses. The context for the establishment of the Select Committee was growing public concern over drunkenness and the association between drink and crime, immorality, pauperism and vice amongst the working classes, all of which were emphasised by the emerging temperance movement and the founding in 1853 of the United Kingdom Alliance, which favoured complete prohibition. The licensing and regulation of, and arbitrary distinction between, the 80,000 public houses and 41,000 beershops in existence by 1852, which had increased substantially in number since the Beer Act of 1830, was regarded as one of the many causes of the problem.[103] On the licensing question, as with the Corn Laws, Villiers again ran counter to the prejudices of great vested interests and monopolists, in this case the brewers, a wealthy class, who owned many public houses, both directly and indirectly. Indeed, it was common for an understanding to exist between the brewers and persons applying for a licence, which perpetuated the brewers' monopoly in the supply of beer to the labouring classes.

Villiers claimed that the Select Committee was fairly constituted, consisting of gentlemen who had been Chairmen of Quarter Sessions, and that there was hardly a member upon it (Villiers excepted) who had not acted in the commission of the peace. The inquiry itself had been promoted by magistrates, and many of the witnesses were magistrates, commissioners of police, and persons of experience in the administration of the law.[104] The Committee was also generally sympathetic to free trade, which ran counter to temperance demands, even though many of Villiers' former colleagues in the Anti-Corn Law League, including Cobden and Bright, had sympathised privately with the teetotal movement, and free-traders, supported by a campaign in the *Morning Chronicle*, strongly influenced not only the Villiers' committee's detailed inquiry into the licensing system but also subsequent parliamentary debates on the licensing question throughout the 1850s.[105] The Committee sat for two years and Villiers himself drew up the Report and framed the recommendations for dealing with the evils disclosed by the evidence. The Committee issued two reports, in 1852–3[106] and in 1854,[107] and years later, in an address at Newcastle-on-Tyne in 1882, Cardinal Manning recalled that

> Till I read these two Blue-books I had no conception of the state of the country and I am confident that you who hear me, if you will only buy and read them, will have your eyes opened to that which hitherto you have never imagined.[108]

The evidence gathered by the Select Committee presented an alarming state of affairs and Villiers later recalled that

> He owned that he went into that inquiry prepossessed himself against interference, and doubting that legislation could do the good intended, but he had been completely converted by the unquestionable proofs to the contrary which had been submitted,[109]

adding that it was

> on account of the startling evidence exposing the evils of the licensing system that he advised the Committee not to report in the first year of the inquiry, in order that this evidence should circulate through the country ... and that the Committee should only make its Report upon the truth,[110]

and which accounted for the subsequent publication of two blue books.

In general, the evidence indicated that there were major anomalies and discrepancies in the licensing, regulation, inspection and monitoring of public houses and beershops, and Villiers stated that,

> in some places the caprice and irregularity that existed in the granting of licences to public houses could not be disputed ... there was favouritism and corruption of every description; that many of the licensed houses were of the lowest description, but that it was in vain to complain against them on account of the interest which the owners of them had with gentlemen on the bench ... almost to preclude any respectable person from obtaining a licence.[111]

He also noted that it had been shown beyond doubt that there were times when the poor were especially tempted to spend their money in drink (which was often adulterated[112]) to the great injury of their families,

> by the circumstances of these houses being open when no public convenience required them to be so – for instance on the nights when they received their wages, followed by a day when they did not work. This was on Saturday night and Sunday morning and in all the great towns of the country, as well as the metropolis, scenes of riot and drunkenness occurred in consequence.[113]

The witnesses who gave evidence to the Select Committee included Gilbert Hogg, the Chief Constable of Villiers' own constituency of Wolverhampton, and with whom Villiers was acquainted, and his evidence is worthy of further comment in view of the fact that his views were largely echoed in the committee's final recommendations. Hogg attributed the marked increase in drunkenness and disorderly behaviour in Wolverhampton to the rapid increase in the population of the town in recent years,[114] whilst acknowledging that the town's police force, established in 1848, was, though vigilant, insufficient in numbers to cope effectively with the problem.[115] His greatest concern, however, lay with the discrepancies in the regulations (under the Beer Act of 1830) for the licensing and monitoring of public houses and beershops, and he drew a sharp distinction between the respectability and good conduct of the owners of the former and the lack of this in regard to the latter. A publican, he observed, had to provide a character reference; he had to meet certain rating criteria; he was required to meet the bench of magistrates once a year on the licensing day before his licence could be renewed; and a police constable was present 'with his black book before him', listing any infringements of the licensing laws and complaints against the publican during the previous year. Indeed, Hogg held that the fear of the licence not being renewed, and the public humiliation which followed, was sufficient to encourage most publicans to maintain good conduct and had 'a very beneficial effect'.[116] By contrast, beerhouse-keepers were not required to provide a character reference, were subject to lower rating criteria, were difficult to prosecute due to the reluctance of people to give evidence against them, and practised a variety of strategies in evading their responsibilities.[117] Accordingly, Hogg argued that beershops should be put on the same legal footing as public houses and that their owners should pay a larger sum for the licence, on a scale proportionate to the size of the population. This, he argued, would make beerhouses more respectable and better conducted.[118] Hogg also noted the increase in Wolverhampton in the number of unlicensed premises – normally private dwellings – which sold liquor and which the police found great difficulty in detecting. These ranged from 'Wabble shops', which sold beer – which was frequently adulterated – at cheap prices,[119] to 'Bush houses', where ale, beer and porter were sold day and night and which were frequented by 'pickpockets, thieves, and prostitutes from neighbouring towns',[120] and to illicit stills in 'Dram shops', 'where persons meet and drink spirits, and are drunk and disorderly the entire night'.[121] The situation was particularly bad in the Irish district of Caribee Island, off Stafford Street, where, as Hogg observed, 'parties coming from Ireland invariably bring spirits with them, and it is sold in those houses; in fact, some instances have been known where parties have been drunk, and serious disturbances have taken place', adding

> I have frequently been obliged to remove the men off duty in different parts of the town and congregate them in the neighbourhood of the Irish; I have been there with 25 men, with cutlasses drawn, all day on Sunday.[122]

Hogg also noted that some Wolverhampton coffee-houses also sold alcohol, which was illegal. Indeed, he added that this practice was also evident in the Metropolis, as he himself had witnessed whilst in London to give evidence before the Committee:

> I acquired that knowledge since I came to London this time myself; at 20 minutes past two on Sunday morning I went to a place [a coffee-shop]. I asked for some gin, and the man said, 'Yes, you shall have it; but you

must drink it out of a cup; we cannot give you a glass, or if the police come in, I shall be fined' ... there was a little milk placed on one side in a cream ewer; and I was instructed, if the constable came in, to put a little of that into it.[123]

Finally, Hogg observed that there were few houses of public entertainment other than public houses and beershops available to the working classes in Wolverhampton, and suggested that the provision of recreational facilities such as public grounds for out-door activities and other opportunities for 'innocent amusement', including cheap concerts, would, in his view, diminish the scale of drunkenness. He was, however, against Sunday closing, which 'would be met with great resistance on the part of the beerhouse-keepers, and the public-house keepers, and by the inhabitants, and by myself'.[124]

In view of the detailed evidence that had been presented, the Select Committee concluded that the licensing system was defective and recommended that it was expedient to put public houses and beershops on the same legal footing by abolishing the arbitrary distinction between them by taking away from the Excise the power of granting licences to beershops and placing it in the hands of the magistrates. The Committee also recommended that magistrates should not only inquire into the character of the applicants for licences but also take proper securities from them, and rely upon the police to enforce the restrictions under which they were to act, in the belief that the best security for public-houses being well conducted was the power of withdrawing a licence. This, it was held, would enable anyone of good character to get a license provided they could pay licence fees related directly to the size of the local population. The Committee further recommended that all coffee-houses should be placed under the supervision of the police and suggested that the police should exercise supervision over such places from nine at night until four in the morning because it was to such places that bad characters resorted after they were expelled from public houses. Finally, in regard to the adulteration of drink, the Committee recommended the establishment of a separate inquiry into the broader question of the adulteration of food, drink and medicines.[125] In short, the Committee recommended the reform of the existing licensing laws through more effective regulation, monitoring, inspection and enforcement by law.[126]

By contrast, on the vexed question of Sunday closing, the Committee concluded that whilst they were bound not to overlook the very strong evidence in favour of closing the public houses on Sunday, they were unwilling to impose restrictions beyond the existing law (which required closure from midnight on Saturday until 1 pm on Sunday) without proposing, at the same time, some relaxation of the law which precluded the people from access to places of innocent recreation on that day. Indeed they suggested that it should be left to the discretion of some appropriate local authority to determine at what places and at what hours this counter-attraction to the public house should be offered. In so doing, the Committee recognised the need for the working classes to be provided with 'rational' recreational facilities as a disincentive to drink, and reflected Villiers' private view that centralised attempts to make men moral were doomed to failure in the absence of rational recreational facilities for working people.[127]

However, these recommendations fell on deaf ears, for the Government, preoccupied with events in the Crimea, failed to legislate, much to the consternation of the members of the Select Committee, as subsequent debates on the licensing question in the House of Commons illustrated. For example, in February 1857, in promoting a Bill to amend the laws relating to the sale of beer and to regulate certain places of public resort, refreshment and entertainment, Mr Hardy, MP, regretted that nothing had resulted from the Select Committee of 1853–4, yet it had been proved before the Committee

> that beershops were places where thieves met, where stolen goods were disposed of, where burglars planned their attacks, and where poachers and sheep-stealers associated before starting on their expeditions. It seemed remarkable that no attempt had yet been made to put beershops on the same footing as licensed public houses by taking away from the Excise the power of granting licenses and placing it in the hands of the magistrates.[128]

It was also noted that the recommendation that all coffee-houses should be placed under the supervision of the police had not been acted upon.[129] During the same debate, the Secretary of State, Sir George Grey, who had been a member of the 1853–4 Committee, also stated that the Committee had taken a great deal of evidence and had come to the same conclusions as to the expediency of abolishing the distinction between public houses and beershops as Mr Hardy,[130] whilst Sir John Pakington, another member of the Committee, stated that he had hoped that after such a long inquiry the Government would have carried through some legislative measures based on the recommendations, but 1855 and 1856 had passed without anything being done and now urged the Government to legislate.[131] Charles Villiers made similar observations in March 1856 when a deputation from Wolverhampton presented him with a petition requesting the repeal of the Sale of Beer (Sunday) Act, Villiers accepted that the public houses being kept open on Sunday night had 'a very injurious effect on the working classes', but doubted whether anything would be done.[132] In particular, Villiers bemoaned the fact that under the present licensing system a man could continue to get a beer-house licence without the certificate of the magistrate as to his being a fit person in point of character to receive it, and could go to the Excise and claim a beer-house licence without his certificate of character on payment of £1.2s.0d, whereas the Committee had recommended that the lowest payment should be £6 and should increase gradually in proportion to the population.[133] In May, when Villiers informed Sir George Grey that there was no chance of carrying the recommendations of the Committee into a Bill, Grey attempted to press Palmerston to direct the government's attention to the unsatisfactory state of the licensing laws, but to no avail.[134]

Nevertheless, Villiers' chairmanship of the Committee and his contribution to subsequent debates was both admired and respected by many of his peers. In May 1860, during the debate in the Commons on the Refreshment Houses and Wine Licenses Bill, Villiers again recalled and endorsed the work of the Select Committee and his observations moved Mr Henley, MP, to comment that

> The right hon. gentleman who had just sat down deserved to be heard on this question, seeing that he had presided over one of the most laborious Committees that ever sat on the question. The Committee occupied two years in their investigation, and extracted many thousand answers from different witnesses. The opinion of the right hon. Gentleman was therefore entitled to great weight.[135]

Later, when attending the annual dinner of the Wolverhampton Licensed Victuallers' Society on 28 October 1861, Villiers reaffirmed his concern on the 'Drink Question' when he stated that many of the misfortunes of the poor could be traced to intemperance, adding that no class had no stronger interest in discouraging excess, intemperance and disorder as the licensed victuallers themselves, since discredit otherwise fell upon them and their business, and their capital would be jeopardised. The answer, he held, lay in the maintenance of existing regulations in regard to the closure of public houses from 11.00 pm on Saturday until 12.00 pm on Sunday, coupled with greater powers to enforce the law against disorderly customers than they at present possessed.[136]

The other major issue with which Charles Villiers had to contend during this period arose from the Crimean War of 1854–5. The main aim of the war, which initially received popular support when war was declared in March 1854 (although opposed by Radicals such as Cobden and Bright), had been the capture of the Russian naval base at Sebastopol in the Crimea in order to prevent Russian naval dominance of the Black Sea, which threatened British naval supremacy in the Mediterranean. However, despite early and qualified military successes at the battles of Alma (20 September), Balaclava (25 October) – famed for the heroic Charge of the Light Brigade – and Inkerman (5 November), Britain and her French allies were forced to postpone an immediate attack on Sebastopol and wintered in the Crimea, where the appalling privations of British troops from death and disease, and from shortages of clothing, medicine and other essentials, exposed the maladministration of military supply. These were highlighted by the reports in the *Times* from the war correspondent, William Howard Russell, and by the activities of Florence Nightingale and her nurses at Scutari, all of which served to discredit the War Office and Aberdeen's government.[137] Public opinion was turning, and in the House of Commons in January 1855, the Radical

J.A. Roebuck, who had supported the war, demanded the establishment of a Select Committee to inquire into the condition of the Army before Sebastopol.[138] The motion was carried by 305 votes to 157, Aberdeen's government promptly resigned and, on 5 February, following protracted discussions in which Villiers' brother George, Lord Clarendon, played an important role, Queen Victoria, with some reluctance, appointed Lord Palmerston as Prime Minister.[139]

Charles Villiers, who held that Britain had plunged into the Crimean War 'without any reason and in defiance of all prudence and sound policy',[140] was drawn into these events by virtue of his position as Judge Advocate General. The course of the war had highlighted the inefficiency and incompetence of, and personal antagonisms between, the military commanders themselves, most notably Lord Raglan, the Commander in Chief of the Army in the Crimea, and the Earl of Cardigan, the Commander of the Light Brigade, and his superior, the Earl of Lucan, the Commander of the Cavalry, who shared a mutual dislike for one another. In particular, Raglan blamed Lucan for misinterpreting his orders prior to the ill-fated charge of the Light Brigade at Balaclava and its catastrophic consequences, and Lucan was recalled home from the Crimea, whilst Cardigan, who had led the charge, was feted as a national hero. On his recall, Lucan sent his son, Lord Bingham, to the Commander-in-Chief, Lord Hardinge, to demand a court-martial in response to the allegations made against him by Raglan in regard to the fate of the Light Brigade. It was refused. A similar request was made to Lord Panmure, who had succeeded the Duke of Newcastle as Minister for War, on 5 March. This was also refused. Lucan then made several speeches in the House of Lords on the subject of his recall, again demanding a court-martial, but the Lords were against him.[141]

However, Lucan's claim for a court-martial was then raised in the House of Commons in a motion presented by the Hon. H. Berkeley, MP for Bristol, on 29 March 1855. Whilst acknowledging that Roebuck's Select Committee had been established to investigate 'the destruction of our gallant countrymen by withholding from them the absolute necessaries of life – fuel, food, raiment, and medical comforts', Berkeley stated that:

> He was not here to inquire into that loss ... He was there to ask for inquiry into the conduct of Lieutenant General the Earl of Lucan, because he believed that, through the misconception of an order received by him, the disaster at Balaclava had been occasioned. In consequence of that fatal mistake not only were 300 soldiers slain, but he might mention, though it was a minor consideration, the country had lost 360 horses, estimated with their equipments at the value of £160 each; and, in point of fact, the Brigade of Light Cavalry had been annihilated.[142]

In seconding the motion, Lord Elcho, who was related to Lord Lucan, stated that

No doubt the House would be told by the right hon. gentleman the Judge Advocate [Charles Villiers] that nothing could be more dangerous than to establish a precedent for bringing the subject of military discipline under discussion in the House of Commons,

but appealed to the House, 'on behalf of his gallant and noble relative', to 'do him that justice which had been denied elsewhere and ... vindicate his conduct, and relieve him from the disgrace under which he now more or less laboured'.[143]

In his reply, Villiers summarised the sequence of communications between Raglan and Lucan, which had led to the latter's recall from the Crimea, observing that

It was upon receipt of these communications that the Minister of War discovered that there were essential differences between the lieutenant general of cavalry and the commander of the forces in the East; and upon that ground, and that ground alone, fortified by the opinion of the Commander in Chief in this country, considering that these differences were detrimental to the public service, and that harmony was essential between officers of rank, the recall of the lieutenant general of cavalry was decided upon.[144]

Villiers then explained on what grounds of military law and practice Lord Lucan had been refused the inquiry by court martial for which Mr Berkeley had asked. He outlined the legal difficulties involved, by reference to precedents in military law, and also noted that there were also technical difficulties which impeded proceedings:

There was nobody to prefer any charge ... if such an inquiry were granted, when must it take place, and where? It certainly could not take place here. The commander of the forces could not be recalled to give evidence, because his presence could not be dispensed with in the Crimea ... Then, could the inquiry take place in the Crimea? It certainly would be most inconvenient at present. Men high in command could hardly be called upon to vindicate their conduct when they had important duties to discharge ... Consequently, an inquiry could only take place when the war was over, and when many of the persons who ought to be examined would not be forthcoming.[145]

Villiers also pointed out that Lord Lucan had not been charged with having wilfully disobeyed orders, and that it was just as much open to Lord Raglan to demand a court-martial upon the charges made by Lord Lucan as it was for Lord Lucan to demand a court-martial upon the charges made by Lord Raglan. The whole matter, he argued, should be left in the hands of the House, but it was his belief that 'there was no ground for calling for a court-martial', whereupon the motion was withdrawn.[146] Two months later, on 28 June 1855, Lord Raglan died in the Crimea, which effectively curtailed Lucan's claims. In the same month, Roebuck's Select Committee had presented its final report to the House of Commons,[147] and, as Saul David observed, its tone was remarkably restrained, praising the valour of the troops and, rather than directing blame at individuals, concentrated on the maladministration of various military branches, including the Commissariat and Medical Departments, which may also have hastened Raglan's death.[148] In the Crimea, the military stalemate was finally broken with the fall of Sebastopol on 8 September and following negotiations between Britain, France and Russia, in which Lord Clarendon, the Foreign Secretary, played a significant role, peace was concluded in March 1856 by the Treaty of Paris, which effectively neutralised the Black Sea and, at least for the time being, appeared to check Russian expansionism.

In the midst of these negotiations, however, Charles Villiers suffered a great personal loss with the death of his beloved mother, Theresa Villiers. 'Mrs George', now in her eightieth year, had been suddenly taken ill at The Grove and had been moved to Lord Clarendon's London home in Grosvenor Crescent, where she lingered for several days in a feeble state before passing away on 12 January 1856. Her children – George, Charles, Henry and Maria Theresa were all at her bedside when she died.[149] On the following day, Queen Victoria noted in her diary, 'We heard that poor Mrs Villiers died last night, and feel much for poor Ld Clarendon, who was so devoted to his mother and wrote him my condolences'.[150] Thomas Thornely extended his sincere condolences to Charles Villiers, stating,

> I do most deeply sympathise with you on this most distressing event ... the loss of your dear Mother will be a dreadful blow to all your family ... I have to acknowledge great kindness from your Mother, for whom I entertained the highest respect. I cannot but think she must have had a very happy life, seeing the high position that her children are holding in the country ... Would you say to Lady Theresa in particular how much I am grieved for this sad event, which I know will afflict her so seriously.[151]

Theresa Villiers, a woman of great drive and energy, had been the mainstay of a closely-knit family and, as Charles Greville, who knew the family well, had once observed

> It is always refreshing, in the midst of the cold hearts and indifferent tempers one sees in the world, to behold such a spectacle of intimate union and warm affection as the Grove presents. A mother (Mrs George) with a tribe of sons and daughters, and their respective husbands and wives, all knit together in the closest union and community of affections, feelings and interests – all, too, very intelligent people, lively, cheerful and

striving to contribute to each other's social enjoyment as well as to their material interests.[152]

Nevertheless, the Grove was to continue to be the focus for family gatherings for many years to come. As Charles Villiers' niece, Maria Theresa Earle (one of the daughters of his late brother Edward and his wife, Elizabeth Liddell) later recalled

> The daily intercourse with my aunt and uncle [The Clarendons] at the Grove, and the interesting company they were constantly receiving at Saturday to Monday parties (now called week-ends), supplied the interest in the outside world and the higher ambition of men which was lacking in our home [nearby Grove Mill] from the fact of our having no father. The conversation at the Grove in those days was the most brilliant that I ever remember in my life. The *habitués* consisted principally of the Villiers family, Lady Theresa Lister and Sir George Cornewall Lewis, Charles Villiers, old Lady Morley, Charles Greville, Henry Reeve, intermixed with young and old.[153]

In the meantime, Lord Palmerston had, in February 1855, commissioned a separate 'Inquiry into the Supplies of the British Army in the Crimea' which was conducted in the Crimea by Sir John McNeill and Colonel Alexander Tulloch. Whilst this investigation took place, *The Times* claimed that there was growing public dissatisfaction with the continuation of the war and that the government should change its policy, although Lord Clarendon informed Queen Victoria that his brother Charles, who was 'almost more acquainted with public feeling than anyone',[154] held that the general feeling of the country was sound, and the Queen remarked in her diary that 'one trembles lest a change should come before we are in a state to make an honourable and secure peace'.[155] In discussing the progress of the Commission of Inquiry with the Queen ('about which he spoke very sensibly'[156]) Charles Villiers stated that although '*The Times* wants a victim … it has lost much influence and no longer guided public opinion', adding that it would be very difficult for the Inquiry 'to fix the blame on anyone'.[157] The Report was published in April 1856 and drew particular attention to the general maladministration of military supplies to the army, for which Charles Villiers privately held Sir Charles Trevelyan, Assistant Secretary at the Treasury, and Lord Panmure, as Minister of War, largely responsible. As he told the Queen, 'Ld P [Panmure] does things in a way I have never seen anything like before … in a rough, coarse manner', and had offended people dreadfully, 'making such bad hits', causing much mischief and offending the army.[158] The Report also blamed the destruction of the cavalry at Balaclava on the inefficiency, indifference and obstinacy of the Earl of Cardigan and Lord Lucan, as a result of which their conduct was bemoaned in the press and there were calls for their dismissal. Cardigan, Lucan and three other officers referred to in the Report demanded redress, and on 3 April 1856 a Board of General Officers, based at Chelsea Hospital, initiated an inquiry which was overseen by Charles Villiers, as Judge Advocate General, and their Report, which ran to over 600 pages, concluded on 4 July that it was the unanimous opinion of the Board that, in regard to the five officers mentioned, 'there does not appear to us to be any ground for further proceedings thereon'.[159] Lucan and Cardigan were therefore exonerated and the Chelsea Board was thereafter referred to as the 'Whitewashing Board'.[160]

Lucan, however, continued to make disparaging remarks about both the Chelsea Board of Generals Report and Charles Villiers in the House of Lords, and when Villiers presented the Report to the House of Commons on 21 July he asked leave to respond to

> a statement of an extraordinary character that I am informed has been made in another place with respect to this Report in connection with myself. I am told that a noble Lord [Lucan], in complaining that the Report had not been placed upon the table sooner, ascribed the delay to the fact that I had drawn the Report, and that I had been dilatory in the matter for the purpose of serving the objects of the Minister of War.[161]

Villiers refuted vigorously these allegations, pointing out that he had not delayed the presentation of the Report, because he had no power to do so even if he had wished it, and had no object or interest whatever in doing so, adding that the General officers had finished their Report as soon as they were able to do so, and were much indebted to the Judge-Advocate's office for the assistance that had been rendered them. He also rejected Lucan's false claim that the inquiry had been 'political in its character, owing to the Judge Advocate General being a Minister and attending Court', declaring that

> so totally opposed is this to the fact, that I solemnly declare that I never, during the whole inquiry, asked or heard what were the politics of the general officers who composed the Board and of which I knew nothing.[162]

The General Officers had, he stated, given 'a careful, anxious, and honest consideration to the evidence which was submitted to them and ... looking to what evidence they had to decide upon, have given a just verdict'.[163]

General Peel, who had also sat at Chelsea, endorsed Villiers' comments: 'I have not the slightest hesitation in expressing my opinion that the charge adverted to the right hon. and learned Gentleman as made by a noble Lord in another place is perfectly unfair and unfounded', adding

> I express the feelings of the whole of the Board – that I am at a loss for language sufficiently powerful to express the opinion of the advantage which the Board derived from the assistance of the right hon. and learned Gentleman.[164]

The Report was welcomed by the House and, two days later, Villiers indicated that he had no intention of continuing the controversy which Lucan had initiated, 'because it will be more respectful to this House not to bandy unmeaning personalities with that noble Lord in this place',[165] and the matter was closed. Lord Lucan duly retired to his Irish estates at Castlebar, County Mayo, where he had acquired an unenviable reputation for the ill-treatment and eviction of his tenants during the Irish Famine, although ironically, like the Earl of Cardigan, he was the recipient of further military honours and was promoted Field Marshal in 1887, the year before he died.[166]

In the meantime, Palmerston's government was facing rising criticism in the House of Commons from the Peelites, and, most notably Gladstone (who felt that Palmerston was abandoning true Liberal principles and who was particularly critical of the administration of income tax by Charles Villiers' brother-in-law, Sir George Cornewall Lewis, the Chancellor), and from the Tory opposition, most notably Disraeli, who disapproved of Palmerston's foreign policy.[167] Events in China brought matters to a head in October 1856 with the arrest and imprisonment by the Chinese of the crew of a British ship, the *Arrow*, which represented a breach of Britain's treaty rights with China. Although the crew were subsequently released and handed over to the British consul in Canton, the Chinese Commissioner for Canton, Yeh Mingchin, refused to apologise for the incident, whereby Sir John Bowring, the Governor of Hong Kong, ordered the naval bombardment of Canton. Palmerston's Cabinet defended Bowring's action in public (whatever their private misgivings) and were supported by the *Times* and the *Morning Post*, who regarded the issue as a commercial one, emphasising the need to uphold treaty rights and to protect British shipping and commerce.[168] However, in Parliament, Richard Cobden moved a vote of censure of the government, supported by Gladstone, Russell, and Disraeli, which was carried by 263 votes to 247.[169] Charles Villiers voted against the motion. His views on foreign policy – and, indeed, political economy and free trade – predated those of the Manchester School and whilst he had made common cause with Cobden and Bright on the economic question of Corn Law repeal he had less sympathy for their wider political objectives post-1846, especially Cobden's foreign policy vision of using free trade as a means towards securing world peace. Villiers hated war but he was not a pacifist and accepted the need to protect British interests by naval or military force as a last resort.[170]

On 5 March 1857, believing that he had sufficient popular support in the country, Palmerston decided to dissolve Parliament and to go to the country on a mandate of peace abroad and progressive improvement in all that concerned the welfare of the nation at home.[171] As David Brown has illustrated, the General Election effectively became a plebiscite on Palmerston, who was still immensely popular in the country at large.[172] Charles Villiers had long regarded Palmerston as something of an adventurer abroad and an opponent of reform at home, but he had gradually come to respect the elderly Whig during his premiership. Indeed, in 1855, after many months grumbling about Whig appointments to Cabinet vacancies, Villiers told John Bright that Palmerston was a changed man:

> It looks to me as if Palmerston is in for his life ... I am bound to say ... I know of no-one that I believe will be better or more peaceful that could fill his place. He has become far more careful and less warlike than he used to be ... far more attentive and able in the House than I ever though possible.[173]

When Gladstone, Sidney Herbert and Sir James Graham resigned from the Cabinet in February 1855, Villiers informed Bright (correctly) that Palmerston 'would fight on till removed by a vote of the House, and would fill up his Govt. as he best could' and, with cabinet vacancies in the offing, Bright advised Villiers 'to get the Colonial Office, even tho' they might not last long; it would help his position for the future'.[174] This was not to be, for Lord John Russell was brought back into the Cabinet as Colonial Secretary and when he resigned in July the post was filled by Sir William Molesworth. However, on Molesworth's death in October, Palmerston evidently considered appointing Charles Villiers as Secretary of State for the Colonies and had sought the private opinion of Sir George Grey, the Home Secretary, who duly snubbed the suggestion:

> I do not think that Charles Villiers has any special recommendation for the Colonial Office, though his being in the Cabinet would, I have to say, be very acceptable to many of the Liberal Party and he has a fair claim to it from the position he has occupied in the house, although not as a member of the Government, in which capacity he has hardly ever shewn himself in debate.[175]

Any hopes which Charles Villiers may have entertained for further political preferment were therefore temporarily dashed. In December 1856, however, Palmerston intimated that the post of American Ambassador might be available to Villiers, should he wish to accept it.[176] Villiers sought the advice of his brother, Lord Clarendon, and Thomas Thornely, who pointed out that although the appointment would be

> entirely popular with the Free Traders in this country and the Americans would be pleased with it ... it must rest entirely with you to decide, whether you would give up your present position and make as total a change in your pursuits as would be required if you were to become Ambassador.[177]

After further consideration, however, Villiers rejected the offer,[178] and in May 1857 he also turned down the opportunity to become Secretary of State for Ireland.[179]

Nevertheless, Charles Villiers defended Palmerston's record in government. At an election meeting at Bilston on 18 March 1857, Villiers made clear to his constituents that 'I am not going to speak of Lord Palmerston with any wonderful enthusiasm. I am not going to speak of him merely with the feelings of a friend, for he is not exactly a private friend of mine', adding that 'It is therefore with some sort of independence that I judge Lord Palmerston'.[180] Nevertheless, he claimed that Palmerston deserved support, being 'about the most popular Minister we have seen for many years', who had undertaken government 'at a most critical time, when the war was raging, when our army was in a desperate state, and when the most fearful excitement prevailed throughout the whole of Europe',[181] and adding that now that the Crimean War was over, Palmerston was entitled to receive the gratitude of the nation. Moreover, Villiers endorsed Palmerston's defence of British trade and commerce in the China Seas; he defended the Income Tax – 'the principle was good and he would not change his opinion to serve his interest'; and he spoke of the benefits of Free Trade, which was creating greater prosperity.[182] In appealing to his constituents, Villiers then reaffirmed his credentials as a principled politician:

> I believe, gentlemen, that as long as a man can stand before the constituency of this borough and say 'I have conscientiously done my duty; I come here to meet my constituents; I ask them to inquire into my conduct; I stand here ready to give an account of that conduct; I ask you to examine every vote I have given; I am ready to account for those votes; I have supported every measure calculated to promote the interests of the community, the interests of this borough; aye, and the interests of mankind at large' – so long as a man can do that he has nothing to fear from the electors of Wolverhampton. During twenty-three years I have supported that policy and, having acted upon those principles, I come before my constituents and say to them 'Re-elect me if you believe me'. All I say is, I have acted in accordance with the principles I have always professed.[183]

The meeting resolved, to popular acclaim, that 'the old members are worthy of the support of the Electors of the Borough of Wolverhampton and it pledges itself to return them again to Parliament triumphantly', and both Villiers and Thomas Thornely were duly elected unopposed.[184] In the country, Palmerston's optimism was proved justified, for the government was returned with a majority of 85 in the House of Commons. Palmerston's victory, however, was short-lived, for his government, faced with financial concerns at home and with the Indian mutiny abroad, as well as continuing opposition from Peelites and Derbyites in the Commons, survived for only eleven months. In February 1858, following acute Anglo–French tensions arising from the Orsini affair,[185] Palmerston was defeated in the Commons by nineteen votes on an amendment to the Conspiracy to Murder Bill and resigned, and Lord Derby formed his second administration. In opposition, as David Brown has shown, Palmerston found difficulty in developing a coherent Liberal programme, which was compounded by the long-standing antipathy between himself and Lord John Russell and the half-hearted support provided by Gladstone.[186] Nevertheless, when the opposition successfully moved a motion of no confidence in Derby's plans for limited parliamentary reform in the Spring of 1859, the government resigned and called a general election.

In Wolverhampton, Charles Villiers' election campaign was the first that he had fought without Thomas Thornely at his side, for his fellow-member of many years, now aged 78, had decided to stand down owing to ill-health. Villiers had known privately of Thornely's impending retirement since December 1856, when Thornely had written to him stating

> And now, my good friend, it behoves me to say with how much satisfaction I have been your colleague for nearly 22 years. I have derived great advantages from it, but do not make any calculation, but the contrary, that I shall stand again. I am now one of the oldest Members in the House of Commons, and shall be 76 years of age in the Spring – I feel that I am failing both in mind and body, and this trembling of the hand, I think is spreading to the lower limb – My Doctor says nothing can be done for it – I think it is a sort of paralysis, but the Doctor did not go into particulars. Depend upon it I will be extremely cautious upon this subject – I do not believe my retirement would affect your seat, but would rather secure it, for People of all Parties in the Borough would vote for you. This we will keep very quiet.[187]

In his open letter of resignation of 5 April, Thornely drew attention to the important reforms which had been passed whilst he had been an MP – repeal of the Corn Laws, adoption of Free Trade, Postal reform, admission of Jews to Parliament, recognition of the principles of civil and religious liberty, and law reform – causes which both he and Villiers had jointly and consistently promoted.[188] Thornely added that 'I esteem it a privilege that, during my political life, I have shared the responsibilities of my position with my excellent colleague, and have invariably enjoyed the benefit of his abilities and kind advice'.[189] The Liberal committee, in accepting Thornely's resignation, expressed their thanks

> for the eminent services he has rendered in the House of Commons during the long period of twenty-four years; to assure him of their unabated regard, and of their admiration of his undeviating political consistency and remarkable attention to business, whether local or national.[190]

Thornely had, they added, proved to be 'a model representative' and 'an excellent man of business' in the House of Commons, 'labouring with untired diligence in committees and being one of the most constant in his attendance'.[191] Charles Villiers was equally complimentary in regard to Thornley, stating:

> He never saw a Member of Parliament more devoted to his duties than he was. He was, as they knew, a single man, and while Parliament was his companion, he regarded everything that concerned the borough as if it was his own family. A more worthy, honourable, and consistent man never, he believed, took his seat in the House of Commons.[192]

Subsequently, the Liberal committee, meeting in private rooms at the Wolverhampton Exchange, selected Sir Richard Bethell (later Lord Westbury),[193] the Attorney-General and MP for Aylesbury, as Thornley's successor. Bethell had been attracted to Wolverhampton not only because he considered it to be a more important constituency than Aylesbury but also because he considered it to be virtually impregnable due to the influence and popularity of Charles Villiers.[194] In April, at election rallies at the National School, Coseley, and the Turk's Head, Willenhall, Villiers, accompanied by Bethell, observed that much had been achieved in Parliament in the name of the Liberal opinions that they all held, and lauded the great improvements made in the district in regard to population growth, civilising influences, sanitary regulations, superior travel, postal and communication facilities, and the more efficient administration of justice. He stressed that he continued to hold the same principles in regard to trade and civil liberty as he had always held, and re-emphasised the great benefits accruing from free trade, which prompted the Rev. Joseph Davies of Willenhall to observe that during the fight for the Repeal of the Corn Laws 'Mr Villiers did the work and Mr Cobden was paid for it'.[195] On parliamentary reform, Villiers mocked Disraeli's abortive Reform Bill, stating that it had been no easy matter for the astute Disraeli to devise a scheme that would satisfy reformers and not offend his own followers and, in the event, 'his bill was certainly not one of his successful productions; his Bill was a Reform Bill, but the part of reform was hardly apparent in it'.[196] Whilst acknowledging that 'great differences' existed amongst Liberals in the House of Commons on the reform question, Villiers stated that he desired to see extensive reform. He thought the county constituencies were too agricultural and the small boroughs too numerous, advocating the elimination of pocket boroughs and the further redistribution of seats whereby small boroughs had one or both MPs transferred to 'large and intelligent constituencies'. When this was done, and the householder or occupants of £10 value were appointed to the county franchise, a better balance would, he argued, be achieved. On franchise reform, his opinion was that 'No people as a class should be excluded from the political franchise, and should at once be admitted, when exhibiting the intelligence and independence requisite to exercise it with advantage to themselves'.[197]

Finally, Villiers, who rarely spoke in public on foreign affairs, referred to the imminent threat of war between France and Austria over the Italian

Question.[198] Villiers stated that since no English interests were at present involved, and believing that this country would never sympathise with despotism in any shape or form, he hoped that there would be 'reasonable and just ground for remaining aloof. A strict neutrality was the proper course to be pursued', an observation that was greeted with cheers.[199] Villiers later elaborated upon this position during the Franco–Austrian war in a speech at Wolverhampton in July, when he stated that there although the British government had honourably endeavoured to avert war, her counsels had been disregarded, as a result of which there was 'a sense of insecurity in every state of Europe … all men were preparing for the *curse* of war visiting their own lands'. The war, he argued, interfered with trade and with the general interests of the whole country, whose general opinion was, 'namely – that they are not in favour generally of extending their forces; that they are not in favour of war; and their greatest desire is to maintain peaceful relations with the rest of the world', adding that 'the people of England were beyond any other nation interested in the welfare, the commercial prosperity, and the freedom of her continental neighbours'.[200]

Indeed, for Villiers, commercial prosperity, which underpinned many of his speeches during this period, was integral to the Liberal belief in the progress of the nation. This was well illustrated in an address Villiers gave later in the year to the Willenhall Exhibition of Fine Art, Models and Manufactures, an event inspired by the Great Exhibition of 1851 (which Villiers had both supported and visited[201]). In his speech, Villiers stated of the exhibits

> They were a tribute to the manufacturing industry of the people and it was impossible for the great and the rich to be contemplating the works of our artisans, the beauty of their productions, and the cleverness of their inventions, without feeling sympathy with, and respect for, the class by whom they were produced. He believed of late years this had already done much to improve the feeling towards the working classes. That feeling, as it existed once, had fortunately much changed. He remembered when it was very different, and most unjust. These classes were thought then by great people to be dangerous, disloyal, and ill-affected to the laws of the land. He had heard men of station say, not wise men, certainly, that it would be a happy thing for this country if the manufacturing towns were all erased from the surface of the earth (Laughter). But how different and much juster was the feeling now, since they had learnt more duly to appreciate the value and the importance of our manufacturing industry, and seen its connection with the wealth and power of the country (Hear, Hear). It was no small advantage, then, of these exhibitions, that they offer an opportunity for different classes to show their goodwill to each other, evoking generosity and confidence on one side, and grateful acknowledgment on the other … in the country at large we observe refinement in taste and habit almost in contrast with what formerly prevailed.[202]

At the hustings, Charles Villiers and Sir Richard Bethell were duly elected unopposed for Wolverhampton (and much to Thomas Thorney's satisfaction[203]), whilst in the country the Liberals secured 356 seats, giving them a majority of 58 over the Tories, and in June 1859 Queen Victoria invited Lord Palmerston to form his second administration, the formation of which was to provide Charles Villiers with the opportunity to return to the political centre stage.

Notes

1. Villiers, *Political Memoir*, lxii.
2. Villiers, *Free Trade Speeches*, I, vii.
3. Winston S. Churchill, *Lord Randolph Churchill* (London, 1907), 236–7.
4. Villiers, *Political Memoir*, lxii.
5. *Cobden Letters*, I, 445–6: Cobden to Joseph Parkes, 6 July 1846.
6. Villiers, *Political Memoir*, xlvi.
7. Ibid., lxvi–lxviii.
8. BLPES/SR1094, Villiers to Thorney, 18 Sep. 1846.
9. *Cobden Letters*, I, 447–8: Cobden to George Wilson, 11 July 1846.
10. See Russell to Cobden, 2 Jul. 1846, concerning the new Liberal administration 'devoted to improvement, both in this country and in Ireland'. Russell noted that Cobden did not wish to join and that 'Mr Charles Villiers has declined to take any office': Morley, *The Life of Richard Cobden*, 403.
11. It should be noted that Villiers was not the only member of his family to embrace radical causes, for his cousin, William Stephen Villiers Sankey (1793–1860), represented the Edinburgh and Mid-Lothian Chartists at the General Convention of the Industrious Class in London in 1839 and thereafter became a staunch Chartist propagandist. For further details, see especially Owen Ashton and Paul Pickering, 'The Aristocrat of Chartism: William Stephen Villiers Sankey (1793–1860)', in Owen R. Ashton and Paul A. Pickering, *Friends of the People: Uneasy Radicals in the Age of the Chartists* (London, 2002), 55–80.
12. *Staffs Advertiser*, 31 Jul. 1847. Thereafter, correspondence between Villiers and Russell appears thin on the ground, since many of Russell's papers disappeared whilst those of Villiers were destroyed. The National Archives, *Lord John Russell: Papers and Correspondence*, PRO 30/22 series only contain passing references by Russell to Villiers in the context of cabinet meetings between 1859 and 1866, two letters from Villiers to Russell (see PRO 30/22/15H/78/ f.230–3, 1865; 16C/1/f.1–2, May 1866), and one from Russell to Villiers on franchise reform (31/29/ f.61–2, 25 Nov. 1859). This probably explains why Villiers is also largely ignored in Walpole's, *Life of Lord John Russell* (1889), apart from five minor references. Significantly, however, in his *Recollections and Suggestions, 1813–1873* (London, 1875), 246–7, Russell, in recalling the Anti-Corn Law and Free Trade movements, refused to even mention Charles Villiers:

    > Men who consult the parliamentary history of England from 1815 to 1873 will rejoice to acknowledge that the most enlightened Members of our Parliament, the Liberal Tories of 1846, together with the Whigs ... together with Cobden and Bright and many Radical members of the House of Commons, have laboured to destroy the restrictions which fettered British industry and British trade, and have thereby conferred immense benefits on their country.

13. BLPES/SR1094, Villiers to Thorney, 18 Sep. 1846.

14 Villiers, *Political Memoir*, lxix. According to Bisset, the East India Company's objections were 'exclusively owing to the political antecedents of Mr Villiers, and the low company he had kept in his communications with the Anti-Corn Law League': *Notes on the Anti-Corn Law Struggle*, 163.
15 BLPES/SR1094, Villiers to Thornely, 18 Sep. 1846.
16 *Wolverhampton Chronicle*, 28 Feb. 1849.
17 Howe, 'Villiers, Charles Pelham', *ODNB*, 28286.
18 *London Standard*, 17 Jan. 1898.
19 *Manchester Times*, 28 May 1847.
20 MALS. George Wilson Papers, GB127, M20/3030: Villiers to George Wilson, nd. May 1847.
21 Ibid., 3032: Villiers to Wilson, 31 May 1847.
22 Ibid., 3034: Villiers to Wilson, 14 Jun. 1847.
23 *Wolverhampton Chronicle*, 16 Jun. 1847.
24 *Cobden Letters*, I, 486–8: Cobden to George Wilson, 21 June 1847.
25 *Staffs Advertiser*, 31 July 1847.
26 *Manchester Times*, 7 Aug. 1847.
27 BLPES/SR1094, Villiers to Thornely, 24 Aug. 1847.
28 Richard Monckton Milnes [later Lord Houghton], Whig MP for Pontefract, recalled a conversation with Villiers during a dinner at the Rothschilds in early September 1847, noting that 'Villiers has determined to sit for Wolverhampton and seemed very angry that Hawes has been spying about for the seat' (Sir Benjamin Hawes, Whig MP for Lambeth, had just lost his seat, which he had held since 1832, and was evidently considering Wolverhampton, should Villiers accept South Lancashire): T. Wemyss Reid, *Richard Monckton Milnes, 1st Lord Houghton: Life, Letters and Friendships* (2 vols, London, 1890), I, 391.
29 *Wolverhampton Chronicle*, 8 Sep. 1847.
30 Ibid., 24 Nov. 1847.
31 *Manchester Times*, 23 Nov. 1847.
32 Cited in *Wolverhampton Chronicle*, 1 Dec. 1847, which reprinted three articles, from the *Economist*, the *Examiner*, and the *Manchester Examiner*, under the heading 'Mr Villiers and his Constituents'.
33 Ibid.
34 Ibid.
35 Howe, *Cobden Letters*, Introduction, xlii. Later, in 1859, when Cobden was en route to France whilst negotiating the Anglo-French Commercial Treaty, which Charles Villiers opposed on the grounds that it marked a break with the free-trade principles of 1846, Cobden told Bright, 'I had a little talk with Villiers – What a complete negation he is, & always has been, on every subject but "total and immediate Repeal"!': Cobden to Bright, 17 Oct. 1859, cited in A. Howe (ed.), *The Letters of Richard Cobden*, vol. III, *1854–59* (Oxford, 2012), 468.
36 *Greville Memoirs*, 7 Jan. 1846.
37 Trevelyan, *The Life of John Bright*, 180.
38 See, for example, Bill Cash, *John Bright: Statesman, Orator, Agitator* (2012). Strangely, there are but a handful of passing references to Villiers in this biography, which also states incorrectly that Villiers 'died in harness' in Wolverhampton at the age of 96: 287.
39 Bright to Villiers, 6 Dec. 1846, cited in Keith Robbins, *Politicians, Diplomacy and War in Modern British History* (London, 1994), ch. 1, 'John Bright and the Middle Classes in Politics', 1–14.
40 Asa Briggs, 'John Bright and the Creed of Reform', in A. Briggs, *Victorian People* (London, 1954), 216–7.
41 Cash, *John Bright: Statesman, Orator, Agitator*, 58.

42 Bright to Villiers, 21 Dec. 1848, in Trevelyan, *The Life of John Bright*, 184.
43 Ibid.
44 Keith Robbins, for example, has argued that Bright's notion that there was or could be a 'popular party' was a myth – 'it was incoherent in an age of incoherent politics': Robbins, *Politicians, Diplomacy and War*, 9.
45 Villiers, *Free Trade Speeches*, II, 445: House of Commons, 23 Nov. 1852.
46 Extract from Roebuck's parliamentary journal, 12 July 1849, cited in Leader, *The Life and Letters of John Arthur Roebuck*, 230.
47 Ibid.
48 Ibid.
49 Ibid.
50 Ibid.
51 S. Maccoby, *English Radicalism, 1832–1852* (London, 1935), 435.
52 Briggs, *Victorian People*, 229.
53 Writing to Thomas Thornely in 1843, Villiers observed

> We both agree as to the necessity of great alterations in the distribution of the Electors and the mode of election, but that is quite consistent with not giving to every Irish peasant and every unlettered wight in this country a vote. I own I have no fears such as have been expressed by some as to the result of that, either as affecting the security of property or person which is the great purpose of law and Government. The day is past when the value of both as a condition of civil society is not manifest to the meanest of the mass. But I believe it would require a revolution to bring it about, and that, in the present state of the Working Class, would only be effected by violence, which would send us back half a century:
> BLPES/SR1094, Villiers to Thornely, 16 Dec. 1843

54 *Staffs Advertiser*, 31 Jul. 1847.
55 *Northern Star*, 14 Aug. 1847.
56 *Wolverhampton Chronicle*, 12 Jul. 1848.
57 *Parl. Debs*, 3rd ser., 100, cc.1225–68, 6 Aug. 1848.
58 Robert Saunders, *Democracy and the Vote in British Politics, 1848–1867: The Making of the Second Reform Act* (Farnham, 2011), 90.
59 Ibid., 91.
60 Baron Lionel Nathan de Rothschild (1808–1879): British banker and Liberal politician; elected as Liberal MP for the City of London in 1847 but barred from taking his seat; finally admitted to Parliament in 1859, re-elected in 1865, defeated in 1868, returned in 1869 and defeated in 1874. Married his cousin Charlotte. For further details, see especially Niall Ferguson, *The World's Banker: The History of the House of Rothschild* (London, 1998).
61 *Parl. Debs*, 3rd ser., 95, cc.1356–401, 17 Dec. 1847; 98, cc.606–70, 4 May 1848; 125, 71–122, 11 Mar. 1853.
62 Ibid., 3rd ser., 118, cc.1144–217, 21 July 1851;118, cc.1574–94, 28 July 1851.
63 *Wolverhampton Chronicle*, 21 Mar. 1857.
64 For example, Charles Villiers attended the marriage of Miss Evelina de Rothschild, second daughter of Baron Lionel, to her cousin Baron Ferdinand de Rothschild (son of Baron Anslem of the great commercial and financial aristocracy of Vienna) in the Baron Lionel's new mansion at Hyde Park corner 'with princely state and ceremony' on 7 Jun. 1865. The guests also included the Disraelis, the Molesworths and other aristocrats. Later in the evening, the Baroness gave a Ball, which was attended by RH the Duke of Cambridge, the Duchesse d'Aumale, 'and by all the leading members of the aristocracy and fashion': *The Times*, 8 Jun. 1865.

65 Ferguson, *The World's Banker*, 1162, n.248.
66 William Flavelle Moneypenny and George Earle Buckle, *The Life of Benjamin Disraeli, Earl of Beaconsfield* (6 vols, London, 1910–20), I, 124.
67 Ibid., I, 203: Disraeli to Sarah Disraeli, 18 Feb. 1832.
68 Ralph Disraeli (ed.), *Lord Beaconsfield's Letters, 1832–52* (London, 1887), 212–3: Disraeli to Sarah Disraeli, 29 Dec. 1848.
69 Ibid., 230–1: Disraeli to Sarah Disraeli, 26 Apr. 1850.
70 Moneypenny and Buckle, *Life of Benjamin Disraeli*, III, 250: Disraeli to Sarah Disraeli, 13 May 1850.
71 Ibid., III, 318: Disraeli to Lord John Manners, 13 Sep. 1850.
72 Disraeli, *Lord George Bentinck*, 534.
73 *Bell's New Weekly Messenger*, 28 Jan. 1850.
74 Villiers, *Free Trade Speeches*, II, 369–404, 31 Jan. 1850.
75 For further details, see Robert Blake, *Disraeli* (London, 1966), 315–6.
76 Matthew, *Gladstone*, 55–8.
77 Gladstone's Library, Hawarden. *Papers of the Prime Ministers of Great Britain, Series 8: The Papers of William Ewart Gladstone* [hereafter *Gladstone Papers*]. Correspondence with C.P. Villiers, 1851–96. Add MSS 44370, folio 23, Villiers to Gladstone, 4 Mar. 1852.
78 Ibid., 44371, 228, Gladstone to Villiers, 4 March 1852.
79 Villiers, *Free Trade Speeches*, II. 405–26, 15 March 1852.
80 *Gladstone Papers*, 44371, 273, Villiers to Gladstone, 1 April 1852.
81 University College London, Ogden MS 65: John Bright's Letters to his wife, Margaret, 1847–1878, 13 Nov. 1852.
82 *Gladstone Papers*, 44373, 55, Villiers to Gladstone, 13 Nov. 1852.
83 Ibid., 44373, 62, Gladstone to Villiers, 15 Nov. 1852.
84 Ibid., 44373, 66, Villiers to Gladstone, 17 Nov. 1852.
85 Villiers, *Free Trade Speeches*, II, 427–8, 23 Nov. 1852.
86 Ibid., 472.
87 Villiers, *Political Memoir*, lxxv.
88 Ogden MS 65: John Bright's Letters to his wife, Margaret, 1847–1878, 23 Nov. 1852.
89 Villiers, *Political Memoir*, lxxi.
90 *Parl. Debs*, 3rd ser., 123, cc.588–705, 26 Nov. 1852.
91 *Gladstone Papers*, 44373, 66, Villiers to Gladstone, 17 Nov. 1852.
92 *Parl. Debs*, 3rd ser., 123, cc.588–705, 26 Nov. 1852.
93 Ibid.
94 Ibid.
95 Ogden MS 65: John Bright's Letters to his wife, Margaret, 1847–1878, 27 Nov. 1852.
96 For further details, see Blake, *Disraeli*, 'The Budget of 1852', 328–48.
97 *The Letters of Queen Victoria*, Benson and Esher (eds), II, 420–2.
98 For further details, see Villiers, *A Vanished Victorian*, 179–88.
99 Trevelyan, *The Life of John Bright*, 180.
100 Stuart J. Reid, *Lord John Russell* (London, 1895), 79.
101 George Douglas [8th Duke of Argyll], *Autobiography and Memoirs, 1823–1900* (2 vols, London, 1906), I, 460.
102 For further details, see the debates on the Office of Examiner (Chancery) Bill, *Parl. Debs*, 3rd ser., 28 Feb. 1853, 124, 772–81; 4 Mar. 1853, 124, 1159–60. In the event, the Office of Examiner (Chancery) Act of 1853 prevented the possibility of this scenario occurring.
103 Brian Harrison, *Drink and the Victorians: The Temperance Question in England, 1815–1872* (London, 1971; 2nd edn. Keele, 1994), 63–84.
104 *Parl. Debs*, 3rd ser., 158, cc.775–833, 7 May 1860.

105 Harrison, 165.
106 *Report of the Select Committee on Public Houses, PP*, 1852–3 (855), XXXVII.
107 *Report of the Select Committee on Public Houses, PP*, 1853–4 (367), XIV.
108 Villiers, *Political Memoir*, lxxviii.
109 *Parl. Debs*, 3rd ser., 139, c.182, 26 Jun. 1855.
110 Ibid., 144, cc.477–88, Jun. 1857.
111 Ibid.
112 *Report of the Select Committee on Public Houses, PP*, 1853–4 (367), XIV, 6523–6975. Villiers returned to this issue later in his career: in May 1875, during the debate on the Sale of Food and Drugs Bill, which sought to extend the appointment of food and drugs analysts in counties and boroughs, Villiers observed that

> Lectures were being delivered in the metropolis which proved that all the evils that ever existed in regard to adulteration were still rampant. It had been stated, indeed, on good authority, that much of the savage ferocity displayed in recent cases of drunken assaults was attributable to the noxious ingredients with which the liquor of the lower classes was adulterated.
> *Parl. Debs*, 3rd ser., 224, cc.196–209, 6 May 1875

113 *Parl. Debs*, 3rd ser., 139, cc.182–206, 26 Jun. 1855.
114 *Report of the Select Committee on Public Houses, PP*, (1852–3), 855, XXXVII, 6537.
115 Ibid., 6671.
116 Ibid., 6715.
117 Ibid., 6621–84.
118 Ibid., 6730.
119 Ibid., 6826.
120 Ibid., 6838.
121 Ibid., 6857.
122 Ibid., 6935.
123 Ibid., 6862–66; see also *Parl. Debs*, 3rd ser., 144, cc.477–88, 10 Feb. 1857.
124 Ibid., 6948–75.
125 This was established in 1855–6. For further details, see *Report of the Select Committee on the Adulteration of Food, PP*, 1855, 480, VIII.
126 *Report of the Select Committee on Public Houses, PP*, 1854 (367), XIV.
127 See also Villiers' contribution to the debate in the House of Commons on Gladstone's Refreshment Houses and Wine Licenses Bill in May 1860: 'There was', he said,

> no country in the world where the Sabbath was so well observed as England. Did not that look as if the people were intelligent beings and good Christians who could pass public-houses without making brutes of themselves? ... There was one way in which they could induce people not to go to drinking-houses, and that was by allowing them innocent recreation ... the truth was that since people had been able to get into the country on Sunday, there had been less drunkenness in large towns than there used to be.
> *Parl. Debs*, 3rd ser., 158, cc.1213–58, 14 May 1860

128 *Parl. Debs*, 3rd ser., 144, cc.477–88, 10 Feb. 1857.
129 Ibid.
130 Ibid.
131 Ibid.
132 *Wolverhampton Chronicle*, 7 Mar. 1856.
133 *Parl. Debs*, 3rd ser., 144, cc.477–88, Jun. 1857.
134 University of Southampton. Special Collections. Palmerston Papers, PP/GC/GR/2491, Grey to Palmerston, 8 May 1857.

152 Interlude

135 *Parl. Debs*, 3rd ser., 158, cc.775–833, 7 May 1860.
136 *The Spectator*, 2 Nov. 1861.
137 For further details on the war and its consequences, see especially C. Woodham Smith, *The Reason Why* (London, 1957), 262–83; Christopher Hibbert, *The Destruction of Lord Raglan: A Tragedy of the Crimean War, 1854–55* (London, 1961); M.E. Chamberlain, *British Foreign Policy in the Age of Palmerston* (London, 1980), 69–75. Trevor Royle, *Crimea: The Great Crimean War, 1854–56* (London, 1999), especially part II, 203–433; Saul David, *Victoria's Wars: The Rise of Empire* (London, 2006), 200–83.
138 *Parl. Debs*, 3rd ser., 136, cc.979–1063, 26 Jan. 1855; see also Asa Briggs, 'John Arthur Roebuck and the Crimean War', in Briggs, *Victorian People*, 60–94.
139 G. Villiers, *A Vanished Victorian*, 243–49: Lord Derby could not form a Tory Ministry and Clarendon informed the Queen that the appointment of Lord John Russell would be very unpopular among many Whigs and that he would not serve under him, whilst Palmerston, who could carry sufficient support (especially at a time of war), would not accept office unless Clarendon accepted the post of Foreign Secretary. See also, A.C. Benson and Viscount Esher, *The Letters of Queen Victoria*, III, 79–97, 30 Jan. 1855 to 5 Feb. 1855.
140 Wilson, *The Greville Diary*, II. 526, 27 Nov. 1855.
141 Woodham Smith, *The Reason Why*, 275–6.
142 *Parl. Debs*, 3rd ser., 137, cc.1310–54, 29 Mar. 1855.
143 Ibid.
144 Ibid.
145 Ibid.
146 Ibid.
147 *The Report from the Select Committee on the Army before Sebastopol*, PP, (1854–5), ix.
148 David, *Victoria's Wars*, 266–8.
149 *Morning Post*, 14 Jan. 1856.
150 *Queen Victoria's Journals*, 41, 23, 13 Jan. 1856.
151 BLPES/SR1094, Thornely to Villiers, 13 Jan. 1855.
152 Villiers, *A Vanished Victorian*, 146.
153 Mrs C.W. Earle, *Memoirs and Memories* (London, 1911), 225. For details of family life at The Grove, see also Dennis Lovett, *The Grove Story* (Watford, 1984).
154 *Queen Victoria's Journals*, 40, 266, 23 Oct. 1855.
155 Ibid.
156 Ibid., 41, 104, 2 Mar. 1856.
157 Ibid.
158 Ibid., 41, 285, 23 June 1856.
159 *The Report of the General Board of Officers appointed to Inquire into the Statements contained in the Reports of Sir John McNeill and Colonel Tulloch, and the evidence taken by them relative hereto, animadverting upon the conduct of certain officers on the General Staff, and others in the Army; Together with Minutes of Evidence taken by the Board; and an Appendix*, PP (1856), xxi, 611.
160 David, *Victoria's Wars*, 280.
161 *Parl. Debs*, 3rd ser., 143, cc.1115–8, 21 Jul. 1856.
162 Ibid.
163 Ibid.
164 Ibid.
165 Ibid., 143, cc.1273–4, 23 Jul. 1856.
166 Woodham Smith, 282–3.
167 David Brown, *Palmerston: A Biography* (Yale, 2012), 400.
168 Ibid., 400–2; see also M.E. Chamberlain, *British Foreign Policy in the Age of Palmerston* (London, 1980), 76–7.

169 *Parl. Debs*, 3rd ser., 144, cc.1726–846, 3 Mar. 1857.
170 The 'Manchester School', an epithet coined by Disraeli after the repeal of the Corn Laws, was far from heterogonous, composed as it was of a variety of different groups with a variety of ideas and whilst the question of Corn Law repeal provided it with a singular and unifying purpose between 1838 and 1846, thereafter, with free trade secured, it consisted of the followers of Cobden and Bright and was less effective. For a useful discussion of this subject, see William Grampp, *The Manchester School of Economics* (Stanford and Oxford, 1960), 1–16. In 1898, the Tory *St James's Gazette*, which favoured protectionism, claimed that

> Mr Villiers saw the birth, rise, culmination, heavy downfall and practical disappearance of Manchesterthum ... The free trade part of the Manchester School is still with us. What Mr Villiers lived to see disappear was its political part – its views of foreign policy and on the subject of war. Mr Villiers took no part in that, and lived it down.
> *St James's Gazette*, 17 Jan. 1898

171 Brown, *Palmerston*, 421.
172 Ibid., 404.
173 E.D. Steele, *Palmerston and Liberalism, 1855–1865* (Cambridge, 1991), 63.
174 Walling, *The Diaries of John Bright*, 181, 20 Feb. 1855.
175 University of Southampton. Special Collections. Palmerston Papers, PP/GC/GR/2452: Grey to Palmerston, 12 Nov. 1855.
176 Fitzmaurice, *The Life of Granville George Leveson Gower* (1905), I., 221, 7 Dec. 1856: 'Ch. Villiers is going as Minister to the United States'.
177 BLPES/SR1094, Thornely to Villiers, 15 Dec. 1856.
178 Fitzmaurice, I, 223, 24 Dec. 1856: 'Washington has been offered to Charles Villiers, who will not have it. Napier is to have it'.
179 *Bell's New Weekly Messenger* 23 May 1857 (Sat): Reported that Charles Villiers had been offered the office of Irish Secretary, but that 'he hesitates in the acceptance of the situation'.
180 *Wolverhampton Chronicle*, 21 Mar. 1857.
181 Ibid.
182 Ibid.
183 Ibid.
184 Ibid., 25 Mar. 1857. The prospective Tory candidate, Rupert Kettle, had withdrawn his candidacy on 21 March on the grounds that although he thought that he would poll well, it would not be enough to secure a majority.
185 In January 1858 an abortive attempt was made on the lives of the Emperor Napoleon and Empress Eugenie in Parish by Felice Orsini, an Italian republican, who had previously been in London, where his bomb had been made. The French government demanded strong action by Britain to prevent such future occurrences and Palmerston, conscious of Britain's traditional role as a home for political exiles, Yet equally anxious to prevent foreign conspiracies being hatched in Britain, decided to strengthen the law by the Conspiracy to Murder Bill (which was perceived by many to constitute a prospective Aliens Act) on condition that the French desisted from sending 'political undesirables' to England: Jasper Ridley, *Lord Palmerston* (London, 1970), 479–82; Chamberlain, *British Foreign Policy*, 77–8; Brown, *Palmerston*, 409–10.
186 Brown, *Palmerston*, 423–29.
187 BLPES/SR1094, Thornely to Villiers, 15 Dec. 1856.
188 *Wolverhampton Chronicle*, 13 April 1859.
189 Ibid.

190 Ibid.
191 Ibid. Thornely later died at his home at Mount Street, Liverpool, in May 1862. For further details, see obituary, *Wolverhampton Chronicle*, 7 May 1862.
192 Ibid., 27 Apr. 1859.
193 Sir Richard Bethell (1800–1873): lawyer, judge and Liberal politician, MP for Aylesbury 1851–9, and for Wolverhampton from 1859–61, Lord Chancellor 1861–5, raised to the peerage as Baron Westbury in 1861.
194 T.A. Nash, *The Life of Richard Lord Westbury, formerly Lord High Chancellor* (2 vols, London, 1888), I, 268.
195 *Wolverhampton Chronicle*, 27 Apr. 1859.
196 Ibid.
197 Ibid.
198 The context was the Franco-Austrian War over Piedmont-Sardinia. In 1858, Napoleon III and Cavour had agreed that France would support Piedmont in a war to expel the Austrians from Italy, whereby Lombardy, Venetia, Parma, Piacenz and the Romagna would be united with Piedmont-Sardinia and France would receive Nice and Savoy in return. The war broke out in April 1859 when the Austrians invaded Sardinian territory and France responded, the Austrians being defeated at Magenta and Solferino in June. The Armistice of Villafranca ended the war in July and France and Austria agreed to the establishment of an Italian Confederation under the Pope. For further details, see Chamberlain, *British Foreign Policy*, 78–9.
199 *Wolverhampton Chronicle*, 27 Apr. 1859.
200 Ibid., 9 Jul. 1859.
201 *Bell's New Weekly Messenger*, 12 Oct. 1851.
202 *Wolverhampton Chronicle*, 15 Sep. 1859.
203 BLPES/SR1094, Thornely to Villiers, nd. May 1859:

> My dear friend – I am greatly obliged by your letter from Wolverhampton, received this morning. I am quite delighted the thing has gone off so well. Without over-rating my own importance, I really did not expect to retire without occasioning more trouble to you or the Borough. Thank God it is all over and beautifully ended ... What a blessing it is there was no contest, and how lucky that Sir R. Bethell took with the people. The People have done me great honour, much more than I deserve, but I am deeply grateful to them ... I congratulate you most sincerely on all that has occurred and I thank you most truly for all your kindness to me for so many years.

Figure 1 'The Hon. Mr Villiers', Pen and ink drawing by A. Bickell, 1840, reproduced by kind permission of ©Wolverhampton Archives and Local Studies.

Figure 2 'Charles Pelham Villiers', Mezzotint steel engraving by J. Cochran, after Charles Allen Du Val, 28 February 1840, reproduced by kind permission of ©National Portrait Gallery, London.

Figure 3 'Charles Pelham Villiers', c. 1846. Oil on canvas. Anon, reproduced by kind permission of Charles N. Villiers, from his private collection.

Figure 4 'Charles Pelham Villiers', Photograph by W. & D. Downey, albumen carte-de-visite, mid-1860s, reproduced by kind permission of ©National Portrait Gallery, London.

Figure 5 'Caricature of the Right Hon. C.P. Villiers, MP', Lithographic print, colour, by James Tissot ['Spy'], in Statesmen Series, No. 123, *Vanity Fair*, 31 August 1872.

Figure 6 'The Late Right Hon. C.P. Villiers, Father of the House of Commons', black and white photograph by Whitlock Bros, Wolverhampton, c.1896, published in *The Graphic*, 22 January 1898.

Figure 7 Statue of Charles Pelham Villiers, by William Theed, in Snow Hill, Wolverhampton, 1879, reproduced by kind permission of ©Wolverhampton Archives and Local Studies.

6 The Cabinet Minister

In July 1859 Lord Palmerston offered Charles Villiers the post of President of the Poor Law Board in the new government (in succession to Milner Gibson, who became President of the Board of Trade), together with a seat in the Cabinet. The appointment clearly pleased Queen Victoria, who noted in her diary, 'Mr C. Villiers (Ld Clarendon's clever brother), President of the Poor Law Bd, with a seat in the Cabinet'.[1] In forming his Cabinet, as Alan Sykes has shown in his examination of the concept of 'Palmerstonian Centrism', Palmerston was aware that previous Whig governments had been frequently criticised, especially by Radicals, for 'aristocratic exclusiveness' and was therefore keen 'to reconstruct the government upon a different principle ... out of a larger range of political parties'.[2] This entailed the creation of a broadly 'Liberal' ministry comprising a coalition of aristocratic Whigs, Peelites and Radicals. This mid-Victorian political consensus, merging the Peelite legacy of impartial government with the Liberal commitment to civil and religious liberty,[3] not only effectively neutralised much Radical discontent but also enabled Radical members of the Cabinet, such as Villiers and Gibson, to espouse their continuing commitment to 'Advanced Liberalism' whilst also arguing the Ministry's case, which made it more acceptable publicly.[4] The new Ministry – described by Villiers' brother, Lord Clarendon, as 'a great bundle of sticks'[5] – proved to be relatively harmonious, although Eric Evans has suggested that it was significant that the only left-wing Liberal in the Cabinet, Charles Villiers, 'was tucked impotently away at the Poor Law Board'.[6]

Nevertheless, Palmerston was clearly delighted when Villiers accepted this post, commenting in a letter to Lord Clarendon:

> I am very glad that your brother Charles has accepted the Poor Law Board with a seat in the Cabinet; and after the precedent set us by Derby of father and son in the same Cabinet, there can no longer be any objection to having two brothers at that mystical table in Downing Street.[7]

For the time being, however, Lord Clarendon was excluded from the Cabinet purely because Lord John Russell had made the post of Foreign Secretary the condition of his appointment by the government (although Clarendon was to return to the Cabinet as Chancellor of the Duchy of Lancaster in 1864 and as Foreign Secretary in Russell's Ministry, 1865–6), and Lord Granville remarked that 'Clarendon is annoyed at losing the Foreign Office, but very friendly, and much pleased at Charles Villiers accession to office. The latter has combed a little, grown fat and a shade pompous on the strength of it'.[8] Sir John Trelawny, the radical MP for Tavistock, whose *Diaries* record his observations of life and proceedings in the House of Commons during Palmerston's second ministry, also noted that:

> The appointment of Charles Villiers considerably improves the position of government. It will go far to engender a disposition to look upon the new Cabinet 'with interest & with hope' to use a phrase Villiers used many years ago when a liberal administration began to look with diminished disfavour on freetraders. Still the men below the gangway may complain that faith has not been kept with them – & middle class people will say Villiers is another aristocratic selection.[9]

The Times also applauded Villiers' appointment:

> Few people who remember the origin of the Free Trade movement will refuse their hearty sanction to this tardy acknowledgment of high desert. It was Mr. Charles Villiers who practically originated the Free Trade movement ... We are glad to hear that he has accepted the office and to think that he has at last an opportunity for displaying those administrative talents which found no scope in the formal duties of Judge Advocate.[10]

Thus Villiers' appointment not only substantially strengthened Palmerston's first 'Liberal' government by including a Radical, but also and finally provided Villiers with a position commensurate with his abilities and interests.

According to convention, Villiers' appointment as a Cabinet Minister necessitated a by-election in Wolverhampton, and at a meeting held on 4 July at the Corn Exchange, Villiers was unanimously re-elected, unopposed, as the Member for Wolverhampton. The Mayor, John Hartley, congratulated Villiers on his appointment and, in returning thanks, Villiers stated that despite 'the pressure of business in London and so great the heat of the weather', he had been determined to attend the proceedings, adding that he had never sought office but could not refuse such a distinguished position, whilst acknowledging that 'the duties of his new post were not slight; indeed, they had formerly been most anxious in their character'.[11]

Charles Villiers' first act as President of the Poor Law Board was to appoint Thomas Thornely's nephew, John Thornely, a graduate of London University and a barrister in the Middle Temple, as his Private Secretary.

Thomas Thornely had not sought this post for his nephew, but was extremely grateful to Villiers nonetheless, stating in a letter of 20 July,

> Almost every friend I meet stops me in the street to congratulate me on the position my nephew has obtained in being appointed your Private Secretary. This shews me how highly the situation is regarded, and I do again most sincerely thank you for giving it to John, to whom I think it may be of great service.[12]

John Thornely retained this post until Villiers left office in 1866, thereafter continuing to serve the Poor Law Board as Auditor for, first, the West Norfolk District[13] and, later, the Hampshire and Wiltshire District.[14]

Peter Wood has argued that the Poor Law Board, which was not as yet a permanent department, was 'pragmatic and rather colourless ... a government department of lowly status which was unlikely to attract the appointment of an ambitious politician'.[15] Nevertheless, Villiers sought from the outset to raise the profile of the Board and his successful seven-year tenure of the post was to be marked by the most important series of poor-law reforms since 1834. These not only modernised the New Poor Law, giving it a slightly less inhumane face, but also witnessed the acceptance of the Poor Law Board as a permanent part of the machinery of government which was subsequently reshaped as the Local Government Board in 1871. Indeed, although often suffering from ill-health – Trelawny observed during a debate in 1865 that 'Villiers looked ghastlier than usual – he always looks very ill and I believe has long had lung disease',[16] Villiers subsequently proved indefatigable in his efforts to meet the challenges faced by the Poor Law Board.[17] Yet, in this context, it is somewhat surprising to observe that the contribution of Charles Villiers to Poor Law reform has been strangely neglected within the historiography of the English Poor Law, including important studies by Michael Rose, Norman Longmate, Peter Wood, Alan Kidd, David Englander and David Green.[18]

As a means for deterring able-bodied males from relief applications, the New Poor Law appeared to be working reasonably well by 1860, although local practice varied both within and between regions,[19] and the number of paupers had fallen from 1.2 million (8.8%) to 845,000 (4.3%) between 1834 and 1860,[20] although a reduction in pauperism was not the same as reducing poverty. Nevertheless, as Villiers later recalled, there had always been a feeling of distrust and jealousy towards the Central Board which had persisted since the inception of the New Poor Law and this antagonism, he held, had inhibited the full development of poor law administration.[21] This hostility was revealed in the Commons in July 1860, when Villiers moved for the renewal of the Poor Law Board for the usual period of five years, which was supported not only by Palmerston, but also by other leading figures with experience of Poor Law administration, including Sir George Cornewall Lewis and Sotheron Estcourt, a former President of the Poor Law Board.

However, during the debates in the Commons, reference was made to a number of petitions submitted from some Boards of Guardians in the Metropolis and the provinces critical of the Poor Law Board. Villiers believed that these petitions sought 'by casting discredit on the central administration, to paralyze its authority in future',[22] and that the discontent was largely the product of some local administrators of the Poor Law who were 'impatient of the control of the Central Board and who wanted to return to the old system of local and uncontrolled management', and who had been stirred up by a 'malcontent union in London', pointing out that only 70 out of the 660 poor law unions had petitioned against the Board.[23] Nevertheless, an amendment to the Poor Law Board Continuance Bill was duly carried which restricted the period of renewal to only three years, on condition that a comprehensive inquiry into the administration of the Poor Laws since 1834 be established. A Select Committee on Poor Relief was duly established by Villiers in the spring of 1861,[24] and this was to develop subsequently into the most comprehensive examination of the poor laws since 1834.

The context for the inquiry arose in part from the fact that the New Poor Law had failed to discriminate effectively between unemployed though otherwise industrious workers and paupers during periods of high unemployment. This was highlighted by the London relief crisis during the harsh winter of 1860–1, when many dockers and other casual labourers became unemployed and, in order to obtain poor relief, were forced to undertake the same workhouse labour 'test', such as stone-breaking or oakum-picking, as ordinary paupers. Many refused to do so and became dependent on private charity, which provoked criticism of the whole poor law system. The Select Committee, which Villiers chaired, was thus established to examine the administration of the relief of the poor under the orders, rules and regulations established in 1834, including the election and activities of guardians, the appointment of officials, the financing of relief and the administration of workhouses, medical relief, and religious and educational provisions. Much of the evidence in this first report pertained to poor relief in London.[25]

However, the Select Committee was reappointed in 1862, 1863 and 1864 with a nationwide brief. The reports of 1862 and 1863 covered a range of issues, including whether poor relief should continue to be administered by the central authority, the Poor Law Board; the religious rights of workhouse inmates, the education of pauper children; the administration of medical relief, the audit of parochial and union accounts, and the equalisation of the poor rate.[26] The 1864 Report, which summarised the evidence on each of these issues, made extensive and sensible recommendations, including the continuation of the central authority as essential for the proper administration of relief and the right of workhouse inmates to receive educational instruction and to practise their religion freely, which was of particular benefit to Catholic pauper children. Indeed, the Catholic Workhouse Committee had long complained that in some London workhouses Catholic, and largely Irish, pauper children had received religious instruction from Anglican clergymen.

When the Catholic Committee presented its evidence to the Select Committee, it was received sympathetically but impartially by Charles Villiers and the Select Committee duly recommended the provision of Creed Registers in all workhouses and their inspection by ministers of all denominations and as well as provisions for the transfer of Catholic pauper children to schools of their own denomination.[27] The Select Committee also made significant recommendations in regard to the administration of poor relief in London, including the extension of the Poor Law Board's authority over committees established under local acts, the setting up of a common fund for the relief of the casual poor, and the equalization of metropolitan poor rates.[28] According to Aschrott, as a result of the final report and recommendations of the committee, presented on 31 May 1864, and the measures taken by Villiers in consequence of it, the Poor Law Board, 'which had hitherto borne an experimental character, was raised to the rank of a substantive department of government'.[29]

This said, the main challenge – indeed crisis – faced by Villiers at the Poor Law Board arose from the American Civil War. During the war, British intervention was initially the Federalists' greatest fear and the Confederacy's greatest hope,[30] and Anglo–American relations were sorely tested by the *Trent* affair in November 1861, when a Union warship, the *San Jacinto*, intercepted a British mail packet, the *Trent*, off the Cuban coast and seized two Confederate envoys, James Mason and John Slidell, who were on *en route* to London to secure support for the Confederacy.[31] This violation of international maritime law caused uproar in Britain and Palmerston, backed by public opinion, demanded an apology and the immediate release of the envoys, threatening a military response against the Union. Villiers privately informed Richard Cobden, who disapproved of the bellicose stance of Palmerston and the popular press and was anxious that peace should prevail at all costs, that 'England has been insulted and defied; she must and will have redress',[32] an assertion that provoked no little disagreement between the two old friends.[33] In the event, the situation was defused in January 1862 when the Lincoln administration repudiated the actions of the captain of the *San Jacinto* and Mason and Slidell were released.[34] Thereafter, private opinions within the Cabinet were divided: Gladstone, for example, sympathised initially with the South and in an infamous speech at Newcastle in October 1862 went as far as stating that 'Jefferson Davis and the leaders of the South have made an army; they are making, it appears, a navy; and they have made, what is more than either – they have made a Nation';[35] by contrast, Charles Villiers, with his strong anti-slavery credentials, sympathised privately with the North.[36] However, Palmerston, who believed that key foreign policy decisions should be made by the entire cabinet, steadfastly pursued a policy of neutrality during the Civil War, and when some Ministers, notably Gladstone and Russell, gave the impression of abandoning neutrality in favour of a negotiated peace they were strongly opposed by Granville, Argyll, Milner Gibson, Grey, Cornwall Lewis and Charles Villiers, who was strongly opposed to British intervention.[37] Indeed, Villiers, who had personal contacts with the American Embassy,[38] publicly endorsed government policy in a speech in Wolverhampton in November 1863, stating that 'in the face of the strongest inducements to take an opposite course, the pledge of neutrality to each contending party in the States of America has been strictly and honourably observed'.[39] Thus Britain remained neutral from start to finish, despite pressures from a divided public opinion to support one side or the other.[40]

However, the Unionist blockade of Southern ports during the war cut off British access to supplies of raw cotton from the Southern States and resulted in the so-called Lancashire 'Cotton Famine', with over 400,000 textile operatives unemployed by November 1862 and more than £65,000 expended by poor-law unions and charitable bodies in the relief of distress.[41] For Villiers, this was a matter of great concern, as he indicated to the Queen.[42] The New Poor Law was ill-equipped to deal with the demands placed upon it by mass urban unemployment in the northern textile districts, and not least because it proved impossible to enforce the workhouse test before relieving able-bodied applicants. But Villiers responded to the challenge with flexibility and imagination.

First, Villiers issued a circular to every union, not only in the cotton districts but also in other localities connected with the American trade, encouraging them to make early provision for an unusual amount of distress and pointing out that the system 'was elastic and capable of being adapted to extraordinary circumstances'.[43] Indeed, initial reports from Boards of Guardians suggested that the system could cope when supplemented by charitable aid. Villiers also relaxed the provisions of the Outdoor Relief Regulation Order of 1852, which allowed out-relief (half in kind and half in cash) to be given to the able-bodied in return for work (the labour test), and guardians were given discretion in interpreting this, hence some applied an 'education' test in differentiating between applicants and provided relief to those men and women who attended adult industrial schools for a period each week. By 1863, 48,000 men and 41,000 women were being relieved in this way, with men attending classes in carpentry, shoemaking and tailoring and women attending sewing classes.

Second, in November 1861, Villiers informed the guardians in the manufacturing districts that the Poor Law Board was considering further measures to relieve distress. In May 1862 he despatched H.B. Farnall as a special commissioner to investigate the state of affairs and, in July, Villiers informed the House of Commons that the contents of Farnall's reports exhibited 'a less hopeful tone as to any mitigation of the present distress, and something like mistrust of that continuous flow of private benevolence on which, together with the poor rate, he and others had relied for support',[44] and indicated that the 'cotton famine' was placing such a heavy financial burden on many parishes that in some districts ratepayers were being excused payment of rates and were being supported by the poor-law authorities. In Oldham, for example, it was reported that two-thirds of the ratepayers were operatives. How, asked Villiers, could these people pay the rates when they were unemployed and what were the shopkeepers to do when their customers (who had often been given credit) no longer received wages?[45] Villiers' solution was the Union Relief Aid Act of 1862, which applied to Cheshire, Lancashire and Derbyshire. It provided that if the cost of poor relief in a parish exceeded a 3s rate then the other parishes within the union should pay the excess, and that if a union spent more than a 3s rate it could apply to the Central Board for permission to borrow the excess from the public works loan commissioners. Finally, if a union's expenses exceeded a 5s rate then the county would be required to pay the excess. Hence the principle was being introduced, gradually, of making the union rather than the parish responsible for poor-law finance.

At this stage, given that it was uncertain how long the American Civil War would last and, therefore, cotton imports curtailed, Villiers did not consider it necessary to introduce a special Parliamentary Grant to relieve distress, which had been suggested by Richard Cobden, who had been very active in relief efforts in Lancashire, variously raising funds in Stockport and visiting soup kitchens and sewing classes.[46] As Villiers told Gladstone, the Chancellor of the Exchequer,

> It would be most unwise on the part of the Government, at this moment, to favour any expectation of a Parliamentary Grant being made – it would in the first place stay this marvellous flow of general charity, which is steadily increasing and which is proving, together with the resources available under the Poor Law, to be ample for the occasion ... The Guardians at present have ample funds at their disposal [and] the funds in the hands of Voluntary Committees are being distributed with method, and will be more so each week as their plans become better matured.[47]

Neither did Villiers regard assisted emigration schemes as a viable response to distress in the cotton districts. As he observed in 1863,

> when we know the large amount of capital in the country, and the great increase of it, and are also cognisant of the demand for labour a few years since, I do not think it would be wise of the Government to expend public money in the provision of emigration,[48]

a statement which re-affirmed the scepticism about the value of rate-aided pauper emigration schemes which Villiers had first espoused as an Assistant Commissioner in 1832–4.

Third, and in the immediate aftermath of short-lived disturbances at Stalybridge, Ashton, Hyde and Dukenfield in March 1863,[49] Villiers despatched the experienced civil engineer, Robert Rawlinson, to Lancashire to consider the feasibility of establishing public works schemes to provide distressed operatives with employment. Rawlinson had originally been appointed a Government Inspector under the Public Health Act of 1848, and his specific mandate was to ascertain the general condition and sanitary arrangements of the towns, the state of their streets, their drainage and water supply, and provisions for parks and pleasure grounds for popular recreation and to 'form an opinion as to the works of utility which could be executed ... both in the improvement of the towns and the employment of the distressed operatives at a fair rate of wages'.[50] Rawlinson duly reported that although there were difficulties to be overcome by local authorities, 'a vast amount of useful work may be beneficially undertaken, and be executed by the best of the distressed men out of employment'.[51] In June 1863, in light of Rawlinson's recommendations, which were supported by the Central Relief Committee at Manchester, Villiers introduced the Public Works (Manufacturing Districts) Bill before the Commons, which was passed in July.[52] This enabled poor-law unions to borrow money, on security of the rates, from the public works loans commissioners for up to thirty years at three and a half per cent interest for the employment of distressed operatives in the construction of various public works schemes. Between 1863 and 1865, over ninety unions subsequently borrowed almost £2 millions in developing such schemes, which included the building of roads, waterworks, sewerage works, cemeteries and recreation grounds, at wages (as opposed to poor-law relief) of around 12s per week (the normal rate for the job). By March 1864, almost 5,000 men were engaged on such schemes and, although this represented but a small proportion of those unemployed (and of the 70,000 operatives whom Villiers had hoped might eventually be relieved in this way), this was nevertheless an innovatory development, foreshadowing some late-nineteenth and twentieth-century responses to mass unemployment.[53] Villiers' efforts were praised by his friend and fellow-Liberal MP, William Torrens, in his treatise of 1864, *Lancashire's Lesson; or the need of a settled Policy in Times of Exceptional Distress*. Torrens, whilst recommending the introduction of an additional Poor Law code to deal with the relief of distress in exceptional circumstances in future, and suggesting that had this been available to Villiers in 1861 the cotton famine could have been more promptly addressed,[54] lauded Villiers for his 'political capital and courage ... in dealing with a concatenation of perplexities for which public policy had made no provision'.[55]

The American Civil War was eventually concluded in April 1865 and cotton supplies were duly restored. When the final meeting of the Lancashire Central Relief Committee was held in June 1865, *The Economist* was moved to comment that the event 'was a legitimate occasion for something more than national rejoicing', adding 'Mr Villiers deserves no little credit, as the Relief Committee were not slow to remark, alike for the conception of the Public Works Act and for the energy and economy with which its details have been carried out'.[56] Moreover, as *The Economist* observed, the Act had provided a major boost to sanitary reform in Lancashire, with 200 miles of streets 'sewered, formed, paved, channelled and flagged', and thereby 'raising the moral standard of the labouring population of our richest county to a new level of decency, respectability, and comfort'.[57]

For Villiers, however, the success of his measures had been overshadowed temporarily by the death on 2 April of his old friend Richard Cobden, who, as Anthony Howe has observed, had sought 'to refurbish his old rapport with his aristocratic coadjutor, C.P. Villiers'.[58] Indeed, in his last letter to Villiers in November 1864, Cobden, then confined to his bed with a bad cold, had welcomed Villiers' 'wise and cheerful views of the future' and, in addition to making some witty observations about the current preoccupation of Gladstone and Disraeli with ecclesiastical questions, had stressed the need for the government to more carefully monitor its finances, since it was only the great expansion of trade and the price of wheat at 40s. that had enabled the government to set the present revenue out of the taxpayers, which *'may not last'*.[59] In his reply, the last communication between the two men, Villiers expressed his concern for Cobden's health, endorsed Cobden's emphasis on the need for economy, and viewed with some distaste the current preoccupation with ecclesiastical matters.[60] Four months later, on 2 April 1865, Cobden died at the age of sixty-one at his Dunford home following an attack of asthma and bronchitis, and on 7 April Villiers attended Cobden's funeral at Lavington, acting as a pall-bearer alongside Bright, Gladstone and Milner Gibson.[61]

In the aftermath of the Lancashire Cotton Famine, Gladstone wrote to Villiers informing him that he had received a request from Robert Rawlinson to be honoured by the Crown in recognition of his efforts in implementing the Public Works Act in Lancashire, and asking for Villiers' opinion on the subject. Villiers replied in support not only of Rawlinson's claim but also on behalf of Mr Farnall, stating:

> I am of opinion that Mr Rawlinson is well entitled to some such honour ... for the valuable services he rendered during the period of the cotton distress, and especially when it is remembered how long Mr Rawlinson has been employed by the Government and how invariably he has given the greatest satisfaction from the manner in which he has performed his work. When the Central Relief Committee met it applauded the work of Mr Rawlinson and Mr Farnall and expressed their obligation to the Government for having appointed such men to assist them ... I feel indebted to Mr Farnall and Mr Rawlinson for the great and good judgment they displayed in giving effect to the means adopted by the Government to meet the calamity which fell upon the Cotton Districts.[62]

Villiers added that he had also received letters from persons of consequence stating that it was felt that the Government should in some way recognise the services of Rawlinson and Farnall, and that he had mentioned this in July to Lord Palmerston, who had said that he should recommend the Queen to confer the honour of CB [Companion of the Most Honourable Order of the Bath] on each of them, although nothing had since transpired, either because

Palmerston had not had an opportunity of doing so, or that it had escaped his memory, and asked Gladstone to again raise the matter with the Prime Minister. Villiers added that Rawlinson had also approached him about the possibility of a knighthood, but expressed doubt to Gladstone as to the propriety of 'having men keen for such honours conferred upon them', an opinion which Gladstone evidently shared.[63] In the event, the award of CB was duly granted to both men later in the year, and a knighthood was eventually awarded to Rawlinson in 1888.

Concurrent with the relief crises in London and Lancashire, Villiers also addressed a range of important issues relating to the laws of settlement and removal, and poor-law rating. Villiers upheld the system of compulsory relief which the New Poor Law of 1834 had established as 'a matter no less of wisdom than of humanity' on the grounds that

> in a densely peopled country like this there must always be a greater number of persons who, from a variety of circumstances – from sickness, infirmity, and bad habits of life – must be in danger of experiencing the extreme consequences of want.[64]

However, he believed that the system required further revision and reform. In particular, he acknowledged that in 1834 the Poor Law Commissioners had wished to dispense with the parochial liability for maintaining the poor, and to have Union administration and Union chargeability commensurate. Much to the Commissioners' disappointment, however, this had been opposed by many influential ratepayers who were not prepared to contribute a greater financial burden than they had formerly. Hence the Poor Law Union fund, the common fund, which was collected by the Guardians from the parishes in proportion to the number of paupers in each parish, had remained distinct from various parochial funds, administered by the parish overseers, which were only applicable to their settled poor. The Select Committee on the Irremovable Poor of 1860, which Villiers chaired, examined that section of the removal laws which prevented the removal of paupers who had lived for five years or more in a parish and recommended that, although the law was operating to the benefit of the poor, not only should the period of residence for irremovability be reduced to three years, but also that the area of residence should be the poor law union rather than the parish, and that pauper orphans should inherit the status of irremovability of their parents.[65]

These recommendations were enshrined in Villiers' Irremoveable Poor Bill, which faced considerable opposition in Parliament. As Villiers later recalled to Sir George Nicholls,

> The two difficulties which had to be contended with in Parliament were the sinister interests (dead against this change), always active and vigilant, and the indifference or disinclination to anything that caused dissatisfaction

to some people on our own side, together with the distaste of the House to these subjects generally, unless connected with party objects.[66]

The Irremovable Poor Act of 1861 duly reduced the period required to claim irremovability from five to three years; the union rather than the parish became the area of residence; and in order to protect poorer parishes, contributions to the common fund were calculated according to the rateable value of parishes rather than their expenditure on poor relief. Clearly relieved, Villiers told Nicholls,

> I may now, however, say how much satisfaction it has given me to think that the very great trouble that I took to get that Bill through meets with the approval of the *father* of the new system under which the Poor Laws are now administered ... as a valuable instalment towards the completion of that more perfect arrangement which he had from the very first advocated.[67]

These reforms were extended by the Union Assessment Committee Act of 1862, which directed Poor Law Unions to set up committees to establish new valuations, thereby achieving a more uniform rating system. The Union Chargeability Act of 1865 completed the process by repealing the provision in the Poor Law Amendment Act of 1834 which had made poor relief a parochial charge and by transferring the whole cost of poor relief to the union common fund. The Act also reduced the period for claiming irremovability to one year.[68]

In introducing his Union Chargeability Bill in the House of Commons on 20 February 1865, Villiers stated that the purpose of the measure was to provide for a better distribution of the charge for the relief of the poor in Unions, adding that, contrary to popular rumours, the object was not to abolish the Laws of Settlement and Removal, a gratuitous assumption which was not made upon the authority of any member of the Government. In providing an historical context for the Bill, Villiers referred to 'the dreadful conditions in the workhouses in the past, which had provoked the agricultural revolts of 1830 in the South of England' and, as Jasper Ridley once observed, this observation was met with a stony silence from Palmerston, 'a relic of the age which had accepted these conditions as desirable and inevitable', who sat alongside Villiers on the Treasury bench.[69] He informed the House, however, that the Irremovable Poor Act of 1861 had created 'a sort of revolution in the whole system of rating the property and of relieving the poor of the parish',[70] with such remarkable results – including a reduction in the number of removals, an increase in the number of irremoveable poor, and the increased augmentation of the common fund – that he now felt justified in requesting the House to make further changes in the same direction, particularly in view of the continued existence of

> malpractices and measures adopted by parishes for reducing their liability, such as that of driving the poor from their own into adjoining parishes,

and the many evil results of that system, and which fall upon the poor in consequence. These have been frequently the subject of complaint both in this House and in the columns of the press, and it is known that many parishes have been overburdened with poor driven there by others to escape their fair share of the burden. This is owing to the parochial chargeability having been continued in deference to the opinions and interests of persons in this House.[71]

Villiers proposed therefore 'that the union fund shall in future be made available for the maintenance of all the poor within the union', adding that 'I propose to extend the area of charge from the parish to the union – and thus to make the charge commensurate with the administration'.[72] In justifying this proposal, Villiers drew particular attention to the experience of the Docking Union of Norfolk, where the Guardians had been unanimous and had formed all parishes into one Union in 1849, as a result of which the average expenditure on relief had been reduced substantially,

> an experience which literally verifies what those who had advocated the systems of uniting the parishes of a union for rating and settlement felt must be the result of its operation, and this experience of fifteen years is a very strong recommendation of the general measure which I now propose.[73]

A reform of poor law administration along these lines, he held,

> is likely to result in even greater advantage, seeing the numerous evils that will be removed by it, seeing what benefits it may confer upon the poor, and in promoting good feeling between labourer and employer, between tenant and landlord, between servant and master, by removing from their mind considerations that spring out of the present system.[74]

In addition, Villiers recommended that the period for claiming irremovability be reduced further, from three years to one year. This recommendation sought in part to address the vexed issue of the removal of Irish paupers from England to Ireland, a subject which had consistently provoked discussion in the House of Commons in the years following the Irish Famine, in light of specific examples of Irish paupers being treated with harshness and inhumanity by local Boards of Guardians in their removal to Ireland.[75] In March 1860, for example, Mr Lanigan, an Irish MP, cited several cases of Irish men and women who, although having lived and worked in England for many years but having now become chargeable on their parish, had been removed back to Ireland, concluding:

> It was extremely cruel that honest, hard-working Irish labourers should toil in this country all their lives ... and then, when poverty and sickness

overtook them, they should be looked upon by their English employers only as so much worn-out machinery, fit only to be cast away. It was shocking to see the steam-vessels which left Ireland laden with cattle and sheep return laden with living skeletons – Irish labourers who, having become chargeable to the parish were torn away from their homes sick and helpless, and hurried on board; whence, after enduring exposure on the decks for days and nights, they were landed on the quays in utter destitution.[76]

Further examples of inhumane removals, including that of Patrick Bourke, an elderly Irishman who had been removed from Leeds workhouse to Westport whilst suffering from bronchitis and diarrhoea, were also raised in the Commons by Lord John Browne, who was moved to comment:

In nearly every manufacturing town in the North of England, and in many of the country districts, there are large numbers of labourers, tradesmen, or work-people in the factories, who, though no doubt Irish by birth, have left that country, with all their friends and families, thirty, forty, or fifty years ago, who during the whole of that time had been labouring to increase the wealth of England ... but who, when they are at last overtaken by old age or infirmity, or disabled by accident, are, as Bourke described it, 'hurled out without mercy'. The English pride themselves on being a humane and just people, but I ask is this humanity or justice?[77]

However, Villiers, who was only too aware of the problems associated with Irish poverty in the Caribee Island district of his own constituency of Wolverhampton,[78] informed the House that of late years 'there had been an earnest wish on the part of the Legislature to mitigate the hardships attending the removal of the Irish poor',[79] and that from 1863 poor law overseers had been obliged by law to convey Irish paupers humanely to the union house nearest to their destination on pain of a £10 fine or six month's imprisonment. He held, therefore, that cases such as that of Patrick Bourke – and, indeed, of Mary Moriarty and Julia Hannon, who had been conveyed on deck from Greenwich Union to Cork in December 1864[80] – were due to violations of poor law regulations by local boards rather than defects in existing laws and should be investigated, and if necessary, prosecuted by the authorities. Moreover, Villiers observed that as a result of the Irremovable Poor Act, not merely thousands, but tens of thousands of Irish had been spared removal from the distressed districts in Lancashire and Yorkshire in 1862–3,[81] and noted that the total number of removals to Ireland had been reduced substantially, from 10,308 in 1858 to 1,212 in 1862, whilst removals from Liverpool alone had fallen from 5,043 in 1856 to fewer than 20 in 1864.[82] Thus Villiers held that a further reduction of the period for claiming irremovability from three years to one year would greatly assist in redressing the issue of Irish pauper removals.[83] The aim of the government was, he claimed, to render the law more humane in the case of Irish pauper removals and he anticipated the Union Chargeability Bill, when enacted, would 'put an end to the removal of the Irish poor altogether'.[84]

The parliamentary debate on the Bill lasted for four months. In March 1865, Sir John Trelawny, the Liberal MP for Tavistock, noted in his diary that Villiers made 'a long & able speech', adding that

> He appeared to be ill – his voice being even weaker than usual & he had a suspicious cough. I fear we shall lose him. However, standing up nobly agt. Fate, he did a good work in the interests of the Poor and unprotected.

However, Villiers' speech appeared to irritate his cabinet colleague, William Gladstone. As Trelawny recalled,

> Failing to hear Villiers' voice where I sat, I went into the gallery opposite to him. Grey sat on one side of V. and Gladstone on Villiers' right hand, leaning back with his eyes upturned & with a certain expression of wearied impatience, which Gladstone, when not in action, has. Villiers was rather humorously adverting to the obstacles always thrown in the way of Reforms by men who harp upon the want of 'more time', 'more facts, more opportunity for deliberation generally', meaning some form of ignorance, indolence or interest – tho' not always. At this moment, a smile of pity, or contempt, or derision played on Gladstone's features, as much as to say, 'what a hopeless task it is to battle with stupidity!' It strikes me [Trelawny] that Genius shd. be tolerant, or not to make stupidity more obstinate by intolerance even in a look.[85]

The Union Chargeability Bill duly cleared the House of Commons, but Villiers, aware of potential opposition in the House of Lords, wrote to his old friend Walter Bagehot, the editor of *The Economist*, requesting his support and enclosing

> a memorandum relating to the memorable Poor Law Bill which after much difficulty has just passed the Commons, but which is now probably in jeopardy in the House of Lords owing to the same interested objects that obstructed its progress in the Commons

and asking Bagehot to insert 'a few lines in the paper favourable to the measure, believing it would be of use while the Bill was under discussion in the Lords'.[86] As Paul Brighton has observed, Charles Villiers was only too aware of the power of the press and was no stranger to press manipulation, having once told Richard Cobden that the press 'was not a self-acting machine and wants, as the Yankees would say, an almighty power of grease to set it going', and needed to be kept on message with appropriate information.[87] Indeed,

Villiers had often fed information to J.T. Delane at *The Times* and was, in fact, through his family connections, part of an influential network of politicians and journalists. His sister, Maria Theresa, had married Sir George Cornewall Lewis, variously Chancellor of the Exchequer (1855–58), Home Secretary and Minister of War (1859–63) under Palmerston and editor of the *Edinburgh Review*; Maria Theresa's daughter, Alice (Villiers' niece) later married (in 1870) Algernon Borthwick (Tory MP for South Kensington, 1885–95, who was raised to the peerage in 1895 as Baron Glenesk), who succeeded his father, Peter Borthwick (a staunch supporter of Palmerston), as editor of the *Morning Post*; whilst Alice's sister, Theresa, had married (in 1859) Sir William Vernon Harcourt, a leader-writer for *The Times* and, later, leader of the Liberals in the House of Commons.[88] Accordingly, and despite some opposition in the Lords,[89] the Union Chargeability Bill was passed on 29 June 1865 and its provisions came into force on 25 March 1866.[90]

The final measure for which Villiers deserved credit whilst President of the Poor Law Board was the Metropolitan Poor Law Act of 1867, which Villiers had largely prepared in 1865–6 but which was carried through Parliament by his successor, Gathorne Hardy. Villiers was only too aware of the problem of metropolitan poverty and had discussed this at a private meeting with Queen Victoria in March 1864,[91] and the condition and administration of London's workhouses, described in the *First Report of the Select Committee on Poor Relief* of 1861, became a matter of public concern in December 1864, when a twenty-eight-year-old Irish railway navvy, Timothy Daly, died in St Bartholomew's Hospital after having been removed there from Holborn Workhouse, where he had been admitted in November with rheumatism. The inquest attributed his death to rheumatic fever and putrid bedsores caused by filthy conditions and gross neglect by the medical officer in the workhouse. The press took up the case, with leading articles in *The Times*[92] and *The Spectator*, which observed that

> the condition of these pauper hospitals has before this attracted attention, and if the smallest inventiveness remained in the Whig government this would long since have been remedied. A workhouse ought not to be a pleasant place, but we may at least care for the sick without danger that people will give themselves painful diseases,[93]

and public scandal followed.[94]

In light of these developments, Florence Nightingale took the opportunity to contact Charles Villiers at the Poor Law Board, stating that the Daly case showed the need for improvements in nursing in workhouse infirmaries and asking if he would like to know about developments at the Brownlow Hill Workhouse Infirmary in Liverpool, where a matron and trained nurses from the Nightingale Training School had been employed since 1861 in collaboration with the Liverpool philanthropist, William Rathbone.[95] Villiers, who, according to Cecil Woodham Smith's classic (but now dated) biography of

Nightingale, 'was a champion of people's rights, his manner was charming, and his powers of conversation were considered unequalled',[96] replied immediately, indicating that he wished to meet her in person and discuss matters.[97] Villiers visited Nightingale in January 1865, and this proved to be the first of a series of personal and written communications between them over the next few years. Indeed, Sir Edward Cook claimed in his biography of Florence Nightingale that

> Her powers inspired him [Villiers] with intense admiration ... bursting out to a friend after he had received one of her memoranda: 'I delight to read the Nightingale's song about it all. If any one of them had a tenth part of her vigour of mind we might expect something.'[98]

Nightingale duly urged Villiers to use the Daly case as an opportunity to instigate an inquiry into the whole question of the treatment of the sick poor and in February 1865 Villiers asked H.B. Farnall, the Poor Law Inspector for the Metropolitan District, to visit Nightingale and discuss matters further, as a result of which it was agreed to instigate an investigation by circulating a 'Form of Enquiry' to all workhouse infirmaries and sick wards in the Metropolis. Cook claimed that, although Villiers 'was becoming an old man ... had many other things to think about, and was apt to see lions in the path', he was, unlike some officials at the Poor Law Board, thoroughly committed to reform and promptly authorised Farnall to impress upon the Guardians the importance of employing competent, trained nurses rather than untrained paupers for attending to the sick in workhouse infirmaries.[99] Villiers also informed the House of Commons in May that he was hopeful that great reforms in nursing might come about.[100]

The *Lancet* also took up the case and in July 1865 appointed a special commission (the Sanitary Commission for Investigating the State of the Infirmaries of Workhouses), comprising Drs Hart, Anstie and Carr, to investigate the state of Metropolitan workhouse infirmaries. Their report revealed an appalling state of affairs in the thirty-nine London workhouses which they visited, with overcrowded and unsanitary wards and inadequate nursing, and it was observed that 22,700 of the 31,000 inmates were officially sick, infirm or insane, with a further 6,000, though nominally fit, either crippled or diseased in some way. 'The state hospitals', they concluded, 'are in workhouse wards'.[101]

In the meantime, the returns to the Poor Law Board's 'Form of enquiry' revealed a startling state of affairs and during the Autumn of 1865 Nightingale developed a scheme for the treatment of the sick poor which could be first applied in London and then extended to other Poor Law Unions. This scheme was based on three basic criteria, which she termed the A B C of workhouse reform: (A) The sick, insane, incurable and children must be dealt with separately in proper institutions and not mixed together in infirmaries and sick wards, as at present: 'once acknowledge this principle and you must have suitable establishments for the cure of the sick and infirm'; (B) There should be a single central administration: 'The entire Medical Relief of London should be under one central management'; (C) Suitable treatment would be expensive and could not be carried by parochial rates, which might lead to jobbery in the appointment of trained staff, hence 'Consolidation and a General Rate are essential'.[102] Villiers received this memorandum in December and, as Farnall duly reported to Nightingale, 'he [Villiers] has decided on adopting your scheme. He thinks it will be popular and just, and I think so also',[103] and in February 1866 Villiers informed Lord Cranborne (Salisbury) that he intended to introduce a Metropolitan Poor Law Bill as soon as possible.[104]

In March 1866, a voluntary Association for the Improvement of the Infirmaries of London Workhouses was formed, with an executive committee which included the Earl of Carnarvon, Lord Cranborne, Lord Shaftesbury and the Archbishop of York, and which was supported by Charles Dickens, Walter Bagehot, Thomas Hughes and John Stuart Mill. In April 1866, Villiers cordially received a deputation from the Association and assured them that legislation might be expected almost immediately. Delane of *The Times* also took up the cause. Following this meeting, Villiers also initiated an investigation into the arrangements for the sick poor in metropolitan workhouses by Farnall and Dr Edward Smith, a medical practitioner who had been appointed by Villiers to the Poor Law Board in February, to inspect all infirmaries in London, and their report was finally submitted to the House of Commons in June.[105] However, although Villiers, Farnall and Smith continued to liaise with Nightingale, the government was now tottering. Moreover, workhouse infirmary reform was a controversial subject and fresh contentious legislation was thought unadvisable, hence the government delayed on the Bill. As Nightingale observed in a letter to Harriet Martineau in May 1866:

> We have been in a fever lately because Ministers were hovering between in and out ... Mr Villiers promised us a Bill quite early in the year for a London uniform poor rate for the sick and consolidated hospitals under a central management (this was before we got our Earls and Archbishops and MPs together to storm him in his den). We shall not get one Bill this Session, for Mr Villiers is afraid of losing the government one vote. But we shall certainly get it in time.[106]

Subsequently, even after his departure from the Poor Law Board following the fall of Russell's Government in June, Charles Villiers continued to support Nightingale, who immediately approached Gathorne Hardy (appointed on 12 July as Villiers' successor), although he replied with a discouraging letter which stated that he was 'very much occupied with other business', although he 'would bear in mind the offer you have made and in all probability avail myself of it to the full'.[107] Hardy was reluctant to be seen to complete the work begun by Villiers and did not wish to appear unduly influenced by

Nightingale, who was kept out of further discussions. Hardy also claimed that the problems of the metropolitan infirmaries were too much for one inspector and unceremoniously removed Mr Farnall from the Metropolitan District to Yorkshire, where he remained until 1870, whilst in private communicating regularly with Nightingale and criticising the Poor Law Board.[108]

Hardy also implied in the House of Commons in October that had Villiers, when President of the Poor Law Board, 'only known how to use, with dexterity and wisdom, the weapon of the law, he would have found it a very sufficient weapon' and that fresh legislation was unnecessary. This apparently made Villiers 'frantically angry', since he had devoted his time at the Board to framing new legislation and took this as a personal attack on himself. He wrote to Nightingale, indicating that he was determined 'not to sit down under this kind of thing', that he would 'catch Mr Gathorne Hardy out', and emphasized that something more was needed to reform Poor Law administration than 'a touch of Mr Gathorne Hardy's magic wand to set all things straight'.[109] According to Cook, Villiers thereafter 'corresponded with her [Nightingale] at great length, saw her repeatedly, reported all he was able to learn of how things were going at Whitehall, and begged her to do the like for him'.[110] Lynn McDonald has made a similar observation: 'He [Villiers] responded with alacrity and became a key collaborator, indeed continuing to work with Nightingale behind the scenes, writing from his home address when he was "turned out."'[111] Nightingale subsequently informed Edwin Chadwick on 28 October that:

> I have had a great deal of clandestine correspondence with my old loves at the Poor Law Board this last two months. The belief among the old loves is that the new master is bent on – doing nothing. There is only one thing of which I am quite sure. And that is that Mr Villiers will lead Mr Gathorne Hardy a merry dance.[112]

Hardy duly appointed a committee of sanitary and medical experts (which excluded Nightingale) to report on Workhouse Infirmaries, and although Nightingale, in a private letter, forwarded to Hardy the scheme that Villiers had supported previously, he failed to respond. However, on 8 February 1867 he introduced his Metropolitan Poor Bill into the House of Commons. Although the Bill fell short of what Villiers and Nightingale had originally envisaged, it nevertheless still owed much to Nightingale's ABC scheme.[113] Villiers wrote immediately to Nightingale asking 'I should amazingly like to hear what you say to this seven months' child born in the Whitehall Workhouse', but admitting that it would at least 'set the ball rolling',[114] and, speaking in the House of Commons on 21 February, Villiers duly paid tribute to Nightingale's contribution to reform, for she had 'pressed upon them [the Poor Law Board] the great importance of training those who attended upon the sick in the workhouse infirmaries'.[115]

Passed in March 1867 as an epidemic of scarlet fever spread across London, the Metropolitan Poor Act gave the central authority – the Metropolitan Asylums Board, composed of guardians and officials – the power to provide separate asylums for the sick, insane and infirm in London workhouses and provided a Metropolitan Common Poor Fund to which Unions and parishes in the metropolitan area contributed according to their rateable value, which supported the maintenance of the sick poor. As Michael Rose has observed, 'The principle had been established that the sick poor required specialist treatment [and] the evolution from workhouse infirmary to municipal hospital had begun'.[116] Florence Nightingale was disappointed by the half-measures in the 1867 Act because it only *enabled* rather than enforced improved nursing in workhouse infirmaries. Nevertheless, according to Lynn McDonald, Nightingale's latest biographer, the introduction of nurses into the workhouse infirmaries was 'perhaps the most significant of Nightingale's achievements' because workhouse infirmaries were the hospitals for the vast majority of the population, the sick poor who could not afford to pay for care, and Nightingale believed that many of them should not be there at all and that with effective nursing their condition could be ameliorated.[117]

During his final months in office, Villiers also assisted Russell and Gladstone in preparations for further parliamentary reform, for it fell to the Poor Law Board to prepare the electoral statistics upon which a Reform Bill would be based. This was an appropriate task for Villiers to undertake, for he had undertaken a similar responsibility in 1860, in preparation for Russell's abortive Reform Bill of March 1860,[118] and had also, in strict privacy, acted as a conduit between the government and the Tories on the reform question.[119] Thereafter, the Cabinet decided to postpone further measures,[120] although, as E.D. Steele has shown, Villiers had kept in touch with Radicals outside the government – including John Bright – during the debates in the Cabinet on parliamentary reform and remained optimistic in regard to future prospects for reform. Villiers reminded Bright, who was frustrated by the apparent apathy of the country on the reform question, that Ministers were fully aware of middle-class opinion on reform, adding that 'the social relations between classes are more than usually friendly [and] it is quite clear that there is nothing in the popular principle in England, as its development proceeds, that is at all subversive in its character'.[121] Villiers also held that the prevalence of authoritarian regimes in many European States and the problems of American democracy meant that Britain was 'After all ... the freest ... wealthiest ... most orderly and progressive nation on earth', and entreated Bright 'to draw it mild ... we should all march together and not divide society into hostile classes believing that causes for permanent antagonism exist'.[122]

As Roland Quinault has shown, popular agitation for parliamentary reform had been somewhat tardy and intermittent during the mid-Victorian period, with progress delayed largely by external factors such as the Crimean War, the Indian Mutiny, the Chinese Wars and the American Civil War.[123] However, by 1865 the need for electoral reform was clearly evident, for the population of England and Wales had risen to more than five millions, yet the number of adult male voters was less than one million, and, whilst the size and geographical distribution of an increasingly urban population had changed since 1832, corresponding changes in the distribution of seats, for which both Liberals and Tories held vested interests,[124] had not occurred. The impetus towards further reform during the 1860s was enhanced by the growth of the trade union movement amongst the labour aristocracy of skilled workers, whose contacts with Radical MPs influenced the establishment of both the Reform Union in 1864, which demanded complete household suffrage, and the Reform League of 1865, which sought universal male suffrage. Moreover, the victory of the North in the Civil War, popularly regarded in Britain as a battle between democracy and slavery, had itself provided an important external stimulus to Liberal demands for further reform, as had the visit of Garibaldi to London in April 1864, when he was received by the Cabinet, including Charles Villiers.[125] Within the Liberal Party, the greatest obstacle to reform had been the presence of Lord Palmerston; however, with his death in October 1865 the Cabinet was now in a position to make a serious commitment to parliamentary reform. Moreover, Lord John Russell, Prime Minister in the House of Lords, wished to give his name to a Reform Bill in his declining years, whilst Gladstone, Leader of the House of Commons, had also accepted the need for reform, famously stating in the Commons that every male 'who is not presumably incapacitated by some consideration of personal unfitness or of political danger, is morally entitled to come within the pale of the constitution',[126] a view which Charles Villiers had already espoused many years earlier.[127] Indeed, there was a growing acceptance among reformers that large sections of the working class were now sufficiently fit, in terms of attitude, education and culture, to be brought within the pale of the constitution. The key question in regard to franchise extension among MPs, many of whom had been born and brought up in the shadow of the French Revolution, and who were averse to sudden and sweeping measures, was how to make the system more representative rather than democratic, and where to draw the line between 'respectable' working men, who were fit to vote, and the 'residuum', who were not (hence the contemporary conundrum as to whether rating or renting criteria should be adopted in extending the franchise).[128]

Taylor has noted that, as an 'Advanced Liberal' in the Russell administration, Villiers sided with Gladstone, Gibson and the Duke of Argyll in attempting to secure a timetable for a genuine political settlement,[129] and in preparing and submitting the electoral statistics, with the assistance of John Lambert,[130] Villiers communicated closely with Gladstone, who praised Villiers for his 'interesting and important papers ... prepared with so much promptitude'.[131] This had not been an easy task, for in some towns the number of working-class £10 occupiers suggested by the Poor Law returns was surprisingly large and at variance with census returns and local intelligence,[132] which Gladstone attributed to the possibility that middle-class feeling against the extension of the franchise had influenced the Clerks of Unions who made the returns.[133] Nevertheless, Gladstone duly introduced his Bill in the House of Commons in March 1866. This was a moderate measure which excluded proposals in regard to redistribution but which sought to extend the franchise to £7 householders in the boroughs (instead of £10) and to tenants paying £14 per annum rent in the counties (instead of £50), thereby increasing the total electorate by some 400,000 voters. The political controversy which ensued has been well documented.[134]

The Bill met with lively opposition in the Commons, not only from Disraeli and the Tories but also from a group of Liberals, led by Robert Lowe, a noted educational reformer and architect of the Revised Code, who feared that the Bill went too far. Indeed, Lowe, as Asa Briggs has shown, feared democracy and held not only that the chief characteristics of the working-classes were 'venality, ignorance and drunkenness', but also that their enfranchisement would lead to bribery, intimidation and mob rule.[135] In supporting the Bill, Charles Villiers, in a lengthy but eloquent speech, which showed that he still retained the radical fervour of his youth, launched a withering attack on Lowe, exposing fully the weaknesses in his arguments:

> What weight is to be attached to all the terrors he [Lowe] has been seeking to awaken in our minds, traceable, strictly and especially according to him, to lowering the elective franchise? He sees in this measure the fatal tendency to Democracy … But I ask why he dreads that, and if he does, what he has been about himself for some years past and what has this House been doing with his entire sanction? Why, that which is most calculated to level the distinction that exists between different classes of society, or rather, between the poor and the rich. What are the great distinctions in society? Are they not those founded on ignorance and poverty on one side, and wealth and knowledge on the other? What has he been urging forward himself especially but the education of the people, and who knows better than the right hon. Gentleman that he has not used a single argument against Parliamentary Reform this evening that has not been used in former times against the education of the working classes?[136]

Villiers stated that the fears that Lowe believed would follow from parliamentary reform were merely speculative, adding

> I advise him to look at the facts before him before he jumps to conclusions again in the way he has done, and he will then discover abundant proofs of late years afforded of the good conduct, patience, and forbearance of the working people that will make him wonder at the chimeras he has conjured up, and almost ashamed of the unjust reproaches he has put upon them. The moment chosen, indeed, for casting a slur upon the working people of this country for their want of conduct, honesty, or intelligence is most unfortunate.[137]

Then, after what amounted to a veritable history lesson on parliamentary reform, reminding the House of all the false arguments that had been used against reform since 1832, Villiers stated that he had endeavoured to show that the people were entitled to the confidence of the House, and above all to the fulfilment of the promises deliberately made to them, concluding 'If we lose the very great advantage which the present opportunity offers to us of passing such a measure, we are totally disregarding the lessons which history and our own personal experience offer to us'.[138]

The Bill passed on its second reading but with a majority of only five, thereby clearly lacking credibility, for thirty-five Liberals had voted with the Tories against the Government. John Bright duly described Lowe and his supporters as 'The Adullamites' (a biblical reference to the discontented Israelites who deserted Saul to join David in the Cave of Adullam). Charles Villiers, whilst lamenting 'the blow with which we have been hit by the defection of our friends', held that at least the Bill had offered 'further proof that the Government have been, and still are, in earnest about Reform', and urged Gladstone to continue to fight for reform and to expose their opponents 'to the country in their true colours, as enemies of Reform'.[139] In May, Gladstone decided to try again, this time by introducing a combined Franchise and Redistribution Bill, which would have marginally affected redistribution in only forty-nine seats, but on 18 June, the Bill was defeated on amendment (proposed by Lord Dunkellin) by 315 votes to 304, with forty-four Adullamites voting with the opposition. As Villiers observed, 'The amendment was devised for the real purpose of enabling those who dreaded the enfranchisement of the working classes to defeat the Bill without committing themselves to a direct hostility to reform'.[140]

In Villiers' own constituency of Wolverhampton, where he had campaigned in support of the Bill, the defeat of the Government was greeted with dismay by local Liberals. Here, as Jon Lawrence has shown in his detailed study of Wolverhampton politics during the Victorian period, the shape of local politics was changing. Hitherto, Wolverhampton Liberalism had been controlled largely by a small group of wealthy manufacturers, merchants and professionals in an 'informal if impenetrable oligarchy known as the Liberal Committee'.[141] During the 1850s and early 1860s this Liberal elite had drawn criticism not only from local Radicals (not least for using their influence to obtain lucrative appointments in local government, including the magistracy and the municipal corporation), but also from Villiers and Thornely, who shared a mutual dislike of demands for preferment. When Sir Richard Bethell vacated his seat in 1861 on his appointment as Lord Chancellor, the Liberal Committee chose Thomas Matthias Weguelin,[142] formerly MP for Southampton and Governor of the Bank of England, as his successor.[143] This aroused the ire of local Radicals, who held that MPs were being brought in from outside by the town's Liberal elite and 'Baron Sam' Griffiths, a wealthy ironmaster, put himself forward against Weguelin as an independent Liberal who, as a local man, could promote the interests of the whole town rather than those of the Committee. Although Weguelin was returned with a majority of 591, the Election reflected growing Radical concern in Wolverhampton with the narrow base and conservative character of local Liberalism.[144]

In particular, working-class radicalism had made considerable progress due to the rapid growth and increasing politicisation of trade societies, and the Wolverhampton Trades Council and the Working Men's Reform Committee, established in March 1866, had mounted a vociferous campaign in support of Gladstone's Bill.[145] In April, Villiers, who had earlier promised his constituents that he would 'secure those privileges which are at present so unjustly held from them',[146] submitted a petition in support of the Reform Bill to Parliament on behalf of the Reform Committee. Indeed, at a Reform meeting held in St George's Hall, Villiers was praised for his efforts to promote the cause of reform and he duly thanked those present at the meeting 'for the flattering manner in which you referred to my humble efforts in seeking to promote the interests of the people', adding that 'It does, I assure you, inspire the representative with fresh courage, a fresh confidence in the justice of his cause, when he knows that his conduct is watched by constituents so competent and so ready to appreciate his intentions'.[147] In June, the Reform Committee reconstituted itself as the Working Men's Liberal Association, with a mandate to take the battle for reform into the factories and workshops and to affiliate with the newly formed and London-based National Reform League, which mounted a strong extra-parliamentary campaign to secure universal male suffrage and the secret ballot.[148] On 23 June, at an open-air meeting of the Wolverhampton branch of the WMLA, chaired by William Parkes and attended by some two thousand people, it was resolved to send a petition to the Queen demanding a dissolution of Parliament and an appeal to the country, whereby the people could declare their opinion on the Reform Question. The meeting was highly critical of the Adullamites, and it was stated that at the next election, the choice should be between the cry of 'Gladstone and Reform' or 'Lowe and no Reform'. Mr E. Davies, a tin-plate worker, moved a vote of thanks to Charles Villiers and Thomas Weguelin for their sincere support of the Reform Bill. Of Villiers, he stated 'Mr Villiers was a man whom the inhabitants of Wolverhampton had tried and proved for many years, and they were all proud of him', adding that 'throughout the country he was acknowledged as one of those earnest champions of the rights and liberties of the labouring classes (Hear, Hear)'.[149] Similar sentiments were expressed at a further meeting of the WWMLA at Willenhall in July, which noted that Villiers had told the Association that 'they would triumph if the people stood firm', and moved a resolution expressing its unqualified approval of the conduct of Villiers and Weguelin during the Reform struggle.[150]

However, at a meeting of the Cabinet on 25 June it was agreed that the Government should resign and Lord John Russell tendered his resignation to Queen Victoria on the following day.[151] In July, Lord Derby duly formed his third Ministry, with Disraeli, now Chancellor of the Exchequer and Leader of the Commons, determined to seize the opportunity for the Tories to carry parliamentary reform.

Thereafter, although he did not know it at the time, Charles Villiers was to be consigned to the backbenches for the remainder of his parliamentary career (a period of thirty-two years), for he was never again to attain ministerial status, despite the fact that his work at the Poor Law Board was much appreciated by his contemporaries. In April 1866, for example, *The Economist* was moved to comment that:

> Mr Villiers ... has introduced great improvements into his department; he takes an interest in it; he is acquainted with it. In the Irremovable Poor Bill, the Casual Poor Bill, the Union Chargeability Bill (not to mention the measures for the relief of distress in Lancashire), he has done more actual good than any Minister in Lord Palmerston's Government, Mr Gladstone alone excepted. And among his defects no one would name a tendency to sentimental philanthropy. When a Minister of this sort admits an evil, directs an inquiry, and promises a remedy, the part of the public which cares for the subject may well be glad and satisfied.[152]

In July, in an article entitled 'The Parliamentary Labours of the Right Hon. C.P. Villiers', *The Examiner* also applauded Villiers' tenure at the Poor Law Board, observing:

> During the period Mr Villiers presided over the Poor Law Board it is computed that no less than fifty-two statutes were passed which were directly or indirectly connected with his department. It is not too much to say of him that he did more to benefit the condition of the poor than any member of the legislature in the present generation. In his official capacity as Minister of poor laws, Mr Villiers was always accessible, and always ready to carry out any measures which were suggested to him for the public advantage. He was at his post early and late; and the wonder was that, with so much parliamentary business on his hands, he was able to give the time he did to the ordinary duties of the department.[153]

In the same month, *The Economist* claimed that 'In no seven years since the new poor law was passed has so much been done to improve the condition and lighten the prospects of the poor than Mr Villiers has effected',[154] whilst in December, even the Tory *Spectator* reluctantly acknowledged that 'It is only fair to Mr Villiers to say that he carried successfully two enormous reforms – Union rating and that change in the law of settlement. Very few Poor Law chiefs in our time have done near as much.'[155]

Charles Villiers' achievements as a poor-law reformer were perhaps almost of equal significance to his work as a pioneer of free trade, for he dealt with two of the most serious crises with which the Poor Law Board had ever been confronted and under his firm guidance the Board had not only weathered these storms but had also used the experience so gained to force Parliament to introduce poor-law reforms of far-reaching importance. Indeed, even John and Barbara Hammond – certainly no friends of the New Poor Law – described Villiers' work at the Poor Law Board as 'admirable' in their classic study of 1934, *The Bleak Age*.[156] Moreover, it was due largely to Villiers's work that the Poor Law Board became a permanent department of state in 1869 (with its responsibilities transferred to the newly created Local Government Board in 1871).[157] Indeed, as Anthony Howe has observed recently, Charles Villiers' career at the Poor Law Board was 'a notable, if unsung, success, belying his reputation as a political weathercock, more interested in gossip than policy-making'.[158]

Yet, for Charles Villiers, these years of relative political advancement and success were clouded by a series of tragedies in his private life. In August 1861, his younger brother, Henry Montagu Villiers, who had been appointed Bishop of Durham by Palmerston in 1860, was suddenly taken ill at his palace at Auckland Castle. Charles and his sister, Maria Theresa, travelled to Durham to comfort their brother, but he died on 9 August, aged forty-eight.[159] In February 1863, Maria Theresa's daughter (and Charles Villiers' niece), Maria, who was married to Villiers' Liberal colleague, Sir William Vernon Harcourt, died in childbirth shortly after giving birth to their second son, Lewis (who later became a prominent Liberal politician).[160] In April 1863, Charles Villiers' brother-in-law and Cabinet colleague, Sir George Cornewall Lewis, the Secretary of State at the War Department, died suddenly on 13 April, aged fifty-six.[161] Lewis had been a long-standing friend of both Lord Clarendon and Charles Villiers even before he had married Maria Theresa Lister in 1844, and his wholly unexpected death came as a great shock to the whole family.[162] Maria Theresa was to survive her husband for merely two years, for in the summer of 1865 she too was taken ill and cancer was diagnosed. In the autumn her condition deteriorated and she was moved to Brasenose College, Oxford, in the care of Dr Cradock. On 7 November, her two brothers, Charles and George, hastened to her bedside, where Lord Clarendon observed that she was so shrunk and changed that he should hardly have known her, and Charles admitted that it was but a question of hours and that all would be over by the evening.[163] Two days later, on 9 November, their much-loved only sister, a renowned hostess and talented writer, peacefully passed away.[164]

Notes

1 *Queen Victoria's Journals*, 47, 225, 3 Jul. 1859. Villiers clearly established a cordial relationship with the Queen and was invited to dine with Victoria and Albert at Buckingham Palace and Windsor Castle on several occasions: see *Journals*, 48, 34, 24 Oct. 1859; 49, 160, 17 Jun. 1859.
2 Alan Sykes, *The Rise and Fall of British Liberalism, 1776–1988* (London, 1997), 146–7.
3 Hawkins, *Victorian Political Culture*, 375.

4 Sykes, *The Rise and Fall of British Liberalism*, 147.
5 N. Gash, *Aristocracy and People, 1815–1865* (London, 1979), 271.
6 E. Evans, *The Forging of the Modern State: Early Industrial Britain, 1783–1870* (London, 1983), 430.
7 Maxwell, II, 187–88: Palmerston to Lord Clarendon [George Villiers], 4 Jul. 1859.
8 Lord Edmund Fitzmaurice, *The Life of Granville George Leveson Gower, Second Earl Granville, K.G., 1815–1891* (2 vols, London, 1905), II, 345.
9 *The Parliamentary Diaries of Sir John Trelawny, 1858–1865*, ed. T.A. Jenkins (Camden Society, 4th ser., 1990), 86, Monday 4 Jul. 1859.
10 Villiers, *Political Memoir*, lxxxi.
11 *Wolverhampton Chronicle*, 13 Jul. 1859.
12 BLPES, SR1094, Thornely to Villiers, 20 Jul. 1859.
13 *London Gazette*, 14 May 1869.
14 Ibid., 11 Nov. 1873. John Thornely (b.1829) retained this post with the Local Government Board until 1879.
15 P. Wood, *Poverty and the Workhouse*, 120.
16 Jenkins, *The Parliamentary Diaries of Sir John Trelawny*, 307, 20 Feb. 1865.
17 For further details, see especially Henderson, *History* (1952), 34–8.
18 M. Rose, *The Relief of Poverty, 1834–1914* (London, 1972); Longmate, *The Workhouse*; Wood, *Poverty and the Workhouse*; Kidd, *State, Society and the Poor*; D. Englander, *Poverty and Poor Law Reform in Nineteenth-Century Britain, 1834–1914: From Chadwick to Booth* (Abingdon, 1998); David R. Green, *Pauper Capital: London and the Poor Law, 1790–1870* (Farnham, 2010). Villiers is not mentioned in any of these works, although he is mentioned once in Anthony Brundage, *The English Poor Laws, 1700–1930* (Basingstoke, 2002), 64.
19 Kidd, *State, Society and the Poor*, 44.
20 Rose, *The Relief of Poverty*, 15.
21 *Parl. Debs*, 3rd ser., 185, cc.746–80, 21 Feb. 1867.
22 Ibid., 3rd Ser., 159, cc.1912–24, 13 Jul. 1860.
23 Ibid., 3rd Ser., 160, cc.88–102, 24 Jul. 1860.
24 Ibid., 3rd Ser., 61, cc.224–47, 8 Feb. 1861; 161, cc.866–8, 22 Feb. 1861.
25 *Report from the Select Committee on Poor Relief (England), with Proceedings, Minutes of Evidence, Appendices and Index, PP* (1861), 180, IX.
26 *Reports from the Select Committees on Poor Relief and Poor Removal, with Proceedings, Minutes of Evidence, Appendices and Indices, PP* (1862): First Report, *PP*, 181, X; Second Report, *PP*, 321, X; Third Report, *PP*, 468, X; (1863), 383, VII.
27 For further details, see J.M. Feheney, 'Towards Religious Equality for Catholic Paper Children, 1861–68', *British Journal of Educational Studies*, 31, 2 (1983), 141–53.
28 *Report from the Select Committees on Poor Relief and Poor Removal, with Proceedings, Minutes of Evidence, Appendices and Indices, PP* (1864), 349, IX.
29 P.F. Aschrott, *The English Poor Law System: Past and Present* (London, 1888), 74.
30 Joshua Levin, 'Much ado About Nothing: British Non-Intervention During the American Civil War', MA Thesis, Department of History, University of Sydney, 2000, 3–4.
31 Kathleen Burk, *Old World, New World The Story of Britain and America* (London, 2007), 270–1.
32 *Cobden Letters*, IV, 244: Villiers to Cobden, 21 Dec. 1861. Villiers added that Cobden tended 'to underrate the pugnacious qualities of our countrymen & rather to overrate the goodness, reasonableness and integrity of the Americans'.
33 Villiers had previously expressed similar views in a letter to John Bright on 14 December, which Bright had forwarded to Cobden. In reply, Cobden stated

> If I did not know the writer of the enclosed & that he is generally in a state of morbid gastric irritation which distempers his mind on every question & generally carries him to erroneous conclusions founded on the most narrow and groundless suspicions, I should be alarmed at what he says:

> *Cobden Letters*, IV, 244: Cobden to Bright, 17 Dec. 1861. In a further letter to Bright, Cobden observed, 'Villiers seems in a queer state of mind, as usual, balancing on everything & bringing himself to a decision on nothing', but he acknowledged that 'he seems rather under the impression that the government have gone too far': *Cobden Letters*, IV, 244, Cobden to Bright, 22 Dec. 1861; In December 1862, however, Cobden reported to Bright that 'When coming through London I saw Villiers and Gibson. So far as I could judge they were equally opposed to any interference with the American quarrel': *Cobden Letters*, IV, 343: Cobden to Bright, 7 Dec. 1862.

34 Burk, *Old World, New World*, 271.
35 Ibid., 272.
36 D. Jordan and E. Pratt, *Europe and the American Civil War* (Oxford, 1931), 88. However, Duncan Campbell, *English Public Opinion and the American Civil War* (Woodbridge, 2003), 247–8, has concluded 'my own interpretation of Villiers' speeches places him in the neutral category'.
37 Levin, *Thesis*, 82–4.
38 J. Levenson, E. Sammels, C. Vandersee and V. Winner (eds), *The Letters of Henry Adams, 1858–92*, 3 vols (Cambridge, MA, 1982), vol. 1, 329–30: Letter from Henry Adams to Charles Francis Adams Jnr., 13 Feb. 1863: Adams noted that the feeling among the upper classes in England 'is more bitter and angry than ever, and the strong popular feeling of sympathy with us is gradually dividing the nation into aristocrats and democrats, and may produce pretty serious results for England'. He also refers to a dinner at the Duke of Argyll's 'who is a warm friend of ours … the party was evidently asked on purpose to meet us' and those invited included Lord Clyde, C.P. Villiers 'a friendly member of the Cabinet', Charles Howard, John Stuart Mill 'about the ablest man in England', and Lord Frederick Cavendish. [Adams was the son of Charles Francis Adams, appointed by Lincoln as US Ambassador to Britain in 1861. Henry Adams accompanied his father to London as his private secretary and his letters to *The Times* argued that the US should be patient with GB. He returned to the US in 1868 and became Professor of Medieval History at Harvard.]
39 *The New York Times*, 24 Nov. 1863, reported Villiers' speech in Wolverhampton, 8 Nov. 1863, which also alluded to the *Trent* affair:

> In the first place, peace during that period had been maintained, (cheers) not at the expense of honour, for when the privilege of the British flag was assailed, as it was in a great question of maritime right by the Americans, it was by universal assent vindicated with spirit and success (cheers). Again, in the face of the strongest inducements to take an opposite course, the pledge of neutrality to each contending party in the States of America has been strictly and honourably observed (Hear, Hear).

40 See especially R.J.M. Blackett, *Divided Hearts: Britain and the American Civil War* (Baton Rouge, 2001). In this study, by reference to over 125 local newspapers, Blackett charts the progress of both pro-Union and pro-Confederate organisations in Britain, suggesting that Dissenters, Radicals and Trade Unionists overwhelmingly supported the North, whilst the Confederacy generally drew support from the aristocracy, the Anglican Church and the mercantile community of Liverpool, although the issue cut across class divisions. He makes no mention of Charles Villiers, however.

41 For further details, see R.A. Arnold, *History of the Cotton Famine* (London, 1865); J. Watts, *The Facts of the Cotton Famine* (Manchester, 1866), 299–302: Arnold claimed that had the Union Chargeability Act of 1865 – 'a wise measure' – existed in 1861, it would have sufficed to meet the distress in many cotton manufacturing unions; W.O. Henderson, *The Lancashire Cotton Famine, 1861–65* (Manchester, 1934; rev. edn, 1969), especially chapter 4, 'Relief of Distress in Lancashire', 52–93, including Poor Law Board policy, 52–59.
42 *Queen Victoria's Journals*, 51, 332, 27 Dec. 1862: 'Saw Mr Villiers, who reports an expanding state of distress in Lancashire, where ½ a million of children and people are being supported by voluntary contributions, but he did not know how long this could go on'.
43 *Parl. Debs*, 3rd ser., 166, cc.1490–522, 9 May 1862.
44 Ibid., 3rd ser., 168, cc.285–90, 14 Jul. 1862.
45 Ibid., 3rd ser., 168, cc.739–78, 24 Jul. 1862.
46 Howe, *Cobden Letters*, IV, introduction, xlvii.
47 *Gladstone Papers*, 44399/242, Villiers to Gladstone, 22 Nov. 1862: Villiers also informed Walter Bagehot that

> as we are as uncertain as ever about the termination of the [American Civil] War, it is *not* an object that the subscription to the Distress should cease, and the account here given would lead people to think that we now have *enough* – which we have till March next no doubt! But will the Distress end then?

Mrs Russell Barrington, *The Works and Life of Walter Bagehot* (London, 1915) vol. 10, 400.
48 Sidney and Beatrice Webb, *English Poor Law Policy* (London, 1910), 142.
49 For further details, see Michael Rose, 'Rochdale Man and the Stalybridge Riot. The Relief and Control of the Unemployed during the Lancashire Cotton Famine', in A.P. Donajgrodzki (ed.), *Social Control in Nineteenth Century Britain* (London, 1977), 185–206.
50 *Parl. Debs*, 3rd ser., 171, cc.1050–87, 18 Jun. 1863.
51 Ibid.
52 Ibid.
53 Indeed, Henderson has suggested that Villiers' scheme was more effective than that of Joseph Chamberlain at the Local Government Board in March 1886, when those engaged on relief works were paid only a 'dole' similar to what would have been given in out-relief rather than proper wages: Henderson, *History*, 38.
54 W.T.M. Torrens, *Lancashire's Lesson; or the need of a settled Policy in Times of Exceptional Distress* (London, 1864), 182. William McCullagh Torrens (1813–1894) was a British/Irish barrister, author and Liberal MP. In 1893 Torrens dedicated his book, *Twenty Years in Parliament* (London, 1893) 'To the Rt Hon. Charles Pelham Villiers, M.P. these pages are inscribed by his faithful friend and comrade in many legislative struggles'.
55 Ibid., 7.
56 *The Economist*, 1 Jul. 1865.
57 Ibid.
58 Howe, *Cobden Letters*, IV, xxiv.
59 Ibid., 563: Cobden to Villiers, 27 Nov. 1864.
60 Ibid., 565: Villiers to Cobden, 3 Dec. 1864. Ecclesiastical issues had recently come to the fore in part due to Disraeli's speech, at the invitation of Samuel Wilberforce, Bishop of Oxford (popularly known as 'Soapy Sam') at a diocesan meeting at the Sheldonian Theatre, Oxford, where Disraeli (who had converted to Anglicanism) presented himself (and by implication, the Conservative Party), as the champion of the Broad Church. Villiers observed: 'Master Dizzy is too

late & and it would require a good deal more soap than Samuel can furnish to get the people of the country to slide back to authority for their belief'. For further details, see Buckle, *Life of Disraeli*, IV, 369–77.
61 R.A.J. Walling (ed.), *The Diaries of John Bright* (London, 1931), 287. Entry for 7 Apr. 1865: 'I was one of the pall-bearers, Mr Gladstone and I walking foremost, Mr Villiers and Mr Gibson next, and others following'. See also Nicholas C. Edsall, *Richard Cobden: Independent Radical* (Cambridge, MA, and London, 1986), 417.
62 Gladstone Papers, 44407/239, Villiers to Gladstone, 9 Sep. 1865.
63 Ibid.
64 *Parl. Debs*, 3rd ser., 177, cc.468–86, 20 Feb. 1865.
65 Report from the Select Committee on Irremovable Poor, with Minutes of Evidence, Appendix and Index, *PP* (1860), 520, XVII.
66 Villiers to Sir George Nicholls, 28 Aug. 1861, cited in G. Nicholls, *A History of the English Poor Law in Connection with the State of the Country and the Condition of the People* (London, 1904), 268.
67 Ibid.; see also Thomas Mackay, *A History of the English Poor Law* (London, 1904), 483.
68 For further details, see also W. Cunningham Glen, *Villiers' Union Chargeability Act, 1865; with an Introduction and Commentary; Also The Practice of Poor Removals, Adapted to the Removal of Union Poor* (London, 1868), which was 'respectfully dedicated to the Rt Hon. Charles Pelham Villiers'; Aschrott, *The English Poor Law System*, 70, claimed that the 1865 Act was 'unquestionably the most important [poor law] Act of this period'.
69 Ridley, *Lord Palmerston*, 578.
70 *Parl. Debs*, 3rd ser., 177, cc.468–86, 20 Feb. 1865.
71 Ibid.
72 Ibid.
73 Ibid.
74 Ibid.
75 For further details, see Frank Neal, 'The English Poor Law, the Irish migrant and the laws of settlement and removal, 1819–1879', in D. George Boyce and Roger Swift (eds), *Problems and Perspectives in Irish History since 1800* (Dublin, 2004), 95–116; Roger Swift, *Irish Migrants in Britain, 1815–1914: A Documentary History* (Cork, 2002), 80–93; Frank Neal, 'The Famine Irish in England and Wales', in P. O'Sullivan (ed.), *The Irish World Wide*, vol. 6, *The Meaning of the Famine* (London, 1997), 56–80.
76 *Parl. Debs*, 3rd ser., 157, cc.738–45, 16 Mar. 1860.
77 Ibid., 169, cc.448–60, 17 Feb. 1863.
78 For further details, see Roger Swift, '"Another Stafford Street Row": Law, Order and the Irish presence in Mid-Victorian Wolverhampton', *Immigrants & Minorities*, 3, 1 (1984), 5–29; see also Alison Hobbs, 'The Irish of Caribee Island: Wolverhampton's Irish District', MPhil thesis, University of Wolverhampton (2003).
79 *Parl. Debs*, 3rd ser., 177, cc.596–8, 23 Feb. 1865.
80 Ibid.
81 Ibid., 169, cc.448–60, 17 Feb. 1863.
82 Ibid., 177, 468–86, 20 Feb. 1865.
83 For further discussion of the problems of poverty encountered by the Irish in Britain during the period, see especially the relevant sections in Roger Swift (ed.), *Irish Migrants in Britain, 1815–1914: A Documentary History* (Cork, 2002); Donald M. MacRaild, *The Irish Diaspora in Britain, 1750–1939* (Basingstoke, 2011).
84 *Parl. Debs*, 3rd ser., 184, cc.299–304, 12 Jun. 1866.

85 Jenkins, *The Parliamentary Diaries of Sir John Trelawny*, 316, 27 Mar. 1865.
86 See Barrington, *The Works and Life of Walter Bagehot*, 10, 399–400. Walter Bagehot (1826–77), political journalist and historian, was editor of *The Economist* from 1859; Mrs Barrington was his sister-in-law and the daughter of James Wilson, Free Trader and leading member of the Anti Corn Law League, and founder of *The Economist*. The Barringtons were very close friends of Sir George Cornewall Lewis and his wife Theresa (Villiers' sister).
87 P. Brighton, *Original Spin: Downing Street and the Press in Victorian Britain* (London, 2016), 89.
88 Ibid., 137. Brighton suggests that this familial nexus at the interface of politics and journalism was indicative of a growing sense of 'dialogue amongst equals' which increasingly characterised the relationship between politics and the press during the period.
89 *Parl. Debs*, House of Lords, 12 Jun. 1865, 180, cc.9–42, 12 Jun. 1865; 180, cc.351–7, 16 Jun. 1865.
90 Union Chargeability Act, 1865, 28 & 29 Vict., c.79.
91 *Queen Victoria's Journals*, 53, 132, 17 Mar. 1864:

> After luncheon saw Mr Villiers & talked for some time with him about various matters, including the dreadful floods near Sheffield, & the S. [Schleswig] Holstein affair, about which I found him sensible, saying the Country was entirely against a war & like all, now looking to a division of Schleswig and Holstein & a separation of the Duchies from Denmark. Lastly, we talked of the distress in London, & of there being no cases of starvation which need have occurred, none in short from neglect, & of the horrible crowding, & vice & depravity in which some of the people live.

92 *The Times*, 24 Dec. 1864; 24 Feb. 1865: 'The Case of Timothy Daly'.
93 *The Spectator*, 31 Dec. 1864.
94 For further details, see Gwendoline M. Ayers, *England's First State Hospitals and the Metropolitan Asylums Board and its Work, 1867–1930* (London, 1971), ch. 1: 'The destitute Sick and the Pursuit of a Policy', 1–16; Christine Hallett, 'Nursing, 1830–1920: Forging a Profession', in Anne Borsay and Billie Hunter (eds), *Nursing and Midwifery in Britain since 1700* (Basingstoke, 2012), 50–56.
95 Florence Nightingale to C.P. Villiers, 30 Dec. 1864, in L. McDonald (ed.), *The Collected Works of Florence Nightingale* (6 vols, Waterloo, Ont. Ca., 2002), VI, 329.
96 C. Woodham Smith, *Florence Nightingale, 1820–1910* (London, 1950), 349.
97 Villiers to Nightingale, 31 Dec. 1864, cited in Sir Edward Cook, *The Life of Florence Nightingale* (2 vols, London, 1913), II, 131.
98 Cook, *Life of Florence Nightingale*, II, 131; see also Woodham Smith, *Florence Nightingale*, 349.
99 Cook, II. 131.
100 *Parl. Debs*, 3rd ser., 178, cc.533–5, 5 May 1865.
101 N. Longmate, *The Workhouse* (London 1974), 204–5; see also Wood, *Poverty and the Workhouse*, 131–6.
102 Woodham Smith, *Florence Nightingale*, 352–4.
103 Cook, *Life of Florence Nightingale*, II, 134.
104 Thomas Mackay, *A History of the English Poor Law* (London, 1904), 489.
105 *Parl. Debs*, 3rd ser., 84, cc.683, 26 Jun. 1866.
106 Nightingale to Harriet Martineau, 2 May 1866, in Cook, *Life of Florence Nightingale*, II, 105.
107 Woodham Smith, *Florence Nightingale*, 355. Gathorne Hardy held the office until 21 May 1867, when he was succeeded by the Earl of Devon, who held the post until 15 Dec. 1868, when he was replaced by G.J. Goschen.

108 Ibid.
109 Cook, *Life of Florence Nightingale*, II, 135.
110 Ibid.
111 McDonald, *The Collected Works of Florence Nightingale*, VI, 326.
112 Cook, *Life of Florence Nightingale*, II, 137.
113 Woodham Smith, *Florence* Nightingale, 356–7.
114 Villiers to Nightingale, 8 Feb. 1867, in Cook, *Life of Florence Nightingale*, II, 137.
115 *Hansard*, Parl. Debs., 3rd Ser., 185, cc.746–80, 21 Feb. 1867.
116 M.E. Rose, *The English Poor Law, 1780–1830* (Newton Abbot, 1971), 162; see also Kidd, *State, Society and the Poor*, 53.
117 Lynn McDonald, 'Florence Nightingale A Hundred Years On: Who She Was and Who She Was Not', *Women's History Review*, 19, 5 (November, 2010), 721–40; see also Lynn McDonald, 'Florence Nightingale as a Social Reformer', *History Today*, 56, 1 (2006).
118 *Parl Debs*, 3rd ser., 157, 1793–805, 3 Apr. 1860; 158, 225–39, 27 Apr. 1860.
119 Disraeli to Derby, 4 Jan. 1860:

> What is most pressing is the Reform Question. It is quite on the cards that an offer will be made out of the House. A Cabinet Minister [Charles Villiers] has sounded me, & said communications would be confined, & strictly confined, to P [Palmerston] and JR [John Russell].

Villiers had informed Disraeli in private that the government 'would be disposed to give a calm and respectful consideration to the views of all parties upon the question', and Disraeli duly forwarded an outline of the government's proposals to Derby (Disraeli to Derby, 8 Jan. 1860). However, on 19 January, Derby observed that there would be 'great and general objection to a very low borough franchise, and it will be rejected', and warned Disraeli 'to be very guarded in your communications with CV [Villiers] on this delicate question': Gunn and Wiebe, *Benjamin Disraeli Letters* (10 vols, Toronto, 1982–2014), 8, *1860–64* (2009). Docs 3340–3342, 9–14.
120 David Brown, *Palmerston: A Biography* (Yale, 2012), 464–6.
121 E.D. Steele, *Palmerston and Liberty, 1855–65* (London, 1991), 128.
122 Ibid., 129.
123 Roland Quinault, 'Democracy and the Mid-Victorians', in Martin Hewitt (ed.), *An Age of Equipoise? Reassessing Mid-Victorian Britain* (Aldershot, 200), 112–13.
124 J.P.D. Dunbabin, 'Electoral Reforms and their Outcome in the United Kingdom, 1865–1900', in T.R. Gourvish and Alan O'Day (eds), *Later Victorian Britain, 1867–1900* (London, 1988), 100–1.
125 Walling, *The Diaries of John Bright*, 275, 13 Apr. 1864: 'To Stafford House: reception in honour of General Garibaldi. A large company ... saw nearly all the Ministers – Duke of Argyll, Lord Granville, Palmerston, Gladstone, Cardwell, Villiers and Gibson'.
126 Matthew, *Gladstone*, 139–41.
127 This questions Gladstone's own claim in May 1860 that in regard to attitudes within the Cabinet on parliamentary reform, Charles Villiers was among those 'most fearful and opposed' to the extension of the franchise and larger disenfranchisement: Gladstone's Memorandum on current opinions of the Cabinet, 30 May 1860, cited in J. Morley, *The Life of William Ewart Gladstone* (3 vols, London, 1903), II, 635.
128 Hawkins, *Victorian Political* Culture, 26; John Garrard, 'Parties, Members and Voters after 1867', in Gourvish and O'Day (eds), *Later Victorian Britain*, 137; Quinault, 'Democracy and the Mid-Victorians', 116–17.

129 E. Taylor, 'The Working Class Movement in the Black Country, 1863–1914', PhD thesis, University of Keele (1974), 363.
130 Sir John Lambert (1815–92), free-trader and sanitary reformer had been appointed a Poor Law Inspector in 1857 and subsequently became a distinguished civil servant as first secretary of the Local Government Board from 1871 to 1882. Knighted in 1879, he was also an accomplished musician and composer. His daughter, Agnes Lambert, edited Charles Villiers' *Free Trade Speeches* in 1883. Following his death in January 1892, Villiers sent a wreath 'in affectionate remembrance' of his former colleague: *The Tablet*, 6 Feb. 1892. For further details, see William Archbold, 'Lambert, John (1815–1892)', *DNB*, vol. 32 (1885–1900), 18–19.
131 *Gladstone Papers*, 44408/259, Gladstone to Villiers, 27 Dec. 1865.
132 Ibid.
133 Ibid., 44409/39, Gladstone to Villiers, 5 Jan. 1866.
134 See, for example, Matthew, *Gladstone*, 139–41; Jenkins, *Gladstone*, 160–4; Shannon, *Gladstone: Heroic Minister*, 14–24.
135 Asa Briggs, 'Robert Lowe and the Fear of Democracy', in A. Briggs, *Victorian People* (London, 1954), 24–271.
136 *Parl. Debs*, 3rd ser., 182, cc.141–241, 13 Mar. 1866.
137 Ibid.
138 Ibid.; Yet Villiers' contributions to the wider debate within the Liberal Party on parliamentary reform have largely been ignored in recent studies of the subject, including the admirable study by Robert Saunders, *Democracy and the Vote in British Politics, 1848–1868: The Making of the Second Reform Act* (Farnham, 2011).
139 *Gladstone Papers*, 4410/112, Villiers to Gladstone, 30 Apr. 1866.
140 *Wolverhampton Chronicle*, 20 Jun. 1866.
141 Jon Lawrence, 'Popular Politics and the Limitations of Party: Wolverhampton, 1867–1900', in Eugenio Biagini and Alastair Reid (eds), *Currents of Radicalism: Popular Radicalism, Organised Labour and Party Politics in Britain, 1850–1914* (Cambridge, 1991), 65–85.
142 Thomas Weguelin (1809–1885): son of William Weguelin, a rich Russian merchant who became Governor of the Bank of England from 1855–59. Thomas Weguelin was Liberal MP for Southampton from 1857–59 and for Wolverhampton from 1861–1880.
143 J. Lawrence, *Speaking for the People: Party, Language and Popular Politics in England, 1867–1914* (Cambridge, 1998), 79.
144 Ibid., 80.
145 Ibid., 82–5.
146 *Wolverhampton Chronicle*, 12 Jul. 1865.
147 Ibid., 18 April 1866.
148 Lawrence, *Speaking for the People*, 85.
149 *Wolverhampton Chronicle*, 27 June 1866.
150 Ibid., 11 Jul. 1866.
151 Shannon, *Gladstone*, 23–4.
152 *The Economist*, 21 Apr. 1866.
153 *The Examiner*, 21 Jul. 1866: 'The Parliamentary Labours of the Right Hon. C.P. Villiers'.
154 *The Economist*, 14 Jul. 1866.
155 *The Spectator*, 12 Dec. 1868.
156 J.L. and B. Hammond, *The Bleak Age* (London, 1934), 225.
157 Henderson, *History* (1952), 34.
158 Howe, 'Villiers, Charles Pelham', *ODNB*, 4–5.

159 *Morning Post*, 10 Aug. 1861. For further details of the career of Henry Villiers, see A.F. Munden, 'The First Palmerston Bishop: Henry Montagu Villiers, Bishop of Carlisle, 1856–1860, and Bishop of Durham, 1860–61', *Northern History*, 26, 1 (1990), 186–206.
160 *Morning Post*, 2 Feb. 1863.
161 Ibid., 15 Apr. 1863.
162 For further details, see Villiers, *A Vanished Victorian*, 150–1, 320.
163 Ibid., 329–30.
164 *Morning Post*, 10 Nov. 1865. *The Birmingham Daily Gazette*, 16 Nov. 1865 reported that Lord Clarendon and Charles Villiers had been absent from Cabinet on the previous day in order to attend the funeral of Lady Theresa Lewis. For further details, see also D.A. Smith, 'Lewis, Lady (Maria) Theresa (1803–1865)', *ODNB*, 16595 (Oct. 2006).

7 The view from the backbenches

In June 1867, at the invitation of Salford Borough Council, Charles Villiers gave the inaugural address at the unveiling of a statue, commissioned by public subscription, in memory of Richard Cobden, in Peel Park, Salford. In opening the proceedings, Alderman Wright Turner stated that the memorial committee held that 'there was no man, either in the House of Commons or out of it, more suitable to inaugurate a memorial to the great apostle of Free Trade than Mr Villiers'.[1] In a warm and generous address to his Salford audience, Villiers subsequently paid tribute to his former colleague, 'whom he so much esteemed', stating that Cobden was regarded by all

> as an enlightened citizen of the world whose capacity and disposition enabled him to benefit his race ... a man who had reflected deeply upon public affairs, and who by travel and study had become well informed on all matters passing around him, and whose views with regard to the improvement of the people of this country were as bold as they were benevolent ... He was a man who believed that peace and good-will amongst the nations of the earth was not merely a sentiment to be reached, but a practical policy, which but for the ignorance and folly of men, and the rulers of men, might prevail; and to the last day of his life he did not despair that that great object might be obtained by generous and enlightened legislation.[2]

Having summarised Cobden's contribution to the success of the Anti-Corn Law League, of which he became its 'presiding genius', Villiers observed that, thereafter, Cobden was devoted consistently to peace, economy and reform and, in particular, praised Cobden's efforts in securing the Anglo-French Commercial Treaty of 1860 (which Villiers, as a strict freetrader, had himself opposed at the time) and which, as Villiers observed, Cobden had entered into less to establish trade than to establish friendly relations between France and England, but which had also had, as they all knew, important commercial results. Villiers' address was warmly received, and in his vote of thanks, the old League campaigner, George Wilson, was moved to comment that:

> England did not contain within her borders a man who felt more earnestly desirous to promote the interests of the people of this country. He recalled the time when, almost single-handed, Mr Villiers held his own against the combined leaders of both parties on behalf of Manchester principles, and against overwhelming majorities he still proclaimed that the day would come when the principles which he then enunciated would be the principles that would prevail in England, if not throughout the entire world. It was easy at the end of a fight to select those to whom belonged the honour of victory, and amongst those who were especially entitled, next to Mr Cobden, he would select Mr Villiers as worthy of their warm consideration.[3]

For Charles Villiers, this event no doubt provided an interlude from hectic parliamentary business, for earlier in the year, in the aftermath of reform demonstrations in London and the provinces, Benjamin Disraeli had introduced, on 11 February, his Parliamentary Reform Bill, which contained a measure of household suffrage complemented by a series of safeguards, or 'fancy franchises', with provisions for voting based on various educational and financial qualifications, and a three-year residential qualification, which militated against many lodgers. These proposals were hotly contested by the Liberals, and Villiers attended a private meeting of leading Liberals at Gladstone's London home at Carlton House Terrace on 25 February, where it was decided to vote for the Bill and to then progressively amend it in committee. Villiers duly informed J.T. Delane at *The Times*,[4]

> The meeting at Gladstone's was remarkable; I have not seen such unanimity in trusting to one man's (Gladstone's) lead for these thirty years. He has got an immense hold now over the Party, and they came today ready to adopt whatever he proposed, and went away delighted with what he had prepared for them, and nothing would have been more judicious, or indeed skilful, than his way, for the House is in a very peculiar state now about this question. They are *afraid all round* of leaving it unsettled, and yet nobody likes to make the sacrifice necessary to settle it [and] I suppose there will be a grand compromise before the session is much older, and *something will pass this session*.[5]

Villiers added that although the Tories might carry reform,

> they cannot last; it is against them that Gladstone is gaining ground at every hour. His judgment and moderation are astonishing everybody ... Our Party will not allow the question to be used as the means of displacing the Government; they want to make them pass it.[6]

In Wolverhampton, Villiers pledged his support for the reform cause to William Parkes, the secretary of the WWMLA, stating that during the long time that he had been in Parliament, he had voted for every practical measure of Reform that purported to widen the basis of representation, and adding

> my opinion in this is wholly unchanged ... On the mode in which the people think it right now to make known their wishes and opinions, I have not a word to offer. It is emphatically their own cause, and they have the fullest right to its management,

although he declined an invitation to attend a branch meeting on 28 January on the grounds that this 'might fetter my independence as a Member of the House of Commons'.[7] By contrast, the town's middle-class Liberal elite, fearing that a £7 borough franchise went too far and would give the vote to 'the idle and improvident',[8] favoured a restriction of the franchise to the 'respectable' and 'intelligent' workers, failed to endorse household suffrage and the secret ballot, and became increasingly estranged from the radical WMLA and was denounced by the Reform League.[9] The rising star of the Liberal Committee was the Sunderland-born Methodist, Alderman Henry Hartley Fowler,[10] a former Mayor of the town, who was anxious to stand for Parliament. This issue was raised in passing at a meeting of the WWMLA on 1 May 1867, chaired by William Parkes, where it was noted that there had been complaints about the representation of the county constituency of South Staffordshire by one of its Liberal MPs, Henry Hodgetts-Foley,[11] one of the Adullamites who had opposed Gladstone's Bill in 1866. The suggestion was then made that Charles Villiers might stand for the county, on the grounds that 'it would be a great honour for Mr Villiers to represent the county', and that Mr Fowler should take his seat in the borough.[12] There was great opposition to this suggestion. William Parkes stated that they should leave well alone and not endanger Mr Villiers seat, for 'he had represented them long and well'.[13] The ex-Chartist, Joseph Linney,[14] of Bilston, said that he was surprised that such a matter should even be discussed: 'He should as soon think of the Old Church being removed as Mr Villiers. He was not going to give up Mr Villiers for Mr Fowler', adding that it was 'a trick' on the part of the borough's Liberal Committee to displace Mr Villiers and to get Fowler in, 'who supported their views'.[15] William Parkes concluded that no such thing should be attempted, adding that 'Mr Villiers had no wish to be removed and put to the trouble of a contest', and it was held that if Mr Fowler wished to become a Member of Parliament then he should stand for the county seat, and the subject was dropped.[16]

In Parliament, against the background of great excitement in the provinces and demonstrations in Hyde Park,[17] Disraeli's Bill was radically altered by various Liberal amendments: the bar to household suffrage was lowered; fancy franchises disappeared; and the residential qualification was reduced. Indeed, Disraeli's Second Reform Bill, which was passed by Parliament in

June, becoming law on 15 August 1867, was in fact more radical than the Liberal Bill of 1866, virtually doubling the size of the electorate and enfranchising a large section of the urban working class. It extended the vote in the boroughs to all rate-paying adult male householders and to lodgers resident for at least one year in lodgings worth £10,[18] whilst the county franchise was lowered to £12. Moreover, fifty-two seats were redistributed, with twenty-five going to the counties, whilst Leeds, Liverpool, Manchester and Birmingham acquired a third member. Although the significance of the 1867 Reform Act remains a matter of dispute among historians,[19] Disraeli's calculation that this measure, described by Robert Cecil as 'a leap in the dark', would be rewarded by the electorate with security of tenure for the Tories proved misplaced, and when Gladstone subsequently carried resolutions in the House of Commons on his proposals for the Disestablishment of the Irish Church, Disraeli (who had succeeded Derby as Prime Minister in February), had little choice but to announce that the government would dissolve in the Autumn and a General Election would take place under the new register.

Charles Villiers had supported Gladstone's proposals to disestablish the Irish Church and in April 1868 he had travelled to Wolverhampton to address a meeting of Liberals on the subject at the Exchange. He was, however, taken ill on the train, and took no part in what proved to be a rowdy event, attended by 2,000 people, during which the police were summoned to restore order.[20] However, in October, in declaring his intention to stand again for Wolverhampton in the event of a dissolution of Parliament, he pointed to the wrongs inflicted on Ireland, adding

> Foremost amongst these is one long since denounced by all English Reformers, namely, the Church, which we maintain there by force, in ascendancy over the People's religion. The experience of centuries appears to afford no defence for this institution. The odium which our rule in that country has too often incurred, has always attached alike to the Church (so closely allied to the State) and has made it a means of checking instead of causing the spread of the Protestant faith.[21]

At a meeting of Liberals at the Swan Hotel, Wolverhampton, during the subsequent election campaign in November, Villiers endorsed Gladstone's Irish policy, but also called for the Liberals to promote further social and political reform. Emphasising that 'the Conservative was an individual who wanted to keep everything to himself, whereas the Liberal wanted some of those blessings which Providence intended for all to be widely diffused',[22] he called for the extension of the suffrage, for the curbing of public expenditure and a review of taxation policy, for the expansion of trade in order to provide more employment for the people, and for the further extension of education 'to the humblest child in the realm'.[23] The meeting duly expressed its confidence in both Villiers – who was praised by Henry Fowler for 'his unwavering consistency and unfaltering fidelity' – and Weguelin, and resolved to work for their return. In the country, the Liberals duly secured a convincing victory over the Tories, with a majority of 112 seats, whilst in Wolverhampton, where the revised franchise had given working-class voters a majority within the electorate, thereby broadening the base of Liberal Party support,[24] both Villiers and Weguelin were returned unopposed.

When Queen Victoria invited William Gladstone to form his first Liberal Ministry in December, Charles Villiers must have held reasonable expectations that, in view of his successful tenure of office at the Poor Law Board, he would again attain political preferment in the new administration. J.T. Delane, the editor of the *Times*, certainly thought so,[25] and it was rumoured in both the *London Standard*[26] and the *Birmingham Daily Post*[27] that Villiers would be appointed Chancellor of the Duchy of Lancaster.

However, when Villiers was called by Gladstone on 6 December he was informed that he would not be appointed to the new Cabinet. Writing to Delane after his meeting with Gladstone, Villiers stated that 'He [Gladstone] sent to see me today, and said that he could not have two members of the same family in the Cabinet!'[28] This explanation, which Villiers found both insincere and unconvincing, was, of course, nonsense, since Charles Villiers and his elder brother George, Earl of Clarendon (who was reappointed as Foreign Secretary by Gladstone) had been cabinet colleagues in the ministries of Palmerston and Russell. According to Villiers, Gladstone 'Then began to talk about attaching a pension to the Poor Law Presidentship, which would operate in favour of any Cabinet Minister who had held the office', but 'I told him not to trouble himself about that, that I had been a long time in the House without thinking of how I could turn it to profit, and I was not myself thinking of doing otherwise now.'[29] What Villiers did regret, he informed Gladstone, was that in view of

> the vast reforms that he [Gladstone] would effect, and that he considered necessary, I should not be by his side; and reminded him that upon every single occasion in which he had on Liberal grounds been at variance with his colleagues in the last Cabinet, I had supported him and might be relied upon to do the same in future.[30]

However, Villiers concluded that Gladstone

> seemed to have made up his mind as to who he would have in his Cabinet, and he gave me the idea of not wishing to hear how much the people expected of him, and talked of the difficulties of his position.[31]

In a sense, Villiers might not have been surprised by his exclusion. Although, on the surface at least, he and Gladstone had much in common, there had been political differences between them,[32] notably during the anti-corn law agitation, when Gladstone, from the Tory opposition benches, had voted consistently against Villiers' motions for repeal (although he gradually became converted to the Free Trade cause and supported Peel on the repeal question) and Villiers never forgot Gladstone's early parliamentary career as a Tory Protectionist,[33] or his Peelite conversion and inheritance, and he subsequently regarded Gladstone's Liberal credentials as somewhat questionable. Indeed, in his biography of Gladstone, Richard Shannon has argued that Gladstone was essentially 'a Peelite, in short, in Liberal guise',[34] a thesis which has itself engendered continuing debate.[35] During the American Civil War, Villiers (with his strong anti-Slavery credentials) sympathised with the Northern States whilst his cabinet colleague Gladstone, at least initially, supported the (pro-slavery) South, although both men had subsequently fallen in line with Palmerston's policy of neutrality. Moreover, Villiers took broad views and was not always seen as a 'sound' Party man within Liberal circles, being regarded as too 'independent', although on matters of foreign policy and colonial expansion, his views were not too dissimilar from those of Gladstone, despite their ambiguities and inconsistencies, and reflected the early influence of George Canning on both men.[36] More significantly, the personal relationship between Gladstone and Villiers was somewhat prickly, as contemporary observers, including Sir John Trelawny,[37] Lord Derby,[38] and Sir Charles Dilke[39] all noted.

Nevertheless, Villiers' exclusion provoked some consternation within Liberal ranks. Lord Clarendon was said to be 'greatly hurt' at his brother's treatment and briefly threatened not to take up office as Foreign Secretary,[40] whilst Lord Granville, a long-standing friend of Villiers and staunch supporter of his Commons motions during the battle for the repeal of the Corn Laws, also bemoaned his exclusion. Indeed, Lord Fitzmaurice, Granville's biographer, observed that Villiers was not only intimately associated in the public mind as one of the great champions of Free Trade but also enjoyed a wide reputation in society owing to his 'caustic but not unkindly wit'. This, he held, in part explained Gladstone's decision, because

> some little weakness in Mr. Gladstone's own panoply had perhaps been too often the object of these winged shafts to make it altogether a matter of astonishment that the inner circles of his admirers sought to justify the exclusion by a sudden discovery that it was a great principle of the Constitution, that two brothers could not sit at the same time in the same Cabinet.[41]

On 9 December, the *Morning Post* still held out the hope 'that some important position may yet be found for Mr Charles Villiers',[42] whilst on 12 December *The Economist* also bemoaned the exclusion of Villiers from the Cabinet and the appointment of G.J. Goschen as President of the Poor Law Board, noting that although Mr Goschen 'has great powers ... though, if it had been possible, we had rather have seen them applied to commerce than to pauperism', and suggesting that Charles Villiers would have been a more suitable appointment:

Mr Villiers passed the Union Rating Bill, the Casual Poor Bill, and the Irremovable Poor Bills; he much improved the position of the stationary poor by one Act, and also the position of the migratory poor by other Acts. Mr Villiers does not attend to what has been called the 'hypocrisy of business'. Instead of looking as if he was doing more than he was, he always seemed to labour less than he did. There are many pompous officials who have made an administrative reputation out of work much less than his at the Poor Law Board.[43]

The Tory *Wolverhampton Chronicle*, in a lengthy editorial, made a similar observation, stating that

We had hoped with the dissolution of the Disraeli government to have seen the return to power of a statesman for whose distinguished and eminently unselfish career we have always felt the greatest respect, and we cannot but express our regret that the exigencies of party or other causes should have operated to prevent it ... To the Right Hon. Charles P. Villiers the cause of poor law reform is much indebted [and] we feel we do him simple justice when we assert that to his tact and industry, combined with his felicitous generalisation of facts, the continuance of the life of the Board as a central controlling power was mainly due.[44]

The editorial praised Villiers for the reforms he had promoted, which had been motivated by 'the profoundest feeling of practical philanthropy', and attributed his absence from office to 'some disfavour he has incurred in certain quarters, owing to the course of public action he has followed', and even intimating (mistakenly) that Villiers had not returned to the Poor Law Board

from a belief that it is impossible for him, with the clear and honest views which he entertains, to work in harmony with those permanent officials of the Board, whose tortuous, obstructing, and selfish policy must be totally abhorrent to his nature.[45]

However, despite his undoubted disappointment, Charles Villiers accepted his rejection by Gladstone with no little stoicism and, as Fitzmaurice observed, it was Villiers' good temper and dry sense of humour which, thereafter, prevented him, if not quite able to conceal a sense of grievance, 'from ever degenerating into a "candid friend" in Parliament, or becoming the inhabitant of a political cave'.[46] In the event, as Colin Matthew observed, the composition of Gladstone's Cabinet of fifteen ministers, comprising seven Whigs (Clarendon, Granville, Fortesque, Hartington, Kimberly, Hatherley and Argyll), three Peelites (Gladstone, Cardwell and de Grey), three Liberals (Childers, Goschen and Bruce) and two Radicals (Bright and Lowe), not only maintained the Whig–Liberal–Peelite alliance evident since 1846 but also (with the absence of Halifax, Russell, George Grey and

Villiers) gave the Cabinet a fresh appearance, since only eight members had previous Cabinet experience.[47]

Villiers, never one to bear grudges, welcomed the appointment of his old friend and colleague John Bright as President of the Board of Trade, noting that 'satisfaction is felt, as he desired to take office, that he has got a good berth ... He made no terms with Gladstone, or stipulated for any person to come in with him', and observing wryly that by accepting this appointment Bright 'has disqualified himself for agitation in future'.[48] By contrast, Villiers was less than complimentary about the appointment of Robert Lowe as Chancellor of the Exchequer. Writing to Delane, Villiers stated that 'the prepossession that I am told existed for Lowe was because he was so bold and right upon the whole system of education, whether for rich or poor', but added 'I question if the idea had ever crossed people's minds of what was his fitness for the office of Chancellor of the Exchequer'.[49]

Thereafter, and despite a discreet representation by Granville to Gladstone on his behalf in February 1869 – 'Chas. Villiers is here. At dinner he held the soundest party doctrines'[50] – Villiers' parliamentary career was consigned to the backbenches. However, Villiers did receive a compensation of sorts for loss of office with the passing of the Political Pensions Act in 1869. On leaving the Poor Law Board, he had claimed that he had always been unlucky and 'I am worse off now than when I began thirty-one years ago',[51] but in July 1869 Gladstone, honouring his intimation of the previous December, reminded Villiers that the Political Pensions Bill would shortly receive Royal assent and Villiers, in reply, asked to what extent he was entitled to claim anything under it.[52] Gladstone affirmed that Villiers should prepare a claim, to which Villiers replied:

> I am very much obliged to you for the trouble you have been good enough to take respecting my claim to a civil pension under the Bill now in progress in the House of Lords. My right to a pension under that Bill would arise apparently from my having held offices in the Civil Service for 12 years, that of Judge Advocate General for five years, and that of President of the Poor Law Board for 7 years, which were remunerated by a salary of £1200 a year, and that I am in a position to make the declaration required ... that my income derived from other sources is so far limited as to bring me within the meaning and intention of that Act.[53]

Villiers added that although he was not entitled, under the terms specified in the 6th section of the Bill, to any 'emolument payable by any monies raised by taxation or out of the public revenue in any part of Her Majesty's Dominions', he was also entitled to an annual payment from the fund of the Court of Chancery of £750. Villiers concluded by stating that he did not desire 'the least favour to be shown to myself in estimating the progress of the claims that may at present be submitted for your consideration', adding 'how heartily I rejoice to hear of the improvement which has taken place in your health and which has admitted of your return to London'.[54] Accordingly, under the terms of the Political Pensions Act of 1869, Villiers was awarded a substantial pension of £2,000 per annum (at least £100,000 in modern currency), backdated to 1866, and which included the £750 payable from the fund of the Court of Chancery.[55] He subsequently drew this pension until his death thirty-two years later, prompting the late Roy Jenkins to observe of Villiers, with no little cynicism, that 'appropriately he had been chairman of the Poor Law Board in the long Palmerston-Russell government and was making sure that he did not swell the numbers of those for whom he had been responsible'.[56]

In 1870, however, Charles Villiers was invited to chair the Select Committee on Conventual and Monastic Institutions, which arose from a campaign spearheaded by Charles Newdegate, the Tory MP for North Warwickshire, against a background of popular anti-Catholic agitation attendant upon the Vatican Council.[57] Newdegate hoped to expose convents as wicked and nefarious institutions which required government inspection and regulation and had initially proposed that the select committee should investigate the existence, character and increase in the number of convents and monastic houses in Britain as well as the terms upon which their income, property and estates were received.[58] However, a motion from Gladstone that the mandate of the committee should be confined solely to the property of Roman Catholic houses was passed by the Commons,[59] thereby preventing the inquiry from becoming, as Villiers observed 'extremely painful and offensive to Roman Catholic subjects of the Queen'.[60] The committee, comprising nine Liberals and six Conservatives (including four Roman Catholics) met for the first time on 17 May 1870 and thereafter on fourteen occasions in May, June and July, examining twenty-nine witnesses.[61] Newdegate was initially invited to chair the committee but insisted that Charles Villiers, as the senior MP and the only member of the committee with ministerial experience, should do so, to which Villiers agreed.

In chairing the committee, Villiers stuck rigidly to the mandate of Gladstone's amendment, acting conscientiously and impartially, despite the fact that during his chairmanship he suffered a personal tragedy with the sudden death of his elder brother, George, Lord Clarendon.[62] The distinguished Foreign Secretary had been taken ill in early June with a severe attack of what was described as gout of the stomach and had been confined to his home in Grosvenor Crescent, but his condition deteriorated and he passed away on 27 June 1870, with his wife Katherine and his eldest son Edward at his bedside.[63] Clarendon's death hit Charles hard, for the two brothers had been very close and George had given staunch support to his brother's political career and had been the first to defend him when he felt that Charles had been unfairly treated. It also left Charles Villiers as the only surviving member of the large family which had once gathered together at Kent House some fifty years earlier, although, in future, his own old age was to be enriched in private by the society of numerous nephews and nieces and their children.[64]

This sad event notwithstanding, Villiers proceeded with the work of the select committee. In particular, he allowed Newdegate plenty of opportunities to contribute to the proceedings (which he duly did, asking no fewer than 1,222 questions during the course of the hearings), but he was eventually left with little alternative but to quash Newdegate's repeated attempts – which occupied an inordinate amount of parliamentary time – to introduce irrelevant and often anecdotal evidence about the character of nunneries into the investigation. The select committee established that the legal status of conventual and monastic houses was imperfect and unclear, especially in regard to the registration of Catholic charities, the administration of endowments, and the transfer of properties. Indeed, as Arnstein has shown, the legal position of Roman Catholic religious orders was 'a complete muddle'.[65]

The 1870 parliamentary session closed before the committee could frame a report and on 17 March 1871, in his five hundredth contribution to parliamentary debates in the House of Commons, Villiers proposed that the committee be reappointed in order to complete its work. Newdegate, however, moved an amendment that the scope of the inquiry be expanded on the grounds that the original mandate of the committee had been restricted and that during the hearings he had been treated unfairly by the committee. It was at this point that Villiers lost patience with Newdegate, reminding him that 'general surprise was felt and expressed by the Committee at the small number of witnesses and the meagre nature of the evidence he produced', and Newdegate's amendment was defeated by 196 to 79 votes.[66] The committee was reappointed, but Newdegate refused to participate and when the committee was reconvened by Villiers in June 1871 it was agreed not to hear further witnesses but to prepare a report.

The final report of the Select Committee noted that because conventual and monastic institutions were not technically charities falling within the remit of the Charity Commission, their Catholic founders had understandably hesitated in enrolling them and, moreover, that whilst the religious orders performed invaluable educational and social functions they were not recognized by law as corporations. The committee concluded, therefore, that the law was inconsistent with the principles of religious liberty and should be changed, with legal protection afforded to convents and monasteries. It also concluded that government inspection and regulation of these religious houses was unnecessary.[67] Thus, in practice, the outcome of the inquiry was the opposite of what Newdegate had originally intended, presenting Roman Catholic institutions, as Arnstein has observed, as victims rather than villains.[68] Newdegate subsequently persisted in his demands for government inspection, introducing an abortive Bill to this effect in the Commons in March 1873 which, as Villiers informed Gladstone 'has, of course, no chance of passing'.[69] Thereafter, as Denis Paz has observed, the convent question was increasingly seen as little more than a joke,[70] and further attempts by Newdegate to perpetuate it came to nothing, serving only to speed up the removal of remaining Catholic disabilities.[71]

In the meantime, Gladstone, engrossed with the 'pacification' of Ireland, had left much domestic legislation in the hands of his Ministers, who duly pushed a raft of reforming measures through Parliament. These included the reform of the army (1868–70), the Education Act (1870), the University Test Act (1871), the Trade Union Act (1871), the Criminal Law Amendment Act (1871), the Ballot Act (1872), the Licensing Act (1872), and the Judicature Act (1873). Whilst supporting some of these measures, both Charles Villiers and Thomas Weguelin took an unequivocal stance on several issues, in stark contrast to the half-hearted stance of Wolverhampton's Liberal elite. Addressing the inaugural meeting of the Wolverhampton Reform Association at St George's Hall, Wolverhampton, on 2 April 1872, Villiers, whilst praising his constituents for their adherence to Liberalism over the previous forty years, stated that of the present [Gladstone's] Ministry, 'He thought that some of their friends in high places were not quite so popular as they were, but he rather thought that it was not because they were too liberal'.[72]

In particular, whilst supporting in broad terms Forster's Education Act of 1870, which had established local board schools in areas where voluntary provision was inadequate, Villiers was critical of the religious clauses of the act, which provided for nondenominational religious teaching in the new schools, and which upset Nonconformists and Roman Catholics alike. He stated that it was a matter of regret that the Act 'had given a great deal of offence to a number of their friends' (the Nonconformists) and promised his support for a forthcoming motion by the Birmingham MP, George Dixon, for a revision of the Act, stating that

> The State must sooner or later look the religious question in the face, that the paying for teaching religion out of the public funds was contrary to principles of religious equality, and that the same teacher ought not to be employed to teach religious and secular subjects.[73]

Villiers also criticised the government for failing to immediately implement the secret ballot (for which he had campaigned continuously since 1835), as a logical corollary of the 1867 Reform Act. The Ballot Bill, he claimed, 'was more needed now than ever', adding that 'it was impossible to conceive anything more irregular' and he 'did not suppose that the ballot would be a panacea for all evils, but believed it would do away with many'.[74] In conclusion, Villiers stated (to loud cheers) that hitherto his constituents had allowed him to exercise his judgement on questions with the most perfect independence, and he hoped he might expect the same indulgence in the future. Directly they wanted someone else with more ability or not so old to represent them, he should retire with no other feeling but satisfaction and gratitude for having been so long trusted as their member, and the meeting resolved unanimously that the Ballot Bill be enacted and that the Education Act should be amended.

Villiers was also critical of the government's record in regard to trade union legislation. First, he pointed to the failure to redress the deficiencies of the

Master and Servant Act of 1867, which had been widely used by employers in the mining, textile, pottery, iron and steel and general building industries in the 1860s and 1870s, whereby workers faced prosecution for aggravated breaches of contract on pain of imprisonment or fines, thereby leaving workers at the mercy of employers keen to enforce discipline and regulate hours of work.[75] Second, although the Trade Union Act of 1871 had legalised trade unions by protecting their funds, Villiers condemned the Criminal Law Amendment Act of 1871, which prohibited peaceful picketing on pain of up to three months imprisonment with hard labour for 'coercing' individuals from working, which rendered the strike weapon ineffective and was opposed by trades unionists.[76] When Villiers addressed a crowd of over 1,500 workers outside the Great Western Railway locomotive works in St Mary's Ward during the election campaign of February 1874, he attacked both pieces of legislation vociferously, to the great delight of his audience.[77] In particular, he not only described the Criminal Law Amendment Act as 'unjust and partial', adding that 'he should most certainly vote for its repeal', but also called for powers to be afforded to working men to obtain compensation or damages from their employers for the support of themselves and their families in cases where it had been proved that employers had been negligent.[78] Indeed, Jon Lawrence has claimed that 'Villiers' ability to gain a sympathetic, even enthusiastic hearing from such a large open air meeting outside the town's largest factory conveyed a powerful symbolic message of popular legitimacy.'[79]

Villiers also supported the emerging campaign for women's suffrage, an issue on which both Liberals and Conservatives were divided.[80] Although he had been absent when John Stuart Mill's amendment to the 1867 Reform Act in regard to women's suffrage was defeated in May 1867,[81] Villiers communicated with Lydia Becker,[82] a leading figure in the Manchester Society for Women's Suffrage, and consistently supported Jacob Bright's Women's Disability Bills of 1870, 1871, 1872 and 1873, which sought to extend the franchise to women ratepayers, who had already achieved the right to vote in municipal elections. These Bills were defeated, Gladstone being one of their chief opponents.[83] Thereafter, as the suffragist Helen Blackburn noted, Villiers' vote was always recorded in favour of the repeal of restrictions on women's suffrage,[84] including the Women's Suffrage Bill of 1889, when he communicated on the subject with Millicent Garrett Fawcett,[85] whilst Florence Balgarnie also later recalled Villiers' contribution to the campaign for women's suffrage.[86] Indeed, both Villiers' niece, Maria Theresa Earle, and his great-niece, Lady Constance Georgina Bulwer-Lytton, were active suffragists, the latter becoming a leading member of the Women's Social and Political Union and suffering greatly from forced feeding during her imprisonment in Holloway in 1909.[87]

Since 1873, however, Gladstone's Ministry had been running out of steam, and Disraeli famously described the Liberal Front Bench as 'a range of exhausted volcanoes'.[88] Gladstone's attempt to introduce an Irish Universities Bill, which was opposed by both Irish Catholics and Presbyterians, was defeated in March, with forty-three Liberals voting against the government, and despite a ministerial reshuffle, a series of by-election defeats followed, which Charles Villiers attributed privately to Gladstone's leadership. Writing to his friend, Frances, Countess Waldegrave, he claimed 'Our party are no doubt *now* hoping that Lord Palmerston's last words have become true & that Mr Gladstone is in a state to be put under restraint'.[89] In January 1874, Gladstone declared his intention to dissolve parliament and at the general election in February the Tories were returned with an overall majority. The defeat of the Liberals lay in part in the fact that the coalition of forces – provincial middle-class liberalism, nonconformism, radicalism and the working-class voter – which had brought them victory in 1868 had, by 1874, been split by contentious legislation.[90] The Education Act angered Liberal nonconformists and Roman Catholics alike; the Criminal Law Amendment Act angered trade unionists and working men; Lowe's Budget of 1871, which proposed a 'match tax' to subsidise Cardwell's army reforms, was opposed by the match manufacturers, and was withdrawn, only for Lowe to raise income tax, which was widely unpopular; and Bruce's Licensing Bills and the Licensing Act of 1872 lost the Liberals support from the lucrative brewing industry on the one hand and from the largely Liberal and nonconformist United Kingdom Temperance Alliance on the other.[91] Hence the Liberals' legislative record lost them support amongst the very people who had helped to bring them to power. It also provided Disraeli's increasingly well-organised Conservatives with opportunities to woo the dissatisfied voter by promising to reduce income tax, to repeal trade union legislation, and to introduce social (rather than institutional) reform, the chief desire of the newly enfranchised working classes.[92] However, for Gladstone, who had become temporarily disillusioned with party politics,[93] the election defeat in part prompted his surprising decision of January 1875 to retire from politics. On 3 February 1875, at a meeting of leading Liberals at the Reform Club, Charles Villiers' proposal that the Marquis of Hartington should undertake the leadership of the Liberal Party in the House of Commons was carried, amidst cheers,[94] and John Bright, who had chaired the meeting, duly informed Hartington of their decision.[95] In private, however, Villiers continued to believe that Gladstone's retirement would be short-lived.[96]

Yet in Wolverhampton, in the first contested general election since 1841, Charles Villiers (10,358) and Thomas Weguelin (10,036) were re-elected with large majorities over the Tory candidate, Captain Walter Williams (3,628). Here, the Liberals' success owed much to the fact that both Villiers and Weguelin had sought to represent the wider interests of an enlarged electorate by dissociating themselves publicly from unpopular Liberal measures.[97] The election was attended (as elsewhere) by some anti-Liberal electoral violence in the Irish district, which may be attributed to Irish Catholic concern over the fate of Catholic voluntary schools and Gladstone's Irish policy,[98] although the disorders also represented a protest against the wealth and privilege of the town's 'west end' and, by implication, the Liberal elite, for elsewhere in the borough the party was clearly perceived as the champion of the dispossessed and marginalised.[99]

This said, the 1874 election offered further proof, if indeed proof were needed, of Charles Villiers' personal standing as a constituency MP, for, as R. Smith has noted, he had endeared himself to the people of Wolverhampton through 'a mixture of political empathy, traditional deference and a recognition of his considerable contribution to the welfare of Wolverhampton'.[100] In this context, the assertions of Lawrence that 'Villiers made little attempt to "nurse" Wolverhampton and was an infrequent visitor even in his youth',[101] of Richard Trainor, who described Villiers as 'a carpetbagger who knew little about local affairs and, even between elections, did little to develop local institutions in Wolverhampton and Bilston',[102] and of Frank Mason, whose fleeting references to Villiers in *The Book of Wolverhampton* imply that he was simply uninterested in his constituency,[103] do not quite hold water. Indeed, this myth should be dispelled. Granted, Villiers was hardly the epitome of the modern-day constituency MP, for he lived in London and, as with many of his contemporaries, largely conducted his duties and responsibilities as an MP from Westminster, where he often received deputations from the borough on a variety of subjects. He had, however, cultivated his constituency prior to 1874 more broadly than has been recognised hitherto, despite chronic ill health. Apart from attending election meetings and addressing free trade rallies in the town, Villiers often returned to Wolverhampton in order to attend important civic functions. The most notable of these were the celebrations attending Queen Victoria's visit to Wolverhampton (her first public provincial excursion since the death of Prince Albert) on 30 November 1866, when a statue of the late Prince Consort was erected in High Green (renamed Queen's Square) and the Queen knighted the Mayor, John Morris,[104] but Villiers also returned to the town annually for various functions, including the dinner of the Corporation for the retiring Mayor, held in November,[105] the dinners of the Wolverhampton Licensed Victuallers Society,[106] and the meetings of the Willenhall Literary and Scientific Society (of which he was the President).[107]

The columns of the *Wolverhampton Chronicle* also indicate that Villiers was a patron of several local societies and charitable institutions, including the Wolverhampton Mechanic's Institute, the Widows and Orphans Provident Society, the Wolverhampton Choral Society, the Wolverhampton Horticultural Society, the Royal Staffs Yeomanry, and the Royal Wolverhampton School, founded in 1850 as an asylum for orphans in the aftermath of the cholera epidemic of 1849. Villiers also frequently made donations towards a variety of other local charitable causes, which included the fund for the erection of a new chapel at Blakenhall;[108] the fund for the Sunday School and Ladies Charity at St George's Church;[109] the fund for the relief of persons suffering from Cholera in Wolverhampton and Bilston;[110] the local Subscription to the Works of the Industry of All Nations Exhibition;[111] the Wolverhampton Fund for the Relief of the Wives and Families of Soldiers ordered abroad on active service during the Crimean War;[112] and the fund for the erection of a Primitive Methodist Chapel at Sedgley.[113] Later, with the opening of the West Park in Wolverhampton in June 1881, Villiers, who had long advocated the enhancement of leisure and recreational facilities for working people, donated an ornate bandstand, made by Steven Bros & Co. of Glasgow, at a cost of £225 (the equivalent of £26,000 in modern currency) which was unveiled in July 1882, although Villiers was unable to attend the celebrations owing to ill-health.[114] Further gifts to local charities continued until 1897 (the year before his death), when Villiers donated a generous sum to the Bilston Technical School.[115]

Villiers had also been a familiar figure at the Wolverhampton Races, held annually each August on Broad Meadow, and attended by the Staffordshire aristocracy and Wolverhampton's civic dignitaries and their guests. Villiers first attended the races in August 1837,[116] and, thereafter, often stayed at Chillington Hall, the country home of T.W. Giffard, Esq., a racehorse enthusiast who did much to both organise and promote Wolverhampton Races. In 1838, it was reported that Villiers was among 150 guests who were provided with 'splendid entertainment' at Chillington Hall prior to the race meeting and, afterwards, with a Gala Ball at the Wolverhampton Assembly Rooms.[117] Villiers attended again in 1840, in the company of Lord George Bentinck,[118] and in 1841.[119] In 1856, Villiers shared the stewardship of the race meeting with the Marquis of Anglesey, thereafter attending the entertainments at Wolverhampton Theatre, where 'he was honoured by a cordial recognition by the audience'.[120] In 1858, due largely to the solicitations of Villiers, Baron Rothschild consented to accept the stewardship of the next Wolverhampton race meeting, in conjunction with the Earl of Stamford and Warrington,[121] and which, accompanied by Villiers, he duly undertook.[122] At the last meeting he attended, in August 1866, Villiers narrowly avoided injury when a temporary stand in which he was ensconced, and which supported 500 people, collapsed during the Wolverhampton Stakes, leaving several spectators seriously injured.[123]

In many respects, however, the election of 1874 marked a watershed in Charles Villiers' political career. Although he visited Willenhall in December 1875 as a private guest of R.D. Gough and was persuaded to open a bazaar in aid of the newly established Free Library (giving a brief address on the benefits of Free Libraries),[124] Villiers never again visited Wolverhampton, despite continuing to represent the borough for a further twenty-three years. Thereafter, the custom was always preserved, even when it was known that there was no possibility of his attendance, of inviting Villiers to take part in any important public ceremonial in the borough, and he invariably and unfailingly replied, apologising for his non-attendance and often writing lengthy letters on political or civic affairs, as the circumstances demanded.[125] Villiers' absence from Wolverhampton during these years is not easy to explain. It could, of course, be ascribed to complacency, for Villiers occupied one of the safest seats in the country and could virtually rely on being returned unopposed, such was his standing in the town. Moreover, with Gladstone's spectacular return to politics in 1876 and his subsequent electoral victory of 1880, it was extremely unlikely that opportunities for further political preferment would arise for Villiers under Gladstone's leadership of the Liberal Party. On the other hand, Villiers continued to display great interest in Wolverhampton politics for the remainder of his life, and the constancy shown towards him by the town's electors was graciously reciprocated by Villiers in 1884, when he dedicated the two volumes of his *Free Trade Speeches* to the constituency of Wolverhampton 'in remembrance of the unbroken trust' which had for close upon half a century connected him with the borough.[126] In this context, the most likely explanation for Villiers' absence from his constituency after 1874 – and the explanation which Villiers himself frequently offered to his constituents – was the precarious state of his health. He was already an old man and, with advancing age, suffered from recurrent bouts of ill health which precluded long-distance travel and forced him to decline (always politely, and by letter) many invitations to events outside London.

Nevertheless, and health permitting, Villiers took full advantage of the attractions of the social, cultural and political milieu of life in his home city of London, which were important for an elderly bachelor who had already outlived all his siblings. Indeed, Villiers clearly enjoyed living the high life in London, where he acquired something akin to celebrity status, and where many of his private friendships were rooted.

One reflection of this lies in the reports contained in the society columns of the *Morning Post*, variously entitled 'Foreign Courts', 'The Fashionable World' and 'Fashionable Entertainments', which contain almost one hundred references to Villiers' presence at grand social functions during the 1870s and 1880s.[127] These indicate that Villiers attended regularly all the great Royal and State occasions, such as the Queen's State Concert and State Ball, held at Buckingham Palace, the Royal Garden Party, held variously at Buckingham Palace, Chiswick and Marlborough House, and the Queen's Levee, held at St James's Palace and hosted by the Prince and Princess of Wales. Victoria was often present at these special events, which were attended by members of the Royal family, foreign ambassadors, the aristocracy and leading politicians.[128] Villiers also attended one of the great Parliamentary occasions, the Speaker's full-dress dinner and levee, which was held annually at Westminster in February or March.[129] Villiers was also present at numerous banquets and receptions at the Foreign Office, hosted variously by the Earl and Countess Granville, Lord and Lady Derby, and the Marquis and Marchioness of Salisbury, and attended by foreign royalty, ambassadors, diplomats and leading British politicians, in the course of which Villiers met, among others, the Emperor of Russia, the Sultan of Turkey, the Shah of Persia, and the Sultan of Zanzibar.[130] Moreover, with his aristocratic connections, he also had private meetings, sometimes at Claridge's, with Foreign Royalty during their visits to England, including Queen Augusta and the Crown Prince and Princess of Prussia, the Queen of Holland, the King of the Belgians, and Prince Henri d'Orleans, Duc d'Aumale, the fifth son of ex-King Louis Philippe of

France.[131] Villiers also attended other receptions for foreign dignitaries and the Liberal and Tory political elite, hosted variously by Lady Margaret Beaumont, at the Terrace, Piccadilly; the Countess of Derby, in St James's Square; Baroness Frances Burdett Coutts, in Piccadilly; the Countess of Granville, at Carlton House Terrace; the Duke and Duchess of Devonshire at Devonshire House; Countess Spencer at Spencer House, St James's; and the Duchess of Northumberland, at Sion House, Isleworth.[132] Moreover, as a renowned and convivial conversationalist, Villiers was also frequently invited to dinner parties in London hosted by his aristocratic circle of intimate friends. These included Frances, Countess Waldegrave,[133] and her husband, Chichester Fortesque (later Lord Carlingford),[134] who frequently invited Villiers to dinner parties and receptions at Strawberry Hill, their Twickenham home, which formed an important part of the London Season and where the mixed company included royalty and Tory, Liberal and Radical politicians.[135] Other hosts included his old friends, Lady Molesworth, Lady Holland, Viscountess Combermere, the Earl and Countess Granville, Lord Derby, and Lord and Lady Egerton of Tatton.[136]

Collectively, the contents of these society columns reflect the status of and respect for the monarchy, both British and Foreign, in the social life of the political elite, and the role of the Speaker of the House of Commons. Moreover, they suggest that the 'Westminster Bubble' was in fact far more exclusive in the Victorian period than today (although this began to change during the late 1880s and beyond, with greater party organisation and discipline), and that within the Westminster elite, Liberals and Tories were often at ease with one another in social circles, thereby reflecting the importance of social class and familial/friendship connections in Victorian politics. They also reflect, as Karen Reynolds has illustrated, the importance and prominence of lady hostesses in Victorian political life.[137]

However, these reports clearly understate the true scale of Villiers' social engagements in London, many of which were private. These included regular attendance at all his London Clubs, most notably the Athenaeum and the Travellers Club in Pall Mall, the Wellington Club in Knightsbridge, the Bachelors Club in Hamilton Place, Brooks's in St James Street, the National Liberal Club in Whitehall Place, and the Reform Club in Pall Mall, 'where his bent figure and shrewd face were very familiar to members'.[138] As Amy Milne-Smith has shown, London's clubland provided a vehicle for political conversations and gossip, shaping political friendships and sometimes diluting personal tensions and disagreements, and Charles Villiers was renowned in these circles not only for his conversation but also for his gossip.[139] There were also meetings at the Cobden Club,[140] the Political Economy Club,[141] and the Law Amendment Society to attend.[142] Then there were many dinner parties and soirées, unrecorded in the popular press, but noted in contemporary memoirs and autobiographies. For example, Villiers was a frequent dinner guest of the Rothschilds, sometimes in the company of Disraeli,[143] who, in 1867, had sought in vain to secure a Peerage for Lionel de Rothschild. Indeed, Baron Lionel was himself reluctant to accept a peerage from

Disraeli, a decision which was greeted with some consternation by Villiers, who, according to Lionel

> could not understand, nor could they at Lady Palmerston's, that I won't accept anything from the present Government. They all fancy Dis is under great obligations to us – so the best thing to do is to hold my tongue and let them think what they like – it is only amusing to hear all their nonsense.[144]

Villiers was also friendly with Sir Charles Dilke,[145] on one occasion, in 1872, attending a dinner party at the Dilke's home in Sloane Street where the guests included William Harcourt, the historian Kinglake, Brookfield, the Queen's Chaplain, and the poet Robert Browning.[146] Indeed, both Dilke and Villiers attended soirees at Countess Waldegrave's Strawberry Hill home and 'the rival establishment' at Holland House.[147]

Villiers also kept in touch with his old friend and colleague, John Bright, now MP for Birmingham, with whom he had maintained a steadfast friendship throughout their lengthy political careers, as Bright's diaries confirm. In May 1868, for example, Bright recorded a dinner

> at Orleans House, Twickenham, with Duke and Duchess d'Aumale. Mr. Villiers went and returned with me. Large party, about 24, to dinner, English and French … it was a grand dinner … wines very choice, I was told, and of special vintages … the party broke up at 11 o'clock, the Duke offering Mr. Villiers and me a fine cigar as we left.[148]

In June 1868 he mentions

> Evening, with C.P. Villiers, to York House, Twickenham, to dine with the Comte de Paris. A large party, several French gentlemen among them … Kinnaird came back with Villiers and me: pleasant talk on Irish Church question.[149]

In June 1883, Villiers was invited to join the celebrations in Birmingham Town Hall to mark the twenty-fifth anniversary of John Bright's election as MP for the city. Owing to ill-health, Villiers was unable to attend but, in rendering his apologies, he paid a warm tribute to his old friend in a letter which was read out at the meeting, and which stated

> I have had the advantage of Mr Bright's acquaintance for upwards of 40 years, during the whole of which time we have sat together in Parliament, and during the celebrated movement against the Corn Laws our relations were necessarily most intimate. With such means of observation I can, of course, never speak but in terms of the most highest admiration, not only of his talents and great qualities for public life, but for the consistent

and conscientious manner in which they have been devoted to the public interest. The appreciation, indeed, of his past career, which is now being so universally manifested, is in my opinion an honour to the country, and especially so to the great constituency that he has had the privilege of representing so long and so worthily.[150]

Bright's Diaries also record that in November 1884 he dined 'with Sir C. Forster, M.P. Mr. Storey and Mr. Burt, and my old friend C.P. Villiers, there; also Miss Tenant [Lady Stanley]',[151] whilst in March 1885 he dined 'with Mr. Speaker: a mixed company of members. I sat between my old friend C.P. Villiers and W.E. Baxter of Montrose',[152] and in March 1886 he attended a dinner 'with Lord Rosebery at Lansdowne House, Berkeley Square: a party of 30. Very pleasant evening. Talk with our host, and with my old friend, C.P. Villiers'.[153] The final reference to Villiers in Bright's diary in August 1887 records a 'Long talk with C.P. Villiers at the Reform Club, mainly on Irish affairs', Bright noting that Villiers 'Speaks well and clearly as ever tho' is said to be in his 86th year'.[154]

Villiers, who in his youth had travelled widely on the Continent, had also valued the occasional time away from London during the parliamentary recess, whether on private trips to Paris with Lionel Rothschild,[155] and others,[156] or, with his old friend Sir Abraham Hayward[157] as a house guest of the Molesworths at their country estate at Pencarrow, near Bodmin.[158] In September 1872, Villiers also accompanied the Derbys from Greenock by steamer for Minard in the Western Highlands for a holiday at the ten thousand acre estate owned by his friend Sir John Pender, the millionaire industrialist with interests in Manchester as well as the Atlantic and Indian telegraphs.[159] In addition to Villiers, the party included the Lowes, the distinguished orientalist Sir Henry Rawlinson, the famous artist, Frederick, Lord Leighton, and the eminent scientist and engineer, Sir William Thompson.[160] Later, in December 1874, Villiers was a house guest of the Duke and Duchess of Cleveland (the Duke also owned substantial property in Wolverhampton) at Raby Castle.[161] Thereafter, however, with advancing age, such excursions beyond London became increasingly rare.

Moreover, London held another attraction for Charles Villiers, for in 1871, and in the best traditions of Victorian melodrama, his private life was enriched by a reconciliation with Catherine Mellish. Their reunion – Miss Mellish was now an old spinster of seventy-five, whilst Villiers was now sixty-nine – was effected over a dinner arranged by a mutual friend, who later recorded the rekindling of their friendship in an interview with the *Evening Telegraph*.[162] The reunion was successful, Catherine evidently 'radiant with joy', and Villiers subsequently dined regularly at her house in Great Stanhope Street, Mayfair, on one occasion shouting at the butler and complaining about the quality of the claret. This intimate friendship lasted for nine years, until Catherine died in February 1880, and in her will, dated June 1878, she bequeathed her entire wealth, which included the 2,000 acre estate at Hammels Park in

Hertfordshire, to Charles Villiers.[163] This was somewhat ironic, given that her wealth had been the purported reason for the break-up of her courtship with Villiers over forty years earlier. The lady interviewee also noted that

> It is equally true that he never touched it, despite the reconciliation ... he shrank from it for the reason that he did not wish to obtain any glory with money which in his early life had been the indirect cause of so much pain to him and his sweetheart.[164]

Indeed, Villiers left the money to accumulate with interest, whilst he lived very simply on his own modest revenue, supplemented by his Cabinet pension and his investments.[165] Catherine Mellish was buried in the churchyard of St Mary's Church, Braughing, where Villiers arranged for the placing of a memorial to Catherine in the chancel,[166] and later, in 1881, donated an acre of land for the extension of the churchyard on the north side.[167] Villiers' relationship with Catherine Mellish was little known to many of his contemporaries, although on the passing of 'Old Miss Mellish', John Wodehouse, First Earl of Kimberley, noted in his journal that Charles Villiers had 'proposed to her in vain as she thought he was after her money', but adding that 'when they both became old they became very intimate again, and she left him all her fortune for life'.[168] Indeed, it was only after Villiers' death in 1898 that the story of this romance was revealed in public in articles in the *Aberdeen Journal*, entitled 'A Villiers Romance: a touching romance in the life of the late Rt. Hon. Charles Pelham Villiers',[169] and *The Star*, entitled 'A Bachelor's Romance',[170] although, by contrast, a sensationalised and largely inaccurate version of this romance was published many years later in the *Portsmouth Evening News*.[171]

Yet the Wolverhampton electorate continued to support Villiers from 1874 onwards, despite his absence from the town and the changing face of local politics. In February 1878 the Wolverhampton Liberal Association was itself reformed along the lines of the 'caucus' system developed by Joseph Chamberlain in Birmingham, with an executive committee comprising delegates elected by local wards, in order to more effectively convey the Liberal message to the enlarged electorate. Yet when Weguelin indicated his intention to stand down in 1880, the Executive still acted as of old, determined to secure a seat for their man, Henry Fowler, who was unanimously appointed, unopposed, as a prospective parliamentary candidate.[172] At the General Election of 1880, which witnessed the fall of Disraeli's government and the triumphant return of Gladstone following his inspired Midlothian campaign in the aftermath of the Bulgarian massacres, Villiers (with 12,197 votes) and Fowler (11,606) were returned, with the unsuccessful Tory, Alfred Hickman, a local ironmaster and colliery owner, polling 5,847 votes.

In the aftermath of the election, Villiers was greatly irritated by a false report published in *The Record*, which was carried by *The Morning Post* on

15 May, which claimed 'on high authority', that in view of the fact that Sir William Vernon Harcourt, the Home Secretary, had recently lost his seat at Oxford to the Tories,

> a fresh arrangement has been made to provide a seat ... It seems that Mr Charles Villiers, the brother of the late Earl of Clarendon, who has represented Wolverhampton since 1835, is to be raised to the peerage, and that Sir William Vernon Harcourt will be welcomed by the electorate as his successor.[173]

Writing to his niece, Alice (whose husband, Algernon Borthwick, was proprietor of the *Morning Chronicle*), Villiers stated:

> Dear Alice, – If Harcourt could be served by somebody else being victimised than me I should be very glad. The lying extract from a religious paper circulated in the *Morning Post* this morning, relating to my making way for him [Harcourt] who has lost his seat at Oxford, has already cost me 4 telegrams in giving it unqualified contradiction, and those that know that you are my niece may possibly think that I was a party to its insertion! So that I suppose it will not be easy (for some days at least) to abate the disturbance at my expense it will cause in the large district I represent![174]

The Liberal victory of 1880 encouraged the further development of popular Liberal organisations in the provinces as a counter to Tory working-men's social clubs and, as Lawrence has shown, Wolverhampton was particularly active in this respect. The Wolverhampton Liberal Club was founded in North Street in 1882, and in January 1883, with financial support from Charles Villiers, the Villiers Reform Club was established at 6 George Street, with Henry Fowler following suit in 1884 with the foundation of the Fowler Reform Club.[175] These political clubs were designed in part to reach out to plebian Liberals and Radicals,[176] and it was through the Villiers Reform Club, and particularly its secretary, William McIlwraith, that Charles Villiers was henceforth able to keep in touch with constituency matters. Indeed, through an extensive mutual correspondence, McIlwraith effectively became Villiers' 'eyes and ears' in his constituency for the remainder of his political career.

Yet paradoxically, during this period, Villiers also received a number of public accolades. In August 1872 a cartoon image of Villiers was included in a series of prints of famous statesmen published in *Vanity Fair*.[177] In September 1877 a full-size marble statue of Villiers, sculpted by William Theed, R.A., of London and commissioned by subscribers, was unveiled in Manchester Town Hall, one of three statues – the others were of John Bright and William Gladstone – commissioned by Manchester Liberals. All three were living statesmen who had made significant contributions to Liberal causes but it is significant that Villiers was the first.[178] In May 1876, on receiving several memorials from prominent Wolverhampton inhabitants suggesting that a statue of Villiers should be erected in the town in recognition of his outstanding service to the community, the Mayor of Wolverhampton, J.C. Major, convened a meeting to discuss the proposal – an unusual honour for a living politician – which was accepted unanimously 'by men of all shades of political opinion'. In October 1876 an executive committee, comprising Major H. Loveridge, H. Underhill and H. Walker, was established to co-ordinate arrangements and £1,000 was duly raised by donations and public subscriptions to commission William Theed to produce a marble statue. Wolverhampton Council granted permission for this to be erected on a site in Snow Hill.[179]

The statue was duly unveiled by Earl Granville on Friday 6 June 1879 in the presence of an immense crowd, numbering several thousands. Unfortunately, on the eve of the celebrations, Villiers was taken ill in London and was unable to attend. The proceedings commenced at half-past three in the afternoon when a procession formed outside the Town Hall, comprising Earl Granville; Lord Wrottesley, the Lord Lieutenant of Staffordshire; Sir Charles Foster, MP; Sir Robert Peel, MP; Mr A. Staveley Hill, QC; Mr T. T. Weguelin, MP; Mr F. Monkton, MP; The Mayor and Aldermen, dressed in their ceremonial robes; the Poor Law Guardians and Corporation Officers, followed by the Memorial Committee and subscribers to the Memorial Fund.[180] It was reported that 'flags and banners were floating gaily and the church bells were rung merrily in honour of the occasion' as the procession made its way to the Agricultural Hall, where several addresses were given, after which the party moved to the site of the statue, where the unveiling ceremony was performed by Earl Granville from a small platform which had been erected for the purpose, surrounded by the Rifle Volunteers on horseback, replete in their scarlet uniforms, to maintain order, although the proceedings throughout were most enthusiastic and orderly. In the evening, a grand banquet was held in the Exchange, where the chair was taken by Lord Wrottesley and further addresses were made in honour of Villiers.

The Spectator reported that in his speech, Granville skilfully brought out 'the shrewd, courageous, witty, easy-going, somewhat slovenly character'[181] of the politician – and great personal friend – who had exercised so salutary an influence over the two great reforms which chiefly affected the interests of the poorest class – the abolition of the corn duties (which he referred to at length) and the reform of the Poor Law in relation to the Law of Settlement. Indeed, Granville added that it had been publicly expressed by Sir James Kay-Shuttleworth and Florence Nightingale, and others most competent to judge, that the legislation passed whilst Villiers was in charge of the Poor Law Board 'exceeded any that had previously been passed (applause)'.[182] As Granville observed, Villiers 'had everything, with one possible exception, namely, that he was possibly not so smartly dressed in the last new dress as he might have been', adding 'Indeed, I myself have some recollections of buttons off his coat; buttons lost forever; buttons not even found at the end of that trenchant blade with which he delighted to lunge at pig-headed opponents'.[183] He also recalled how John Bright (who had tendered his great regret at being unable to attend the unveiling) had once told him

> That while Richard Cobden, George Wilson and himself and others had worked the question (repeal) out of doors, they had always considered Mr Villiers as the man who had made the question his own in the House of Commons. He told me how Mr Villiers had attended many of their most important public meetings, and how he was ready always with his advice, which Mr Bright described as excellent, practical, shrewd, and useful in proportion to its fruits, for he added that there was only one thing on which Mr Villiers was earnestly intent, which was that the thing should be done.[184]

At the Banquet, Earl Granville, in reverting to the subject of the House of Lords, was moved to state that the members of that House would be exceedingly glad to see Mr Villiers amongst them, a statement which drew much applause from the audience, although Sir Charles Foster, speaking on behalf of the House of Commons, added that 'Greatly should he regret to lose Mr Villiers from the House of Commons by an elevation to the House of Lords, which had been hinted at'.[185]

Alderman Henry Hartley Fowler (soon to be elected as Villiers' fellow Liberal Member of Parliament for the borough) also delivered a lengthy eulogy of Villiers, which is worth citing in full. Fowler stated:

> True to his party, true to his leaders, true to his policy, he had yet combined with party allegiance such a faithful, such an impartial discharge of all those duties ... that he had won, retained and justified that public confidence, that unanimous respect, which the proceedings of today are intended to express and perpetuate. Wolverhampton is proud of such a man, and I venture to say that Mr Villiers is, and ought to be, proud of Wolverhampton. At the second contest which took place in this borough, Wolverhampton sent Mr Villiers, an inexperienced, untried and comparatively speaking, unknown politician to take the seat for the first time in the House of Commons. During the long succession of elections – I think eleven – that choice had never been regretted and never recalled. In the heat of the conflict, in the hour of the most brilliant triumph of his parliamentary life, Wolverhampton rendered and repeated her confidence in the indomitable champion of Free Trade, who never sheathed the sword until the victory was final and complete; and when at length the talents, the experience, the cultured common sense, the political sagacity, the broad and enlightened statesmanship, which had for so many years been developed to the public good were required in the higher services of the State, the borough gladly continued to the Minister of the Crown the same

admiration and support which it had so freely accorded to the unofficial Member of Parliament. Mr Villiers can look Wolverhampton in the face, and Wolverhampton can look Mr Villiers in the face, with a consciousness that no stain of corruption has ever dimmed the purity of the tie by which they are bound together. A free Member and a free choice, they paint a bright and enduring example to those vast constituencies by which the destinies of this Empire are so materially controlled, and in future days, when that statue, standing in the centre of this great hive of industry, shall tell the story of honourable, brilliant, faithful, successful statesmanship, it will tell with tones equally distinguished, equally forceful, the story of an enlightened, trusting, patriotic constituency.[186]

In May 1881, a marble bust of Villiers, sculpted by Neville Burnard and commissioned by Sir Thomas Bazley (who also commissioned similar busts of Cobden, Bright and Gladstone) was unveiled for display in Manchester City Reference Library and in 1885 a portrait of Villiers, painted by Cope, was exhibited in the Royal Academy (this was moved later to the Reform Club in Pall Mall).[187] In January 1885, Villiers celebrated the fiftieth anniversary of his election as the Member for Wolverhampton and on 10 January the town's Liberals met to celebrate the occasion. Once again, Villiers was unable to attend the event owing to ill-health, but Henry Fowler, who chaired the meeting, praised Villiers' long-standing commitment to reform and Henry Walker proposed a resolution congratulating Villiers on his achievement. This was duly telegraphed to Villiers at his London home and he expressed his 'pride and deep satisfaction' with the honour accorded to him, whilst again regretting his inability to attend the meeting.[188]

Of greater significance, perhaps, was Gladstone's offer to put Villiers' name forward for a Knighthood in November 1884. In reply, Villiers, whilst stating that he appreciated 'the flattering offer you have made me, of submitting my name to her Majesty for the honour of securing a Grand Cross of the Bath', and adding that 'certainly no pedantic objection would prevent my accepting a distinction of this character', he requested that Gladstone postpone the offer on the somewhat dubious grounds that he was unsure how long he would continue to serve as a Member of Parliament.[189] In June 1885 (before the Liberal split over the question of Irish Home Rule), Gladstone tried again, this time with the offer of a Peerage. Gladstone, who might well have wished to see Villiers despatched to the Lords, should have known better, for Villiers, who had showed disdain for privilege, honours and titles throughout his career, declined the offer. As he explained to Gladstone,

> The fact is that arrangements have already been made for my re-election at Wolverhampton, and under circumstances so friendly to myself that I should find it difficult at this moment to withdraw, or rather that I should be unwilling to put the Election to inconvenience or appear to do what would be

ungracious on my part. What may happen during the next months when the Election will take place, no-one can tell, but for this which I would ask you to allow what you kindly propose to remain in abeyance.[190]

Villiers rejection of a Peerage resulted in considerable public surprise, reports of his decision even reaching the Australian press.[191]

Later, on Monday 17 August 1885, a delegation of representatives from Liberal working-men's clubs in Wolverhampton, Bilston, Willenhall and Wednesbury, who had travelled to London by a special excursion train, visited Villiers in Sloane Street and presented him with an elaborately designed and illuminated address marking his fifty years as their MP, expressing their affection and gratitude, and thanking him for 'the constant support he had always given to Liberal principles'.[192] In the afternoon, Villiers accompanied the delegation to the Albert Hall, where a larger body of Wulfrunians had assembled, and where, according to the special correspondent of the Liberal *Northern Echo*, 'there was witnessed an unusual commotion'. He continued:

> As soon as the news spread throughout the vast building and along the crowded courts of the Inventories that the veteran free trader was in the Albert Hall, many gentlemen, and several ladies too, pressed forward and begged to be personally introduced, that they might have the honour of shaking him by the hand. Mr Villiers, whose great age no-one could imagine from his appearance yesterday, took up his position in the midst of a knot of friends on the floor of the amphitheatre, in front of the grand organ, and went through this ordeal with quiet dignity and composure, now and again warming up to the fire of former years, as in subdued conversation one and another of his courtiers told him of their ardour in the good old cause.[193]

This incident says much about Charles Villiers' public reputation. Indeed, one old delegate, who recalled Villiers' initial election in Wolverhampton, told how the working men of the day could hardly understand how an Earl's son could feel for them in their terrible subjection, 'but long since they had learned that the love of justice lent its animating spirits to every Liberal thought and deed'.[194]

During these years, despite his advancing age and frequent ill-health, Charles Villiers was a frequent presence in the House of Commons, where, as Justin McCarthy observed, he could be safely relied upon by his political friends to vote in the lobby during an important division, receiving a warm welcome from members of all parties at such times.[195] He was, however, rarely heard in the House (although, as we shall see, he continued to have much to say about contemporary politics in private). Indeed, there was a ten-year gap between his penultimate speech in the Commons, in April 1875, on the Sale of Food and Drugs Bill,[196] and what proved to be Villiers' final contribution to parliamentary debates on 10 April 1885.

The subject which prompted Villiers' final speech was the question of further parliamentary reform, which he had long supported. In 1883 he had welcomed the Corrupt and Illegal Practices Act, which had marked the death-blow of old corruption by imposing severe penalties for bribery, excessive expenses and other malpractices during elections. As such, the Act was a logical corollary of the 1872 Ballot Act and subsequently transformed electioneering. In the following year, following discussions between Gladstone and Hartington, for the Liberals, and Salisbury and Northcote, for the Tories, it was agreed that further franchise reform, coupled with redistribution of seats, was desirable. Accordingly, the Representation of the People Act of 1884 extended the principle of household suffrage and virtually doubled the size of the electorate to 2.5 millions, including rural tradesmen and agricultural labourers (excluded in 1867).[197] Again, Villiers welcomed this measure as a means towards manhood suffrage. However, he held some reservations about the Redistribution of Seats Act of 1885, which created new electoral districts roughly equal in size, as a result of which 142 new seats were created and new boundaries were designated.[198] More significantly, the Act split Wolverhampton into three separate constituencies (Wolverhampton East, West and South), much to the annoyance of both Villiers and Henry Fowler, for the redesignated boundaries in fact challenged Liberal hegemony in the borough by offering the Conservatives a good opportunity to capture the new constituency of Wolverhampton West, where the growth of middle-class suburbia in this more affluent 'West End' offered the Tories potentially rich pickings (and which ultimately proved to be the case).

Villiers stated that, as his fellow Liberal MP, Henry Fowler, had indicated, Wolverhampton, which now had a population of 105,000, had not sought to become a three-member borough, but that when the proposal was made initially the question had been discussed in the borough and the local Liberals and Tories had planned accordingly. However, when the Boundary Commissioners had visited the town, they had rejected the proposals of the two Parties and proposed one of their own. Villiers added that

> I am not particularly wedded to the system which involves the division of the borough, and I do not particularly approve of the single Member system; but I do think that we should submit to certain rules or judgments when they are laid down by sufficient authority.[199]

Both he and Fowler were, therefore, willing to accept the decision of the Commissioners, who were 'gentlemen opposed in opinion to myself, but willing to do their duty in a most fair and impartial manner ... and the borough has submitted respectfully and quietly to their decision',[200] and the borough was subsequently divided into the three parliamentary constituencies of Wolverhampton East, Wolverhampton West and Wolverhampton South.

The General Election of November 1885, the first under the new system, witnessed the fall of Gladstone's second ministry, for although the Liberals were the largest party (with 335 seats) the Conservatives under Salisbury (with 249) were able to forge an alliance with Parnell's Irish Nationalist Party, who held the balance of power (with 86 seats) in the House of Commons, and Salisbury duly formed his first ministry. Like many Radicals, Charles Villiers had found aspects of Gladstone's foreign policy since 1880 very difficult to digest, since it appeared to continue Disraeli's imperialism in South Africa, where the first Boer War erupted in 1881, whilst the occupation of Egypt in 1882 (which occasioned John Bright's resignation from the government) and the forward policy in the Sudan appeared to be unwarranted and illiberal, for how could Liberals justify the use of armed force against native peoples? Nevertheless, Villiers was returned unopposed for Wolverhampton South, with Henry Fowler elected for Wolverhampton East and the Tory, Sir Alfred Hickman, returned in Wolverhampton West.[201]

In his written address to the Southern Division on 7 November, Villiers recalled that during the fifty-one years that he had represented the town he had submitted himself for re-election on thirteen occasions and each time he had been returned either unopposed or by an increasing majority. He noted that when the town became a three-member constituency he had received a distinct invitation from the Liberal Association in each of the divisions to become their candidate and that his choice was not made until he had sought the assistance and friendly advice 'of those best acquainted with the opinion and interests of the borough'. He added that of all the issues shadowed for consideration in the next Parliament, he considered that of first importance was

> a better arrangement for the conduct of the business of Parliament, the want of which has seriously impaired the credit of the House of Commons ... it is essential that it should be dealt with before we can expect to carry effectually any other measures of reform.[202]

Finally, Villiers expressed his gratitude to the electors of the borough 'for their forbearance under the circumstances of my indisposition during the last few years', adding

> Through ill-health alone have I been deprived of the pleasure of visiting the borough and paying my respects in person to the electors. Indeed, but for the interest I feel in public affairs and my ability still to attend daily in the House of Commons, I should have scrupled to accept the proud distinction you now so generously propose to me.[203]

Within twelve months, however, this 'proud distinction' was to be temporarily jeopardised by the Home Rule crisis of 1886.

Notes

1 *Manchester Courier*, 27 Jun. 1867.
2 Ibid.
3 Ibid. See also *Morning Post*, 27 Jun. 1867.
4 Sir Edward Cook, *Delane of 'The Times'* (London, 1915), 215.

5 Villiers to Delane, 26 Feb. 1867, cited in A.I. Dasent, *John Thadeus Delane, Editor of 'The Times': His Life and Correspondence* (2 vols, London, 1908), II, 189–90.
6 Ibid., 90. Villiers also observed that the 'Adullamites' had returned to the Liberal fold:

> Lord Grosvenor gave us a new view of the 'cave' – that they left their Party because we had not gone low enough, and had found no resting place! He says he objects to the Government now because their Bill is worse than ours was last year, and therefore he comes back to his friends, who have not changed their opinions.

7 *Wolverhampton Chronicle*, 26 Jan. 1867.
8 Taylor, 'The Working-Class Movement', 366.
9 J. Lawrence, *Speaking for the People: Party, Language and Popular Politics in England, 1867–1914* (Cambridge, 1998), 82–8. Lawrence notes that subsequently, in May 1871, the Liberal elite sought to democratise their organisation by forming the Wolverhampton Liberal Association, with delegates elected through open ward meetings, although in reality the new Executive Committee still comprised the inner circle of the old Liberal Committee, prolonging tensions between moderate and radical Liberals.
10 Henry Hartley Fowler (1830–1911): Born in Sunderland. Wesleyan Methodist, Solicitor and Liberal politician, town councillor and Mayor of Wolverhampton in 1866, MP for Wolverhampton 1880–5 and for Wolverhampton East 1885–1908, Secretary of State for India 1894–5, Chancellor of the Duchy of Lancaster 1905–08 and Lord President of the Council 1908–10, raised to the peerage as first Viscount Wolverhampton in 1908.
11 Henry John Wentworth Hodgetts Foley (1828–94), Liberal politician, MP for South Staffordshire, 1857–68, owner of the Prestwood estate, High Sheriff of Staffordshire, 1877.
12 *Wolverhampton Chronicle*, 8 May 1867; *Birmingham Daily Gazette*, 2 May 1867.
13 Ibid.
14 Joseph Linney (1808–85), Bilston Chartist, convicted at Stafford in 1842 and imprisoned for fifteen months, later supported the Liberal Party, died in Wolverhampton Workhouse. His fellow ex-Chartists Thomas Cooper and Arthur O'Neill paid his funeral expenses and conducted the service at his graveside. See S. Roberts, *The Chartist Prisoners: The Radical Livers of Thomas Cooper and Arthur O'Neill* (Bern, 2008), 21–2.
15 *Wolverhampton Chronicle*, 8 May 1867; *Birmingham Daily Gazette*, 2 May 1867.
16 Ibid. There was particular opposition to this proposal in the working-class district of Wednesbury: see Taylor, 'The Working-Class Movement', 369. In the event, the constituency of South Staffordshire was abolished by the 1867 Reform Act and replaced by two new county constituencies, East Staffordshire and South Staffordshire. Henry Fowler had to wait for a further thirteen years before becoming an MP.
17 D. Richter, *Riotous Victorians* (London, 1981), 51–62.
18 Villiers had actually supported the McCullough-Torrens Amendment, which reduced the residential qualification for the lodger franchise to six months rather than twelve: *Birmingham Daily Post*, 8 July 1867.
19 For a useful discussion of the debate, see C. Hall, K. McLelland and J. Rendall, 'Historians and the 1867 Reform Act', in Catherine Hall, Keith McLelland and Jane Rendall, *Defining the Victorian Nation: Class, Race, Gender and the Reform Act of 1867* (Cambridge, 2000), 1–19.
20 *Wolverhampton Chronicle*, 29 April 1868. Villiers was actually in the building during the meeting, and it was reported that 'nothing but a severe indisposition would have prevented him from showing himself'.

21 Ibid., 28 Oct. 1868.
22 Ibid., 18 Nov. 1868.
23 Ibid. In this context, Villiers was reiterating a plea he had made earlier in the year when addressing a meeting at the Willenhall Literary Institute, where he emphasised the need to improve the intellectual and social education of the people, including provisions for technical education, including mechanical drawing and design: *Wolverhampton Chronicle*, 15 Jan. 1868; 29 Jan. 1868.
24 See Taylor, 'The Working-Class Movement', 370–4. Taylor argues that, more broadly, the Liberal victory in 1868 provided the basis of an alliance between Gladstonian Liberalism and an enlarged working-class electorate in the Black Country which was to last until 1886, when it was undermined by the further extension of the franchise by the third Reform Act and Gladstone's conversion to Irish Home Rule: Taylor, 387–98.
25 Villiers to Delane, 6 Dec. 1868: 'You were kind enough the other day to name me amongst those likely to be called, if not chosen, for the new Cabinet', cited in Dasent, *John Thadeus Delane*, II, 230.
26 *London Standard*, 7 Dec. 1868.
27 *Birmingham Daily Post*, 7 Dec. 1868.
28 Villiers to Delane, 7 Dec. 1868, in Dasent, *John Thadeus Delane*, II, 231–2.
29 Ibid.
30 Ibid.
31 Ibid.
32 Roger Swift, 'Gladstone and Charles Pelham Villiers', unpublished paper, Gladstone's Library (2009).
33 Gladstone acknowledged this at the end of his career in a speech he gave at the Cobden Club in honour of Thomas Bayley Potter in May 1890:

> Although I was brought up to admire the incipient Free Trade of Mr Huskisson and Mr Canning, yet the traditions of Protectionism were not so completely shaken but that some of its fetters and some of its recollections hung about me in the earliest years of my public life:
> *Glasgow Herald*, 13 May 1890

34 Richard Shannon, *Gladstone: Heroic Minister, 1865–1898* (London, 1999), xv: 'The attraction of Liberalism for Gladstone was in essence that it offered him the only plausible prospect of Peelite government. He became a Liberal, in short, the better to be a Peelite'.
35 See especially Eric Evans, 'The Strict Line of Political Succession? Gladstone's relationship with Peel: An Apt Pupil?' in David Bebbington and Roger Swift (eds), *Gladstone Centenary Essays* (Liverpool, 2000), 29–56; Richard A. Gaunt, 'Gladstone and Peel's Mantle', in Quinault, Swift and Windscheffel, *William Gladstone*, 31–50.
36 For further details, see Eugenio Biagini, 'Exporting "Western & Beneficent Institutions": Gladstone and Empire, 1880–1885', in David Bebbington and Roger Swift (eds), *Gladstone Centenary Essays* (Liverpool, 2000), 202–25.
37 Jenkins, *The Parliamentary Diaries of Sir John Trelawny*, Jenkins (ed.), 316, 27 Mar. 1865.
38 *The Diaries of Edward Henry Stanley, 15th Earl of Derby (1826–93) between 1878 and 1893*, John Vincent (ed.) (Oxford, 2003), 369, 29 Oct. 1881. Derby recalled that in his conversations with Gladstone,

> He spoke much of Cobden, of whom a biography has just appeared; thought his intellect over-rated, his views more narrow and mistaken than his admirers would readily allow, but praised in vehement terms what he called the nobleness of his moral nature. On this Pender tells me that, when asked on

some occasion to pay public compliment to the leaders of the anti-corn law movement, he [Gladstone] had done so warmly as regards Cobden, moderately in respect of Bright but, though the name of Charles Villiers was repeatedly pressed upon him as that of the real pioneer of the movement, he would take no notice of him whatever; which Pender and his friends ascribed to the fact of Villiers being a shrewd cynical man of the world, a character specially odious to G.

39 S. Gwynn and G. Tuckwell, *The Life of the Rt. Hon. Sir Charles Dilke, Bart, MP,* 2 vols (London, 1917) I, 283–4. Dilke recalled that 'Villiers, who was another good talker, "Mr G" could not abide'.
40 Henderson, *History* (1952), 38.
41 Fitzmaurice, *The Life of Granville George Leveson Gower,* II, 536–7.
42 *Morning Post*, 9 Dec. 1868.
43 *The Economist*, 12 Dec. 1868.
44 *Wolverhampton Chronicle*, 23 Dec. 1868: 'Mr Villiers and the Poor Law Board'.
45 Ibid.
46 Fitzmaurice, *The Life of Granville George Leveson Gower,* II, 536–7.
47 Colin Matthew, *Gladstone* (Oxford, 1997), 176–7.
48 Villiers to Delane, 7 Dec. 1868, in Dasent, *John Thadeus Delane,* II, 231–2.
49 Ibid.
50 Granville to Gladstone, 14 Feb. 1869, cited in Agatha Ramm (ed.), *The Gladstone-Granville Correspondence* (Cambridge, 1998), 12.
51 Howe, 'Villiers, Charles Pelham', *ODNB*, 7.
52 *Gladstone Papers*, 44421/207, Villiers to Gladstone, 28 Jul. 1869.
53 Ibid., 44421/223, Villiers to Gladstone, 31 Jul. 1869.
54 Ibid. Gladstone, exhausted by the final stages of the Irish Church Disestablishment Bill, had been unwell with a persistent cold throughout July 1869 and Lord Granville had finalised negotiations over the Bill with the House of Lords on his behalf. For further details, see Jenny West, 'The Health of a Prime Minister: Gladstone, 1868–85', in Quinault, Swift and Windscheffel (eds), *William Gladstone: New Studies and Perspectives* (Farnham, 2012), 177–98.
55 This was finally confirmed by the Treasury in 1874. For further details, *Gladstone Papers*, 44442/316, Villiers to Gladstone, 20 Feb. 1874:

> I have received a communication from the Treasury in which I am informed that the question, which in my statement to you, I said I was precluded (by the form of the warrant) from submitting to the Council of Law, has been referred by the commissioners of the hearing to their legal adviser, and that he has given the opinion that the charge which I have upon the Suitors Free Fund in the Court of Chancery cannot be legally deducted from the political pension provided for under the Act (32 Vict. c.91) ... The consideration of this matter however by the Treasury, and the reference which has been made in consequence by their legal adviser, I cannot but ascribe to a direction given by yourself, and I beg in consequence to offer you my best acknowledgments for having, in the midst of all the care of the past few weeks, remembered the requisition to which I called your attention.

56 Roy Jenkins, *Gladstone* (London, 1995), 617.
57 For further details, see especially Walter L. Arnstein, *Protestant versus Catholic in Mid-Victorian England: Mr Newdegate and the Nuns* (Columbia, 1982); E.R. Norman, *Anti-Catholicism in Victorian England* (London, 1968); Rene Kollar, *A Foreign and Wicked Institution?: The Campaign Against Convents in Victorian England* (Cambridge, 2011), 16–17.
58 *Parl. Debs*, 3rd ser., 205, cc.179–203, 17 Mar. 1871; 200, cc.872–908, 29 Mar. 1870.

59 *The Tablet*, 7 May 1870.
60 *Parl. Debs*, 3rd ser., 205, cc.179–203, 17 Mar. 1870.
61 Arnstein, *Protestant versus Catholic*, 149.
62 For further details, see Maxwell, II, 356–62; Villiers, *A Vanished Victoria*, 362–4.
63 Charles Villiers attended his brother's funeral at Watford on 9 July: *Bell's Weekly Messenger*, 9 Jul. 1870. Clarendon was succeeded at the Foreign Office by Granville.
64 See Chapter 9, this volume.
65 Arnstein, 155.
66 *Parl. Debs*, 3rd ser., 205, cc.179–203, 17 Mar. 1870.
67 *Report from the Select Committee on the Law Respecting Conventual and Monastic Institutions*, PP, vol. 7 (1871), iii–xv.
68 Arnstein, 162.
69 *Gladstone Papers*, 44438/14, Villiers to Gladstone, 3 Mar. 1873; 44438/20, Villiers to Gladstone, 4 Mar. 1873.
70 D.G. Paz, *Popular Anti-Catholicism in Mid-Victorian England* (Stanford, 1992), 17–18.
71 *Parl. Debs*, 3rd ser., 219, cc.1053–4, 5 Jun. 1874; 219, cc.1498–526, 12 Jun. 1874. See Also Arnstein, 176–97.
72 *Morning Post*, 4 April 1872.
73 Ibid.
74 Ibid.
75 G.J. Barnsby, *Social Conditions in the Black Country, 1800–1900* (Wolverhampton, 1980), 46, observes that there were 10,000 prosecutions in Staffordshire under this Act between 1858 and 1867, and that Wolverhampton had a higher incidence of these prosecutions than any other borough in the country. For further details, see D.C. Woods, 'The Operation of the Master and Servant Act in the Black Country', *Midland History*, 7/1 (1982), 93–115; R.J. Steinfeld, *Coercion, Contract and free Labour in the Nineteenth Century* (Cambridge, 2001), 73–5.
76 For opposition to this legislation between 1871 and 1875, see E.F. Biagini, *Liberty, Retrenchment and Reform: Popular Liberalism in the Age of Gladstone* (Cambridge, 1992), 152–9.
77 *Wolverhampton Chronicle*, 4 Feb. 1874; 11 Feb. 1874.
78 Ibid., 4 Feb. 1874.
79 Lawrence, *Speaking for the People*, 92.
80 For further details of the Women's Movement for political representation during the 1860s and 1870s, see especially Jane Rendall, 'The citizenship of women and the 1867 Reform Act', in Hall, McLelland and Rendall, *Defining the Victorian Nation*, 119–78.
81 *Parl. Debs*, 3rd ser., 187, cc.779–852, 20 May 1867. The House was poorly attended on this occasion.
82 MALS. Women's Suffrage Collection. Lydia Becker and the Manchester Society for Women's Suffrage. M50/1/2/31, letter from Villiers to Lydia Becker, 8 Dec. 1868: 'He must see a Bill for giving women the franchise before he can support it'.
83 *Parl. Debs*, 3rd ser., 201, cc.237–9, 4 May 1870; 206, cc.68–123, 3 May 1871; 211, cc.1–72, 1 May 1872; 215, cc.1194–258, 30 April 1873.
84 Helen Blackburn, *Women's Suffrage: A Record of the Women's Suffrage Movement in the British Isles, with Biographical Sketches of Miss Becker* (Oxford, 1901), 18 & 221.
85 London School of Economics. Women's Library. Autograph Letter Collection: Women's Suffrage. GB/106/9/1/0025, Villiers to Millicent Garrett Fawcett, 28 Feb. 1889, on Women's Suffrage Bill of 22 Feb. 1889. Millicent Garrett Fawcett (1847–1929): suffragist, writer, union leader; married Liberal MP Henry

Fawcett, 1867; joined London Suffrage Committee, 1868; co-founder of Newnham College, 1875; joined Liberal Unionists, 1886; President of the National Union of Women's Suffrage Societies, 1897–1919.

86 Florence Balgarnie, 'The Women's Suffrage Movement in the Nineteenth Century', in Brougham Villiers (ed.), *The Case for Women's Suffrage* (London, 1907), 26. Charles Villiers also supported the admission of women to university degree courses. In February 1896, for example, several memorials were sent to the Council of Senate at Cambridge University in support of those presented by some members of the Senate in favour of the admission of women to degrees. One was submitted by students at Girton and Newnham Colleges, another by headmistresses in endowed and proprietary schools, and a third was signed by a host of eminent public figures, including Charles Villiers: *Morning Post*, 10 Feb. 1896.

87 Constance Lytton subsequently recorded her life in Holloway in *Prisons and Prisoners —Some Personal Experience* (London, 1914).

88 R. Blake, *Disraeli* (London, 1966), 523.

89 O.W. Hewett, *Strawberry Fair: A Biography of Frances, Countess Waldegrave, 1821– 1879* (London, 1956), 243. As Hewett shows, Countess Waldegrave was very close to the Villiers' family and, in particular, to Lord Clarendon (prior to his death) and Charles Villiers. See also n.133 below.

90 See, for example, D. Beales, 'Gladstone and his First Ministry', *Historical Journal*, 26 (1983), 987–98; J.P. Parry, 'Gladstone, Liberalism and the Government of 1868–1874', in D. Bebbington and R. Swift (eds), *Gladstone Centenary Essays* (Liverpool, 2000), 94–112.

91 Harrison, *Drink and the Victorians*, 242–89.

92 P. Adelman, *Gladstone, Disraeli and Later Victorian Politics* (London, 1979), 8–19.

93 For further details, see Matthew, *Gladstone*, 222–39.

94 Fagan, *The Reform Club*, 113.

95 Bright to Hartington, 3 Feb. 1875, cited in Holland, *The Life of Spencer Compton, Eighth Duke of Devonshire* (2 vols, London, 1911), I, 147.

96 See, for example, Walling, *The Diaries of John Bright*, 378, 8 April 1876:

> Evening dined with Sir D. Marjoribanks, Park Lane. A grand house and a large party ... Long chat with C.P. Villiers. His criticisms as usual severe and not friendly on Mr. Gladstone, whom he charges with wishing to get back to the place of leader of the Liberal Party, etc.

97 See also Taylor, 'The Working-Class Movement', 378.

98 For further details, see Swift, *Immigrants & Minorities*, 3/1 (1984), 5–29.

99 Lawrence, *Speaking for the People*, 93.

100 R. Smith, 'The Governance of Wolverhampton, 1848–1888', PhD thesis, University of Leicester (2001), 134, n.27.

101 Ibid.

102 R. Trainor, 'Conflict, Community and Identity in Victorian and Edwardian Politics: A Case Study of the Black Country', in Barry M. Doyle (ed.), *Urban Politics and Space in the Nineteenth and Twentieth Centuries: Regional Perspectives* (Cambridge, 2007), 42.

103 F. Mason, *The Book of Wolverhampton: The Story of an Industrial Town* (Buckingham, 1979), 77, 91.

104 For further details, see *Wolverhampton Chronicle, Staffs Advertiser, Morning Post*, 1 Dec. 1866; *Illustrated London News*, 8 Dec. 1866.

105 See, for example, *Wolverhampton Chronicle*, 16 Nov. 1853.

106 *The Spectator*, 2 Nov. 1861. This was not always possible. In 1859 both Villiers and Sir Richard Bethell declined an invitation, Villiers due to 'to business in

London', and Bethell, 'having been shot through the leg and knee whilst pheasant shooting ... which has greatly disabled me': *Wolverhampton Chronicle*, 26 Oct. 1859.

107 For example, it was reported that

> On Monday [30 Dec. 1867] the Rt. Hon. C.P. Villiers presided at a public soiree held in celebration of the third anniversary of the Willenhall Literary Institute ... there was a numerous company, including Mr Wegulin, MP, and Sir John Morris [Mayor]:

Illustrated London News, 4 Jan. 1868. In his address, Villiers emphasised the need for improvements in technical education, particularly in regard to mechanical drawing and design, and praised the efforts of the late Prince Albert in promoting the technical and social education of the country: *Wolverhampton Chronicle*, 15 Jan. 1868; 29 Jan. 1868.

108 *Wolverhampton Chronicle*, 5 Sep. 1838.
109 Ibid., 15 Jan. 1840; 24 Nov. 1841.
110 Ibid., 31 Oct. 1849.
111 Ibid., 20 Mar. 1850.
112 Ibid., 25 Apr. 1854.
113 Ibid., 4 Nov. 1857.
114 For further details, see Mason, *The Book of Wolverhampton*, 92; Upton, *A History of Wolverhampton*, 99; *The Builder*, 1 July 1882. The Bandstand was later designated a Grade II listed building. Charles Villiers' statue was moved from Snow Hill to the West Park in 1932.
115 *Staffs Advertiser*, 22 Jan. 1898.
116 *Wolverhampton Chronicle*, 17 Aug. 1837.
117 Ibid., 18 Aug. 1838.
118 Ibid., 12 Aug. 1840.
119 Ibid., 18 Aug. 1841; see also *Bell's Life in London and Sporting Chronicle*, 15 Aug. 1841.
120 Ibid., 20 Aug. 1856.
121 Ibid., 8 Sept. 1858.
122 Ibid., 10 Aug. 1859. This was Mayer Amschel de Rothschild, Lionel's youngest brother, a famous racehorse owner and member of the Jockey Club, with stables at Newmarket, whose horses won four of the five 'Classics': see Ferguson, *The World's Banker*, 357–8.
123 *Hertfordshire Express and General Advertiser*, 18 Aug. 1866: Report of 'A Shocking accident at a Racecourse'; *Wolverhampton Chronicle*, 22 Aug. 1866.
124 *Wolverhampton Chronicle*, 19 Jan. 1898.
125 *The Times*, 17 Jan. 1898.
126 *Free Trade Speeches*, I, preface.
127 This is based on a detailed analysis of the *Morning Post* from January 1870 to December 1889. However, it is important to note that these reports were based on lists of invitations to functions which were circulated to the press prior to the actual event, so there is no certainty that Villiers attended all of these functions, particularly when he was ill, and it is significant that his presence at these functions declined during the 1880s, with advancing age and infirmity. They do, nevertheless, reflect the social world within which Villiers was ensconced, particularly during the London Season.
128 See, for example, *Morning Post*, 16 May 1871; 3 Jul. 1872; 1 Jul. 1874; 10 Jul. 1877; 14 Jun. 1883; 5 Jul. 1889.
129 Ibid., 6 Mar. 1873; 21 Feb. 1878; 8 May 1884.
130 Ibid., 25 Jun. 1873; 21 May 1874; 18 Jun. 1875.

131 Ibid., 11 Jul. 1871; 7 May 1872; 14 May 1872; 7 July 1881.
132 Ibid., 29 Feb. 1872; 19 Mar. 1874; 25 Apr. 1874; 29 Apr. 1875; 7 Jul. 1876; 15 Jun. 1882.
133 Countess Frances Elizabeth Anne Waldegrave (1821–79): Noted Liberal society hostess; inherited (and restored) the Waldegrave estates from her second husband, George, Seventh Earl Waldegrave (d. 1846); remarried George Granville Harcourt (d. 1861); in 1863 she married her fourth husband, Chichester Fortescue (later Lord Carlingford), and her salon at Strawberry Hill and London residence at Carlton Gardens were an important focus for Liberal politicians. For further details, see Henry Grenfell, 'Waldegrave, Frances Elizabeth Anne', *DNB*, vol. 59, 1885–1900 (London, 1900).
134 Chichester Parkinson Fortescue, 1st Baron Carlingford (1823–98): British Liberal politician; MP for Louth, 1847–74; Under Secretary for the Colonies, 1857–8, 1859–65; Chief Secretary for Ireland, 1865–6, 1868–71; President of Board of Trade, 1871–4; Raised to the peerage as Baron Carlingford in 1874; Lord Privy Seal, 1881–5; Lord President of the Council, 1883–5; split with Gladstone over Irish Home Rule in 1886. For further details, see H.C.G. Matthew, 'Fortescue, Chichester Samuel Parkinson, Baron Carlingford and second Baron Clermont', *ODNB, 9938* (Oxford, 2004).
135 L. Davidoff, *The Best Circles: Society Etiquette and the Season* (London, 1973), 26.
136 For further details of dinner parties at Lady Molesworth's London home at Eaton Place and at Pencarrow in Cornwall, see Adburgham, *A Radical Aristocrat*, 189–204.
137 K.D. Reynolds, 'Politics Without Feminism: The Victorian Political Hostess', in C.C. Orr (ed.), *Wollstonecraft's Daughters: Womenhood in England and France, 1780–1920* (London, 1996), 94–108; K.D. Reynolds, *Aristocratic Women and Political Society in Victorian Britain* (Oxford, 1998), especially ch. 5, 'Party Politics: Metropolitan Political Society', 156–77, which considers the roles of Charles Villiers' friends, Lady Molesworth and Countess Waldegrave.
138 *Sunday Times*, 17 Jan. 1898.
139 Amy Milne-Smith, *London Clubland: A Cultural History of Gender and Class in Late-Victorian Britain* (London, 2011), 94. Milne-Smith states that Sir Edward Hamilton, Gladstone's private secretary, recalled in his diary that, during a conversation with Villiers at Brookes Club, his companion freely expressed pessimistic opinions on contemporary politics.
140 Villiers attended the inaugural meeting of the Cobden Club at the Star and Garter Hotel, Richmond, where Gladstone gave the address: *Bell's New Weekly Messenger*, 28 July 1866. When Villiers addressed the Cobden Club on 1 July 1868, the *Wolverhampton Chronicle* was moved to comment:

> Mr Villiers excels as an antagonist. He hits straight and he hits hard; and if anything so unlikely were to happen as that free trade policy, or poor law reform, or Liberal principles, were assailed at the Cobden Club tonight, those present would hear a better speech than if merely conventional compliments were exchanged:

Wolverhampton Chronicle, 1 July 1868. See also the letter from Villiers to Andrew Bissett, 3 Jun. 1884, on the purpose, merits and achievements of the Cobden Club, which received 'a good deal of money, and much of this has been expended in the publication and circulation of works on Free Trade, and on speeches of certain public men': A. Bissett, *Notes on the Anti-Corn Law Struggle* (London, 1884), 177.
141 Villiers had attended meetings of the Political Economy Club, founded by James Mill in 1821, since his university days, and continued to do so. See Adelaide Weinberg, 'A Meeting of the Political Economy Club on 7 May 1857', *The Mill Newsletter*, 1/2 (Spring 1966), 11–16.

142 Lawrence Goldman, *Science, Reform and Politics in Victorian Britain: The Social Science Association, 1857–1886* (Cambridge, 2004), 33–4: The Law Amendment Society had been founded in 1844 'to promote careful and cautious improvement in the Law of England' and by the 1860s had around 300 members, including 50 MPs and 120 barristers and solicitors, including Charles Villiers.
143 *Life of Benjamin Disraeli*, Moneypenny and Buckle, V. 234: Letter from Disraeli to Montagu Corry, 10 Feb. 1873. Disraeli had dined at Baron Lionel de Rothschild's the night before. Charles Villiers was also present; V. 430: Letter to Lady Bradford, 19 July 1875. Disraeli reported having dined at Lionel de Rothschild's house at Piccadilly Terrace the previous evening: 'a most amusing party'. Villiers was also present.
144 Lionel de Rothschild to Charlotte Rothschild, 9 Mar. 1868, cited in Ferguson, *The World's Banker*, 773. Disraeli's intimation of 1867 that Lionel be raised to the Peerage was resisted strongly by Queen Victoria, and when Gladstone tried to do so in 1868 and 1873, he was also overruled by the Queen. Lionel de Rothschild died a commoner, although Lord Salisbury secured a peerage for his son, Nathan, in 1885. Charles Villiers' letters to Charlotte Rothschild are preserved in the Rothschild Archive.
145 Sir Charles Dilke (1843–1911): Radical Liberal politician; educated at Trinity College, Cambridge; MP for Chelsea, 1868–85; Under-Secretary for Foreign Affairs, 1880–2; President of Local Government Board, 1883–5; promising political career effectively ended by the infamous Crawford divorce case of 1886, after which he lost his Chelsea seat; thereafter MP for Forest of Dean, 1892–1911. See R. Jenkins, 'Dilke, Sir Charles Wentworth, second baronet (1843–1911), writer and politician', *ODNB*, 32824 (2008).
146 S. Gwynn and G. Tuckwell, *The Life of the Rt. Hon. Sir Charles Dilke, Bart, MP* (2 vols, London, 1917), I, 160.
147 Ibid., I, 199. Dilke and Villiers were present at other dinner parties, as on 22 Jan. 1878, at Mrs Inwood Jones (Lady Morgan's niece), in the company of Robert Browning and Lady Hamilton, and on 7 Mar. 1880, when he dined at Cyril Flowers in the company of Lord Hartington and expressed his amazement at Villiers 'at eighty, walking over from Tring Park': Gwynn and Tuckwell, I, 241; 302.
148 Walling, *The Diaries of John Bright*, 323, 13 May 1868.
149 Ibid., 327, 6 Jun. 1868.
150 *Staffs Advertiser*, 16 Jun. 1883.
151 Walling, 520, 20 Nov. 1884.
152 Ibid., 524, 18 Mar. 1885.
153 Ibid., 535, 17 Mar. 1886.
154 Ibid., 560, 10 Aug. 1887.
155 Delane to Bernal Osborne, 25 Nov. 1858: 'the Rothschilds are well and jolly ... Lionel has been a month in Paris with C. Villiers', cited in Dasent, *John Thadeus Delane* (1908), 1. 304.
156 Ibid., Delane to G.W. Dasent 25 Oct. 1867: Delane was on holiday in Paris: 'Milnes, Villiers, Wyke, Stanhope and a host of others are here': ii, 210; see also letter from Richard Monckton Milnes [1st Lord Houghton] to Lady Houghton, 19 Oct. 1867, from Paris: 'Queen of Holland very agreeable yesterday ... I found Charles Villiers sitting with her', cited in Wemyss Reid, *Richard Monckton Milnes, 1st Lord Houghton* (1890), ii, 184.
157 Sir Abraham Hayward (1801–84) was a Lawyer, man of letters, and political observer. Initially a Tory, and friend of the Duke of Newcastle, he became a Peelite, and contributed articles to the *Morning Chronicle* and *Quarterly Review*. An influential member of the Athenaeum, friend and confidant of great ladies and politicians, and friend of Villiers, who he first met at the London Debating Society in 1832. Following Hayward's death in 1884, Villiers provided Henry

Carlisle with some material for his biography, as did Gladstone. For further details, see P. Harling, 'Hayward, Abraham (1801–1884)', *ODNB*, 12793 (2004).
158 See Henry E. Carlisle, *A Selection from the Correspondence of Abraham Hayward, Q.C., from 1834 to 1884* (2 vols, London, 1886), I, 195: letter from Abraham Hayward to Sir John Young, 11 Oct. 1853:

> From Pencarrow ... I came down with C. Villiers on Saturday last ... our party here are the Fords, Lord and Lady Vivian, Miss Damer, Fleming, C. Villiers and myself. Villiers and I stay until the beginning of next week.

Sir William Molesworth died in 1855 and thereafter Lady Molesworth received friends, including Charles Villiers, at her London home.
159 Sir John Pender (1815–96): Textile merchant in Glasgow and Manchester; pioneer of submarine technology; founder of Anglo-American Cable Company and, later, chairman of Metropolitan Electrical Supply Company; Liberal MP for Totnes, 1865–6, and Wick Burghs, 1872–85 and 1892–6 (as a Liberal Unionist); Knighted, 1888. See George Stronach, 'Pender, John (1815–1896)', *DNB* (London, 1901). Villiers was a family friend of the Penders and attended the wedding of Mr W. des Voeux and Ms Marion Denison, Pender's daughter, at St James's Church, Piccadilly and the wedding reception at Pender's London residence in Arlington Street on 24 July 1875: *Morning Post*, 26 Jul. 1875.
160 *A Selection from The Diaries of Edward Henry Stanley, 15th Earl of Derby (1826–93) between September 1869 and March 1878*, ed. John Vincent (Camden Society, 5th ser., 4, 1994), 117. See also *Morning Post*, 21 Sep. 1872.
161 *Morning Post*, 7 Dec. 1974.
162 *Evening Telegraph*, 5 Feb. 1898.
163 *Morning Post*, 2 April 1880:

> The Will (Dated June 14 1878), of Miss Catherine Martha Mellish, late of Hammels Park, Herts, and of 11 Great Stanhope Street, Park Lane, who died on February 17 last, was proved on the 6th ult. by the Rt. Hon. Charles Pelham Villiers, Hamilton Fane Gladwin, and Charles Reynolds Williams, the executors, the personal estate being sworn under £120,000. The testatrix ... bequeaths all her personal estate to the Rt. Hon. Charles Pelham Villiers for life.

164 *Evening Telegraph*, 5 Feb. 1898.
165 Villiers had been on the boards of, and had invested in, several railway companies during the 1840s and 1850s: see, for example, *Wolverhampton Chronicle*, 16 Oct. 1844; 26 Nov. 1845. He also took out an annuity for £3,500 p/a with the Scottish Union and National Insurance Company and on his death in 1898 the Company claimed that, due to Villiers' longevity, it had lost £49,395. 18s. 2d. on the policy.
166 This read: 'In Memoriam. Catherine Martha Mellish of Hammels Park. Daughter of John Mellish of the Same Place. She Died on 17th February 1880, Aged 84'.
167 http://www.hertfordshire-genealogy.co.uk/data/places/braughing-st-mary.
168 *The Journal of John Wodehouse, First Earl of Kimberley, for 1862–1902*, Angus Hawkins and John Powell (eds), Camden Fifth Series, vol. 9 (Cambridge, 1997), nd. Feb. 1880, 495.
169 *Aberdeen Journal*, 16 Feb. 1898:

> A Villiers Romance: A touching romance in the life of the late Rt Hon. Charles Pelham Villiers has (says the *Daily Telegraph*) been disclosed by his death. In early life he fell deeply in love with a Miss Mellish, and his affection was returned as far as could be done by a lady who for some reason had taken

a vow to lead a single life. Mr Villiers remained true to his first love, and never married, and his constancy so touched Miss Mellish that in her will she left all her fortune – a considerable one – to him absolutely. He, however, never touched the money, leaving it to accumulate with interest, while he lived very simply on his own modest revenue, supplemented by his Cabinet pension.

170 *The Star*, 2 April 1898: 'A Bachelor's Romance'.
171 Herbert Watson, 'Lives of Great Men: Two Strange "Fathers" of the House of Commons', *Portsmouth Evening News*, 25 April 1939. The article stated:

> Charles Pelham Villiers was still young and handsome when, at a dinner given by the wife of the leader of his party, he met the beautiful daughter of a city magnate, who fell in love with the charming politician's easy grace and fascinating manners. It mattered nothing to her – or she may not have known it – that for years he had been resisting the allurements of some of the prettiest girls in society. The girl in this instance, however, was serious, deadly serious. When her covert advances met with no response she became bolder, and he broke her heart by indifference. Finally, driven by desperation, she actually proposed to him and, as gracefully as he could, he gave her to understand that he had made up his mind never to marry. He never did marry, and neither did she, for in a few years she was dead. Whether Villiers knew of it at the time or not, one cannot say, but he was reminded of it when her solicitors wrote to inform him that shortly before her death she had made a will bequeathing the whole of her fortune to him. The legatee instantly replied that in no circumstances would he accept a penny of the money. He argued that it would be dishonourable to accept the money, even with the intention of giving it away, and so he refused to acknowledge its existence. The executors, therefore, placed the money in a bank in his name, but throughout all the years that followed he never spoke of it, completely ignoring the fortune which was growing larger and larger every year, the fortune that was revealed by his will, though that will contained no reference to it. The money left by Villiers himself did not amount to a few thousand pounds. It is an extraordinary story, and I hope that it is true.

172 Lawrence, *Speaking for the People*, 94.
173 *Morning Post*, 15 May 1880.
174 Villiers to Alice Borthwick, 15 May 1880, in Lucas, *Lord Glenesk and the Morning Post* (London, 1910). 227.
175 Lawrence, *Speaking for the People*, 110–114.
176 Ibid., 113. Subsequently, the Villiers club was particularly active during the 'Labour revival' of 1890–1, hosting meetings addressed by national Labour and socialist leaders, and providing lectures by the local Fabian Society, whilst the Fowler club led the local campaign in support of the London dockers in 1889.
177 *Vanity Fair*, 31 Aug. 1872. Statesmen 123. The caption beneath this cartoon, drawn by 'Spy', read 'He advocated Free Trade before it was safe to attack Protection'.
178 Public Monument and Sculpture Association. National Recording Project: 'Charles Pelham Villiers'. http://pmsa.cch.kcl.ac.uk. Prior to its unveiling, Bright called on Mr. William Theed, sculptor, to inspect the statue, which, he remarked, was 'very good': Walling, *The Diaries of John Bright*, 361.
179 *Birmingham Daily Post*, 7 Jun. 1879.
180 *Staffordshire Advertiser*, 7 Jun. 1879.
181 *The Spectator*, 14 Jun. 1879.
182 *London Standard*, 7 Jun. 1879.
183 *The Spectator*, 14 Jun. 1879.

184 Robertson, *The Life and Times of John Bright*, 316–17.
185 *Birmingham Daily Post*, 7 Jun. 1879.
186 Edith Fowler, *The Life of Henry Hartley Fowler, First Viscount Wolverhampton* (London, 1912), 106–7.
187 PMSA, NRP, 'Charles Pelham Villiers'.
188 *Morning Chronicle*, 12 Jan. 1885.
189 *Gladstone Papers*, 44488/27, Villiers to Gladstone, 4 Nov. 1884.
190 Ibid., 44490/242, Villiers to Gladstone, 21 May 1885.
191 *South Australian Times*, 29 June 1885; see also the *Clutha Leader*, 23 Oct. 1885, which commented:

> The general public is disposed to regard this refusal of titled honours with approbation, considering it as an indication of good sense rather than otherwise. Certainly the acceptance by the poet Tennyson of a Peerage was not generally regarded with favour.

192 *Morning Chronicle*, 18 Aug. 1885.
193 *Northern Echo*, 18 Aug. 1885: 'Hon. C.P. Villiers and his Constituents: Pleasing Episode in Political Life'.
194 Ibid.
195 McCarthy, *A History of Our Own Times*, 234–5.
196 *Parl. Debs*, 3rd ser., 224, cc.196–209, 6 May 1875. This Bill had sought to extend the appointment of food and drugs analysts in counties and boroughs. Villiers stated that:

> If the Committee were really in earnest in preventing the enormous evils of adulteration of food, they should take care that their legislation should be effective, compulsory, and general. At present, nothing could be more capricious than the operation of the existing law ... the consequence was that the unscrupulous traders sent their adulterated goods to the latter places [where there were no analysts] and enormous injury was inflicted upon the community ... Lectures were being delivered in the metropolis which proved that all the evils that ever existed in regard to adulteration were still rampant. It had been stated, indeed, on good authority, that much of the savage ferocity displayed in recent cases of drunken assaults was attributable to the noxious ingredients with which the liquor of the lower classes was adulterated.

197 D.G. Wright, *Democracy and Reform, 1815–1885* (London, 1981), 95–6.
198 Ibid., 97–9.
199 *Parl. Debs*, 3rd ser., 296, cc.1338–431, 10 Apr. 1885.
200 Ibid.
201 Hickman defeated Sir William Plowden (Lib) by 3,722 votes to 3,569 and Fowler defeated W. Bird (Tory) by 3,935 votes to 2,648. Hickman briefly lost the seat to Plowden in July 1886 (3,706–3,583) but regained it July 1892 by 4,772–3,656, with Fowler and Villiers unopposed, and retained it in July 1895 (over George Thorne (Lib) by 4,770–3,947, with Villiers unopposed and Fowler defeating R. Kettle (Liberal Unionist) 4011–2977. Thereafter, Wolverhampton West became a Tory stronghold well into the twentieth century. For further details see G.W.Jones, *Borough Politics: A Study of the Wolverhampton Town Council, 1888–1960* (London, 1969).
202 *The Spectator*, 21 Nov. 1885.
203 Ibid.

8 Gladstone and the Home Rule crisis

Throughout their long and distinguished parliamentary careers, the relationship between Charles Villiers and William Gladstone[1] was problematic and did not always run smoothly, frequently blowing hot and cold, although – in public at least – both were usually civil towards one another. Although both men had a Liberal Tory upbringing, they had entered Parliament in the early 1830s, Gladstone as a devout Tory and Villiers as a Benthamite Radical. Indeed, at least initially, Gladstone had little sympathy for the essential causes of nineteenth-century Liberalism, such as democracy, equality and social improvement, whilst Villiers was, from the outset, very much associated with radical reform and the notion of social progress. Their careers had converged as Cabinet colleagues in the ministries of Palmerston and Russell between 1859 and 1866, and both were stalwarts in the emergent Liberal Party thereafter. Yet they were to end their parliamentary careers as political opponents within a Liberal Party divided by the issue of Irish Home Rule, and from 1886 onwards Villiers supported the Liberal Unionists.

As we have seen, there had been long-standing personal and political differences between Villiers and Gladstone, a situation which was exacerbated by Villiers' exclusion from cabinet office in 1868, despite Gladstone's subsequent efforts to secure a political pension for Villiers, and the offer of a knighthood and a peerage in the 1880s. Moreover, Villiers had been critical not only of some Liberal measures introduced during Gladstone's First Ministry of 1868–74,[2] but also of Gladstone's forward foreign policy between 1880 and 1885.[3] This said, the one major issue which really exposed the personal and political differences between Gladstone and Villiers during their later careers was the question of Irish Home Rule. The primary evidence for this lies not with Villiers' speeches in Parliament (for he last spoke in the Commons in 1885) or in his *Political Memoir* of 1883 (which predated the Liberal split of 1886), but in a hitherto unpublished and extensive collection of letters, located in Wolverhampton Archives, written by Charles Villiers to his trusted friend, William McIlwraith,[4] the Secretary of the Villiers Reform Club in Wolverhampton, between 1884 and 1898. With their explicit emphasis on privacy and confidentiality, these rare and hitherto largely unexplored letters (recall, the bulk of Villiers vast correspondence having been destroyed by his housekeeper after his death) shed a unique light on Villiers' views on Gladstone's Irish policy and its divisive impact on the Liberal Party. Moreover, they illuminate, both wittingly and unwittingly, not only aspects of Villiers' character and beliefs but also his private views of Gladstone.

Charles Villiers had developed a sincere interest in, and knowledge of, Ireland – as well as a sympathy for the Irish people – long before Gladstone's 'mission to pacify Ireland'. In his inaugural address to his constituents in Wolverhampton in January 1836, Villiers had devoted much time to Ireland and its problems,[5] and in 1838 Villiers was moved to comment in the House of Commons that 'In common with many English Members, he felt that a great debt was due to Ireland for the manner in which we have long misgoverned her'.[6] Indeed, as Agnes Lambert, the editor of Villiers' *Political Memoir*, recalled

> His language relating to Ireland and the intolerable injustice it had sustained at our hands was distinguished by a largeness of mind so exceptional in those days that it is difficult to realize its full significance now that we have grown accustomed to generous acts of reparation which, under presently existing circumstances, seem to the impatient to have been made in vain to heal the wounds of that unhappy country.[7]

Moreover, Villiers was well-informed on Irish matters. His brother, George, fourth Earl of Clarendon, had been Lord Lieutenant of Ireland from 1847 to 1852, at the time of the Irish Famine, the Young Ireland movement, and the Smith O'Brien rising, and Charles Villiers was present when Queen Victoria and Prince Albert visited Ireland and stayed at Viceregal Lodge as guests of the Clarendons in July and August 1849.[8] Furthermore, his brother-in-law was Sir George Cornewall Lewis, the Poor Law Commissioner responsible for preparing the *Report on the State of the Irish Poor* of 1836, who had married Villiers' widowed sister, Lady Maria Theresa Lister, in 1844.[9]

Villiers had always held that Ireland's problems, particularly the depressed economy, the evils of landlordism, and the penury of the peasantry, could only be solved by improvement, by progressive reforms, within the Union of Great Britain and Ireland rather than by the Irish themselves. Subsequently, the state of the Irish economy and the plight of the Irish poor formed an important component of his campaign for the repeal of the Corn Laws, which also drew support from leading Irish MPs, including the Irish nationalist, Daniel O'Connell – 'the Great Liberator' – and the Ulster Liberal, Sharman Crawford.[10] Villiers also supported Lord John Russell's Irish reforms, including the sale of encumbered estates,[11] and defended the implementation and further amelioration of the Poor Law in Ireland, stating in 1850 that this was

> a measure of policy as well as of humanity. I believe that it has already removed from the people one great pretext for crime; that it has diminished an evil only next to crime – the frightful extent of mendacity in

that country; that it has secured comparative safety to life and property; and that therefore the people have ceased to feel desperate from being destitute. And all this, taken together with the facilities that have been given to the sale and transfer of property, will, it is to be hoped, soon tempt men of capital to invest their fortunes in land in Ireland, and agriculture there will become a profitable enterprise engaged in by persons from all parts of the United Kingdom.[12]

Thereafter, this mixture of benevolent paternalism and free trade principles characterised Villiers' – and indeed the Liberal Party's – essential position in regard to Ireland, and Villiers broadly supported Gladstone's reforming policies, including the Disestablishment of the Irish Church in 1869 and the Land Acts of 1870 and 1881, although he was strongly critical of the adoption of Irish coercion policies in the face of agrarian outrages in Ireland.[13]

However, when Herbert Gladstone flew the 'Hawarden Kite' in December 1885, announcing his father's conversion to Home Rule, Villiers felt betrayed. In February 1886, Gladstone duly formed his third ministry and put forward his first Home Rule Bill in March. This, in essence, provided for the establishment of a two-chamber Irish Parliament in Dublin, the removal of Irish MPs from Westminster, the payment by Ireland of one-fifteenth of imperial expenditure, and a Land Bill to buy out Irish landlords. The Bill was defeated on its second reading in the Commons on 8 June 1886, by 343 votes to 313, with 99 Liberals, including the Radical Unionist wing led by Joseph Chamberlain, voting in the majority. Three members did not vote: Grosvenor (who had been elevated to the peerage), Mr Speaker Peel, and Charles Villiers. Torn between loyalty to his party and loyalty to his principles, Villiers abstained,[14] and Colin Matthew has suggested that Gladstone 'seems to have worried more about the defection of old cronies, such as C.P. Villiers than that of the Chamberlain clique'.[15] Nevertheless, the issue had split the Liberal Party. Gladstone dissolved Parliament and at the subsequent General Election, the Tories under Lord Salisbury were returned by 394 seats (including 78 Liberal Unionists) to 276 (191 Liberals and 85 Irish Nationalists).[16] Thereafter, in opposition, Gladstone, now in close negotiation with Parnell via Mrs O'Shea,[17] continued to campaign for Home Rule with a revised prospectus which included the notion of 'Dual Parliaments' (one in Westminster and another in Dublin) and the provision for Irish MPs to continue to sit in the House of Commons (though reduced in number to 80).

For Charles Villiers, the Union between Great Britain and Ireland was sacrosanct. He believed that the historic injustices suffered by the Irish could and should be redressed by remedial legislation within the Union, and his criticisms of Gladstone's Home Rule policy in many respects echoed those embodied in the Unionist academic A.V. Dicey's masterly analysis of 1886, *England's Case against Home Rule*.[18] Villiers held that Gladstone's 'New Departure' marked a breach with traditional policy towards Ireland, remarking to McIlwraith,

> I can only say that I am the same Liberal now that I have been for sixty years past, but that I have an objection to Mr Gladstone's scheme for the severance of the Legislative Union between the two Islands, and chiefly from my conviction that it would be prejudicial to Ireland and I believe we might do much still for Ireland without repealing the Union.[19]

Moreover, he held that Gladstone, after more than fifty years having deliberately viewed with satisfaction the course pursued by the British Government towards Ireland, had

> put himself at the head of the Rebel Party in Ireland, and at the same time stating that their demand against the Union is and always has been not only reasonable but justified by the cruel and unjust policy pursued by this country towards them,[20]

an explanation which Villiers rejected, since he believed not only that at present there was 'not a single case in which Ireland has to complain of England' but also that Ireland's future prospects under the Union 'from the goodwill of this country towards her' were generally good.[21]

Thus, for Villiers, to oppose Home Rule was not a sign of neglect of, or hostility to, the interests of Ireland; indeed, from his perspective, it was an honourable position to take. In this context, Villiers and other Liberals, including Ulster Liberals, who opposed Home Rule could claim to be the 'true' Liberals; after all, was it 'Liberal' to place Ulster Protestants, who represented a quarter of the Irish population, under the heel of the nationalists, which Gladstone's Bill threatened to do?[22] Yet here, as Shannon has argued, Gladstone was 'candidly dismissive' of the Irish Protestants.[23] Indeed, as Eugenio Biagini has argued, the fundamental flaw in Gladstone's Irish strategy was that it completely neglected the reality of Ulster,[24] for Gladstone believed that Parnell's home rule movement represented the Irish nation in political terms (with 86 out of 103 Irish MPs) and he could not allow a Protestant minority – which he regarded as an obstacle to progress – to dictate the larger Irish question, and therefore saw no reason for excluding Ulster from his Bill. Indeed, as D. George Boyce has shown, Gladstone believed (mistakenly, as subsequent events were to show) that the Ulster Protestants – who did not, in his view, form a separate nationality – would in due course (with appropriate safeguards) become reconciled to his scheme and play their part in a moderate home rule parliament.[25]

Moreover, Villiers held that any form of Home Rule was fundamentally impractical, due largely to the internal divisions within Irish society (to which he repeatedly alluded), which made the Irish incapable of self-government. This belief was compounded by a mistrust of Irish nationalism for its association with a lack of respect for law and order, and property, and a predilection for agrarian violence and outrage, which Villiers (and other Liberal Unionists) frequently condemned.[26] Writing to McIlwraith in January 1888, for example, he observed

> The course avowed, of recognising a distinct nationality in the inhabitants of Ireland and of deciding upon the form in which that people, so inveterately divided amongst themselves, should be governed has not yet been seriously or sincerely considered,[27]

adding that 'Gladstone's New Departure ... may break down, as so many have done before and for the same reason of "Internal Dissention"',[28] whilst in May he remarked

> Not that I believe that the immediate concession of a National Parliament in Dublin would do much to remove the evils said now to be pressing upon that country, for really what their real quarrels are run more with each other than with this country.[29]

Such quarrels, Villiers argued, were also evident amongst Irish Nationalist MPs themselves, noting that even Parnell's leadership was not without question:

> It is pretty nearly an open secret abroad that several amongst his supporters (a few of the ablest in his Party) are dissatisfied with his lead and charge him with want of pluck and energy, of which they believe themselves possessed, and that some would be better in his place,

adding that 'there are signs of discontent amongst them such as were manifested against the best man they ever had or could have, which was Dan O'Connell.'[30]

Villiers also held that the question of Home Rule for Ireland was a matter of national security and that any scheme

> should honourably have in view the interests of that country itself and also as well what can be surrendered on the part of Great Britain, with a view to its safety and its relations with every other part of the world in which it is in any way connected.[31]

He believed that Home Rule 'would be a means of really weakening our own national defences, should we ever be in danger',[32] and argued that, if there were not other reasons for resisting the division of the Empire, 'the geographical one, in this case, seems to me almost sufficient, and for us to retain the real power we now possess, without a simple reason for expecting that Ireland would in any way be benefited by it.'[33] Above all, Villiers was concerned that an independent Ireland, having anything but a friendly feeling towards England ... possibly upon being refused powers that we might consider to impair our own safety, would listen, as they have done before, to overtures made to them by foreign countries with whom we might be at war.[34]

In this context, Villiers was particularly concerned that Ireland might be susceptible to overtures from France, Britain's colonial rival in Egypt and West Africa, who had supported the Irish Rising of 1798. Villiers, whose childhood had coincided with the Napoleonic Wars, had little time for the French, and John Bright was once moved to observe of Villiers, 'He is desperately and absurdly anti-French'.[35]

Villiers also regarded Gladstone's 'New Departure' as prejudicial to British parliamentary democracy on the grounds that the idea of Dual Parliaments in Dublin and Westminster, but with Irish MPs continuing to sit at Westminster, effectively gave Irish members control over the House of Commons. As he remarked to McIlwraith (somewhat facetiously) in July 1888:

> Mr G is probably as much puzzled as he said he was two years ago by 'discovering' that it was possible to have an independent Parliament in Dublin and a Parliament in England dependent on an Irish Party getting its way and which of course would be guided in the support it gave to either political party by the compliance with the demands of the Dublin Parliament. This is however all solved, namely that the national Irish Parliament should be established all the same and that, if it please the timid English, there might be always an Irish contingent in our House in Westminster, elected by Irish constituencies!![36]

For Villiers, this had been made a party question,

> for the sake of 85 men returned to the House and who promise to support the party that has promised to give it [Home Rule] to them, and by which means many persons will profit by patronage in the gift of their chief,[37]

adding that, if Gladstone's scheme was adopted, Irish MPs could

> at any moment they choose ... transfer themselves from one side to the other, like ballast in a vessel, and thus ruin or rescue any Ministry according to their pleasure, and in fact subordinating the rule in England to that of Ireland.[38]

Neither did Villiers believe that Gladstone's 'Union of Hearts' would satisfy Irish demands in the long term, for he saw Home Rule as leading inexorably to Separation.[39] In essence, Villiers believed that Gladstone had been effectively terrorised by Irish nationalists (and their supporters in the USA[40]) into making concessions and that this served only to further encourage them to believe 'that the best way of getting any thing out of England is by frightening her.'[41] Moreover, he saw that it was the recognition of distinct nationality that was called for by the leading opponents of the Union, and that Parnell had been consistent in stating 'that his claim still for his country is a Parliament in all its senses, which should recognise them as a distinct nation, and secure for them this acknowledgement of governing themselves as all other Countries of the Earth', and that he would 'not allow Mr Gladstone to deceive themselves or others by the fallacious term of "Home Rule", if that is to mean anything less than what he said at first'.[42] Villiers made a similar observation (after the fall of Parnell in 1891) during the drafting of Gladstone's Home Rule Bill in 1893, claiming

> The Bill is, one suspects, craftily drawn but there is not a line that offers any assurance that the people that have exacted the concession (made by it) will ever regard it in any other light than as a means of obtaining much more, in fact much more than they have over and over again asked for. The ground for their agitation every one of them have avowed the same is that they will not submit any longer to the control of England and that they seek the establishment of an Irish Parliament as a means of obtaining that object.[43]

Thus, for Villiers, Home Rule was merely a half-way house between the Union and an independent Ireland, irrespective of any guarantees to the contrary which might be provided in the Home Rule Bill. In this context, he argued that the mere insertion of a few lines in any clause declaring that the English Parliament may at any time have the right to control the legislature of the new Parliament in Dublin would in practice be a worthless safeguard, and was designed merely 'to reconcile the fears of those who have not yet lost their heads'.[44]

In short, Villiers regarded Gladstone's 'New Departure', which he held to be motivated in part by Gladstone's desire not only to retain his leadership of the Liberal Party but also as a means to regain the Premiership,[45] as an unmitigated disaster. As he remarked to McIlwraith, 'It is impossible therefore not to see that the aspect of the Old Question between us now is being changed for the worse'.[46] Villiers believed that Gladstone's Home Rule scheme was fundamentally wrong, misguided, impractical, 'proposed in haste ... by appeals to ignorance and passion',[47] and lacking in public support,[48] and would not 'as his friends say, relieve all England of fear and spread contentment in Ireland!'[49] Moreover, Villiers believed that the whole question of Irish Home Rule had impeded the real work of the House of Commons, not least through the routine obstructionism of Irish MPs,[50] and had distracted the House from attending to other important domestic issues.[51]

Above all else, Villiers bemoaned the divisive impact of Gladstone's 'New Departure' on the Liberal Party. In particular, as with many Radicals within the Liberal ranks, Villiers disliked the Party's focus on single-issue politics (which Home Rule represented), believing that the Liberals should be identified with a broad programme of reform.[52] Writing to McIlwraith in March 1888, Villiers observed:

> To be in the House of Commons now, with any approach to independence of mind or memory of the past, when the struggle against abuse, and mischievous and obsolete laws, was clear and never left an honest politician in doubt, or to his course, is certainly not agreeable, and all the friends with whom I acted formerly with so much satisfaction are gone, and though their successors assume the name of the Party with which it was my delight to be connected, yet one cannot deceive oneself as to the object in former times which was simply for principles and well-considered Liberal policy. At present I can understand what the Liberal members are chiefly fighting for is to recover place and power without finitely stating what they would do, whether perhaps could do, if the men who were in office three years ago were placed there again![53]

His sincere wish was that 'what used to be called the "Liberal Party" should once again appear as an honestly organised power, united in opinion, and ready for the field',[54] and he held that the division within the party which had commenced in 1886 was entirely the fault of Gladstone and his supporters – 'the Gladstonites'. These men, he argued, had abandoned Liberal principles: 'The Liberalism which the substantial and educated portion of the community would desire to see again connected with official power is not that which W. Gladstone is at present guiding',[55] Thus, for Villiers, it was the Gladstonites who were the real turncoats rather than the Liberal Unionists and it was they, 'by their peculiar tactics and proceedings' who had forced the Old Liberals,

> into a position, when it is neither dishonourable or impolite on their part, to cooperate with their former opponents and to separate themselves from those who claim the severance of the Legislative Union with this country, and who are impatiently demanding organic changes in the constitution of both countries.[56]

By contrast, Villiers claimed that he had

> declared my firm adherence to the principles on which I had acted throughout my life and that my objection to the Dual Parliament was not now in order to act with them but in constancy to the principles that I had held for 50 years before and which I had adopted in common with the most earnest and most advanced Liberals that ever sat in Parliament.[57]

Support for Liberal Unionism was, therefore, a logical, consistent and principled position for Villiers to take and endorses Cawood's assertion that the only true definition of a Liberal Unionist was one who rejected Gladstone's Irish policy and looked back to the Liberal Party of 1885 as the true embodiment of orthodox Liberal principles before these were jettisoned by Gladstone.[58] Thereafter, Villiers was prepared to give Salisbury's government (1886–1892) the benefit of the doubt; as he told McIlwraith,

> One is striving now to consider whether one ought not to take what the present government are willing to give (whether they like it or not) to benefit the country, or reject it simply because they are Tories and we are Liberals,[59]

adding that it seemed 'paltry now to obstruct the action of this Gov in every way, simply because Mr Gladstone's government has broken down.'[60] Moreover, Villiers claimed that there was now

> a considerable change in the spirit and purpose of the Conservative Party, and which is peculiarly to be observed, since they have sought and accepted the cooperation of the well-known and distinguished section who have hitherto uniformly supported Liberal policy! – and who contend that in maintaining the Parliamentary Union of the two countries, they are acting in strict consistency with the opinions of every distinguished statesman that in all past time has ever led or belonged to their party.[61]

In short, the Tories were now adopting traditional (pre-1886) policies towards the Irish Question (and were influenced by some of Chamberlain's proposals which Gladstone had previously rejected).

This said, when Arthur Balfour, the new Chief Secretary for Ireland introduced his Perpetual Crimes (Coercion) Bill in March 1887, it was not supported by Villiers. Balfour claimed that the Bill was necessary to quell increased agrarian crime and disorder in Ireland, although the evidence for this was debatable,[62] and was torn to shreds by Gladstone in the House of Commons, where he described the measure as 'a deplorable proposal'.[63] Gladstone also wrote to Villiers, seeking his opinion on the Bill. Villiers replied 'I am only flattered, I assure you, at your having addressed me on the subject' and expressed his wish 'that this whole Liberal Party will unite again in seeking to accomplish complete redress', but explained to Gladstone that 'I never vote for any of these Coercive measures without great regret and I am ashamed to think how often I have voted with the Party in doing so'.[64] The demand for such measures, he claimed, invariably came from the authorities in Ireland, who were always alleging that such measures were essential for the preservation of order and the preservation of life and property and that the Tory Government might well feel that their position was in danger if they did not propose them. Moreover, in reflecting on previous Irish Coercion Acts, Villiers regarded the measure as futile, stating

> It is from my recollection of what has occurred before and may therefore resume, and that upon any change of Government the policy will change, and this measure, like any other, may be rescinded or amended, and if that occurs after any temporary suppression of perpetual crimes, thereupon the recurrence of any great distress and the reappearance of the same disorders, the cry again for repressive measures will be revived.[65]

The Coercion Act became law in July 1887 but was accompanied by Chamberlain's Land Act which, intended as a 'softener' to coercion, enabled county courts in Ireland to grant stays of evictions and guaranteed Irish tenants what were described as 'judicial rents', based on market conditions.[66] As Villiers remarked to Gladstone, 'I am afraid that it cannot be said that it is the first time that measures of advantage to Ireland have been accompanied with what implies mistrust of the people and is distasteful to many', recalling

> If I remember rightly when the restrictions on Catholics on account of their religion were removed [1829], the Catholic Association (to which they were so much indebted) was suppressed and Electors were then deprived of the Franchise (they have lately been added to the Electorate).[67]

Nevertheless, Villiers believed that the Gladstonites were exacerbating Liberal disunity by their behaviour and tactics. Noting that there was 'nothing whatever of any compromise (of opinion at least) between the several sections of the Liberal Party',[68] Villiers bemoaned the Gladstonites for

> their personal and passionate abuse of their old friends who had done so much to keep them, and which has been substituted for anything like a grave consideration of the very important question that has now been raised between the two Islands![69]

Indeed, the failure of the Gladstonites to fully discuss and explain their position was not lost on *The Spectator*:

> The failure of the Gladstonian leaders in their public utterances to make out a case for Home Rule is one of the most striking features of the present political situation ... as exponents of their cause by argument and by appeals to the reasoning faculty of their hearers, they entirely fail ... though they have arguments in reserve, they consider that appeals to party feeling and to sentiment, ridicule of opponents, imputation of motives, the calling of names, and the copious use of rhetoric, are the most potent instruments in political controversy.[70]

Finally, during the Summer of 1888 the Liberal party embarked on a campaign to target Liberal Unionists in their constituencies and to undermine their position. As Villiers observed,

> W.G. has some very devoted tools, for though they are not many, they are now used on every occasion and if one is correctly informed, they are now required to visit every Liberal Unionist constituency now at ease to stir up strife,

adding that 'the game has been lately played in several places besides our Boro',[71] and that

> where a man is called a 'Unionist', to talk of his conduct of treason to Liberalism and desertion of party, but carefully avoiding anything of the practicability of the Dual Parliament project, about which most reasonable persons have their doubts.[72]

This practice was particularly evident in the Liberal Unionist stronghold of Birmingham and the West Midlands, and Joseph Chamberlain, in particular, was the prime target for Liberal venom, both within Parliament and without. Writing to McIlwraith in May 1888, for example, Villiers referred to the

> singular interchange of hospitality and hard blows that have lately passed between Mr Chamberlain and Sir W. Harcourt. If they are not really to fight, without their gloves next week, I don't see the point of their shaking hands before the battle begins. Some thought it had to do with Joseph's married state, but upon something like authority I heard that this, like the fishing question, is yet quite unsettled, and though Lady Harcourt comes from Bankers land, she is in no way interested in the fortunes of Miss Endicott.[73]

This was in fact a reference to a spat between Sir William Harcourt, a leading Gladstonite and former Chancellor of the Exchequer,[74] and Chamberlain, who had described Harcourt as 'a soldier of fortune', whose boisterous humour made him difficult to take seriously, adding 'whilst he is belabouring us we cannot doubt that he would have an equal pleasure in slashing at his employers if his term of service with them had happened to have expired'.[75] Later, during the debates on the Local Government Bill (which the Liberals opposed), Harcourt stated that Chamberlain 'had lost all real capacity of gauging public opinion', and was 'only a butterfly without antennae and nothing to warn him of his flutterings'.[76] *The Spectator* duly observed,

> Appearances may be deceptive, and the inference drawn from them incorrect; but, at any rate, Sir William Harcourt's unswerving practice of

abusing the exponents of Unionism rather than of attempting to found Home Rule on the sure rock of argument, does a good deal to encourage the notion.[77]

Whilst illustrating the enmity between Liberals and Liberal Unionists more broadly, Villiers' personalised explanation of this particular episode to some extent endorses his reputation amongst his opponents as a gossip (as well as his wit: 'Bankers land' being another sarcastic reference to the USA). This said, although there is little surviving correspondence between Villiers and Chamberlain, it appears that Villiers – at least initially – thought well of Chamberlain's leadership of the Unionists and on the eve of the second Home Rule Bill he told McIlwraith (with no little foresight) that

> his [Chamberlain's] service in continuing the Union cause has been invaluable and if his body strength does not fail him he is most certainly booked for some very high office in this country. For some reason, he was only a favourite some time ago but he is becoming immense. Each of his speeches seem better than the last that he makes.[78]

Nevertheless, the General Election of August 1892 saw Gladstone return to power with an overall majority of forty-two over the Tories and Liberal Unionists (albeit with the support of the Irish Nationalists, who were themselves divided between Parnellites and Anti-Parnellites). During a protracted debate in the House of Commons in response to the address in answer to Her Majesty's speech on 11 August (which endorsed the government's commitment to Irish Home Rule), the Liberal Unionist, Sir Henry James (the MP for Bury) responded to an allegation by the new Home Secretary, Herbert Asquith, that Liberal Unionism illustrated 'perverted fidelity unexampled in the history of apostasy'.[79] James charged Asquith (elected as the MP for East Fife in 1886) with

> too much self-confidence – perhaps, I may say, of arrogance, when he charges such men with such a Liberal past as John Bright or the Right Hon. Member for South Wolverhampton [C.P. Villiers] with being guilty of political apostasy. What does an apostate mean? Is it a man who changes his faith or opinions for gain, for office, for power? Who are the men who have done that?

James added, 'I would ask him to consider whether it is becoming in him to use such language to such distinguished – I may add illustrious – men as the men I have mentioned – John Bright and Charles Pelham Villiers'.[80] James also berated Sir William Harcourt for his sustained attacks on his former Liberal colleagues, especially Joseph Chamberlain.[81] Personal enmities between Liberals and Liberal Unionists notwithstanding, however, Gladstone's fourth administration subsequently faced a range of difficulties and was riven by internal disagreements over policy, as David Brooks has shown,[82] but Gladstone's parliamentary majority was sufficient for him to carry a second Home Rule Bill through the Commons. As Villiers observed, 'unless the Irish contingent prove faithless to the old man, in the Committee the Bill will get through the Commons',[83] which, he held, would satisfy Gladstone:

> I expect that with the closure in his hand and a thorough 'Union of Hearts' between himself and his Irish Allies that the Old Gentleman will have his way, and knowing that when it is passed he will not be here, but only seeing, as many do in their latter days, that it will do for him and that the D … l take the hindmost.[84]

Whilst acknowledging Gladstone's immense standing and public popularity – 'he is now greater than ever'[85] – Villiers held that Gladstone had not been 'much affected by his eccentricities, or by his mistakes or misstatements!'[86] and confided in McIlwraith that 'I never thought Gladstone a safe pair of hands, but now I think him really dangerous for he is evidently afraid of his own hounds and will be devoured by them … to escape the ridicule attaching to failure!'[87]

In July 1893, following eighty-two days of debate in the Commons, where, according to Villiers there was 'a sort of Donneybrook scene every night',[88] the Home Rule Bill was carried on its third reading by a majority of thirty-four. Charles Villiers voted against the Bill. *The Morning Post* later recalled that his appearance in the Commons – he was now aged ninety-one – 'excited great interest among the members, who loudly cheered him as he passed the tellers',[89] whilst the London correspondent of the *Leicester Chronicle* was moved to comment that

> After the second round the gallant old gentleman was obliged to cave in. His still abundant white hair, and his crooked figure, literally pressed down by the heavy hand of Time, finally disappearing from the scene … For more than a generation he had been a sort of Parliamentary ghost.[90]

By contrast, Henry Lucy,[91] the renowned parliamentary correspondent, who greatly admired Gladstone, described Villiers presence in a different vein, commenting sarcastically that

> So high did Party feeling run at the moment, that Mr Villiers came down to the House and voted in the first two rounds taken immediately after ten o'clock, when the closure came into operation. After that, he reasonably thought he had done enough to save his country, and went off home. But although Ninety judiciously retired, two members of more than Eighty stopped to the last, going round and round the lobbies for two hours on a sultry night. One was Mr Gladstone, then approaching his eighty-fifth year.[92]

Villiers himself informed McIlwraith that 'I stopped past 12 to vote and have hardly been well since', adding that 'After the surrender that Mr Gladstone has made to them [Irish], they would think it ignoble if ever they were quiet again', and noting that 'Mr Morley mentioned with glee that what had been now done in forcing the Bill through the House of Commons could never be undone.'[93] However, it was widely acknowledged that the Bill would be defeated by a large majority in the House of Lords who, as Villiers had foreseen, would 'deal the well-merited blow',[94] and on 8 September 1893 the House of Lords rejected the Bill by 419 votes to 41, much to Villiers' relief, although he had correctly prophesied that this would open up once again the old question of the reform of the House of Lords.[95]

On 27 February 1894, William Gladstone announced his intention to stand down as Prime Minister and on 1 March he made his final speech and last appearance in the House of Commons where, as Villiers observed

> the language was almost exhausted in lavish eulogy at the retirement of the Grand Old Gentleman, and the open avowal by his Parliamentary friends of a steady adherence to every line of his past policy, so far as it is known, with regard to the United Kingdom, or, perhaps, of the mode of severing the Union between England and Ireland.[96]

For Villiers, Gladstone's retirement was timely. As he told MacIlwraith

> From all the speeches that I refer to, as well as to most educated people that one converses with, I should only suppose that a relief has been felt from being ruled most arbitrarily by great genius, certainly by a man who had evidently outlived the judgment which he was supposed to have possessed in his earlier years, when he was going on what he would do next, which was a matter of doubt, if not apprehension, on the part of interested and thoughtful people in every part of the country ... I never pretend to see further into a millstone than my neighbour, but I have had an idea for some time past that the country very generally wanted *rest* rather than *fresh turmoil*, and many, I am sure, had the idea of putting Lord Rosebery in the place of the old man, and something of this kind must follow from it.[97]

The Home Rule Question and divisions within the Liberal Party had implications for Villiers' position in his constituency in Wolverhampton, which was a Liberal stronghold for much of the Victorian period.[98] Here, as Jon Lawrence has observed, Liberalism meant loyalty not to an organisation but to a set of principles and to individuals thought to embody those principles, namely Gladstone and Villiers, who 'symbolised the historic Liberal victories of earlier decades, and thereby reinforced the idea that Liberalism was a dynamic political movement dedicated to securing the political, religious and social emancipation of working people'.[99] In 1886, Villiers' fellow Liberal MPs were Sir William Plowden[100] (for Wolverhampton West) and Henry

Fowler (for Wolverhampton East). Both men were staunch Gladstonites and pro-Home Rulers, (Fowler, in particular, seems to have had little time for Villiers after 1886 following his desertion of the Gladstone ship, although he remained on friendly terms with both Chamberlain and Hartington and privately hoped for Liberal reunion[101]) but Villiers (representing Wolverhampton South), who held an iconic status in the district, was clearly not, and from 1886 onwards he became the target of a vigorous campaign in support of both Gladstone and Irish Home Rule mounted by the leading Wolverhampton newspaper, the *Express & Star,* under the direction of its owner, Andrew Carnegie (1835–1919) and manager, Thomas Graham (1841–1909).

Dunfermline-born Thomas Graham was the son of a hand-loom weaver, whose family moved to Wolverhampton in the 1850s and who set up a bacon-curing business at Wadhams Hill in 1862. Graham subsequently became a successful pork merchant, member of the Borough Council, J.P., and prominent radical local Liberal. Disappointed at the Conservative politics of the local paper, *The Evening Express,* Graham sought to establish or acquire a newspaper that would espouse his Liberal principles, but he needed financial support. The opportunity to do so arose as a result of Graham's friendship with Andrew Carnegie,[102] the multi-millionaire industrialist, philanthropist and republican, which had commenced by chance during a train journey from London following one of Graham's regular visits to the Liberal Reform Club. Carnegie had also been born in Dunfermline, and during the 1870s the two struck up a firm friendship.[103] Carnegie had also been looking for an opportunity to invest in the expanding British newspaper industry in order to disseminate his political views. Having made his money through his vast Pittsburg steel empire, Carnegie compared the wealth of the USA with the poverty and deprivation he had experienced as a youth in Scotland and which he believed still existed in Britain, and concluded that the British Constitutional Monarchy should be replaced with an American-style constitution (and the Royal Family sent back to Germany). In June 1880, Graham and fellow local Liberals had launched *The Evening Star* as 'a reliable and efficient representative of the United Liberal Party', but further funds were required and Graham was keen to persuade Carnegie to invest in the newspaper.[104]

The opportunity arose in June 1881, when Carnegie brought a party of American friends to Britain, where Graham had arranged a sightseeing trip for them. Landing at Liverpool, they went to Brighton where they collected a stagecoach drawn by four bays, which took the party, dubbed the 'Gay Charioteers' by Carnegie, to Oxford, Stratford and then Wolverhampton, where they stayed with Graham at his Parkdale home, before leaving for Inverness. In 1882, in association with Samuel Storey, a newspaper owner and Liberal MP from Sunderland, Carnegie duly invested in the *Evening Star* and in September 1883 a new company was formed, the Midland News Association, with Carnegie and Storey as principal shareholders and Thomas Graham, Hugh Reid, Theodore Fry and William White (all Liberals) as members of the syndicate.[105] The MNA subsequently bought up the *Evening*

Express in February 1884 for £20,000 and the merger of the *Express* and the *Star* took place in July, becoming thereafter the *Evening Express & Star*, until 15 April 1889, when the word 'Evening' was dropped from the title.[106] Edited by Andrew Meikle, another Dunfermline-born Scot, the *Express & Star* was strongly pro-Gladstone and pro-Irish Home Rule, Graham often inviting leading Irish Nationalist MPs to speak at the Wolverhampton Liberal Club and entertaining them at his Parkdale home. Carnegie's interest in the MNA and *Express & Star* lasted until 1902, when he sold his shares in the business, the paper remaining in the Graham family thereafter.[107]

Charles Villiers had little personal sympathy for Carnegie, who he regarded as another American 'Robber Baron' and who he described variously in his letters – with biting sarcasm– as 'Andrew', 'The Coach and Four', 'The Old Goose', 'Our Patron', 'The Millionaire', 'Protectionist Yankee Millionaire', 'the Grand Chief', and 'the Paymaster'. He resented Carnegie's support for Irish Home Rule and his apparent influence in British politics as 'foreign' interference, observing that 'he has, ever since his return, been meddling where he has no business, to favour his object, and he has been in intimate relation with some of the GOMs appendages'.[108] Villiers was also irritated by Carnegie's constant references to the virtues of the New World as opposed to the supposed evils of the Old. For example, in January 1888 the *Pittsburgh Volksblatt* published a letter from Carnegie which stated:

> The old European continent is an armed camp, its millions training how best to kill each other. The new American continent is a smiling garden, its millions cultivating the arts of peace. The dynasties of the Old World sink deeper and deeper under the load of debt. The New World is troubled how to dispose of its surplus. In despotic Europe anarchists and Nihilists abound, the natural result of unjust laws. The germs of these pernicious growths transplanted to the Republic wither and die. For these and many other mercies, rejoice; for of all lands America is the most favoured.[109]

On reading this, Villiers remarked to McIlwraith that

> I see that old goose (Andrew), Our Patron, (as one in the Borough styled him, in fact) is now again out against all Europe, where all the States (as he says) are now succumbing to the Dark, crushed by debt, and must now be confronted with the splendid picture presented by the 'States', who are prosperous, contented and without a debt.[110]

In a further letter, Villiers added that Mr Carnegie needed to remember that it had been a quarter of a century since the 'smiling garden' had been

> engaged in a civil war far more horrid than any in which any state in Europe had been engaged during the present century and the purpose of

which was to suppress a hideous system of human bondage existing for the sake of the commercial advantage of the sections of 'the Garden' who were fiercely contending for its continuation, that an enormous debt was thereby contracted, and which for the sinister purpose of maintaining a high tariff, a majority in 'the Garden' object to pay off.[111]

He also pointed out that during the present century, the United States had annexed a huge territory 'to which they have no right and which belonged to another power', adding that, 'with respect to the suppression of a party among themselves advocating Nihilism if not Anarchism they have only just been obliged to visit four of their leaders with capital punishment', (A reference to the so-called Chicago 'Anarchists' who had been hanged in November 1887 in consequence of their role in an industrial dispute).[112] Villers concluded, 'So much for Andrew's judgments, who urges upon England to change her form of government and adopt the one under which he lives!'[113]

Moreover, as a staunch supporter of the Monarchy, Villiers found Carnegie's criticisms of the Royal Family particularly distasteful, attacking the *Express & Star*, (which he regarded as Carnegie's mouthpiece, and which he variously described as 'the American Organ', 'the Carnegie Luminary' or 'the Pittsburg Luminary')

> for going the whole hog in supporting the Yankee's views of our social and political system, and beginning with his peculiar fancy that a Royal Family was a deliberate insult to every other family; yet he said that he might not object to our Queen taking tea with his wife (for he had heard that she was a respectable woman).[114]

When, in the summer of 1893, the Carnegies were invited by Gladstone to visit Hawarden, Villiers remarked, 'I don't think it was wise for the First Minister to have him as his guest just now. I doubt very much whether the working classes appreciate what vulgar impertinence he sends to the Royal Family'.[115]

Although Villiers had strong personal support not only within his constituency but also within the town of Wolverhampton, he was also aware of Gladstone's popularity in the district, remarking to McIlwraith that

> I am of course aware of the universality of the Gladstone worship throughout the Boro, and as I think that I ought to forbear from openly differing from a constituency, with which I have been so long by connection, I do not wish to put views forward as differing from theirs. Perhaps I have a hope that they may abate their passion for Man-worship by following W.E. Gladstone.[116]

Nevertheless, he was clearly irked by the politics of the *Express & Star* and, more especially by the personal attacks made upon him in editorials, which reached their peak in 1888, and for which he held Carnegie and Graham responsible:

> I wish the said Andrew had sown the seeds of all that is prejudicial to England in any other town than ours ... It is melancholy to see into whose hands the Liberal organ [*The Express & Star*] has now fallen, and by what means it is supported! But what is it that money may not and will not do? However, I don't want this Butcher [Graham] to be more hostile to us than he is already, therefore I only say these things privately.[117]

Moreover, it is clear from Villiers' correspondence with McIlwraith that Carnegie, Graham, and a pressure group of Gladstone supporters within the local Liberal Association, described by Villiers as 'The Circus', and led by W.M. Fuller, the leading light in the Fowler Reform Club (founded in 1884), were seeking not merely to impugn his reputation in Liberal circles, but also, and by various means, to replace him as the MP for the Southern Division.[118] In this, they were to fail.

The Graham–Fuller campaign aimed to put pressure on Villiers, in the hope that he might ultimately be replaced by a local representative of sound Gladstonite views,[119] and the implications of the editorials printed in the *Express & Star* during the summer and autumn of 1888, were that Villiers was disloyal in supporting Liberal Unionism (and was therefore of unsound views); that he was too old and frequently unwell, which prevented him from attending the House of Commons regularly (and was therefore guilty of dereliction of duty); that, as an absentee MP who lived in London and confined himself to Westminster politics, he was out of touch with the feelings of his constituents; and that there was a popular demand within the Southern Division for his removal. In responding to these 'mean and malicious attacks devised and encouraged in others by Mr Graham's paper' on behalf of 'the paltry ungenerous purposes of an ill conditioned clique',[120] Villiers could (and did) justifiably claim that, far from being disloyal, he had always been loyal to the Liberal principles upon which he had been elected in 1835 (and for which he had been continuously re-elected thereafter), principles which Gladstone's conversion to Home Rule had betrayed; that, though he was often unwell (suffering from colds and bouts of gout, in particular), his attendance and voting record at Westminster were generally good; that his residency in London had always enabled him to operate where it mattered, at the core of British politics in the House of Commons, and that he was fully cognisant with the views of his constituents through his correspondence with the local Liberal Association (and, in private, through William McIlwraith); and that demands for his removal were exaggerated.

Villiers (understandably) deplored the means employed by his opponents. For example, he noted that the Liberal Association were inviting Irish Nationalist MPs, 'and other persons whose views on political matters are at variance with those of the people generally' to speak at the Villiers Reform

Club (which he had supported financially) rather than at the pro-Gladstone Fowler Club. These included Justin McCarthy, MP: 'Why did he not go next door, since he be of Mr Fowler's politics?', queried Villiers, adding

> it looks as if there was some purpose in it ... there would have been a propriety in the Fowler Club proposing to a close ally of Mr Fowler's, to speak at that club – with Mr Fuller in the Chair.[121]

In April he noted that Fuller, the Chairman of the Eastern Division, was 'stepping out of his own beat to talk about Ireland' at Sedgley, within Villiers' own constituency, adding that 'the object of the meeting is probably again to tell them [the Electors] of someone more worthy to represent them'.[122] In June, Villiers observed that the 'local tools' were preparing for their intended 'rout' in the Southern Division where 'with the illness of the present member, an easy conquest is to be made of a seat in favour of repeal' and that a 'pompous article' had been published in the 'Carnegie Luminary' [*Express & Star*] which stated

> that the representation of that Division must be immediately altered, that there was still a corner of the old Boro that the member had represented so long that was not ready to revel in the worship of their Demigod [Gladstone]

and that the Division 'was pining to be relieved from one with whom they agreed so little!'[123] Indeed, on 12 July the *Express & Star* stated that the state of the Liberal Party in the Southern Division was unsatisfactory and that 'many leading members of it are of this opinion and are quite aware of what is needed to be done', adding that there was enough energy, enthusiasm and intelligence in the Division 'which, if properly directed, will be more than enough to make the Liberalism of Wolverhampton South invincible'.[124]

The future of the Southern Division was also raised by Graham in July at meetings in London with key Gladstone supporters, including John Morley, Francis Schnadhorst, the Secretary of the National Liberal Federation (who was anxious to keep the NLF Gladstonian rather than Chamberlainite) and Philip Stanhope, the Liberal MP for Wednesbury (later Baron Weardale) and an influential member of the National Liberal Club. Their purpose, according to Villiers, was, in the event of a dissolution of Parliament (which seemed possible should the Local Government Bill be defeated), 'of putting Mr Gladstone in office again, and of putting in my place anybody whatever who will add to the list of those that he regards as Toadies.'[125] When Villiers inquired of McIlwraith 'who you think the wise men, who seem to have "GOM" on the brain and as their only prophet, think of for a candidate for my Southern Division?' the reply was that it was rumoured that a certain Mr. Charles Shaw was a possible candidate.[126] A local man, a graduate of Balliol College, Oxford, and a Captain in the 3rd Voluntary Battalion of the South Staffordshire Regiment, Shaw was the Managing Director and Chairman of John Shaw & Sons Ltd, hardware manufacturers, and was a member of Wolverhampton Town Council.[127] It transpired that Shaw was also a close friend of Margaret Plowden, daughter of Sir William Plowden, the Gladstonite MP for Wolverhampton West, (described by Villiers as 'the rejected of the Western Division'[128]) which prompted Villiers to later remark, with his usual sarcasm,

> The local member of the Privy Council [Plowden] is ... prominent in the Boro at home. Did you hear that C.E. Shaw is named in the running for Ms Plowden's hand when she recovers from the typhoid fever she has had lately?[129]

Villiers was clearly disappointed by these developments, for which he held Carnegie and Graham ultimately responsible. In August he noted

> I was told that their Grand Chief [Carnegie] has never encouraged these attacks upon me and has acknowledged that I have never spoke publicly against him – but I suppose one may say, as Lord Cross once said in the House of Commons, 'There is a lying spirit abroad just now that makes it difficult to discern the truth', for I don't think he is often charged with being generous or true. I don't believe it.[130]

and later he informed McIlwraith that

> I must think that all this work of Carnegie's agents in the Division is mean and paltry to the last degree and what is unfortunate is that though he [Carnegie] 'pays the piper' there are men whom one would like to think were honest and earnest in the Liberal cause that dance to his piping really for personal ends. If there is any party in the Division that have any good ground of quarrel with me, it has not arisen from what has passed of late on my part, but does seem to result from the communications that have been going on lately between Graham, Schnadhorst and Carnegie! And considering what they are about, in order to get the approval of Gladstone namely, to turn out a man who has served them faithfully for 53 years, at very great sacrifices of time and health and personal prospects, in order to put in some favoured local man in my place without experience, and in whose past career they can see no reason for confidence, and to get the thanks of the ambitious and unscrupulous Chief in whose restorative power they would see their own advantage ... I could hardly conceive anything more miserable.[131]

On 27 August, however, an editorial in the *Birmingham Daily Post* came to Villiers' defence and provided him with some relief from the rumours and innuendos published in the *Express & Star*. 'It is interesting to note', it observed

Gladstone and the Home Rule crisis 249

'how eager a certain class of politicians are to provide for vacancies which have not occurred'. It continued:

> We hear from the Wolverhampton papers that some restless spirits in that borough, either acting on their own fancies, or prompted from outside, are extremely desirous to deal with the seat of Mr Villiers. They do not, as we understand, propose to ask him to resign, nor do they avow a desire to oust him at the next election. It is put in this way – that a good Liberal ought to be found who, being accepted by the constituency, might succeed Mr Villiers if he were wanted – a sort of political coadjutor, with a right of succession; in other words, someone who will be waiting to step into Mr Villiers' shoes, and who may quietly take them off, if opportunities offer. It has been said that Mr Villiers assents to this arrangement; but we are told, as a matter of fact, that he does nothing of the kind. Mr Villiers, we are informed, has no intention of giving up his seat for Wolverhampton; nor does he intend to take part, or in any way to sanction, any transaction as to his successor whenever he may wish to retire ... We have no doubt that Mr Villiers may and will retain the confidence of the electors as long as he is still willing to represent them in the House of Commons.[132]

On the following day, the *Express & Star* responded to this editorial by stating that whilst it might be the hope of the *Birmingham Daily Post* that there would be no 'loose talk' about finding Mr Villiers a successor, this had not always been the feeling of the local Tories who, it alleged, demanded that Villiers should pledge his unstinting support for Unionism 'in no uncertain terms' if his seat was to be unchallenged.[133] Moreover, on 30 August, in the context of Villiers' impending change of address from Sloan Street (which was scheduled for redevelopment by the owner, Lord Cadogan) to 50 Cadogan Square, the *Star* carried a sarcastic editorial entitled 'Mr Villiers to be Evicted':

> From his seat in Wolverhampton? – No. This is not the kind of eviction that is impending, but came from his old home in Sloan Street, Chelsea ... What with Lord Cadogan's turning him out of his house, and the Tories of Wolverhampton suggesting that he should be self-evicted from his Liberalism, the old gentleman is in circumstances which call for sincere commiseration. We hope that Mr Villiers will find a new and comfortable home in London and that he will to the end of his days find a truly Liberal environment his only congenial surroundings.[134]

As Villiers duly remarked to McIlwraith,

> I saw the paltry spite exhibited in the 'Star' remarking about my change of residence the other day and I thought it characteristic of the style of this mean dependent organ for the grand independent party which they

profess to represent and which, as you say, directs the nature and spirit of those who prompt (and I suppose pay for) such rubbish.[135]

In fact, Villiers was both irritated and upset by

> the impudent malicious reference to me in the paper of the Porkman [Graham] with the object, as it is said, of driving me to resign or to enter the ranks of the Tories, and then to find an excuse for going at me (poker and tongs),[136]

and actually asked McIlwraith, 'If you could by any chance ascertain what this Mr Graham says himself on the cause of his personal hostility to me I should be glad to hear it.'[137]

Nevertheless, Villiers was reassured in September by communications from Colonel Gough, the Chairman of the Conservative Association, which indicated that the Tories were disinclined to contest the South Division in the event of an election 'if they can decently avoid it and, I suppose, if they also have no hope of succeeding if they do so'.[138] However, he informed McIlwraith that he continued to be 'unusually worried by communications from the Division I sent for, and chiefly on account of people who are panting for my resignation, that the vacancy might be filled by some tool of the Gladstone party', adding that

> the taste of these men ... is like the stupid way they proceed in bringing about my resignation. Without having regard to consistency, they say two things. One is that 4/5ths of the Electors in the South are Gladstonians, and for the Repeal of the Union, and also that the Tories are gaining ground so fast that it is necessary to appoint certain people especially to attend any meetings to keep them straight upon the Irish Question, and because I don't at present approve of having a Dual Parliament.[139]

In October, his fears were tempered by news from McIlwraith, garnered from his contacts in Wolverhampton, that the prevailing feeling towards Villiers in the Southern Division was, despite the assertions of the *Express & Star*, generally favourable.[140] Any thought of resignation was, for Villiers, now out of the question and, as he reported to McIlwraith, 'I have told them on both sides that I have no intention of resigning my seat',[141] although he also expressed his concerns about the devious ways in which the Liberal caucus had operated in Wolverhampton during the campaign against him (in which he suspected that both Plowden and Fowler had also been complicit[142]), adding that 'from what I hear from other places, this caucus system will not be easily distinguished from the old nomination in rotten Boroughs'.[143]

By December, when the prospect of a dissolution of Parliament had receded, Villiers was able to observe not only that 'just now, what one may call the Gladstonian agitation hangs fire',[144] but also that the Liberal Unionists 'have not lost ground of late and whose position ... is firmer than it has been yet'.[145] In fact, with insufficient support for Shaw within the local Liberal Association, (where Villiers was still considered to be a *bona fide* Liberal who might slip back into the fold, despite his split with Gladstone over Home Rule[146]), the campaign against Villiers had fizzled out and, as Villiers observed at the end of December, 'my critics in the Southern Division have laid down their arms, as far as I am concerned, for which I am obliged to them', whilst adding 'there are still Grahamites on the ground, I daresay'.[147]

Nevertheless, on the eve of the General Election of 1892, Villiers was nominated overwhelmingly by the Southern Division as its candidate, with only five dissentient voices,[148] and was returned unopposed, whilst Henry Fowler was returned for Wolverhampton East, although the Tories made a significant gain in Wolverhampton West – the rich 'West End' of the town, where a local industrialist, Sir Alfred Hickman defeated Plowden.[149] Indeed, such was Villiers' status and authority in Wolverhampton South – a largely working-class district – that his was one of the safest seats in the country, for the Conservatives had no interest in contesting it and the Liberals had no chance of putting forward a candidate who could defeat him. Indeed, as Taylor has observed, no Gladstonite had dared to openly challenge this 'grand old man'.[150] This said, Villiers clearly benefited from the Tories not standing a candidate against him, which sheds some doubt on the Cawood thesis that, in the West Midlands at least, the victories of the Liberal Unionists at elections owed absolutely nothing to the alliance with the Tories.[151]

Although 'The Circus' had been defeated, it should be remembered that Andrew Carnegie had, since 1882, also established a friendship with Gladstone (as well as with other leading Liberals, including John Morley).[152] Colin Matthew has suggested that this friendship was not only rooted in their joint enthusiasm for their Scottish roots but also reflected the rapprochement that was taking place between the British governing class and East Coast American wealth and politics.[153] Moreover, Gladstone saw merit in Carnegie's 'Gospel of Wealth', which decreed that provided men were given the opportunity to become rich, thereby assisting economic development and prosperity, they would be able to diminish the widening gulf between the classes by benevolent philanthropy – which Carnegie undertook on a vast scale, and which was much admired by Gladstone (although he disagreed with Carnegie's view that inherited wealth was fundamentally bad).[154] Carnegie subsequently gave donations to the Liberal Party, offered Gladstone the (then) enormous sum of £100,000 for the full rights to an autobiography (which was declined), and even, as Gladstone recalled in his Diary 'offered as a loan "any sum" needed to place me in a state of abundance, without interest, repayable at my death, if my estate would bear it; if not, then to be cancelled altogether'.[155] According to Shannon, Carnegie, who stayed at Hawarden on several occasions, wished fervently for Gladstone to strengthen the United Kingdom 'by giving to Ireland the rights of an American State, by giving self-government to Scotland through a Grand Committee, and "justice in religious matters" to Wales'.[156]

In particular, during one conversation with Gladstone, Carnegie expressed disapproval of the 1886 Home Rule Bill on the grounds that it excluded Irish MPs from Westminster (unlike the Bill of 1893).[157]

In this context, the question arises as to whether Gladstone was in any way implicated in the efforts to drive Villiers from his constituency. As far as Villiers was concerned, this was not the case. Writing to McIlwraith in October 1888, he observed

> One has heard of some people who were called more Catholic than the Pope, and I am not sure that this may not be the case with some of the followers of the Great Man, whose faith and hope in his return to power is something expected and ... I have an idea that it was not at his bidding exactly that they were hurrying on to insult and eject me, for it might have given the risk of exhibiting some personal feeling towards myself ... but sentiment, after a long service, has actually some influence.[158]

This said, and given the friendships not only between Gladstone and Carnegie but also between Carnegie, Graham and Henry Fowler (who was a house guest at Carnegie's Highland home at Skibo Castle[159]), not to mention Graham's frequent discussions with Schnadhorst, Stanhope and Morley at the National Liberal Club, it is almost inconceivable that Gladstone was unaware of the efforts of some of his own supporters to eject Villiers from his seat. In the event, however, he (and his Diaries) remained silent on the matter.

Charles Villiers' letters to William McIlwraith are illustrative of the impact of the Home Rule crisis on Liberal politics. In the first place, Villiers' split with Gladstone, and its consequences, perhaps offer a new way of approaching the Home Rule crisis, for too often the narrative has focused on the Tory opponents of Home Rule, emphasising the imperial dimension of national integrity, whereas some of the most significant Liberal Unionists, including Villiers, held equally strong views about developmental and governing responsibilities towards Ireland and Irish society. Second, the difficulties encountered by Villiers in his Wolverhampton constituency well illustrate how the Home Rule battle was fought out at the local level, in constituencies and communities, involving interest groups, party factions and the media (although the experience of Black Country constituencies was not necessarily representative of all). Moreover, they serve to highlight the problem of the often fraught relationship between the Liberal Party at Westminster, the National Liberal Federation, and provincial Liberalism. Third, Villiers' letters suggest that Home Rule was far from being a natural step in Gladstone's thinking about nationality, self-government and religious nationality; rather, it was a sudden and dramatic gesture by the 'Grand Old Man', based as much on tactical and personal impulses as by claims over any strategic statesmanship involving a devolutionary plan for the United Kingdom. Indeed, as Villiers observed, Gladstone wholly excluded the Ulster Liberals from his scheme, regarding them as an irrelevance and treating them with contempt, and they were subsequently swept away as Irish politics entered the binary system of Unionism versus Nationalism.

Finally, the Villiers–McIlwraith correspondence serves as a salutary reminder that the acrimonious rupture of 1886 was clearly difficult for all concerned and the break-up between Villiers and Gladstone is painful to read even at this distance in time. Clearly, both men disagreed profoundly with one another on the question of Irish Home Rule, which, for both, was a matter of principle. As far as Villiers was concerned, Gladstone's stance was an example of political misjudgement which had damaged the Liberal Party, and it is in this context, perhaps (and despite their personal differences, which were real rather than imagined), that the marvellously fruity language which Villiers deploys in his letters and his sarcastic descriptions of Gladstone as 'the Great Man', 'the Demigod', 'the Grand Mystery Man', 'the Gifted Man', 'the crafty Old Gentleman', 'the Champion of the Masses', and 'the Grand Old Man', should be understood.

This said, outside the political arena Gladstone and Villiers were relatively cordial towards one another in public, and on one occasion Gladstone even referred to Villiers as 'a marvel'.[160] Both men were well-connected in London society and had shared a mutual acquaintance in Laura Thistlethwayte, a reformed prostitute whose salon was frequented by both men during the 1880s.[161] Writing to his wife in October 1882, Gladstone remarked 'Last night, at Thistlethwayte Hall, I was really amazed at the freshness, nimbleness and force of Villiers, past eighty but perfectly young and extremely shrewd';[162] in 1886 he observed, 'Saw Mrs Th. Who told me very interesting things about C. Villiers' (the nature of which one can only surmise);[163] and in 1887 he noted, 'Dined at Miss Ponsonbys (a friend of Mrs Thistlethwayte and a Liberal Unionist). No rise to be had out of C. Villiers'.[164] Moreover, near the end of his parliamentary career, Gladstone acknowledged Villiers' vast political experience and knowledge, as he indicated in a letter to Lord Acton in February 1894,[165] and, following Gladstone's resignation, these two veteran parliamentarians, Gladstone (then aged 85) and Villiers (now 92) 'paired' in the House of Commons,[166] until Gladstone cancelled the pairing in June 1895 due to his reservations on 'points of detail' and his wish 'to keep an open mind' about the Welsh Church Disestablishment Bill.[167]

Moreover, it is also worth noting that Gladstone could be very unpleasant and embittered towards former colleagues who he felt had betrayed him,[168] and even snobbish and mean to cabinet colleagues. These included Villiers' fellow Wulfrunian MP, Henry Fowler, the President of the Local Government Board in Gladstone's last ministry, who was at pains to defend Gladstone's record before his constituents in 1893, but of whom Gladstone said 'the idea of cabinet loyalty of an able Wolverhampton solicitor were not quite the same as those of a highly cultivated statesman of an elder stamp', adding that 'a man like Sir Henry Fowler, with the pronounced servility of a certain kind of provincial attorney, was bad for the Queen, though infinitely less so than Disraeli'.[169] Gladstone also dropped some of his friends when it suited him.[170] Yet Charles Villiers, an aristocratic elder statesman, and now 'Father of the House', was not the recipient of such disapprobation, at least in public. However, it is clear that the relationship between Gladstone and Villiers was inhibited by mutual personal tensions as well as by political differences, unlike Gladstone's relationships with other Parliamentary opponents, such as Benjamin Disraeli and Joseph Chamberlain, which were, as Roland Quinault has shown, determined primarily by political rather than personal considerations.[171]

Notes

1 For Gladstone, see for example, R. Jenkins, *Gladstone* (London, 1995); H.C.G. Matthew, *Gladstone* (Oxford, 1997); Peter J. Jagger (ed.), *Gladstone* (London, 1998); Richard Shannon, *Gladstone: Heroic Minister, 1865–1898* (London, 1999); David Bebbington and Roger Swift (eds), *Gladstone Centenary* Essays (Liverpool, 2000); E.F. Biagini, *Gladstone* (London, 2000); W. Gladstone, *Gladstone: A Bicentenary Portrait* (Norwich, 2009); Roland Quinault, Roger Swift and Ruth Clayton Windscheffel (eds), *William Gladstone: New Studies and Perspectives* (Farnham, 2012).
2 *Wolverhampton Chronicle*, 4 Feb. 1874; 11 Feb. 1874.
3 Lawrence, *Speaking for the People*, 114.
4 Born in Kirkconnel, Dumfrieshire, in 1845, McIlwraith established a successful business as a clothier and draper in Wolverhampton. The Electoral Register of 1879–80 records him as living at 31 St John's Square, but by 1894 he had moved to 13 George Street. McIlwraith produced a short biography of George Grote in 1884. See W. McIlwraith, *The Life and Writings of George Grote: An Essay* (Wolverhampton, 1884); R. Simms (ed.), *Biblioteca Staffordiensis* (Lichfield, 1894), 295.
5 *Speech of C.P. Villiers, Esq, M.P. at a Dinner given by the Constituency of Wolverhampton to the Representatives of that Borough, January 26, 1836* (J. Bridgen, Wolverhampton, 1836).
6 *Parl. Debs*, 3rd Ser., 44, cc.322–72, 19 Jul. 1838.
7 Villiers, *Political Memoir*, xviii–xx.
8 Villiers, *Free Trade Speeches*, II, 377–8. House of Commons, 31 January 1850: Villiers observed,

> Having been present in the capital myself when Her Majesty was there, I am bound to say that I never saw so vast a concourse of people congregated together who demeaned themselves with so much order and propriety. People from all quarters of the country and of all opinions assembled in Dublin on the occasion, and, without yielding to any extravagance of feeling or losing their self-respect, they seemed to have come together for the common object of manifesting regard for the person and character of Her Majesty. According to information that I have received, nothing has occurred amongst the Irish people generally since Her Majesty's departure from Ireland to shake those feelings of attachment and loyalty that were evinced in her presence; for further details of the visit, see also Villiers, *A Vanished Victorian*, 179–87; Christine Kinealy, 'Famine Queen or Faery?: Queen Victoria and Ireland', in Roger Swift and Christine Kinealy (eds), *Politics and Power in Victorian Ireland* (Dublin, 2006), 21–53.

9 Gilbert Frankland Lewis, *Letters of the Right Hon. Sir George Cornewall Lewis, Bart. to Various Friends* (London, 1870), 29–31.
10 See, for example, *Free Trade Speeches*, I, 172–3. House of Commons, 1 Apr. 1840; I, 257–8. House of Commons, 27 Aug. 1841; II, 56–7. Colchester, 8 Jul. 1843; II. 159. House of Commons, 25 Jun. 1844; II. 189–90. Covent Garden Theatre, 3 Jul. 1844.
11 See letter from George Villiers [Clarendon] to Russell, 26 Jan. 1844, cited in Spencer Walpole, *The Life of Lord John Russell* (2 vols, London, 1889), I, 440. This contained an extract from a letter which he had received from Charles Villiers praising Russell's speech in the House of Commons on this subject:

> Lord John's tone, and the judgment and ability with which he proposed his measures, thoroughly conciliated the House, and all people felt pleased. He gains every day wonderfully upon the House. He has made no speech that is not a good one, and the absence of the Peel egotism (always displayed on such occasions) was much remarked upon.

12 Villiers, *Free Trade Speeches*, II, 400–403. House of Commons, 31 Jan. 1850.
13 There is an extensive historiography on Gladstone and Ireland. The classic work is J.L. Hammond, *Gladstone and the Irish Nation* (London, 1938), but important recent studies include Alan O'Day. 'Gladstone and Irish Nationalism: Achievement and Reputation', in David Bebbington and Roger Swift (eds), *Gladstone Centenary Essays* (Liverpool 2000), 163–83; D. George Boyce, 'in the Front Rank of the Nation: Gladstone and the Unionists of Ireland, 1868–93', in Bebbington and Swift, *Gladstone Centenary Essays,* 184–201; D. George Boyce and Alan O'Day (eds), *Gladstone and Ireland: Politics, Religion and Nationality in the Victorian Age* (London, 2010); Mary E. Daly and K. Theodore Hoppen (eds), *Gladstone: Ireland and Beyond* (Dublin, 2011). For an excellent overview of Prime Ministerial policy towards Ireland, see especially, Roland Quinault, 'Victorian Prime Ministers and Ireland', in Swift and Kinealy, *Politics and Power*, 54–68.
14 T.A. Jenkins, *Gladstone, Whiggery and the Liberal Party, 1874–1886* (Oxford, 1988), 290. Jenkins notes that of 105 Liberal MPs defined as 'Aristocratic-Landowning' (the class to whom Villiers belonged), 43 (41%) voted against the Bill.
15 Matthew, *Gladstone*, 559.
16 For the Home Rule crisis of 1886, see especially D.A. Hamer, 'The Irish Question and Liberal Politics, 1886–1894', *Historical Journal*, 12 (1969), 511–32; T.W. Heyck, 'Home Rule, Radicalism and the Liberal Party, 1886–95', *Journal of British Studies*, 13 (1974), 66–91; W.C. Lubenow, 'Irish Home Rule and the Great Separation of the Liberal Party in 1886: the Dimensions of Parliamentary Liberalism', *Victorian Studies*, 26 (1983), 161–80; J. Loughlin (ed.), *Gladstone, Home Rule and the Ulster Question, 1882–93* (Dublin, 1986); W.C. Lubenow, *Parliamentary Politics and the Home Rule Crisis: the British House of Commons in 1886* (Oxford, 1988); R.T. Shannon, 'Gladstone and Home Rule, 1886', in *Ireland after the Union: Proceedings of the Second Joint Meeting of the Royal Irish Academy and the British Academy, London 1986* (Oxford, 1989), 45–59; J. Parry, *The Rise and Fall of Liberal Government in Victorian Britain* (London, 1993); D. George Boyce, *The Irish Question and British Politics, 1886–1996* (London, 1998); M.R.D. Foot, 'The Hawarden Kite', *Journal of Liberal Democrat History*, 20 (1998), 26–32; E.F. Biagini, *British Democracy and Irish Nationalism, 1876–1906* (Cambridge, 2007); David Bebbington, 'The Union of Hearts depicted: Gladstone, Home Rule and *United Ireland*', in Boyce and O'Day, *Gladstone and Ireland*, 186–207; Ian Cawood, *The Liberal Unionist Party: A History* (London, 2012).

17 See especially, Jane Jordan, 'The English Delilah: Katharine O'Shea and Irish Politics, 1880–1891', in Roger Swift and Christine Kinealy (eds), *Politics and Power in Victorian Ireland* (Dublin, 2006), 69–83.
18 A.V. Dicey, *England's Case against Home Rule* (London, 1886; rev. edn, Richmond, 1973, with an introduction by E.J. Feuchtwanger).
19 W[olverhampton] A[rchives] and L[ocal] S[tudies], Villiers-McIlwraith Correspondence, MSS. DX60/5/25, Villiers to McIlwraith, nd. July? 1888.
20 WALS. DX60/5/8, Villiers to McIlwraith, 15 Mar. 1888.
21 Ibid., DX60/10/12, Villiers to McIlwraith, 19 May 1893.
22 For a recent discussion of the views of Liberal Unionists towards Irish Home Rule, see Wesley Ferris, 'The Liberal Unionist Party, 1886–1912', (PhD thesis, McMaster University, Ontario, 2008), ch. 5, 'Liberal Unionist Identity', 280–326.
23 Shannon, *Gladstone: Heroic Minister*, 427.
24 Biagini, *British Democracy and Irish Nationalism*, 17–18.
25 D. George Boyce, 'Gladstone and the Unionists of Ireland', in Bebbington and Swift, *Gladstone Centenary* Essays, 184–201.
26 A similar observation has been made recently by Graham Goodlad, 'British Liberals and the Irish Home Rule Crisis: The Dynamics of Division', in Boyce and O'Day (eds), *Gladstone and Ireland*, 86–109.
27 DX60/5/1,Villiers to McIlwraith, 7 Jan. 1888.
28 DX/60/5/3, Villiers to McIlwraith, 23 Jan. 1888.
29 DX60/5/13, Villiers to McIlwraith, 17 May 1888.
30 DX60/5/8, Villiers to McIlwraith, 15 Mar. 1888.
31 DX60/5/1,Villiers to McIlwraith, 7 Jan. 1888; see also Dicey, *England's Case*, 128–56.
32 DX60/10/6, Villiers to McIlwraith, 23 Feb. 1893.
33 DX60/10/8, Villiers to McIlwraith, 1 Mar. 1893.
34 Ibid.
35 Steele, *Palmerston and Liberalism*, 97.
36 DX60/5/24, Villiers to McIlwraith, 19 Jul. 1888.
37 DX60/5/25, Villiers to McIlwraith, nd. July? 1888.
38 DX60/10/6, Villiers to McIlwraith, 23 Feb. 1893.
39 See also Dicey, *England's Case*, 142–56.
40 DX60/5/8, Villiers to McIlwraith, 15 Mar. 1888:

> It is the recognition of distinct nationality that is called for by the leading opponents of the Union, and as such would be regarded by foreign nations; and thus the means of ever threatening, or terrorising England, to which they entertain, here and everywhere else where they are found and collected all over the Earth, an undying hate. This was asserted by some able letters written by the Editor (inserted I think in the *Times*) of the *New York Tribune*, who truly, I believe, asserted that they never identified themselves, but at least called for their instructions, and that how they could in some way injure England was their only thought from year's end and even since they have thronged in the United States – where also it is admitted that they have brought with them their own internal feuds, which are manifested in their usual style on particular occasions by sanguinary riot – and that they collect funds for carrying on their tactics in Ireland against England, there is no doubt of. And by which, from the general insecurity in Ireland, which they occasion, we are at a hideous expense in preserving order by means of a large military force.

41 DX60/5/24, Villiers to McIlwraith, 19 Jul. 1888; see also Loughlin, *Gladstone, Home Rule and the Ulster Question*, who argues that Gladstone, rather than

undergoing a dramatic conversion to Home Rule, was panicked into concessions by alarming reports of the state of Ireland.
42 DX60/5/13, Villiers to McIlwraith, 17 May 1888.
43 DX60/10/8, Villiers to McIlwraith, 1 Mar. 1893.
44 DX60/10/12, Villiers to McIlwraith, 19 May 1893.
45 DX60/5/8: Villiers to McIlwraith,15 Mar. 1888; see also DX60/10/14: Villiers to McIlwraith, nd. Jun. 1893: 'What effect is being produced by what the GOM is pleased to call a "New Departure", in other words, by degrading all Parliamentary precedent in order to secure his retention of office for some time longer by a new device'.
46 DX60/5/8, Villiers to McIlwraith, 15 Mar. 1888.
47 DX60/5/1, Villiers to McIlwraith, 7 Jan. 1888; DX/60/5/7, V-M, 20 Feb. 1888.
48 DX60/5/39, Villiers to McIlwraith, 12 Dec. 1888:

> Up to this moment neither WG or any of his followers have attempted, or if so, have certainly not succeeded in persuading the substantial classes of this country that the important constitutional change which he has proposed for both England and Ireland, at the insistence of the 85 Irishmen now sitting in the House of Commons, can be effected without inconvenience or disadvantage to England, or with the smallest chance of enduring satisfaction to Ireland.

49 DX60/10/6, Villiers to McIlwraith, 23 Feb. 1893.
50 See, for example, DX/60/5/6, Villiers to McIlwraith, 22 Apr. 1888:

> The company of 'Farmers' (of Cork) [Irish Nationalists] all sat again; I think we had about 14 obstructive notices last night and I think we did not adjourn till close upon 3 a.m., and the rules of the House have been every night disobeyed. In fact I believe Doctor Johnson, if writing his Dictionary now, would probably describe the H of Commons as a place distinguished for 'bad language and late hours'. What is already whispered, though not openly avowed, is that if all real business is progressively obstructed, as it was last year, there must be a dissolution.

51 DX60/10/8, Villiers to McIlwraith, 1 Mar. 1893:

> It is quite possible however that the measure will pass the House of Commons and more than probable that it will either be much altered or would be rejected by the other House – but what an interruption will all this be to the real business requiring attention in Great Britain.

52 D.A. Hamer, 'The Irish Question and Liberal Politics, 1886–1894', *Historical Journal*, xii (1969), 511–32; see also T.W. Heyck, 'Home Rule, Radicalism, and the Liberal Party, 1886–1895', *Journal of British Studies,* 13 (1974), 66–91.
53 DX60/5/8, Villiers to McIlwraith, 15 Mar. 1888.
54 DX60/5/24, Villiers to McIlwraith, 19 Jul. 1888.
55 DX60/5/40, Villiers to McIlwraith, 27 Dec. 1888.
56 DX60/5/40, Villiers to McIlwraith, 27 Dec. 1888.
57 DX60/5/35, Villiers to McIlwraith, 28 Oct. 1888.
58 Cawood, *The Liberal Unionist Party*, 243.
59 DX60/5/8, Villiers to McIlwraith, 15 Mar. 1888.
60 DX60/5/26, Villiers to McIlwraith, nd. Aug. 1888.
61 DX60/5/14, Villiers to McIlwraith, 28 May 1888.
62 See J.B. O'Reilly, 'The Coercion Bill', *North American Review*, 144, 366 (May 1887), 528–39. O'Reilly showed, for example, that between 1885 and 1886 there had only been an increase in the circulation of threatening letters in

Ireland from 432 to 497 and in offences other than threatening letters from 512 to 518.
63 Ibid., 529.
64 *Gladstone Papers*, 844501/163, Villiers to Gladstone, 9 Jul. 1887.
65 Ibid.
66 For further details, see Travis L. Crosby, *Joseph Chamberlain: A Most Radical Imperialist* (London and New York, 2011), 76.
67 *Gladstone Papers*, 844501/163, Villiers to Gladstone, 9 July 1887.
68 Ibid.
69 DX60/5/24, Villiers to McIlwraith, 19 Jul. 1888.
70 *The Spectator*, 6 Oct. 1888.
71 DX60/5/23, Villiers to McIlwraith, 6 Jul. 1888.
72 DX60/5/28, Villiers to McIlwraith, 20 Sep. 1888.
73 DX60/5/14, Villiers to McIlwraith, 28 May 1888: Chamberlain's second wife, whom he married in November 1888, was Mary Endicott, the daughter of William Endicott, the American Secretary of State for War: see J.L. Garvin, *The Life of Joseph Chamberlain* (3 vols, London, 1933), II, 370.
74 Sir William Vernon Harcourt (1827–1904): Lawyer, journalist and Liberal politician; Professor of International Law at Cambridge, 1869; Home Secretary, 1880–5; Chancellor of the Exchequer, 1886, 1892–5; Leader of the Opposition, 1896–8. Harcourt's first wife, whom he married in 1859, was Charles Villiers' niece, Therese Lister (the daughter of Villiers' sister, Lady Maria Theresa Villiers, and Thomas Lister). Therese died in 1863. Their son, Lewis Harcourt, also a noted Liberal politician, was Villiers' great-nephew, whilst his stepfather was Sir George Cornewall Lewis. Sir William Harcourt was often a companion of Villiers at the Waldegrave soirées. Harcourt's second wife, whom he married in 1876, was Elizabeth Cabot Motley, the daughter of the American historian, John Motley For further details see the relevant sections in A.G. Gardiner, *The Life of Sir William Harcourt* (London 1923).
75 Patrick Jackson, *Harcourt and Son: A Political Biography of Sir William Harcourt, 1827–1904* (New Jersey, 2004), 181.
76 Ibid., 182.
77 *The Spectator*, 6 Oct. 1888.
78 DX60/10/20, Villiers to McIlwraith, nd. Jul. 1893.
79 *Parl. Debs.*, 3rd ser., 7/332-430, 11 Aug. 1892.
80 Ibid.
81 Ibid.
82 David Brooks, 'Gladstone's Fourth Administration, 1892–1894', in Bebbington and Swift (eds), *Gladstone Centenary Essays*, 223–42.
83 DX60/10/9, Villiers to McIlwraith, 11 Apr. 1893.
84 DX60/10/15, Villiers to McIlwraith, 1 Jul. 1893.
85 DX60/10/17, Villiers to McIlwraith, nd. Jul. 1893.
86 DX60/5/40, Villiers to McIlwraith, 27 Dec. 1888.
87 DX60/10/17, Villiers to McIlwraith, nd. Jul. 1893.
88 DX60/10/15, Villiers to McIlwraith, 1 Jul. 1893.
89 *Morning Post*, 17 Jan. 1898.
90 *Leicester Chronicle*, 22 Jan. 1898.
91 Sir Henry William Lucy (1843–1924): Journalist and the greatest parliamentary lobby correspondent of his age. Lucy wrote for *Punch* (under the nom-de-plume 'Toby, M.P.'), the *Pall Mall Gazette* and *The Strand Magazine*, and edited the *Daily News* from 1873. A staunch Liberal, he denounced the Liberal Unionists as 'Dissentient Liberals'. Lucy was knighted in 1909 and became extremely rich, leaving over £250,000 in his will. See Herbert B. Grimsditch and Colin

Matthew, 'Lucy, Sir Henry William (1843–1924), Journalist', *ODNB*, 34626 (Oct. 2008).
92 H.W. Lucy, *Later Peeps at Parliament: From Behind the Speaker's Chair* (London, 1905), 123.
93 DX60/10/20, Villiers to McIlwraith, nd. Jul. 1893.
94 DX60/10/9, Villiers to McIlwraith, 11 Apr. 1893.
95 DX60/10/19, Villiers to McIlwraith, nd. Jul. 1893:

> There are now I believe 540 Peers entitled to vote in their House, the greater part of whom I should say were quite equal in terms of intelligence to those who sit in the Lower House! The fault of their position is of course that they are not representative and therefore not equal to giving effect to the wishes of the people, but this has nothing to do with what may be considered and the Peers will decide ... honestly and fairly according to the best of their ability and judgment ... But can you say what the country expects of them at their crisis? If they throw the Bill out, they will of course be pelted with all the stuff that Nationalists, Socialists, Anarchists and Gladstonites generally can find on their ground to fling at them! Not a kind of treatment agreeable to ordinary men, and particularly distasteful to those who believe that they have consciences as well as Titles! But if there are still a considerable body of thinking men, of whom some we used always to speak of with pride and gratitude, in the middle class of society, will they give any countenance to the course which is (I believe) pretty generally expected to be pursued by the House of Peers in the next month? I have a notion myself that the public generally is averse to the Irish Bill, though only a few perhaps avow it, but under the circumstances is it not possible that the grand attack upon the House of Lords which will happen (possibly) before the end of the century will not take place now upon the signals given by Tim Healy or Kier Hardie on what would indeed be serious, if such a thing could happen, for GOM?

96 DX60/11/12, Villiers to McIlwraith, 4 Mar. 1894.
97 Ibid.
98 For the Home Rule crisis and the development of Liberal Unionism in a local context, see R.A. Wright, 'Liberal Party Organisation and Politics in Birmingham, Coventry and Wolverhampton, 1886–1914, with particular reference to the development of Independent Labour Representation', PhD thesis, University of Birmingham (1977), Ch. 4 & 5, 101–34; 135–72.
99 Jon Lawrence, 'Popular Politics and the Limitations of Party: Wolverhampton, 1867–1900', in Eugenio Biagini and Alastair Reid (eds), *Currents of Radicalism: Popular Radicalism, Organised Labour and Party Politics in Britain, 1850–1914* (Cambridge, 1991), 68.
100 Sir William Plowden (1832–1915): Civil servant in India and Liberal politician, MP for Wolverhampton 1886–92, knighted in 1886.
101 Fowler, *Life of Henry Hartley Fowler*, 221–70. Fowler's biography of her father contains only two passing references to Villiers and there is no surviving correspondence between Henry Fowler and Villiers. It is not without significance that Fowler was conspicuous by his absence from Villiers' funeral in 1898, despite the attendance of many civic dignitaries from Wolverhampton: *The Times*, 21 Jan. 1898.
102 For Carnegie, see G. Tweedale, 'Carnegie, Andrew (1835–1919)', *ODNB*, 32296 (May 2012).
103 Peter Rhodes, *The Loaded Hour: A History of the Express & Star* (Worcester, 1992), 21–4.
104 Ibid., 26.

105 For further details, see Raymond Lamont-Brown, *Carnegie: The Richest Man in the World* (Stroud, 2005), ch. 12, 99–110.
106 Rhodes, *The Loaded Hour*, 30–2.
107 Ibid., 32–7.
108 DX60/5/17, Villiers to McIlwraith, 2 Jun. 1888.
109 Letter from Andrew Carnegie to the Editor, *Pittsburgh Volksblatt*, 20 Jan. 1888, p. 24.
110 DX/60/5/3, Villiers to McIlwraith, 23 Jan. 1888.
111 DX60/5/4, Villiers to McIlwraith, nd. Jan. 1888.
112 Ibid.
113 Ibid.
114 DX60/5/17, Villiers to McIlwraith, 2 Jun. 1888.
115 DX60/10/19, Villiers to McIlwraith, nd. Jul. 1893.
116 DX60/5/1, Villiers to McIlwraith, 7 Jan. 1888.
117 DX60/5/20, Villiers to McIlwraith, 6 Jul. 1888.
118 Lamont-Brown also suggests that it was widely rumoured that Carnegie sought to oust Villiers from his seat, although Carnegie denied this: Lamont-Brown, *Carnegie*, 109.
119 This campaign is ignored by Taylor, 'The Working-Class Movement', and is only briefly referred to by Wright, 'Liberal Party Organisation and Politics', 107.
120 DX60/5/30, Villiers to McIlwraith, nd. Aug. 1888.
121 DX60/5/7, Villiers to McIlwraith, 20 Feb. 1888.
122 DX60/5/6, Villiers to McIlwraith, 22 Apr. 1888.
123 DX60/5/19, Villiers to McIlwraith, 29 Jun. 1888.
124 *Express & Star*, 12 Jul. 1888.
125 DX60/5/30, Villiers to McIlwraith, nd. Aug. 1888:

> At present, I do not believe that the most noisy of them have any personal purpose beyond putting Mr Gladstone in office again, and of putting in my place anybody whatever who will add to the list of those that he regards as Toadies. It seems (at least I am told so) that Graham is constantly in London and in communication with the Gladstone caucus (Morley and Stanhope) and that amongst those whose seats they could get, as they say, would be that of the Southern Division.

126 DX60/5/20, Villiers to McIlwraith, 6 Jul. 1888.
127 Sir Charles Shaw (1859–1942) was Liberal MP for Stafford from 1892 to 1910, and was created first Baronet in 1908.
128 Ibid. This was a reference to Plowden's defeat in the Western Division at the hands of the Tory Sir Alfred Hickman at the 1885 General Election, although Plowden was victorious in 1886, losing the seat to Hickman in 1892.
129 DX60/5/35, Villiers to McIlwraith, 28 Oct. 1888. In the event, Margaret Plowden married Hubert Mostyn, 7th Lord Vaugh, whilst Shaw married Emily Bursill of Hampstead in 1900.
130 DX60/5/30, Villiers to McIlwraith, nd. Aug. 1888.
131 DX60/5/31, Villiers to McIlwraith, 7 Sep. 1888.
132 *Birmingham Daily Post*, 27 Aug. 1888.
133 *Express & Star*, 28 Aug. 1888.
134 Ibid., 30 Aug. 1888.
135 DX60/5/30, Villiers to McIlwraith, nd. Aug. 1888.
136 DX60/5/28, Villiers to McIlwraith, 20 Sep. 1888.
137 DX60/5/31, Villiers to McIlwraith, 7 Sep. 1888.
138 DX60/5/28, Villiers to McIlwraith, 20 Sep. 1888.
139 DX60/5/34, Villiers to McIlwraith, 13 Oct. 1888.

140 DX60/5/35, Villiers to McIlwraith, 28 Oct. 1888.
141 DX60/5/28, Villiers to McIlwraith, 20 Sep. 1888.
142 DX60/5/31, Villiers to McIlwraith, 7 Sep. 1888:

> Do you think that Fowler has had anything to do with this move in the South? I suppose Fuller has, and he is the Chairman of the Fowler Division, is he not? I think it is cool of the Secretary of the Fowler Club writing to you for a donation after the troubles of the Fowler Club, where Fuller is the chief personage.

143 DX60/5/34, Villiers to McIlwraith, 13 Oct. 1888.
144 DX60/5/39, Villiers to McIlwraith, 12 Dec. 1888.
145 DX60/5/40, Villiers to McIlwraith, 27 Dec. 1888.
146 Lawrence, *Speaking for the People*, 196.
147 DX60/5/40, Villiers to McIlwraith, 27 December 1888. Villiers was correct in this assumption: as late as December 1893, after Gladstone's second Home Rule Bill had been rejected by the House of Lords, Villiers, who had been suffering from influenza at the time, bemoaned the 'malicious' references to his illness (and therefore the possibility of him vacating his seat) made by Graham in the *Express & Star*: DX60/10/37, 29 Dec. 1893. Charles Shaw subsequently stood successfully as the Liberal (Gladstonite) candidate at Stafford in 1892.
148 *Express and Star*, 20 Jun. 1892.
149 Sir Alfred Hickman (1830–1910): Local colliery proprietor, ironmaster and industrialist who formed the Staffordshire Steel Ingot and Iron Company and became President of the British Iron Trades Council, Conservative MP for Wolverhampton West 1885–6 and 1892–1906, and created a baronet in 1892. Of Hickman, Villiers observed,

> Sir A. Hickman an able, steady sort of man of business who had a good right to expect the favour of the educated class in such a place of business as Wolverhampton ... his accuracy on matters on which he came into conflict with his political opponents was maintained. His local interests throughout the Boro were considerable and he must have given employment to many:
>
> DX60/9, Villiers to McIlwraith, 14 Jul. 1892.

150 Taylor, 'The Working-Class Movement', 411.
151 Cawood, *The Liberal Unionist Party*, 39.
152 GD., 10, 306–7: (Monday) 31 Jul. 1882: Their initial meeting was arranged by Lord Rosebery.
153 Matthew, *Gladstone*, 569.
154 Philip Magnus, *Gladstone* (London, 1954), 258.
155 GD., 12 Jun. 1887; Matthew, *Gladstone*, 621–2.
156 Shannon, *Gladstone: Heroic Minister*, 526.
157 Andrew Carnegie, *The Autobiography of Andrew Carnegie* (London, 1920), 327: 'I objected to the exclusion of the Irish members from Parliament as being a practical separation. I said we should never have allowed the Southern States to cease sending representatives to Washington'.
158 DX60/5/35, Villiers to McIlwraith, 28 Oct. 1888.
159 Fowler, *The Life of Henry Hartley Fowler*, 154.
160 GD, 10, 306: (Tuesday) 1 Aug. 1882: 'Saw ... Mr C. Villiers (a marvel)'.
161 For further details, see especially Jenny West, 'Gladstone and Laura Thistlethwayte, 1865–1875', *Historical Research*, 80, 209 (August 2007), 368–92.
162 GD, 10, 353: (Friday) 20 Oct. 1882; 10, 354: Gladstone to Mrs Gladstone, 21 Oct. 1882.
163 GD, 11, 514: (Saturday) 20 Mar. 1886.

164 *GD*, 12, 20: (Monday) 21 Mar. 1887.
165 *GD*, 13, 371: (Tuesday) 6 Feb. 1894.
166 Shannon, *Gladstone: Heroic Minister*, 574.
167 *The Times*, 19 June 1895; see also cartoon 'William! Ahoy!' in *Punch*, 29 June 1895.
168 Timothy Moore, 'Anti-Gladstonianism and the pre-1886 Liberal Secession', in Boyce and O'Day (eds), *Gladstone and Ireland*, 65–85.
169 Brooks, 'Gladstone's Fourth Administration', 228.
170 Denis Paz, 'Gladstone as Friend', in Quinault, Swift and Windscheffel, *William Gladstone*, 129–54.
171 Roland Quinault, 'Gladstone and Disraeli: A Reappraisal of their Relationship', *History*, 91, 304 (2006), 557–76; Roland Quinault, 'Joseph Chamberlain: A Reassessment', in T.R. Gourvish and Alan O'Day (eds), *Later Victorian Britain, 1867–1900* (London, 1988), 69–92; Roland Quinault, 'Chamberlain and Gladstone: An overview of their Relationship', unpublished paper delivered at the Joseph Chamberlain: Imperial Standard Bearer, National Leader, Local Icon Conference, Newman University, Birmingham, June 2014.

9   The Father of the House

In 1890 Charles Villiers, at the advanced age of eighty-eight, and having sat continuously for Wolverhampton since first elected in 1835, had succeeded Christopher Rice Mansel Talbot, South Wales industrialist and Liberal MP for Mid-Glamorganshire, as 'Father of the House of Commons'. Henry Lucy, who had never forgiven the Liberal Unionists for deserting Gladstone in 1886, observed that Villiers had now 'grown out of Liberalism into the Fatherhood of the House',[1] and pointedly, and rather ungraciously remarked that 'in a Parliamentary sense Mr Gladstone was born before his father, seeing that he took his seat for Newark in the year 1832', adding that

> whilst Mr Villiers, literally bent under the weight of his more than ninety years, has long withdrawn from regular attendance upon Parliamentary duties, Mr Gladstone was, up to the end of last Session, daily in his place, actively directing affairs and ready at a moment's notice to deliver a speech which, standing alone, would make a Parliamentary reputation.[2]

However, unlike Villiers, Gladstone had not sat continuously in the Commons since first elected in 1832, having been briefly out of the House for a period of eighteen months prior to his election for Oxford University in 1847,[3] hence Villiers was fully entitled to his new status.

In his old age, Charles Villiers lived quietly at 50 Cadogan Place, Chelsea, (to where he had moved from Sloane Square in 1888). Here, he was attended by his housekeeper, Maria Walsh, and servants, and became increasingly reclusive, occupying himself with his books, correspondence and newspapers, receiving friends and family on occasions, and otherwise enjoying a retirement upon which few were permitted to intrude.[4] Indeed, the *Sunday Times* observed that

> Never seeking a reputation among the people, less has been written about him [Villiers] than about any other public man; he has steadfastly declined to figure as a 'celebrity' at home, and the society journalist has found it necessary to leave him severely alone.[5]

By this time, many of Villiers' close friends had passed away, including Frances, Countess Waldegrave and Baron Lionel de Rothschild (both in 1879), Sir Abraham Hayward (1884), Sir Henry Taylor (1886), Andalusia, Lady Molesworth (1888), Mary, Lady Holland (1889), Edward Stanley, 15th Earl of Derby (1893), Henry, 3rd Earl Grey (1894), and Sir John Pender (1896). However, in private he continued to maintain close relations with, and receive visits from, his many nephews and nieces – and great-nephews and nieces – in an ever-expanding aristocratic family, and, when possible, attended family celebrations and weddings.[6] One regular visitor to Cadogan Place was Villiers' young great-niece, Lady Edith Villiers, who observed

> Always a great reader of the newspaper, Mr Villiers could have been seen day after day seated in his hard, straight-backed chair – the one of his choice – surrounded by newspapers of every variety. Every article of interest was perused, every debate followed to the letter, and the sum of things discoursed upon afterwards with that rare brilliancy which characterised his speech and an accuracy of memory balanced by a soundness of judgment not often to be found in the children of his third and fourth generation.[7]

Lady Edith added that, as Villiers' great-niece she enjoyed many advantages from his company:

> It was a liberal education in itself to hear him speak of the men and manners, the changes and chances of nearly a full century; of history and biography, and matters both private and public – all things were touched upon, treated and disputed by his master-mind; and the readiest wit illuminated the driest topic. Before everything, Mr Villiers was a humourist; and that subtle sense of fun which underlay so many of his sayings, and was so much enjoyed by the sayer, can never be forgotten by those who have been privileged to share it.[8]

In addition to reading his newspapers – it was rumoured that he glanced at upwards of thirty national and provincial newspapers which were delivered to his home each day – Villiers spent much time writing letters to friends and family. This was a family trait for, as his niece, Maria Theresa Earle (who was a great admirer of her uncle[9]) once observed,

> The Villiers family were very clever people, but they wrote too many letters, met each other too often, were too much engrossed in each other's health and domestic affairs, to touch in their correspondence on subjects which they considered belonged to official life.[10]

Charles Villiers was no exception, and was, according to Mrs Earle, 'an immense hoarder of old papers and letters' so much so that on calling at his house on one occasion to inquire after him she was told by his housekeeper that 'Mr Villiers is quite well and much more comfortable, for he has hired a house opposite for his letters and papers'.[11] Sadly, however, relatively few of Villiers' private letters to his family have survived.[12]

During his later years, Villiers continued to suffer from bouts of ill-health, which he had long claimed were the main reason for his failure to visit his Wolverhampton constituency since 1874, and which, in his declining years, he continued to proffer as the reason for his occasional absences from the House of Commons,[13] his non-attendance at Liberal Unionist meetings,[14] and, in a letter to Millicent Garrett Fawcett in May 1892 (when he was then in his ninetieth year) for his inability to attend a Suffragist rally.[15] Villiers had always been particularly vulnerable to coughs and colds, which confined him to his home from time to time, and for which he blamed the inclement weather. For example, in April 1888 he told William McIlwraith that

> I wish I could be certain of being well tomorrow ... but I have not been out of the House for the last 3 days and one day I did not get up till the evening, I was suffering so much from cold and cough and it is by not being out at all in this weather that I hope soon to be myself again.[16]

Again, in August 1888, he reported that 'I have been shut up for the past few days and confined to the house with a severe cold',[17] adding that 'What with the variations in the weather and the effect on my health ... I have not been able yet to acknowledge and thank you for the letter you were good enough to write'.[18] In October 1891, Villiers suffered a serious fall, but recovered, the Press Association duly reporting that his general health was good.[19] Later, in the winter of 1893-4, when there was an influenza epidemic in London, Villiers was, somewhat predictably, a victim, informing McIlwraith that 'I have had a touch (and not much more) of what the professional oracles call influenza', adding that 'having depended far more upon very early closing in a warm room than upon fresh medical prescriptions I am nearly myself again', whilst expressing his concern that

> it is not easy to disregard the influences that are at work around us, be they atmospheric or any other, in the extraordinary number of fatal and sudden attacks that are now of hourly occurrence, and one only wonders at the great increase of deaths that are now occurring in all the surrounding counties of England.[20]

On this occasion, it was widely rumoured in the provincial press, including the Wolverhampton *Express & Star*, that Villiers' illness was critical, as a result of which Villiers informed McIlwraith 'Of course, I am not better than other people who have had the influenza and never quite recovered from it, but it has not yet placed me, by it, in the position the *Star* hopes, no doubt, for'.[21]

Nevertheless, Villiers was too unwell to attend a debate in the Commons on the Parish Councils Bill and, as he told McIlwraith,

> What good could I do by putting in an appearance in the middle of the night on such a measure as that which the House is wasting so much time about. Of course, if you began attending it would be worse than useless to wait till the last minutes of the sitting of the House to await the eternal questions that arise upon every clause of it,

adding that 'the Speaker himself is not well enough to attend, and several servants of the House are laid up, and there are no worse places than Palace Yard (so near the river for fog) to be unwell'.[22] In January 1896, Villiers was once more struck with influenza and rumours abounded that he might not survive; once more, he recovered, subsequently spending much time in writing personally to many correspondents who had sent letters of goodwill during his illness.[23] In July 1897 Villiers was again taken ill, informing McIlwraith that he was sleeping downstairs and was unable to leave his room, and adding 'The Doctor says I shall recover, but they are not always right'.[24] Villiers recovered, only to suffer a relapse in December, when he informed McIlwraith that 'I am myself very tried by the weather, which I venture to say is worse in Chelsea than in the Black Country', adding 'I must postpone my correspondence for a day or two longer'.[25]

Villiers had long suffered badly from gout in his hands, which seriously impaired his handwriting and for which he frequently apologised. For example, in July 1888 he informed McIlwraith that 'I shall be better myself in a few days if the weather keeps mild and will write again – at present I can't write legibly having gout in my fingers'.[26] This condition worsened in time and in January 1893 Villiers complained 'I have been a great deal inconvenienced by the unusually disagreeable weather and ... what with depression of spirit and difficulty in writing by means of gout in the hand my correspondence has got terribly in arrears';[27] in March he again complained that 'This capricious weather doesn't suit me at all, but I believe I shall pull through for some time' and apologised for 'the dreadful scrawl', adding 'but I can't do better today';[28] in May he reported that 'I have not attended the House [of Commons] lately and got leave of absence for a few weeks, ... I am still very feeble, and particularly in my hands, so you must excuse all this bad writing';[29] whilst in November he admitted 'I ought to excuse myself for my handwriting, but really it is due to the failure of my sight, which is fast coming on me, and also to having been very much out of repair for the last week', adding 'I doubt if it is legible at all and I hope you will burn it if you find it so'.[30] Indeed, the very form and style of Villiers' numerous and frequently lengthy letters to McIlwraith themselves testify to the problems he faced in addressing his correspondence, for they often commence with a relatively bold and legible handwriting before progressively deteriorating into a miniscule and sometimes illegible scrawl, punctuated by various blots, deletions and insertions, and for which Villiers blamed his weak eyesight,[31] of which he also frequently complained, informing McIlwraith in July 1897 that 'My eyes are weaker than ever, and I do like to read again and again'.[32]

Villiers' concerns about his health also featured in his letters to his niece, Alice Borthwick [Lady Glenesk], and in October 1895, for example, he bemoaned 'the cold and damp fogs with which we are afflicted (certainly in Chelsea)', adding that

> I have been so completely laid up, or rather knocked down, during the last week or two by the effects of this most unseasonable and detestable weather, with which we have been and still are afflicted, that I have been obliged to postpone all the duties the performance of which depends upon the use of pen, ink, and paper; but the wind and the weather having changed somewhat today for the better.[33]

That Charles Villiers was able, throughout his life, to overcome the many illnesses that he encountered with such resilience is quite remarkable, particularly in view of the fact that it was reported that he was 'an irreclaimable smoker', and, as the *Yorkshire Evening Post* observed, he afforded 'an example of the fact that delicate youths may not only outlive their weakness, but outlive also their strongest contemporaries'.[34] In July 1891, on meeting Charles Villiers at a garden party at Marlborough House, Queen Victoria expressed some surprise that 'Old Mr Villiers, uncle to Lady Ampthill, is a great age and in possession of all his faculties'.[35] Moreover, periodic illness does not appear to have prevented Villiers from maintaining the social and cultural habits of a lifetime well into old age. In particular, Villiers, once popularly described as 'the Prince of Bachelors', had long been a familiar and frequent figure in London's political and gentlemen's clubs, and, despite bouts of ill-health, he continued to visit his clubs well into his nineties. This habit was not without its risks for a nonagenarian. On 6 July 1894, whilst passing though the crowds assembled in St James's Square in celebration of the Royal Wedding of Prince George, Duke of York, and Princess Mary of Teck, Villiers, who was en route to one of his clubs, was robbed of his watch and chain. It was reported that Villiers identified the thief and cried out to a policeman standing nearby, 'He has got my watch', whereupon the watch and chain were retrieved and the thief – a porter named Dunford – was duly arrested and was subsequently convicted at Marlborough Street Magistrates Court and sentenced to three months' imprisonment.[36] In March 1894, at the age of ninety-two, Villiers suffered a fainting fit at the Wellington Club, and it was reported that the services of Dr Reggie Jones and an assistant had to be called upon and, after conferring for some time, they decided to permit the removal of the patient to his town residence.[37] On another occasion, Villiers was observed by the London correspondent of the *Leicester Chronicle*, who recalled

> He [Villiers] happened to be crossing the most dangerous roadway in London, that bifurcated by the many thoroughfares that meet in front of

the Mansion House. Notable by reason of his figure, almost bent double, the Father of the House of Commons attracted attention by the agility with which he dived in and out, eluding the conflicting currents of cabs, carts, omnibuses, and carriages.[38]

Villiers, as a diner-out of great renown, was particularly fond of the cuisine at the Bachelors Club, informing Alice Borthwick in 1895 that 'the Bachelors is the healthiest spot in London (that is Hamilton Place) and the materials of the dinner are superior to the others, and when I can, I crawl there'.[39] Here, as Reginald Lucas observed, it must have been a strange sight

> to see this figure, bowed with age and clothed in the morning dress of seventy years ago, seated in the Club dining room amongst a number of very young gentlemen scrupulously attired for ball-going, and utterly unable to account for such an unfamiliar presence.[40]

In London's clubs, Villiers was widely acknowledged by members to be the most brilliant of conversationalists,[41] and it was noted that men of all parties found it pleasant to listen to him.[42] As a conversationalist, it was said that he was slightly cynical, was fond of epigram, and had a fund of amusing and inimitable anecdotes, always told good-humouredly, of his early experiences in Parliament, and of great parliamentary events and personalities.[43] The biographer (and Villiers' fellow Liberal MP during the 1880s) George Russell once observed, in a generous tribute

> I hold it to be an axiom that a man who is only a member of society can never be so agreeable as one who is something else as well. And Mr Villiers, though 'a man about town', a story-teller, and a diner-out of high renown, has had seventy years of practical business and parliamentary life. Thus the resources of his knowledge have been perpetually enlarged, and, learning much, he has forgotten nothing. The stores of his memory are full of treasures new and old. He has taken part in the making of history, and can estimate the great men of the present day by a comparison with the political immortals ... and nowhere is his mastery of the art of conversation more conspicuous than in his knack of implying dislike and insinuating contempt without crude abuse or noisy denunciation. He has a delicate sense of fun, a keen eye for incongruities and absurdities, and that genuine cynicism which springs, not from the poor desire to be thought worldly-wise, but from a lifelong acquaintance with the foibles of political men. To these gifts must be added a voice which age has not robbed of its sympathetic qualities, a style of diction and a habit of pronunciation which belong to the eighteenth century, and that formal yet facile courtesy which no one less than eighty years old seems capable of even imitating.[44]

Indeed, as late as January 1898, the *London Standard* observed that

> Notwithstanding Mr Villiers' advanced years, a breezy freshness characterizes his conversation, which at times becomes charmingly reminiscent. Being endowed with a retentive memory, he is able to entertain his friends for hours, narrating many of the stirring scenes which he witnessed in the House of Commons.[45]

These included the Cato Street conspiracy of 1820, which aimed at the slaughter of Lord Liverpool's cabinet,[46] the duel between the Duke of Wellington and Lord Winchelsea in a London suburb, which arose from his Lordship calling the hero of Waterloo a traitor in connection with Catholic Emancipation, and the attack by the mob on the Duke of Wellington's home during the reform bill crisis of 1830.[47]

In June 1895, with the fall of Rosebery's short-lived Liberal Ministry in March 1895, Charles Villiers was once again returned unopposed as the Member for Wolverhampton South at the General Election, thereby becoming the oldest candidate ever to be returned as a Member of Parliament (a record which still stands), and the Tory *Wolverhampton Chronicle* later claimed that 'it had never been seriously proposed, even in the moment of greatest irritation, to condemn, much less to supersede him [Villiers]'.[48] However, whilst Villiers continued to take a keen interest in Wolverhampton affairs, he eschewed practical involvement in formal Liberal Unionist politics and organisations and remained aloof from the squabbles over the leadership of the party between the aristocratic Lord Hartington, with whom Villiers had always been on friendly terms, and Joseph Chamberlain, whose radical social policies and increasingly imperialistic tendencies Villiers had little sympathy for. Indeed, Chamberlain was moved to observe (in an implied criticism of Villiers) that 'Wolverhampton was a town where the local Liberal Unionists have hitherto had no encouragement and where organisation wants stimulus'.[49] Moreover, Wright has suggested not only that Liberal Unionist meetings in Wolverhampton were conspicuous by their absence but also that Villiers' impregnable position in the Southern Division – which had become almost a personal fiefdom – ensured that Liberal Party organisation in the constituency simply stagnated, not even being canvassed or worked by an agent, and subsequently hampered the development of the 'modern' party system in the town.[50]

Nevertheless, despite his increasingly irregular attendance in the House of Commons during the changing political world of the 1890s, when his detachment from many of his old Liberal friends had become almost complete,[51] Villiers continued to retain a lively interest in contemporary politics and, as Lady Edith Villiers observed, 'politics were the chief topic of conversation with him'.[52] This is well illustrated not only in his letters to William McIlwraith but also in a rare interview he gave to a correspondent of the *Northern Echo* in April 1895.

Reflecting upon his long career, Villiers spoke warmly of his former colleagues, Richard Cobden and John Bright. Cobden, he stated, 'was a remarkable man ... He could speak really well, and with great power. I remember Disraeli praising him for his lucidity',[53] whilst Bright was 'a really able speaker' who 'rendered magnificent service in our Corn Law struggle' and who 'always spoke best when attacked ... His appeal, his vindication, stamped him as a noble orator'.[54] By contrast, when asked if he remembered anything special of Mr Gladstone as a young man, Villiers' reply was less fulsome, but nonetheless insightful:

> He was in Parliament before I was. His friends expected great things of him. He had been distinguished at Eton and Oxford, and a great career was anticipated. I cannot recall his early speeches, but Macaulay's description of him as the hope of the 'stern, unbending Tories' was accurate, and then suited him. What Mr Gladstone has been writing lately recalls my early idea about him and the ecclesiastical bent of his mind. He seemed to me passionately devoted to the Church, and many think it is singular that he should have been drawn into politics. I could compare him to Fox from the influence he acquired by speaking. When he had a great subject to deal with he used his power in explaining, analysing, and clearing up difficulties. I think he was pre-eminently the sort of man to be a member for a University, and this came out when he stood before a Lancashire audience as a candidate. He was too refined for that time, and a few coarse jokes would have gone down better than his style of speaking. Apparently, he has done with politics, unless the Armenian atrocities should draw him out, as seems probable; but he is swinging back to his early love and tendency – religious discussion.[55]

When asked for his opinion of the modern-day House of Commons, Villiers stated that he felt that the House had, in some respects, lost credit with the country:

> It does not hold the position in men's minds that it used to do. It has not the same power. The influences outside are greater and more developed, and there are some popular leaders who do not find a place in it – I mean leaders on social questions; and newspapers and organisations of one kind or another are nearly as powerful as the House of Commons is in the shaping of opinion. It was not so in my early days – then Parliament was paramount in its education of the public mind ... Governments do not now start the great reforms which are required, and they have, rather, become the instruments, the executors, of the popular will.[56]

Yet he also believed that the Commons now exercised greater vigilance over public business than formerly, because the extension of democracy had brought member and constituency closer together, although it possessed 'fewer stars than it used to have, its modern life probably being rather against the rise of individual men'.[57] Villiers also claimed that the style of speaking in the Commons had changed, due largely to the increased representation of 'commercial men' (of whom he held Cobden and Bright to have been the forerunners) in the House:

> Everybody can speak now. It used not to be so. A young man made a reputation at his University, and his friends said: 'he must go into Parliament'; and he went as a prodigy, because it was held to be a remarkable gift to be able to speak well. A good speaker now is more common, but he gets on by speaking, just as the young University men did.[58]

Villiers, who recalled that the greatest orators he had witnessed in Parliament were George Canning, Lord Grey and Lord Lyndhurst,[59] observed that examples of the old oratory still remained, citing in particular Joseph Chamberlain's debating power, which 'resembles Pitt's in clearness and furnish of detail'.[60] This said, Villiers believed that the major problem which the House of Commons now faced lay in increasing the representation of working men in the House and, once in, keeping them there, an issue which underlay the continuing debate over the payment of MPs. Villiers held that there was considerable popular indifference on this subject, adding that the French paid their members, 'but they are always disparaging them. They might do so here'.[61] His solution was that payment of members should be optional rather than mandatory, for men of wealth and leisure, coming from the classes that did not need payment, would continue to seek to enter Parliament, 'even though as a Club it is not much, and hard work is expected', although he added that 'it may not be so in the future'.[62]

In regard to the complex and contentious issue of the future of the House of Lords, a subject which, as David Cannadine has shown, had been exacerbated by the passing of the Third Reform Act and the defeat of Gladstone's second Home Rule Bill,[63] Villiers reluctantly supported the *status quo*. In essence, he held the view that the majority of Peers were 'quite equal in terms of intelligence to those who sit in the Lower House' but, as an unelected body, they were 'not representative and therefore not equal to giving effect to the wishes of the people'. In consequence, as he informed Wiliam McIlwraith, the Lords were 'pelted with all the stuff that Nationalists, Socialists, Anarchists and Gladstonites generally can find on their ground to fling at them!'[64] However, whilst acknowledging that the abolition of the House of Lords was 'an intelligible issue to raise', he observed that it would not be easy to realise its abolition, due principally to the absence of a viable alternative. Indeed, his great fear was that its replacement would be another, yet different 'aristocracy', comprising 'only the "superb" (who are sometimes the most selfish) people ... and which perhaps stupidly attaches to the importance of family'.[65]

Villiers was equally pessimistic about the rising tide of socialism, exemplified by the joint forces of the 'New Unionism' of unskilled and semi-skilled workers and the advent of the Independent Labour Party in 1893,[66] which he regarded with anathema.[67] 'I have a notion', he told McIlwraith,

> that equality is just what the English hate or don't care about and ... I have no fancy for creating common funds, out of which the honest and the idle are to have their share alike, and that is what plain people believe,

adding, 'What some venture to call "Progress" now is in my opinion only a retrograde movement and if not arrested soon we should be in a lane that has no turning'.[68] In a staunch defence of capitalism, Villiers reproached the ILP for 'practising for a while on the credulity of our uneducated, encouraging them to believe that their condition is not temporary but resulting from the tyranny of the classes', adding 'I suppose the fools will discover that capital is the fund out of which wages are derived and the value of labour will be determined by the proportion which it bears to the demand for it'.[69] The socialists were, he held, 'setting the working class against the middle class', adding

> I should like to know where the working class would be but for the capitalists (the favourite aversion now of the populace), and where would the 'Upper ten' be either but for the middle section of society who are, above others, interested both in order and freedom, and progress.[70]

These remarks were prompted, in part, by the prolonged strike of 1893 called by the Miners' Federation of Great Britain against a twenty-five per cent wage cut imposed by colliery owners at a time of falling prices. Villiers deplored the strike and its associated violence, which he blamed in part on the intransigence of the colliery owners and their supporters, who had caused the miners 'to act with rashness and in ways injurious to themselves'.[71] Indeed, Villiers held that such strikes served only to spread socialism, 'of which I suspect there is more about in this country than people like to admit', and regarded arbitration, 'by some authority previously agreed upon between employers and employees, and from which any departure or restriction by either side should be declared illegal', as the only viable solution.[72] This proved to be the case, for, following direct intervention by Gladstone's government (which was in itself unusual) the miners were allowed to return to work at their original wage and a Conciliation Board was established to resolve outstanding issues.[73]

By contrast, on the subject of the general depression in agriculture which currently afflicted the nation, and which, as Alun Howkins has shown, was complex, regionally specific and variable in its effects,[74] Villiers held that the situation was due not only to the fall in prices, which in turn reduced both the profits of farmers and the rental income of landed estates, but also to tenancy arrangements in the countryside. Unlike the great landlords, who were tenants for life, most farmers were, he observed, tenants at will and annual tenancies, rather than long-term leases, had become the general rule, 'a condition not favourable to agriculture'.[75] Moreover, he believed that the material condition of 'Hodge', the rural labourer, who had once 'suffered under a Poor Law system extravagant and full of abuses',[76] and had 'burnt the farmer's stacks to get an advance of wages and to save him and his large family from starving',[77] had improved substantially, with the result that the labourer was much better off than at any time in living memory.[78] He was, however, sceptical in regard to the Parish Councils Act of 1894, the open object of which was 'to democratise the people living in villages … and make "Hodge" into a sort of parochial statesman'.[79] Indeed, Villiers held that the village labourer had been humbled too much by ignorance and poverty for him to be felt of any importance, and feared that he would readily give way to the influence of persons in better station than himself within the new Councils, adding

> He may have had a little education of late years, and he may be able to stand upright, but I don't believe that he has ever had much reason to care for his Parish, and he would readily leave it if that would better his condition, and quite right too.[80]

As Villiers informed McIlwraith, the 'sudden and intense affection for the village labourer' was nothing other than a blatant attempt to secure his vote in Elections.[81] Villiers also absolved the rural poor of complicity in the great contemporary social question of urban poverty and degeneration, which had been highlighted by the pioneering social investigations of Charles Booth in London, the first volume of which had been published in 1889,[82] and which contributed to the subsequent redefinition of the concept of poverty itself during the late-Victorian and Edwardian years.[83] As he told McIlwraith,

> About every night in the House of Commons some member asserts that the cause of the poverty of great towns is that the agricultural labourers fly there in order to live, which they are unable to do in their parish [yet] I see nothing of degradation in any of our towns owing to the contact with the man of the village.[84]

Indeed, Villiers claimed that, despite their social problems, the great towns and cities now offered 'proof of what is called a "higher civilisation"',[85] which was in part the product of 'the enormous wealth of our country, the wealth we see daily in London', and which he attributed to the success of free trade policies.[86] 'Whether the people are happier in consequence', he added, 'is another thing, but it is a reason why we should not be in a present hurry to pull down, or rather change everything'.[87] Indeed, Villiers, who had always been sceptical of the ability of government alone to change society, opposed much of the 'New Liberalism' of the period, epitomised by the Newcastle Programme of 1891, which, in response to the growth of popular Toryism and the spread of socialist ideas, advocated greater state intervention in social policy and which caused tensions between moderate and Radical Liberals in the municipalities,[88] including Wolverhampton.[89] Yet Villiers remained optimistic that the socialist advance could be checked by social and moral progress, with the middle classes taking the lead.[90]

In regard to British foreign policy, Villiers retained broad views, which, in many respects, continued to echo those of his late brother, Lord Clarendon, with an emphasis on the maintenance of the balance of power in Europe, non-intervention in the internal affairs of other nations, and negotiation and arbitration to settle international disputes.[91] In private, however, he observed the changing balance of power in Europe during the late-nineteenth century – evidenced by the Triple Alliance of 1882 between Germany, Austria and Italy and the Dual Alliance of 1894 between Britain's traditional rivals, France and Russia, which left Britain increasingly isolated – with some concern, and held that the best hopes for peace in Europe in the short term lay in a general fear of war among the European powers, coupled with their mutual distrust of one another.[92] With regard to the emergence of Germany, under Bismarck's direction, as the dominant continental power, Villiers had hoped initially that the elderly German Chancellor would keep the new Kaiser, Wilhelm II, in check, informing McIlwraith in 1888

> I think the young gentleman who has succeeded to the throne is mistaken if he fancies that all the people now in the Garrison into which his country has been converted by Bismarck (perhaps wisely for a time) are panting for war,[93]

whilst adding 'Bismarck may keep him in order, but though his will is strong, his health is very far from being so'.[94] However, Bismarck resigned in 1890 after prolonged disagreements with the Kaiser and his militaristic and imperialistic advisors and, thereafter, Germany became fully involved in achieving overseas and colonial ambitions, much to Villiers' consternation.[95] When local crises, such as the Armenian massacres of 1895[96] and the Greco-Turkish War of 1897,[97] appeared to threaten the peace of Europe, Villiers expressed the hope that both affairs would not result in '*War*, the greatest of all curses',[98] and would be settled peaceably by negotiation without armed intervention by the Powers, which proved to be the case. Moreover, whilst acknowledging that there were different views within the government with regard to foreign policy,[99] by 1897 Villiers, with no little foresight, had come to the conclusion that it was time for Britain to settle her differences with France, a colonial rival in East and West Africa, and Russia, whose continued expansion threatened British interests in the Eastern Mediterranean and India, by negotiation.[100] Indeed, as Eric Hobsbawm observed, whilst a British alliance with France was once regarded as improbable, and one with Russia almost unthinkable, the implausible subsequently became reality,[101] through the Entente Cordiale of 1904 and the Anglo-Russian Entente of 1907.[102]

Villiers continued to have little sympathy for the expansion of empire and imperial adventures, contending that as long as Britain maintained a navy powerful enough to defend her shores, her manufacturing supremacy was sufficient to attract other nations to trade with her without incurring the cost of acquiring and safeguarding a large colonial empire.[103] In particular, he was critical of the expansionist policies of Rosebery and the Liberal imperialists, remarking to McIlwraith that 'He [Rosebery] does not seem to know that more than 2/3rds of our external trade is with foreign countries, not Colonies', adding 'Our Colonies have never thriven so well as since we have ceased to govern them'.[104] Villiers deplored the forward policy in Egypt during the early 1890s – 'I should think it better we have no right really to be there' – although acknowledging that 'the good that our occupation has done already for that country is hardly to be disputed'[105] – and supported (as he had for John Bright in 1882) Sir Charles Dilke's stance against British expansion in the Nile Valley.[106] In regard to India, Villiers held that 'there is much in our government of India that is difficult to defend, and, in my opinion, the extravagancies of our administration ought to be checked – I mean our military expenditure – as much as anything', whilst adding 'We must keep our promise to the natives'.[107] Villiers also bemoaned the escalating tensions between the British and the Boers in South Africa, which he believed to have been exacerbated by the desire of Germany 'to have a finger in the pie',[108] and following the ill-fated Jameson Raid in the Transvaal in December 1895, in which both Chamberlain and Cecil Rhodes were implicated, he remarked to McIlwraith that 'things are looking very shady, *quo* S. Africa',[109] and questioned Rhodes' right to remain a Privy Councillor in view of his role in the embarrassing affair.[110]

Villiers had once remarked to William McIlwraith that he believed that Lord Salisbury had more influence with the powers of Europe than any other man in Parliament,[111] and from 1895 onwards he certainly regarded the Conservative Prime Minister as 'the safest pilot to weather the storm which he sometimes feared might at a moment's notice burst upon the Empire'.[112] In particular, Villiers applauded the cessation of party strife about increased naval expenditure, informing the correspondent of the *Northern Echo*,

> I am glad of it. We have been getting behindhand ... and our supremacy at sea must be maintained as in the old days. I am delighted we are going back to our old determination to have a powerful navy.[113]

In January 1895, Villiers celebrated the sixtieth anniversary of his election as Member of Parliament for Wolverhampton, prompting *The Times* to comment that

> it will probably be interesting to politicians in particular, and to the public in general, to learn that 'the Father of the House of Commons' has completed his 'record' by having continuously represented in Parliament

the same constituency for a longer period than has ever been the fortune of any member of the House since its constitution in the reign of Henry II,

adding that

> Of Mr Villiers it may emphatically be said that he never 'to party gave up what was meant for mankind' and after 60 years of Parliamentary service he has the proud satisfaction of knowing that as 'Father of the House of Commons' he still enjoys in a singular degree the 'public confidence' which he so happily described as the 'reward of public services'.[114]

On 27 June 1896, a lavish banquet was held by the Cobden Club at the Ship Hotel, Greenwich, in celebration of the 50th (Jubilee) Anniversary of the Repeal of the Corn Laws and in order to present an address to Charles Pelham Villiers, the sole survivor of the four statesmen – Peel, Villiers, Cobden and Bright – to whom the passing of the measure was mainly due. It was noted that due to Villiers' great age and present state of health, he was unable to attend but it had been arranged for Richard Gowling, the Secretary of the Cobden Club, to present the address to Villiers at his residence, 50 Cadogan Place, prior to the banquet. The address included the following statement:

> In celebrating triumphs which have become part of our national history, it is an exceptional privilege to be able to address congratulations to one who not only played a leading part in the final contest, but who led a forlorn hope when the fortress of prejudice and privilege might well appear unassailable. The cause of which you have been so persevering an advocate – the cause of all that we know under the name of Freedom of Trade – the cause which achieved its final triumph in the repeal of the taxes on food, has, like other great causes, gone through various stages, and owes its ultimate victory to a succession of heroic efforts ... You, sir, and you alone of living men, have had the privilege of playing a leading part in these stages ... Neither your own constituents nor the people of the country have forgotten what you have done for them.[115]

On 26 June, Villiers penned his reply, with two appendices, which was read at the banquet, attended by 175 members and guests, and chaired by the Rt. Hon. Leonard Courtney, MP, and which featured, at the end of the room, a life-sized portrait of Mr Villiers, sent by Messrs Guggeridge and Whitlock, photographers, of Wolverhampton. In acknowledging the honour which the Cobden Club had bestowed on him, Villiers observed, in a quite remarkable statement from a 96 year old – shrewd, articulate, insightful, wise, and revealing a clear memory of past events – that the fifty years that had elapsed since the repeal, 'in furnishing abundant proofs of the wisdom of that policy, constitute as powerful an ally to Free Traders of today as was famine, in the words of my good friend Mr. Bright, to those of fifty years ago'.[116] He recalled both Sir Robert Peel's memorable speech of 27 January 1846 in moving his Free Trade Budget and Peel's exhaustive delineation, in his speech of 6 July 1849 (included as an appendix), of the facts and reasons which justified the Free Trade policy that he had set forth, and of his declaration that 'the principle of Protection to domestic industry – meaning thereby duties on imports imposed for that purpose and not for revenue – was a vicious principle, and that the best way to compete with hostile tariffs was to encourage free imports'.[117]

He then moved on to consider the justification of the policy, 'so admirably expressed' by Peel, which had been afforded by fifty years' experience, stating that:

> Free Trade has become during the fifty years of our experience a living force of incalculable energy. Of this fact no stronger proof can be urged than the belief in its principles of a succession of eminent Conservative statesmen, including Lord Beaconsfield, Mr. W.H. Smith, and Lord Randolph Churchill among those who have passed away, as well as the leading members and the great bulk of the Conservative party of the present day; and no-one has ever questioned Mr. Gladstone's firm adherence to Free Trade since the repeal of the Corn Laws. Nor must we forget Lord Salisbury's expression of opinion that Protection is impossible again in favour of one single interest.[118]

He then turned to 'the abounding proofs' of the benefits enjoyed by the country as a result of the policy of Free Trade, citing various statistics. These were also summarised in an appendix to his reply.[119] In particular, Villiers emphasised the importance of Free Trade in regard to the 'Condition of England Question'. He noted that during the thirty years that the Corn Laws were in operation, there had been constant distress in the country, often accompanied by incendiary outbreaks, whereas following repeal 'very slowly the condition of the people then improved; until prosperity at last advanced "by leaps and bounds"'.[120] The people had, he maintained, 'benefited in their every day lives, as may be seen from their largely increased consumption of articles of food, and by their being better clothed, better housed, and better educated'.[121] Moreover, he held that Free Trade had resulted the extended employment of the working classes, who were now able to obtain more and better articles, both of necessity and luxury, from the importation of goods from every quarter of the globe, adding (in an implicit reference to his famous exchange with Disraeli in 1852) that:

> In face of such facts as these, substantial as they are by figures taken from the official records, who can venture to dispute that the country has benefited, and continues to benefit, under the fiscal system known as Free Trade, which few would *now* deny to be 'just, wise, and beneficial?'[122]

In conclusion, Villiers reaffirmed his belief in the primacy of Free Trade over Protectionism, stating:

> To you, gentlemen, and to those who share your convictions, it remains as a sacred duty to secure that the millions of electors in this country are not seduced in the future from their allegiance to Free Trade, which would assuredly result in a condition more disastrous to our multiplied millions than even was experienced in the evil days of the supremacy of Protection. Of such a result I have no fear; and in the words of Sir Robert Peel, I say, 'It is my consolation that *never* will such a Corn Law be re-enacted in England'.[123]

Villiers' reply to the address was subsequently printed and circulated by the Cobden Club and, as *The Times* observed,

> It was a fine specimen of close and spirited reasoning for a statesman in his 95th year. It set forth in clear terms the soundness of the policy on which the nation entered in 1846, and the vast benefits which had resulted from that policy.[124]

Villiers' reply is perhaps of greater significance, however, by virtue of the fact that he had sought Gladstone's advice in preparing it, for Villiers had sent Gladstone a draft of his address in advance of the Cobden Club banquet. Gladstone had replied with a 'friendly and acceptable letter', which approved of the draft and also made reference to Villiers' remarkable longevity. In his reply, written on Cobden Club notepaper, Villiers stated

> It is certainly a long time that I have exceeded the term allotted by the 'Psalmist' for the duration of life, 'tho I have never forgotten the insuperable design of nature as to its termination, or that I expect that I shall shortly be assured completely of nothing,

adding

> I am much pleased, I assure you, that you approved of my reply to the address ... I was glad to learn what I certainly expected, that nothing has occurred to shake your judgment upon this important question of leaving nothing to chance in providing a dependable supply of food for the people.[125]

Then, on a personal note, Villiers remarked

> The only drawback that I discovered in the contents of your letter was the admission on your own part of suffering from some of the inconveniences that usually attach to advanced age and that you are already

conscious of some defect both in hearing and sight. With respect to the latter, you must no doubt have done much to expect it! But as we know, that loss can be repaired artificially, but with respect to deafness, it does interfere with the pleasure of society and is not easily to be remedied ... I only wish I could sign my name half as well as yours ... I ought to apologise to those I address for deciphering what I have written. Thanking you again for your letter.[126]

This, the last known correspondence between Villiers and Gladstone, perhaps suggests that these two elderly parliamentarians, still united in their mutual support for Free Trade, but both now well past their primes and nearing the end of their lives, yet discussing freely their respective ailments and reflecting on their own mortality, had at least reached a kind of *modus vivendi* or grudging tolerance of one another.

Charles Villiers was last seen in the Commons on 13 August 1895, when he attended to take the oath of allegiance and his seat in the new parliament, as the only sitting member to have been elected during the reign of William IV. As Henry Lucy observed, 'Mr Villiers, arriving just before two o'clock, was spared the crush at the table, the oath being specially administered to him at the Clerk's table'.[127] Nevertheless, as the *Walsall Advertiser* observed on the occasion of Villiers' ninety-fifth birthday in January 1897, he continued to take the keenest interest in politics and was especially '*au courant* with everything of consequence that takes place in the social world'.[128] The newspaper added that

> Age has naturally bowed his figure, and his hearing is now somewhat dull, but his intellect is as alert and his conversation as keen and instructive as in days of yore; and, whenever the weather is not too unfavourable, he may be seen at the 'Bachelors' in Hamilton Place, where his visits are always welcome.[129]

In the same month, Wolverhampton Borough Council decided to confer the honorary freedom of Wolverhampton on Charles Villiers in recognition of his unique service to the borough as a Member of Parliament,[130] an accolade which was presented (in absentia) in May.[131] Finally, in June, in his capacity as 'Father of the House', Villiers presented Queen Victoria with the present of an ebony-handled umbrella encrusted with diamonds on the occasion of her Diamond Jubilee.[132] This was said to be the only present of its kind ever accepted by Her Majesty from a subject,[133] and was used by the Queen during the grand procession through London on 22 June, although Villiers was himself too unwell to attend the celebrations. As he told McIlwraith,

> I was not well enough to go out and did not see the procession. I am told that nothing was ever seen in London equal to the enthusiasm with

which she was received when she left her Palace this morning. It is said that the Queen appeared to be in good spirits and was bowing to the people right and left as she would have done 40 years ago.[134]

On 3 January 1898, Villiers celebrated his ninety-sixth birthday with a party for family and friends at Cadogan Place. The *London Standard* reported that Villiers had received a large number of congratulatory messages and 'continues to enjoy comparatively good health, and was in excellent spirits', adding that 'His interest in public affairs is as keen as ever and he spends much time in attending to his correspondence',[135] whilst the *Sunday Times* observed:

> He is of course greatly bowed with age, and at times very feeble; but his mental rigour is astonishing. In appearance now he reminds one very much of the late Mr Bright. His long white hair is parted in exactly the same way, and except that the features are not so sharply cut, and that the cheeks are more fleshy, there has grown to be a wonderful resemblance between the two ... Mr Villiers is a fine old English gentleman – 'one of the good old days'. The venerable recluse of Cadogan Place still wears the shirt-frill, recalling the good old times when he and his fellow-MPs wore coats with high collars and tight sleeves. He has worn these frills now for close on 80 years. He has grown stout, and looks different to the thin and rather dandified young aristocrat, brother of a Peer, who went down to Hull when George IV was on the Throne.[136]

On the following day, Villiers wrote to his old friend William McIlwraith in Wolverhampton. The contents were significant. 'What Disraeli used to say about England's history', he observed,

> was that it ought to be termed the History of Reaction, and that not long after the public had possessed itself with a cause and had gone all lengths to give it effect, then all of a sudden are apt to regret what they have done and a 'new departure' (my expression) becomes all the go.[137]

This was, of course, a reference to the recent debate within Liberal Unionist ranks over Joseph Chamberlain's proposals for the creation of a free-trade empire with tariffs against foreign countries which, for Villiers, represented a departure from the Free-Trade principles which he had consistently upheld and which he again re-affirmed. He bemoaned the fact that the public appeared to

> now speak with a faltering voice about the advantages of having abolished the Corn Laws and recognising fully the advantages of opening our ports to all comers and finding after 50 years experience that the country is generally in a far better condition that it ever was and the working classes are more peaceful than they have been before during this century.[138]

'What', he asked McIlwraith, 'is Lord Hartington wishing to substitute for Mr Chamberlain's scheme for free trade? I long to have your notion of what is going on'.[139] Strangely, and unlike all previous correspondence between Villiers and McIlwraith, the envelope containing this letter was bordered in black, of the kind normally reserved for denoting a bereavement, and it proved to be the last of the many letters sent by Villiers during their friendship, for within a fortnight, Charles Pelham Villiers was dead.

During the following week, Villiers had been taken ill with a cold at 50 Cadogan Place, where he was attended by Dr Reginald Harrison, but his condition rapidly deteriorated. When previously ill, Villiers had declined the aid of professional nurses and, during this last illness, he requested that only his own servants should attend upon him. Despite their constant and unremitting attention, however, he was unable to eat, became increasingly weak and lapsed into a comatose state on 14 January,[140] passing away peacefully on the evening of Sunday 16 January.[141] According to one report, supplied by a relative who was present,

> A great peace seemed to settle on Mr Villiers at the end and to those of whom he was dear his last words will be of comfort, for, acknowledging the little assistance rendered to him by a faithful attendant, he said 'Thank ye, thank ye, I think I will go to sleep now'. His lips never moved again.[142]

On his passing, numerous callers visited the house, including messengers from the Queen (who noted in her diary that 'Mr Charles Villiers, aged 97, uncle of Emily Ampthill, had died last night. He had given me a very handsome parasol at my Jubilee'[143]), the Prince of Wales and other members of the Royal Family.[144]

News of Villiers' death prompted generous and often affectionate tributes in obituaries in the national and provincial press in Britain and beyond.[145] In general, these provided a summary of his long career, with particular reference to his critical contribution to the fight for Free Trade and the Repeal of the Corn Laws, his work at the Poor Law Board, and his split with Gladstone over Home Rule in 1886. The most comprehensive of these was provided by *The Times*, in a detailed and lengthy obituary of some four thousand words, which, after praising his achievements, observed that

> Mr Villiers was content to lead the life of an unselfish politician. He cared nothing for office as such. Though belonging to the aristocracy by birth, he found many of his warmest friends outside of its circle. He was highly esteemed by men of all parties, and he enjoyed the reputation of being one of the best talkers of the day,

and which concluded:

> The great political events of the early part of our century are fast receding into that distance whence they assume to the eyes of all men their due

relative proportions, and whence those who have taken the lead in them are estimated with a judgment that cannot be biased by the prejudices of party, nor distorted by the glamour of self-interest.[146]

The *London Daily News* reported that 'every politician will be recalling the brilliant services of the veteran member of Parliament who has just died', adding that Villiers' career 'was almost singular in its combined consistency and duration', that he had been 'a master of lucid exposition and logical argument, an excellent administrator [and] the living embodiment of a great and triumphant cause', and concluding that he was 'an extremely favourable specimen of the high and dry Whig, clear headed and courageous'.[147] Writing in similar vein, the *London Standard* observed that Villiers had the rare fortune of witnessing the realisation of all the great schemes that comprised his political programme at the commencement of his public career, including Free Trade, Poor Law reform, Municipal reform, the extension of the Franchise, the Ballot, Irish Disestablishment, and a system of National Education.[148] Indeed, as the *Glasgow Herald* noted 'He took a prominent part in promoting many useful and serviceable reforms … and in all his Parliamentary career strove to win "the greatest good for the greatest number"'.[149]

In Lancashire, the home of the Anti-Corn Law League, tributes were equally fulsome. The *Manchester Times*, for example, observed that 'One of the remarkable figures of the age has passed away', adding that

> It is to the credit of the electors of Wolverhampton of both parties that his connection with the constituency, begun over sixty years ago, continued until his death. The consideration extended to him, even after he had ceased to reflect the opinions of many Liberals on one great question of the day [Home Rule] was a tribute to the great services he had rendered to the commonwealth.

In particular, the newspaper emphasised his contribution to the Free Trade movement, noting that,

> as the last of the great Free-Trade trio, he retained to the close of his long life the deep respect, and even affection, of his countrymen of all classes, for whom he stood, after Cobden and Bright, as the representative of a principle that has conferred enormous benefits on the nation.[150]

By contrast, the *Blackburn Standard* recalled Villiers' work at the Poor Law Board, noting that during the Lancashire Cotton Famine, 'the wise and humane administration of Mr Villiers enabled the period to be surmounted with far less permanent harm than seemed at one time possible'.[151]

Most obituaries drew attention to Villiers as a conviction politician, a man of principle, and to the singular political courage he had evinced over the Corn Laws and Home Rule issues. In regard to the Corn Laws, *The Spectator*, in describing Villiers as 'a man of good sense coupled with singular courage and independence', observed that 'A young man of the landlord class wanted something more than ordinary pluck when he stood up and denounced the Corn Laws', adding that Villiers career in Parliament was 'a standing proof that Democracy is not always forgetful or ungrateful, and the electors [of Wolverhampton] stuck to him with absolute loyalty'.[152] The *Nottinghamshire Guardian* made a similar observation, claiming that Villiers deserved equal praise with Cobden and Bright in securing Free Trade and that it had required 'no small courage in a Whig aristocrat in those days to identify himself with that cause', adding that 'Few of Mr Villiers friends agreed with him, and of those few hardly one was prepared to face the obloquy incurred by giving expression to their views',[153] whilst the *Glasgow Herald* described Villiers as 'the public man who more than any other had suffered in his practical associations by his undeviating advocacy of what, to him, at least, seemed a great and sacred question'.[154] On Home Rule, the *Glasgow Evening Telegraph* noted that even in his old age, Villiers 'showed the courage of his convictions by refusing to follow Mr Gladstone when he took over the bulk of the Liberal Party into Mr Parnell's camp', adding that 'While Mr Villiers had no great love for Mr Gladstone, and often jested at his expense, he fully recognised the Parliamentary supremacy of the Liberal leader',[155] whilst the *London Standard* observed that although Villiers, who was anxious for a conciliatory policy towards Ireland, had been subjected to very angry remonstrances from his (former) Home Rule friends throughout the duration of Lord Salisbury's Ministry, he had stuck to his principles because 'he did not see how any measure of Home Rule could succeed while Ireland was torn with internal dissentions, and needed the strong hand of Great Britain to prevent a civil war'.[156]

This said, it was appreciations of, and affection for, Villiers' character and personal qualities which received both unanimity and approbation in his obituaries. As the *Pall Mall Gazette* observed,

> What impressed every one honoured with the friendship of Mr Villiers was his unfailing spirit of breezy cheerfulness. No one could pass many minutes in his company without recognizing that he was in the presence of a rare, almost of a unique, personality. In him were happily blended the exquisite manners of a polished man of the world and the charm of a great intellect.[157]

Likewise, the *Newcastle Courant* remarked that

> He was a typical fine old English gentleman, with all the dignity and gentle, winning courtesy associated with the name. His urbanity, broad sympathies, tolerance of others and their views, made him a favourite in the House, and won for him the ready and affectionate deference of every individual member,[158]

whilst the *Isle of Wight Observer* described him as 'A gentleman of the old school, a courtly gentleman, who loved his Queen and his country', adding that:

> There was nothing *fin-de-siecle* about him, and, indeed, he seemed almost, as it were, out of place in these vulgarised days. He belonged to that kind which has almost died out now, to those to whom honour and honestly earned fame came before anything else, who entered Parliament in order to work for the good of England, and who kept that object ever before their eyes. Self-advertisement was abhorrent to him.[159]

The Morning Post recalled that in his youth Villiers had been 'something of a Dandy', adding that 'if so the Dandyism was transitory, and with advancing years he grew less careful of mere outward appearance', noting that 'for honours he never cared' and emphasising the genuine affection he generated within both Parliament and his constituency:

> Loyalty of character was one of Mr Villiers most charming characteristics. He had a caustic tongue in debate but a kindly heart, and in the constituency he represented so long was, by the generation now passed away, most idolised. Stories of his generosity, his bonhomie, his transparent honesty, were the common talk of the Black Country.[160]

In Wolverhampton, news of Villiers' death prompted a wave of sympathy and, as a mark of respect, flags were lowered to half-mast at the Town Hall, St Peter's Church, and at the Liberal and Conservative Clubs, and fulsome tributes to Villiers were made at a meeting of the Borough Council, where it was said that Villiers' distinguished career had 'added lustre' to Wolverhampton.[161] Indeed, the Mayor, Alexander McBean, stated that the life of Wolverhampton's senior parliamentary representative had been contemporaneous with the history of the century, adding

> His national work was accomplished during a past generation, but the present generation was reaping the benefit of the splendid labours of this great statesman in the advantages and blessings of Free Trade ... He was of sterling worth, and the world would be the poorer for having lost such a conscientious gentleman.[162]

The *Wolverhampton Chronicle*, in a generous and lengthy obituary, which included a comprehensive summary of Villiers' career, was moved to comment that

> The death of Mr Villiers is the sundering of a tie, vital and visible, that has long connected the politics of the present hour with the unforgotten controversies and conflicts of a period which seems far remote from the eager spirits of this generation. The continuity of national life, its

thought and action, finds always most acceptable representation in the personalities of our aged men, who by reason of their abilities, their opportunities, their good fortune, or their services, have become indisputably distinguished ... The remarkably long life of Mr Villiers took us by one clean sweep right to the childhood, the infancy of this now very old and almost worn-out century. The century, viewed in the light of Mr Villiers' career, has a wholeness, a homogenousness, a consistency which is instructive to contemplate.[163]

In praising Villiers' contributions to reform, the *Chronicle* noted that Charles Villiers had been 'the life and soul' of the movement for the repeal of the Corn Laws: 'In season, out of season, by speech and pamphlet, by public advocacy and personal intercourse, he sowed broadcast that good seed of well-expounded truth which ripened with phenomenal rapidity into a glorious harvest'.[164] Whilst observing that in later years Villiers had parted from the Party with whom he had been 'so long and so honourably identified', the *Chronicle* declared that it had never been seriously proposed, 'even in the moment of greatest irritation, to condemn him, much less to supersede him', and that because of his years, and the great services of a singularly useful life, 'the hesitancy of his later years was sympathetically borne with'.[165] Indeed, the *Chronicle* pointed out that although in recent years Villiers had been unable to attend to his political duties with the assiduity and regularity that had marked his previous career, owing to advanced age and the precarious state of his health, 'He never failed, when any subject of importance either to the nation at large, or affecting the interests of his constituents in Wolverhampton, was under discussion, to be in his place in the House'.[166] In conclusion, the *Chronicle* acknowledged that Charles Villiers was 'on all occasions faithfully devoted to the traditional principles of the Liberal Party' and that 'throughout his long political career not one single instance can be adduced in which he made a sacrifice of his principles to gain a temporary triumph, or to aid in securing a Party vote'.[167] Similar sentiments were expressed by the *Staffordshire Advertiser*, which recalled that Villiers had entered the House of Commons 'as a fighting man, as the hardy and unflinching champion of a cause, then unpopular, which he lived to see crowned with success', adding that 'his clear and logical intellect was especially fitted to develop and popularize the doctrines of the orthodox political economy of Adam Smith in the struggle against old world Protectionism'.[168] By contrast, and somewhat predictably, the *Express & Star* published a shorter and less generous obituary, supplemented by a brief biographical sketch, which concluded that

> For many years past, Mr Villiers had been unable to take that active part in the political life of the country that perhaps his constituents would have wished, but remembering the great work he had done for the nation in times gone by, they were proud to have been able to retain him as their representative in the House of Commons.[169]

Charles Villiers' funeral service took place on Thursday 20 January at St Paul's Church, Wilton Place, 'amid many manifestations of public interest and sympathy', and he was buried at Kensal Green Cemetery where, 'despite the unpleasantness of the weather – the frequent showers of rain and the mud and slush under foot – a large crowd of the general public assembled'.[170] Among the several hundred mourners who attended the funeral or were represented were the Earl of Clarendon (who also represented the Queen) and the wider Villiers family, Sir Francis Knollys (representing the Prince of Wales), the Duke of Devonshire, the Earl and Countess of Derby, Lord Stanley, Lord Hyde, Lord and Lady Skelmersdale, Lord and Lady Glenesk, Lady Ampthill, Viscount Peel and Mr John Bright Jnr (son of John Bright) and Mrs Fisher Unwin (daughter of Richard Cobden), whilst wreaths were sent by Lord Rosebery and Lord Rothschild. The mourners also included a contingent of representatives from Wolverhampton, most notably Alexander McBean, Thomas Graham, William McIlwraith, and representatives of the Liberal and Conservative & Unionist Clubs, and deputations from the Cobden Club and the Reform Club. Mrs Maria Walsh, who had been Charles Villiers' housekeeper for upwards of thirty years, also attended and placed a wreath on the coffin with the inscription 'An affectionate tribute to a valued master, one of Nature's noblemen'.[171]

A fortnight later, at the by-election held in the constituency of Wolverhampton South on 3 February, the Liberal Unionist candidate, John Lloyd Gibbons, whose campaign had sought to attract former supporters of Villiers whilst also playing on divisions within the Liberal Party,[172] defeated the Liberal-Radical candidate, George Thorne, by 4,115 votes to 4,004 in a closely contested election.[173]

Charles Villiers died an extremely wealthy man, leaving an estate valued at £354,678.15s.9d (the equivalent of £41.8 millions in modern currency), the bulk of which was left in equal shares to two of his nephews, the Revd. Henry Villiers (the son of Henry Montagu Villiers) and Colonel Ernest Villiers (the son of Edward Ernest Villiers).[174] The publication of his will in March 1898 aroused controversy in some quarters, not least because Villiers, having been bequeathed a fortune by Catherine Mellish, had also continued to draw his Cabinet pension of £2,000 per annum. Predictably, Henry Lucy, who had earlier remarked that it was only due to Gladstone's concern for the welfare of his old friends and colleagues that Villiers had been granted a pension in the first place, thereby enabling him to live to 'green old age',[175] described the situation as nothing short of a scandal. 'Mr Villiers', he claimed, 'had been for so long in receipt of a pension granted in recognition of a few years' service at the Poor Law Board that he came to regard it as a matter of course', and, 'as an honourable man, should have relinquished the pension, possibly even have repaid what he had inadvertently overdrawn'.[176]

In April, the matter was raised in the House of Commons by Sir John Leng, the Member for Dundee, who tabled a question to Arthur Balfour, the First Lord of the Treasury, asking whether an ex-Minister of the Crown, having received a pension on making a declaration to the effect that his means are insufficient to maintain the dignity of his position, is ever required to renew the declaration, and, if not, whether, having in view that such a pensioner, recently deceased, left upwards of £350,000 of personal estate, will he consider the propriety of ex-Ministers in receipt of State pensions periodically reviewing their declarations of insufficiency of means?[177]

Balfour replied that for the past fifteen years (since 1883) the rule had been that Ministerial pensions should be relinquished in the event of a pensioner acceding to a fortune, but that in Villiers' case his was an older pension which pre-dated the new rule.[178] Balfour also informed Leng in private that the published statement of Mr Villiers' will did not affect the question of the pension. He had, Mr Balfour said, been enriched by the bequeathal of the fortune of a lady, but had resolutely declined to benefit by the bequest, now transferred to his heirs.[179] Villiers had, therefore, behaved in an honourable manner and was exonerated of having acted with impropriety. Significantly, Villiers' will also made a generous provision for Mrs Maria Welsh, his Irish housekeeper, who was bequeathed £3,000 (£354,000 in modern currency), plus the contents of his house, a life annuity of £300, and his vast correspondence, which Mrs Walsh subsequently destroyed, whilst the sum of £1,000 (£118,000 in modern currency) was bequeathed to various charities in Wolverhampton.[180]

Notes

1 H.W. Lucy, 'From Behind the Speaker's Chair', II, *The Strand Magazine*, vol. 5 (Jan.–June, 1893), 202.
2 H.W. Lucy, 'From Behind the Speaker's Chair', XIII, *The Strand Magazine*, vol. 7 (Jan.–June, 1894), 388.
3 Matthew, *Gladstone*, 45–6, 70–3.
4 *Isle of Wight Observer*, 29 Jan. 1898.
5 *Sunday Times*, 3 Jan. 1898.
6 For example, in 1887 he attended both the wedding of Revd. Lord William Cecil, second son of Lord Salisbury, to Lady Florence Bootle-Wilbraham, daughter of the Earl of Lathom, at St Andrew's Church, Oxford Street, and the reception at Lathom's home in Portland Square on Tuesday 16 August: *Morning Post*, 17 Aug. 1887; in May 1890 he attended the wedding of Ernest Farquhar and Theresa Lister (daughter of Sir Villiers Lister) in St Paul's Church, Knightsbridge, on Thursday 22 May: *Morning Post*, 24 May 1890.
7 *St James's Gazette*, 17 Jan. 1898: 'Charles Pelham Villiers: A Personal Recollection'. Although the author of this article remained anonymous, it was almost most certainly Lady Edith Villiers (1878–1925). Mrs Earle cited this article in *Memoirs and Memories*, 202–3, where she stated that the author was a twenty-year-old great-niece of Charles Villiers. In 1898, Lady Edith was the only twenty-year old great-niece in the Villiers' family.
8 *St. James's Gazette*, 17 Jan. 1898.
9 In 1911, Mrs Earle recalled,

> In Paris [in 1854] I first felt I got to know my uncle, Charles Pelham Villiers. I was seventeen and a half, and he took notice of me, which a young girl so appreciates. He offered to take me to a French *jeune fille* play; this my mother would not allow. She said no one would know he was my uncle; this seemed to me very hard then, and I think now it was certainly conceding too much to the fashion of the country we were in; we do not bind up the faces of our girls if we take them to Constantinople. From this time I took great interest in this uncle and his distinguished political career, and swelled with pride as I realised the part he had taken in wringing from a reluctant legislature the repeal of the Corn Laws ... All my youthful sympathies were then and have been ever since with the extreme Liberal party, and my Whig relations at the Grove chaffed me unmercifully for taking in Bright's *Morning Star*, the most radical paper of the day, out of my pocket-money, at eighteen:
>
> *Memoirs and Memories*, 199.

10 Ibid., ix.
11 Ibid., 203.
12 The Clarendon Papers, housed in the Bodleian Library at the University of Oxford do contain some of Charles Villiers' private letters on family matters. See, for example, Clarendon Papers, MS. Eng. c.2160, B.6. Letters to Lady Clarendon from Lord Clarendon's family, 1838–65, Fols. 1–17: Letters from C.P. Villiers. The Clarendon Papers were used extensively by George Villiers when writing his biography of the 4th Earl Clarendon, *A Vanished Victorian*. Although this was an illuminating and original study, it was, however, devoid of notes and references, and there is clearly further and ample scope for further research on the wider Villiers family during the Victorian period based on this valuable archive.
13 Villiers' voting record in the House of Commons is indicative of this. In August 1890, for example, it was reported that during the Parliamentary Session of 1890 there had been 260 Divisions in the House on which Villiers only voted on four occasions. Only four MPs (three of whom never voted) had a poorer record: *Morning Post*, 21 Aug. 1890.
14 See, for example, *Morning Post*, 6 Aug. 1886, 6 Aug. 1887, 9 Dec. 1887.
15 Villiers to Millicent Garrett Fawcett, 7 May 1892: 'His health prevents him from promising to attend the suffrage meeting on 31 May'. MCL, Women's Suffrage, Part 2, Correspondence: Letters to Millicent Garret Fawcett, M50/2/1/170.
16 DX60/5/6, Villiers to McIlwraith, 22 Apr. 1888.
17 DX60/5/26, Villiers to McIlwraith, nd. Aug. 1888.
18 DX60/5/30, Villiers to McIlwraith, nd. Aug. 1888.
19 *South Wales Echo*, 14 Nov. 1891: 'The Press Association is requested to state that the general health of Mr C.P. Villiers, MP, is good. The right hon. gentleman, who is in his 90th year, has quite recovered from the effects of the fall he had three weeks ago'.
20 DX60/10/32, Villiers to McIlwraith, nd. Nov. 1893.
21 DX60/10/36, Villiers to McIlwraith, 28 Dec. 1893.
22 DX60/10/37, Villiers to McIlwraith, 29 Dec. 1893.
23 *Leeds Mercury*, 18 Jan. 1896.
24 DX60/14/39, Villiers to McIlwraith, 3 Jul. 1897.
25 DX20/14/120, Villiers to McIlwraith, 27 Dec. 1897.
26 DX60/5/15, Villiers to McIlwraith, 8 Jul. 1888.
27 DX60/10/1, Villiers to McIlwraith, 17 Jan. 1893.
28 DX60/10/8, Villiers to McIlwraith, 1 Mar. 1893.
29 DX60/10/12, Villiers to McIlwraith, 19 May 1893.
30 DX60/10/29, Villiers to McIlwraith, 15 Nov. 1893.

31 See, for example, DX60/5/28, Villiers to McIlwraith, 20 Sep. 1888: 'Excuse all this bad writing, for my eyes are very weak just now'.
32 DX-60/14/73, Villiers to McIlwraith, 18 Jul. 1897.
33 Villiers to Alice Borthwick [Glenesk], 21 Oct. 1895, cited in Reginald Lucas, *Lord Glenesk and the Morning Post* (London, 1910). 252–3.
34 *Yorkshire Evening Post*, 17 Jan. 1898.
35 *Queen Victoria's Journals*, 94, 22, 9 Jul. 1891.
36 *Staffs Advertiser*, 15 Jul. 1893.
37 *Glasgow Herald*, 1 Mar. 1894.
38 *Leicester Chronicle*, 22 Jan. 1898.
39 Villiers to Alice Borthwick, (nd) 1895, cited in Lucas, *Lord Glenesk and the Morning Post*, 228.
40 Ibid., 228.
41 *The Times*, 17 Jan. 1898; *Manchester Times*, 21 Jan. 1898.
42 *The Brooklyn Daily Eagle*, 23 Jan. 1898; *San Francisco Call*, 17 Jan. 1898.
43 *Leamington Spa Courier*, 22 Jan. 1898; *Reynold's Newspaper*, 23 Jan. 1898.
44 G.W.E. Russell, *Collections and Recollections* (London, 1903), 66.
45 *London Standard*, 4 Jan. 1898.
46 *The Pall Mall Gazette*, 18 Jan. 1898.
47 *London Standard*, 4 Jan. 1898; *San Francisco Call*, 17 Jan. 1898.
48 *Wolverhampton Chronicle*, 19 Jan. 1898.
49 Wright, 'Liberal Party Organisation and Politics', 112. The relationship between Villiers and Joseph Chamberlain remains obscure. Although they clearly knew one another, there is certainly no surviving evidence in Chamberlain's papers [University of Birmingham, Cadbury Research Library, Special Collections, The Joseph Chamberlain Collection, GB/150/JC] of any direct correspondence between them.
50 Ibid., 15–17.
51 Villiers to Alice Borthwick, (nd. 1894), cited in Lucas, *Lord Glenesk and the Morning Post*, 227: 'Where we are all going now your husband may be able to tell you, but it strikes me that it is very distinctly downwards under our present rulers'. Lucas suggests that this indicates that Villiers' detachment from his old Liberal friends had become complete.
52 *St. James's Gazette*, 17 Jan. 1898.
53 *Northern Echo*, 17 Apr. 1895.
54 Ibid.
55 Ibid. The reference to Charles James Fox is interesting in that Villiers had moved in Whig circles at Holland House in his youth and would have been familiar with the Foxite legacy.
56 Ibid.
57 *Morning Post*, 17 Jan. 1898.
58 *Northern Echo*, 17 Apr. 1895.
59 *Pall Mall Gazette*, 18 Jan. 1898.
60 *Northern Echo*, 17 Apr. 1895.
61 Ibid.
62 Ibid.
63 D. Cannadine, *The Decline and Fall of the British Aristocracy* (London, 1992), ch. 2, 'The Embattled Elite', 35–87, contains an excellent appraisal of the arguments for and against abolition, explaining why Lord Salisbury's 'referendal theory', which placed the Lords on the side of democracy rather than against it, was largely accepted after 1895.
64 DX60/10/19, Villiers to McIlwraith, nd. Jul. 1893.
65 DX60/10/22, Villiers to McIlwraith, nd. Sep. 1893.

66 For further details see, for example, H. Browne, *The Rise of British Trade Unions, 1825–1914* (London, 1980), 71–6; P. Adelman, *The Rise of the Labour Party, 1880–1945* (London, 1980), 20–36.
67 Wright, 'Liberal Party Organisation and Politics', 138.
68 DX60/10/17, Villiers to McIlwraith, nd. Jul. 1893.
69 DX60/10/25 Villiers to McIlwraith, nd. Sep. 1893.
70 DX60/11/2, Villiers to McIlwraith, 19 Jan. 1894.
71 DX60/10/25, Villiers to McIlwraith, nd. Sep. 1893.
72 Ibid.
73 Browne, *The Rise of British Trade Unions*, 74–6.
74 A. Howkins, *Reshaping Rural England: A Social History, 1850–1925* (London, 1991), ch. 6, 'The Crisis of Rural Society', 138–65.
75 *Northern Echo*, 17 Apr. 1895.
76 Ibid.
77 DX60/10/34, Villiers to McIlwraith, nd. Dec. 1893.
78 *Northern Echo*, 17 Apr. 1895.
79 DX60/10/32, Villiers to McIlwraith, nd. Nov. 1893. The Act was largely the work of Villiers' fellow-MP, Henry Fowler, then President of the Local Government Board.
80 DX60/10/34, Villiers to McIlwraith, nd. Dec. 1893.
81 Ibid.
82 Charles Booth, *The Life and Labour of the People in London*, 17 vols (London, 1903).
83 There is an extensive historiography on this subject, but see especially David Englander and Rosemary O'Day, *Retrieved Riches: Social Investigation in Britain, 1840–1914* (Aldershot, 1995), Part II, 105–240; see also Rose, *The Relief of Poverty, 1834–1914*, 34–52.
84 DX60/10/32, Villiers to McIlwraith, nd. Nov. 1893.
85 Ibid.
86 *Northern Echo*, 17 Apr. 1895.
87 DX60/10/32, Villiers to McIlwraith, nd. Nov. 1893.
88 James R. Moore, *The Transformation of Urban Liberalism: Party Politics and Urban Governance in Late Nineteenth Century England* (Aldershot, 2006), 264–5.
89 For further details, see Lawrence, *Speaking for the People*, 112–22.
90 Wright, 'Liberal Party Organisation and Politics', 138. Wright also observes that an increasingly conservative Sir Henry Fowler held similar views.
91 See, for example, letter from Lord Torrington to J.T. Delane, 2 May 1864, in Dasent, *John Thadeus Delane*, 2, 103–4; see also, Steele, *Palmerston and Liberalism*, 117.
92 DX60/5/8,Villiers to McIlwraith, 5 Mar. 1888:

> We must hope, however, for the best and, above all, that nothing will happen to disturb the peace of Europe ... At this moment the appearance of the Continent (as against War) is favourable; fortunately there is no State in Europe that can feel certain of the result of a general disturbance (like that of war), as well as the mistrust all the crowned heads have of each other may keep things straight for some time.
>
> See also DX60/5/24, V-M, 19 Jul. 1888

93 DX60/5/16, Villiers to McIlwraith, 18 Jun. 1888.
94 DX60/5/28, Villiers to McIlwraith, 20 Sep. 1888.
95 DX60/11/8, Villiers to McIlwraith, 7 Feb. 1894; DX60/14/120, V-M, 27 Dec. 1897.
96 DX60/12/23, Villiers to McIlwraith, 22 May 1895. The Armenians had demanded independence from the Turkish Empire but were put down in a series

of bloody massacres by Kurdish and Turkish troops. Britain and France protested, but Russia, Austro-Hungary and Germany refused to intervene. Villiers feared that this might encourage Gladstone to return to politics (as he had done in 1878 over the Bulgarian massacres).
97 DX60/14/72, Villiers to McIlwraith, 16 July 1897. The Greek–Turkish War of 1897 resulted from the revolt against Turkish rule in Crete. Britain, France, Italy and Russia duly forced Turkey to accept an armistice and to grant Crete independence.
98 Ibid.
99 DX60/10/32, Villiers to McIlwraith, nd. Nov. 1893: 'While some have full confidence in the present sincerity of Russia towards us, there are others who chiefly rely upon the strength and unity and natural goodwill towards us of Germany, as the great and powerful centre of Europe'.
100 DX60/14/101, Villiers to McIlwraith, 8 Oct. 1897.
101 E.J. Hobsbawm, *The Age of Empire, 1875–1914* (London, 1987), 314–15.
102 For Britain's changing diplomatic relationships with France, Russia and Germany during the 1890s, see especially Christopher Clark, *The Sleepwalkers: How Europe went to War in 1914* (London, 2013), 136–52.
103 Robinson, 'Villiers, Charles Pelham', *DNB*, 58.
104 DX60/5/34, Villiers to McIlwraith, 13 Oct. 1888.
105 DX60/10/3, Villiers to McIlwraith, 28 Jan. 1893.
106 DX60/10/11, Villiers to McIlwraith, 1 May 1893.
107 *Northern Echo*, 17 Apr. 1895. In particular, Villiers was critical of the burden imposed by Indian Cotton Duties, which 'will not be tolerated for long, and as soon as deficiencies in revenue have been made, they must go. They are a kind of Protection, and I do not like them'. The Cotton Duties, which were opposed by the Lancashire cotton manufacturers, were defended in the House of Commons by Henry Fowler, who had been appointed Secretary of State for India in Rosebery's Ministry: Fowler, *Life of Henry Hartley Fowler*, 284–335.
108 DX60/11/8, Villiers to McIlwraith, 7 Feb. 1894: 'I am not sure that the Uitlanders would prefer us to the Germans if we were to meddle in their affairs'.
109 DX60/13/37, Villiers to McIlwraith, 28 Jul. 1896.
110 DX60/14/77, Villiers to McIlwraith, 18 Sep. 1897.
111 DX60/5/8,Villiers to McIlwraith, 5 March 1888.
112 *Pall Mall Gazette*, 18 Jan. 1898.
113 *Northern Echo*, 17 Apr. 1895; see also *Pall Mall Gazette*, 18 Jan. 1898.
114 *The Times*, 10 Jan. 1895.
115 *The Fiftieth Anniversary of the Repeal of the Corn Laws. The Full Official Report of the Cobden Club Banquet and Presentation to the Right Honourable Charles Pelham Villiers, M.P.* (Cassell & Co., London, August 1896), 4–6.
116 Ibid., 7.
117 Ibid., 8.
118 Ibid., 10.
119 Ibid., 15–16:

> Facts relating to Fifty Years of Free Trade: I. That the value of our Export Trade rose rapidly after the Repeal of the Corn Laws and the introduction of Free Trade; II. That the value of our Import Trade rose even more rapidly after 1848 than did our export Trade; III. That under the operation of the Free Trade tariff we have imported a far higher amount of gold and silver than we have exported; IV. That the general wealth of the nation has immensely increased, as is proved by the growth of property assessable to the Income Tax; V. That the savings of the people have increased enormously; VI. That pauperism has diminished by one-half in the last 40 years; VII. That the

consumption of food has greatly increased per head of the population; VIII. That this nation is the best fed nation in the world, though the country produces the smallest amount of food stuffs; IX. That the National Debt has been diminished by £177,000,000 in the last forty years.

120 Ibid., 12–13.
121 Ibid., 11.
122 Ibid., 12.
123 Ibid., 13.
124 *The Times*, 17 Jan. 1898.
125 *Gladstone Papers*, 44523/189, Villiers to Gladstone, 11 Aug. 1896.
126 Ibid.
127 H.W. Lucy, *A Diary of the Unionist Parliament, 1895–1900* (London, 1901), 7.
128 *Walsall Advertiser*, 9 Jan. 1897.
129 Ibid.
130 *Staffs Advertiser*, 30 Jan. 1897.
131 The Wolverhampton Corporation Act of 1891, for which Henry Fowler deserved much credit, included a clause that enabled the Corporation to bestow the Freedom of the Borough to distinguished persons who had made a significant contribution to the town. Fowler was the first recipient of this honour, in February 1892: Fowler, *Life of Henry Hartley Fowler*, 244. Villiers received this honour on 11 May 1897.
132 *The Times*, 17 Jan. 1898.
133 *The Thames Star*, 19 Jan. 1898.
134 DX60/14/65, Villiers to McIlwraith, 22 Jun. 1897.
135 *London Standard*, 4 Jan. 1898; see also *The Times*, 17 Jan. 1898.
136 *Sunday Times*, 3 Jan. 1898.
137 DX-60/14/123, Villiers to McIlwraith, 4 Jan. 1898.
138 Ibid.
139 Ibid.
140 *Pall Mall Gazette*, 14 Jan. 1898.
141 *The Times*, 17 Jan. 1898.
142 *Manchester Courier*, 22 Jan. 1898.
143 *Queen Victoria's Journals*, 107, 16, 17 Jan. 1898.
144 *London Standard*, 17 Jan. 1898.
145 These included tributes in the USA: see, for example, *The Brooklyn Daily Eagle*, 23 Jan. 1898, which carried a lengthy obituary entitled 'An Old Legislator', which also stated 'He was one of the most brilliant conversationalists in Great Britain and this fame had clung to him since he was 25'; see also the *San Francisco Call*, 17 Jan. 1898; *New York Times*, 17 Jan. 1898.
146 *The Times*, 17 Jan. 1898.
147 *London Daily News*, 17 Jan. 1898.
148 *London Standard*, 17 Jan. 1898.
149 *Glasgow Herald*, 17 Jan. 1898.
150 *Manchester Times*, 21 Jan. 1898; see also *Manchester Courier*, 22 Jan. 1898.
151 *Blackburn Standard*, 22 Jan. 1898.
152 *The Spectator*, 22 Jan. 1898.
153 *Nottinghamshire Guardian*, 22 Jan. 1898.
154 *Glasgow Herald*, 17 Jan. 1898.
155 *Glasgow Evening Telegraph*, 17 Jan. 1898.
156 *London Standard*, 17 Jan. 1898.
157 *Pall Mall Gazette*, 18 Jan. 1898.
158 *Newcastle Courant*, 22 Jan. 1898; see also *Dover Express*, 21 Jan. 1898: 'He was a genial cultured gentleman of the old school whose company was greatly enjoyed by politicians of every shade of thought'.

159 *Isle of Wight Observer*, 29 Jan. 1898.
160 *The Morning Post*, 17 Jan. 1898.
161 *Express & Star*, 18 Jan. 1898.
162 *Staffs Advertiser*, 22 Jan. 1898.
163 *Wolverhampton Chronicle*, 19 Jan. 1898.
164 Ibid.
165 Ibid.
166 Ibid.
167 Ibid.
168 *Staffs Advertiser*, 22 Jan. 1898.
169 *Express & Star*, 17 Jan. 1898.
170 *The Times*, 21 Jan. 1898.
171 Ibid.
172 Wright, 'Liberal Party Organisation and Politics', 236.
173 *Express &* Star, 4 Feb. 1898. John Lloyd Gibbons (1837–1919) was an engineering surveyor and, from 1891, had been a county councillor for North Bilston, a Staffordshire JP, and President of the South Wolverhampton Liberal Unionist Association. He held the seat for two years. George Rennie Thorne (1853–1934), a Baptist and a local solicitor, was a long-serving Liberal member of the Borough Council, serving as Mayor in 1902. He was eventually elected as Liberal MP for Wolverhampton East in 1908 on Henry Fowler's elevation to the House of Lords. For further details of Wolverhampton politics during this period, see especially Jon Lawrence, 'The Complexities of English Progressivism: Wolverhampton Politics in the Early Twentieth Century', *Midland History*, 24 (1999), 147–66.
174 *Morning Post*, 30 Mar. 1898: C.P. Villiers: Estate: £354,678; Executors: Mrs Maria Walsh & Mr John Thornely; To Maria Walsh £1000 and £2000, plus contents of his house and a life annuity of £300; To Wolverhampton charities, £1000; To William Hardman, £2000; To Rev. Henry Villiers (nephew), £1000; To Francis Villiers (nephew), £500; To Col. Ernest Villiers (nephew), £1000; To Thomas Villiers (nephew), £1000. The residue of all his property was left in equal shares to the Rev. Henry Villiers and Colonel Ernest Villiers.
175 H.W. Lucy, 'From Behind the Speaker's Chair', XVI, *The Strand Magazine*, vol. 8 (July–Dec, 1894), 39–40.
176 H.W. Lucy, *Later Peeps at Parliament: From Behind the Speaker's Chair* (London, 1905), 261–4.
177 *Parl. Debs*, 3rd ser., vol. 56, cc.48–9, 4 Apr. 1898.
178 Ibid.
179 Lucy, *Later Peeps at Parliament*, 261–4.
180 *Morning Post*, 30 Mar. 1898.

Epilogue

Charles Pelham Villiers' long life coincided with an age of dramatic change and connects almost a whole century of tumultuous and formative transformations in British politics. Villiers was certainly an enigmatic figure: aristocratic yet radical; gregarious yet independent and unmarried; plagued by ill-health for much of his life and yet extremely resilient, surviving to a ripe old age and outliving all his siblings and most of his friends and colleagues; and a man who constantly bemoaned and worried about his lack of money, which was probably a legacy of his childhood upbringing and especially his father's financial difficulties, yet one who bequeathed an estate valued at a small fortune. Indeed, his long and distinguished parliamentary career, for which he declined honours (which he despised), was characterised by many paradoxes and contradictions, and not least in its unusual trajectory.

Brought up as a Liberal Tory, he had entered Parliament as a fervent Benthamite Radical, becoming a noted reformer within the Liberal Party, yet he ended his political career as a Liberal Unionist. His early career, which illustrated the importance of patronage, connections and networks in social and political circles, was devoted to radical causes which he supported with a pertinacity that shocked the class to which he belonged, made him many political enemies, and long cut him off from political preferment, a situation which was exacerbated by the quick wit, sharp tongue and biting sarcasm that he frequently directed towards his political opponents.[1]

His greatest achievement, which came early in his career, was undoubtedly as the acknowledged parliamentary champion of Free Trade, on which his subsequent reputation rested. For Villiers, the repeal of the Corn Laws was no less than a personal crusade and, particularly (but not exclusively) in the years before Cobden and Bright entered Parliament, Villiers served as a vital link between Westminster, with its small group of Liberal free-traders, and the leaders of the Anti-Corn Law League in Manchester and the northern manufacturing districts. Although he lacked the fiery and impassioned oratory of Cobden and Bright, Villiers (who, as a lawyer, was particularly adept at marshalling a case) literally hammered away, year after year, against a hostile audience in the House of Commons. Here, his annual motions, not to mention his other speeches in the House, articulated and reiterated, with increasing sophistication, and backed up by a veritable battery of facts and figures, the arguments for repeal on commercial, economic, financial, social, political and moral grounds. These, in addition to his speeches in the provinces and his close co-operation with Cobden and Bright, helped to set the agenda for a national debate and allowed the Anti-Corn Law League to exert pressure on Parliament in such a way as to gradually erode the Protectionist majority by 1846. Yet in the hour of victory, Villiers' achievement was to some extent undermined by the credit afforded by Peel to Richard Cobden in the League's success. This legacy, by minimising Villiers' role, duly informed historical narratives and interpretations of the Free Trade movement, notwithstanding the fact that Villiers also played a significant role, which was graciously acknowledged by Disraeli, in the final settlement of the Free Trade question in 1852, for he prepared much of the groundwork for the debates in the House of Commons, even if it was Palmerston's milder resolution that eventually won the day.

From the outset of his career, Villiers' political outlook was too independent to enable him to be regarded as a 'sound' party man – he could be awkward and compromise did not come easily to him – and he was viewed with some suspicion by many Whig and Liberal grandees, as his relationships with Melbourne, Russell and, more especially, Gladstone, illustrated. Yet when presented with the opportunity to serve in the Liberal ministries of Palmerston and Russell, he did so with great distinction, serving as a cabinet minister for seven years (a longer period than his Radical friend and colleague, John Bright, experienced in office[2]) and introducing the most important series of reforms to the New Poor Law since 1834. Indeed, in transforming a backward and unpopular government department into one of substance and repute, Villiers displayed administrative and organisational abilities of a high order (skills which, as Henderson observed, Gladstone later failed to deploy[3]) yet his achievement has been largely ignored by historians.

By contrast, although Villiers successfully championed many reforms, there were occasions when he sided with the opposition, and in his declining years he regarded Salisbury (a fellow aristocrat and a Tory) as a much safer custodian of the national interest than either Gladstone or Rosebery. Indeed, in many respects Villiers embodied the 'Golden Age of the Independent Member', suspicious of Party organisation, rules, and procedures. His personal rubric as an MP was always to judge an issue on the balance of the evidence, reflecting his lawyer's mindset, rather than according to Party dictat, as illustrated by his later attitudes towards 'the caucus' system and the development of tighter party discipline, which increasingly limited the independent discretion of individual MPs. In 1898, even the Tory *St James's Gazette* was moved to observe that

> Mr Villiers was the last survivor in the House of Commons, and, with the exception of Mr Gladstone, the last in public life of a generation in which the well-born gentleman who devoted himself to politics was able

to take his place with a certain air of superiority much less possible for him now, when he must strive and beg (to say nothing of intrigue) for the footing which came to his predecessor almost as a right.[4]

The editorial added that, unlike Villiers, Gladstone had entered public life 'by the most convenient of doorways, a pocket borough' and that, of the two, Villiers had proved the more consistent politician and that his enduring relationship with his Wolverhampton constituents offered 'a pleasant example of the kindly loyalties of English public life'.[5]

This said, Charles Villiers' parliamentary career sheds a unique light on the rise and decline of the Liberal Party, with its fluctuating fortunes, internal conflicts and personal rivalries, during the Victorian period. In particular, it highlights the tensions both between and within the Liberal Party at Westminster, the National Liberal Federation and provincial Liberalism arising from the Home Rule crisis of 1886, which was clearly a painful experience for all concerned. Indeed, Villiers' 'apostasy' (as Gladstonian Liberals regarded it), but which, for Villiers, represented the true Liberal faith, sheds an alternate light on Gladstone himself – a man with whom Villiers had served conscientiously but with whom he disagreed profoundly on the question of Irish Home Rule (displaying in private some marvellously fruity language in the process). In this context, Villiers' claim to be representing 'true' Liberalism, and his critique of some of Gladstone's policies, touches on Richard Shannon's important distinction between Gladstone's Liberalism and Gladstonian Liberalism,[6] for Gladstone's 'liberalism', as Villiers observed, was hardly 'liberal' in the widest sense, containing as it did elements of conservative thought inherited in part from Peel. Indeed, Villiers had, from the outset of his career, allied himself with progressive forces at a time when Gladstone, as a Peelite Tory, had opposed them. Yet Gladstone's admirers liked to project an image of Gladstone's creativity in the making of the Liberal idea and of its finest principles, including his 'internationalism', which contrasts rather with his forward policies in Egypt, the Sudan, and South Africa, and which were opposed by Villiers and other Radicals. Moreover, Villiers' critique of 'Gladstonism' after 1886 gives credence to Lord Randolph Churchill's famous assertion that by this time Gladstone was very much 'an old man in a hurry',[7] a view endorsed by Gladstone's most recent biographer, Ian St. John.[8]

Nevertheless, Charles Villiers' 'desertion' of the Liberal Party in 1886 should not detract from his immense contribution to parliamentary life during his long career. As a member of important parliamentary select committees, he was invariably diligent and conscientious and, as a chairman, scrupulously impartial. Of greater importance, however, was the concern for the well-being of the British people, which characterised many of his speeches in the House of Commons. As Justin McCarthy observed, Villiers was motivated by 'a sincere and unvarying desire to improve the conditions of existence for the poor and the dependent', and he held fast throughout his life to the reforming principles he had first outlined to his constituents in Wolverhampton in 1835, displaying 'a marvellous power of arraying telling arguments, and of compelling the attention even of the most listless and the least sympathetic audience' in the process.[9] Moreover, most of the reforming causes he fought for in his youth – Catholic emancipation, parliamentary reform, universal male suffrage, Corn Law repeal, Free Trade, postal reform, Poor Law reform, the abolition of slavery, and the provision of popular education – were actually achieved during his lifetime, whilst women's suffrage, which he supported later in life, was achieved after his death. Indeed, as Henderson observed, the reforms which Villiers helped to bring about 'lightened the cares of thousands who hardly knew his name'.[10] Indeed, in this context, Charles Pelham Villiers made a difference.

Yet, whilst Villiers was sympathetic to the working classes, he was never of them and, apart from his visits to Wolverhampton, rarely lived among them, although it was known to many of his friends that he privately made quiet visits to the poorer districts of London in order to gain some practical knowledge of the ways and the lives of the inhabitants.[11] His life was largely ensconced in Westminster and London's aristocratic society, where he felt comfortable, and which also helps to explain why he declined ambassadorial opportunities abroad. In his Wolverhampton constituency, Villiers worked closely and conscientiously with his fellow Liberal MPs, most notably Thomas Thorneley and Thomas Weguelin, although his relationship with Henry Fowler appears to have been less harmonious after 1886. Yet his initial attitude to his Wolverhampton constituents, which in part reflected the right of a privileged man to become an MP, in some respects displayed all the hallmarks of youthful arrogance. Nevertheless, Villiers, regarded initially as an aristocratic 'outsider', developed both a genuine affection for, and an excellent rapport with, this largely working-class constituency, albeit at a time when constituency associations were increasingly selecting local men as parliamentary candidates.[12] This respect was reciprocated in equal measure, and Wolverhampton – where he was returned unopposed on all but four occasions – became one of the safest Liberal seats in the country, despite the fact that prolonged bouts of ill-health prevented him from visiting the town after 1875. Here, perhaps, the comparison with John Bright is not without significance, for, as Roland Quinault has shown, Bright too only paid rare and short visits to his Birmingham constituency in his later career, yet that, if anything, increased his popularity in the borough.[13] Both Villiers and Bright (who also turned to Liberal Unionism after 1886) benefited from the hero status accorded to the fathers of Free Trade in the later Victorian period, which may well have reflected growing contemporary concerns with the revival of Protectionism in the Conservative Party.

Yet Villiers' fundamental paternalism, reflecting his aristocratic background and upbringing, never really deserted him, as his political language illustrated. David Cannadine has suggested that Victorian politicians talked constantly in the language of class, which was synonymous with the language of hierarchy (and therefore of social stability), although there was also a darker, more fearful meaning attached to the term 'class', as something divisive and potentially socially disruptive, which explains why many politicians were also at pains to emphasise the need for social harmony.[14] Villiers was no exception to this. As Dorothy Thompson noted, Villiers' speeches suggest that his concept of 'the people' was essentially selective, embracing variously the disenfranchised, the working classes, and the lower orders,[15] and as he once observed,

> the people, being neither Whig nor Tory, were disposed to think that the monopolies springing out of what they termed 'class legislation' had so far exhausted their means and restricted their energies as to be answerable for the decline of this great industrial nation.[16]

Thus, in his general approach to politics, Villiers consistently emphasised inclusiveness as opposed to class conflict, asserting that 'We should all march together and not divide society into hostile classes believing that causes for permanent antagonism exist'.[17] This was, in itself, a legacy of his upbringing during the Napoleonic Wars in the shadow of the French Revolution, and reflected Villiers' fundamental fear of the revolutionary potential of the masses. In consequence, although he once advocated 'the brickbat' argument during the struggle for the repeal of the Corn Laws (which was in itself partly a question of class relations), Charles Villiers favoured constitutionalism and gradualism in achieving his political objectives.

Villiers endured disappointments in his career, most notably the initial failure of the Anti-Corn Law League to acknowledge his role in 1846, his failure to achieve Ministerial status until 1859, and his exclusion from Gladstone's Cabinet in 1868, an event which effectively marked the end of his active political career by consigning him to the backbenches for a further thirty years. Indeed, Villiers' later career presents a salutary reminder of what politics looked like from the position of backbenchers, or of those worthy MPs who served in the constitutional system over a long period of time. Such men did not become the great 'political animals' of the Victorian governing jungle (who subsequently became a focal point for historical study) but they were, nonetheless, critical to the operation of Victorian public life.

Nevertheless, Villiers accepted his disappointments with stoicism and, though inclined towards cynicism and pessimism on political matters, he was renowned for a cheerful and convivial disposition in social circles. Despite advancing age and frequent illness, he continued to enjoy the camaraderie of life at Westminster and at his London Clubs, becoming a noted personality in London society, 'ill-dressed but witty, informed, civilized, at times mischievous, well loved in his family circle, and widely popular outside it'.[18] Writing in 1938 of Charles Villiers' elder brother, Lord Clarendon, in 1868 (shortly before his death in 1870), Clarendon's grandson, George Villiers, observed of his grandfather:

> A generation of statesmen was failing and a generation was rising – a generation brilliant but different, inspired by new standards and principles, faced with new problems ... And in this new orientation of things Clarendon had indeed no part. His politics were all of the past, and his principles were inspired by the great figures of the past who had been his friends and his associates. We picture him at this time – or, rather, in 1868 – an aristocratic old figure, tall but shrunken, failing a little in health; gay and irritable by turns as the gout approached or receded; but courteous and charming as ever ... and quite unaware that the old political summer was over ... a solitary bloom left over from more spacious days. A rising generation had already relegated him to the past.[19]

A very similar picture could be painted of Charles Villiers during the *fin de siècle* years of the 1890s, although he was by now frailer and much older than Clarendon had been in 1868. As 'Father of the House of Commons', Villiers remained a man of principle, integrity and honesty, always loyal to his friends, who still clung to the Liberal and Radical beliefs and values of his youth and who carried his Benthamite principles, garnered during the Regency period, to the grave. Indeed, his consistency was remarkable. As W.H. Greenleaf once observed, one should never assume consistency and uniformity in political behaviour, for politicians get older and face changing circumstances,[20] yet whilst Charles Villiers mellowed in private,[21] becoming a kindly and much-loved figure within family circles, in public he remained true to his political principles. Admirable though this may well have been (as his numerous obituaries testify), Villiers was now out of step with a changing world. He, like John Bright, was an 'old' Radical, for his radicalism belonged to the 1830s and 1840s rather than to the 1890s, as illustrated by his suspicion both of 'new' Radicals like Chamberlain, whose 'Advanced Liberalism', emphasising greater state intervention in social policy, he had little sympathy for, and of socialists, whose creed, which he regarded as divisive, he detested.[22] In a sense, and somewhat paradoxically, Villiers, once a great champion of reform, had become an anachronism in a new age of progress, which may well explain occasional contemporary descriptions of him as an 'Old Whig'. Such descriptions were both unfair and misleading, and should be understood in the relative contexts of the times. Indeed, although Villiers no longer spoke in the House of Commons, his frequently insightful letters to William McIlwraith, not to mention his address to the Cobden Club in 1896, indicate that in private he retained a lively interest in contemporary politics at home and abroad during his declining years, when, as Anthony Howe has shown, Villiers was more important as a political symbol of the great Liberal victories of the past than as an active participant in the Commons, and was revered as such both within Parliament and without.[23]

Charles Villiers remains a somewhat distant and elusive figure, neglected by and not easily accessible to scholars of the Victorian period. Yet his life and work provide a unique window not only on the 'Condition of England' Question and responses to it but also on the Victorian political world and political culture, and especially Victorian Liberalism, with its shifting allegiances, perceptions and priorities. For his unstinting and principled support for radical causes, for his immense contribution to the free trade movement, for his considerable, if understated, contribution to the administration and development of the poor law, and – as the longest serving Member of Parliament in British history – for his remarkable contribution to parliamentary life over a period of sixty-three years, Charles Pelham Villiers merits much more than the occasional footnote in Victorian historiography.

Notes

1 See also Henderson, *History*, 39.
2 Bright served as President of the Board of Trade for two years (1868–70) in Gladstone's First Ministry and as Chancellor of the Duchy of Lancaster for two years (1880–2) in Gladstone's Second Ministry, resigning from office on both occasions.
3 Henderson, *History*, 38.
4 *St James's Gazette*, 17 Jan. 1898. Walter Bagehot had made a similar observation of Villiers' entry into politics: see W. Bagehot, 'Politics as a Profession', *The Economist*, 17 Jun. 1865, 33–8.
5 Ibid.
6 Shannon, *Gladstone: Heroic Minister*, 3–5.
7 W.S. Churchill, *Lord Randolph Churchill*, 860.
8 Ian St. John, *Gladstone and the Logic of Victorian Politics* (London, 2010), 344.
9 McCarthy, *A History of Our Own Times*, IV, 234–37.
10 Henderson, *History*, 39.
11 McCarthy, *A History of Our Own Times*, IV, 237.
12 Trainor, 'Conflict, Community and Identity', in Doyle (ed.), *Urban Politics and Space in the Nineteenth and Twentieth Centuries*, 42.
13 Roland Quinault, 'John Bright and Joseph Chamberlain', *The Historical Journal*, 28 (1985), 639–45.
14 David Cannadine, *Class in Britain* (London, 1998), 98–9.
15 Dorothy Thompson, 'Who were "the People" in 1842?', in M. Chase and I. Dyke (eds), *Living and Learning: Essays in Honour of J.F.C. Harrison* (Aldershot, 1996), 118–132. For further discussion of the language of class, see especially Asa Briggs, 'The Language of "Class" in Early Nineteenth-Century England', in A. Briggs and J. Saville (eds), *Essays in Labour History* (London, 1967), 43–73; Gertrude Himmelfarb, *The Idea of Poverty: England in the Early Industrial Age* (London and Toronto, 1984), 288–306; Dorothy Thompson, 'The Languages of Class', in S. Roberts (ed.), *The Dignity of Chartism: Essays by Dorothy Thompson* (London, 2015), 13–20.
16 Villiers, *Free Trade Speeches*, 322.
17 Cited in Cannadine, *Class in Britain*, 99.
18 Howe, 'Villiers, Charles Pelham', *ODNB*, 28286.
19 G. Villiers, *A Vanished Victorian*, 342.
20 W.H. Greenleaf, *The British Political Tradition* (2 vols, London, 1983), I, *The Rise of Collectivism*, 9–10.

21 As Lady Edith Villiers observed,

> In early life he was a little caustic, perhaps, and apt to sharpen his wit on the edged tool of sarcasm at the expense of his enemies; but this gave place, as years increased, to a quiet humour. 'Grey hairs bring milder moods', and no one could have talked to Mr Villiers latterly or have listened to his comments on a national or individual error without being struck by their leniency:
>
> *St James's Gazette*, 17 Jan. 1898

22 As the *Staffs Advertiser* observed, 'the new questions which have come to the front were not those especially congenial to a heriditary Whig trained in Benthamite Radicalism': *Staffs Advertiser*, 22 Jan. 1898.

23 Howe, 'Villiers, Charles Pelham', *ODNB*, 28286.

Bibliography

Primary Sources

Manuscripts

British Library of Political and Economic Science, GB0097R/SR1094, The Thornely-Villiers Correspondence, 1835–61.

The Bodleian Library, University of Oxford. Clarendon Papers, MS. Eng. c.2160, B.6. Letters to Lady Clarendon from Lord Clarendon's family, 1838–65, Fols. 1–17: Letters from C.P. Villiers.

The Gladstone Library, Hawarden. *Papers of the Prime Ministers of Great Britain*, Series 8: *The Papers of William Ewart Gladstone.* Correspondence with C.P. Villiers, 1851–96.

Manchester Archives and Local Studies, The George Wilson (1808–70) Papers, GB127. M20/3018–3036; Women's Suffrage Collection. Lydia Becker and the Manchester Society for Women's Suffrage. M50/1/2/31.

The National Archives, *Lord John Russell: Papers and Correspondence*, PRO 30/22.

University College London, Special Collections, Ogden MS 65: John Bright's letters to his wife, Margaret, 1847–78.

University of Nottingham, Manuscripts and Special Collections: Mellish Family Biographies: William Mellish (1764–1838).

University of Southampton. Special Collections. The Palmerston Papers. MS62.

Wolverhampton Archives and Local Studies. DX-60/1–15. Letters addressed to William McIlwraith, mainly from the Right Hon. Charles Pelham Villiers, MP, 1884–98.

Parliamentary Debates

Hansard, *Parliamentary Debates*, Third Series (1830–91).

Parliamentary Papers

First Report of the Select Committee on Sugar and Coffee Planting, together with Minutes of Evidence and Appendix (1848).

First and Third Reports from the Select Committee on Postage, together with Minutes of Evidence, Appendix and Index (1837–8), 278, XX. Part I.

304 Bibliography

Report from His Majesty's Commissioners for Inquiring into the Administration and Practical Operation of the Poor Laws: Appendix (A), Reports of Assistant Commissioners, Part II (1834), No. 23., Report from C.P. Villiers, Esq., 1–82.
Report of the Select Committee on Import Duties (1840), V.
Report from the Select Committee on Payment of Wages, together with Minutes of Evidence, Appendix and Index, (1843), 38.
Report of the Select Committee on Public Houses (1852–3), 855, XXXVII.
Report of the Select Committee on Public Houses (1853–4), 367, XIV.
Report from the Select Committee on the Army before Sebastopol (1854–5), IX.
Report of the General Board of Officers appointed to Inquire into the Statements contained in the Reports of Sir John McNeil and Colonel Tulloch, and the evidence taken by them relative hereto, animadverting upon the conduct of certain officers on the General Staff, and others in the Army; Together with Minutes of Evidence taken by the Board; and an Appendix (1856), XXI.
Report from the Select Committee on Poor Relief (England), with Proceedings, Minutes of Evidence, Appendices and Index (1861), 180, IX.
Reports from the Select Committees on Poor Relief and Poor Removal, with Proceedings, Minutes of Evidence, Appendices and Indices: First Report (1862), 181, X; *Second Report* (1862), 321, X; (1862) *Third Report* (1862), 468, X.
Report from the Select Committees on Poor Relief and Poor Removal, with Proceedings, Minutes of Evidence, Appendices and Indices (1863), 383, VII.
Report from the Select Committees on Poor Relief and Poor Removal, with Proceedings, Minutes of Evidence, Appendices and Indices (1864), 349, IX.
Report from the Select Committee on the Law Respecting Conventual and Monastic Institutions (1871), VII.
Second Report from the Select Committee on Postage, together with Minutes of Evidence, Appendix and Index (1837–8), 658, XX. Part II.
The Wolverhampton Inquiry: Copy of the Minutes taken at Wolverhampton, XLVI (1835).

Electoral Handbills

DX-559/2/7, Handbill, 29 Dec. 1834. 'A Few plain words to the Electors of Wolverhampton', for Nicholson against Thornely and Villiers.
DX-584/5/7, Dec. 1834, Address supporting Nicholson and Thornely, true friends of the people, against Villiers, a wolf in sheep's clothing.
DX-584/5/4, Dec. 1834, Address stating Nicholson was a more fit and proper person than Villiers to be MP.
DX-584/5/10. Handbill. Address of Charles Villiers to the Electors of the Borough of Wolverhampton, 29 Dec. 1834.
DX-584/5/16. Handbill. Address supporting Charles Villiers.
DX-584/5/17. Handbill, Dec. 1834, Address supporting Charles Villiers – a friend to all Liberal measures, an enemy to all sinecures and pensions.
DX-559/2/10. Handbill, 30 Dec. 1834. Address: Parliament is Dissolved – for Villiers (and the Laurel).
DX-559/2/8, Handbill, 30 Dec. 1834, Address: 'Vilest and most malicious scandals', in support of Villiers.
DX-584/5/24. Handbill, Jan. 1835, Address from the Committees of Thornely and Villiers, giving their support as united they are invincible and must be victorious – they are the men!!
Wolverhampton Archives and Local Studies. DX-559/584.

Newspapers and Periodicals

Aberdeen Journal
The Annual Register
Bell's Life in London and Sporting Chronicle
Birmingham Daily Post
Birmingham Gazette
Birmingham Journal
Blackburn Standard
Brooklyn Daily Eagle
The Britannia
Caledonian Mercury
Clutha Leader
Dover Express
The Economist
Evening Telegraph
Fraser's Magazine
Glasgow Evening Telegraph
Glasgow Herald
The Graphic
Hertfordshire Express and General Advertiser
Hull Packet
Illustrated London News
International Herald Tribune
Isle of Wight Observer
Leamington Spa Courier
Leeds Mercury
Leicester Chronicle
London Daily News
London Gazette
London Standard
Manchester Courier
Manchester Times
Morning Post
Newcastle Courant
New York Times
Northern Echo
Northern Star
Nottinghamshire Guardian
Pall Mall Gazette
Portsmouth Evening News
Reynold's Newspaper
San Francisco Call
South Wales Echo
South Australian Times
The Spectator
Staffordshire Advertiser
The Star
St James's Gazette

The Strand Magazine
The Sunday Times
The Tablet
The Thames Star
The Times
Vanity Fair
Walsall Advertiser
Wolverhampton Chronicle
Wolverhampton Express & Star
Yorkshire Evening Post
Yorkshire Gazette

Contemporary Diaries, Letters, Memoirs and Tracts

Arnold, R.A., *History of the Cotton Famine* (London, 1865).
Aschrott, P.F., *The English Poor Law System: Past and Present* (London, 1888).
Bagehot, W., 'Politics as a Profession', *The Economist*, 17 June 1865, 33–8.
Barrington, Mrs Russell, *The Works and Life of Walter Bagehot* (London, 1915).
Barrow, J.H. (ed.), *The Mirror of Parliament, Second Series, Commencing with the Reign of Queen Victoria* (2 vols, London, 1838).
Benson, A.C. and Viscount Esher (eds), *The Letters of Queen Victoria* (3 vols, London, 1908).
Bisset, A., *Notes on the Anti-Corn Law Struggle* (London, 1884).
Blackburn, H., *Women's Suffrage: A Record of the Women's Suffrage Movement in the British Isles, with Biographical Sketches of Miss Becker* (Oxford, 1901).
Carlisle, H.E. *A Selection from the Correspondence of Abraham Hayward, Q.C., from 1834 to 1884* (2 vols, London, 1886).
Dasent, A.I., *"John Thadeus Delane, Editor of The Times": His Life and Correspondence* (2 vols, London, 1908).
Dicey, A.V., *England's Case against Home Rule* (London, 1886).
Disraeli, B., *Lord George Bentinck: A Political Biography* (London, 1852).
Douglas, George [8th Duke of Argyll], *Autobiography and Memoirs, 1823–1900* (2 vols, London, 1906).
Earle, C.W., *Memoirs and Memories* (London, 1911).
Fagan, L., *The Reform Club: Its Founders and Architect, 1836–1886* (London, 1887).
Fawcett, M.G., *The Life of the Right Hon. Sir William Molesworth* (London, 1901).
Fielding, K.J., Ryals, C de L., Campbell, I., Christiansen, A., and Sorenson, D., *The Collected Letters of Thomas and Jane Carlyle* (43 vols, Durham, N.C. and Edinburgh, 1970–2015); online edition, B. Kinser (ed.), *The Carlyle Letters Online* (2012).
Fitzmaurice, Lord Edmund, *The Life of Granville George Leveson Gower, Second Earl Granville, K.G., 1815–1891*, (2 vols, London, 1905).
Foot, M.R.D. (ed.), (vols 1–2); Foot, M.R.D. and Matthew, H.G.C. (eds), (vols 3–4); Matthew, H.G.C. (ed.), (vols 5–14). *The Gladstone Diaries* (14 vols, Oxford, 1968–94).
Fowler, E., *The Life of Henry Hartley Fowler, First Viscount Wolverhampton* (London, 1912).
Gardiner, A.G., *The Life of Sir William Harcourt* (London, 1923).

Glen, W. Cunningham., *Villiers' Union Chargeability Act, 1865; with an Introduction and Commentary; Also The Practice of Poor Removals, Adapted to the Removal of Union Poor* (London, 1868).
Grant, J., *St Stephens, or Pencillings of Politicians* (London, 1839).
Grote, Mrs H., *The Personal Life of George Grote* (London, 1878).
Gunn, J.A.W. and Wiebe, M.G. (eds), *Benjamin Disraeli Letters* (10 vols, Toronto, 1982–2014).
Harrison, F., *Autobiographical Memoirs* (2 vols, London, 1911).
Hawkins, A. and Powell, J. (eds), *The Journal of John Wodehouse, First Earl of Kimberley, for 1862–1902*. Camden Fifth Series, 9 (Cambridge, 1997).
Hill, R. and Hill, G.B., *The Life of Sir Rowland Hill and the History of the Penny Postage* (2 vols, London, 1880).
Henry, R., *Memoirs of Joseph Sturge* (London, 1864).
Howe, A. (ed.), *The Letters of Richard Cobden* (4 vols, Oxford, 2007–15).
Jenkins, T.A. (ed.), *The Parliamentary Diaries of Sir John Trelawny, 1858–1865*, Camden Fourth Series, 40 (London, 1990).
Laughton, J.K. (ed.), *Memoirs of the Life and Correspondence of Henry Reeve* (2 vols, London, 1898).
Leach, Sir J., *Reports of Cases decided in the High Court of Chancery* (London, 1843), 138–47: Mellish v Mellish.
Leader, R.E. (ed.), *The Life and Letters of John Arthur Roebuck* (London, 1897).
Lewis, G.F., *Letters of the Right Hon. Sir George Cornewall Lewis, Bart. to Various Friends* (London, 1870).
Levenson, J., Sammels, E., Vandersee, C., and Winner, V. (eds), *The Letters of Henry Adams, 1858–92* (3 vols, Cambridge, MA, 1982).
Lucy, H.W., 'From Behind the Speaker's Chair', II, *The Strand Magazine*, vol. 5 (January–June, 1893), 202.
Lucy, H.W., 'From Behind the Speaker's Chair', XIII, *The Strand Magazine*, vol. 7 (January–June, 1894), 388.
Lucy, H.W., 'From Behind the Speaker's Chair', XVI, *The Strand Magazine*, vol. 8 (July–December, 1894), 39–40.
Lucy, H.W., *A Diary of the Unionist Parliament, 1895–1900* (London, 1901).
Lucy, H.W., *Later Peeps at Parliament: From Behind the Speaker's Chair* (London, 1905), 261–4.
McCarthy, J., *A History of Our Own Times: From the Diamond Jubilee, 1897, to the Accession of King Edward VII* (London, 1905).
McDonald, L. (ed.), *The Collected Works of Florence Nightingale*, (6 vols, Waterloo, Ontario, 2002).
Martineau, H., *History of the Thirty Years Peace* (London, 1877).
Maxwell, Sir H., *The Life and Letters of George William Frederick, Fourth Earl of Clarendon* (2 vols, London, 1913).
Mill, J.S., *Autobiography* (London, 1873).
Moneypenny, W.F. and Buckle, G.E., *The Life of Benjamin Disraeli, Earl of Beaconsfield* (6 vols, London, 1910–20).
Morley, J., *The Life of Richard Cobden* (London, 1879).
Morrison, J.C., *Macaulay* (London, 1882).
Nash, T.A., *The Life of Richard Lord Westbury, formerly Lord High Chancellor* (2 vols, London, 1888).

O'Reilly, J.B., 'The Coercion Bill', *North American Review*, 144, 366 (May 1887), 528–39.
Prentice, A., *History of the Anti-Corn Law League* (2 vols, London, 1853).
Proceedings of the Anti-Slavery Convention (London, 1841).
Queen Victoria's Journals, 1832–1901 (Oxford and London, 2012), Online (https://www.queenvictoriasjournals.org).
Ramm, A. (ed.), *The Gladstone–Granville Correspondence* (Cambridge, 1998).
Rathbone, E.F., *William Rathbone: A Memoir* (London, 1905).
Reid, S.J., *Lord John Russell* (London, 1895).
Reeves, H. (ed.), *The Greville Memoirs* (London, 1896).
Redding, C., *Fifty Years' Recollections, Literary and Personal, with Observations on Men and Things* (3 vols, London, 1858).
Richard, H., *Memoirs of Joseph Sturge* (2 vols, London, 1865).
Rueben [Alexander Somerville], *A Brief History of the Rise and Progress of the Anti-Corn Law League, with Personal Sketches of its Leading Members* (London, 1845).
Russell, G.W.E., *Collections and Recollections* (London, 1903).
Russell, Lord John., *Recollections and Suggestions, 1813–1873* (London, 1875).
Robertson, W., *The Life and Times of John Bright* (London, 1877).
Simms, R. (ed.), *Bibliotheca Staffordiensis* (Lichfield, 1894).
Smyth, E.C., *Sir Rowland Hill: The Story of a Great Reform, told by his Daughter* (London, 1907).
Somerville, A., *The Whistler at the Plough: Containing Travels, Statistics and Descriptions of Scenery & Agricultural Customs in most Parts of England* (1852, reprinted London, 1989), with an introduction by K.D.M. Snell.
Stephen, L.S. and Lee, S. (eds), *Dictionary of National Biography*, LVIII (1899): 'Villiers, Charles Pelham', 318–23.
Taylor, Sir H., *Autobiography* (London, 1865).
Taylor, W.C., *Life and Times of Sir Robert Peel* (London, 1849).
Torrens, W.T.M., *Lancashire's Lesson: or the Need of a settled Policy in Times of Exceptional Distress* (London, 1864).
Trevelyan, Sir G., *Life and Letters of Lord Macaulay* (2 vols, London, 1876).
Trevelyan, G.M., *The Life of John Bright* (London, 1913).
Trumbull, M.M., *The Free Trade Struggle in England* (Chicago, 1892).
Villiers, C.P., *Speech of C.P. Villiers, Esq, M.P. at a Dinner given by the Constituency of Wolverhampton to the Representatives of that Borough, January 26, 1836* (Wolverhampton, 1836).
Villiers, C.P., *The Free Trade Speeches of the Right Hon. Charles Pelham Villiers, M.P., with a Political Memoir*. Edited by a Member of the Cobden Club (London, 1883).
Villiers, C.P. and the Cobden Club, *The Fiftieth Anniversary of the Repeal of the Corn Laws. The Full Official Report of the Cobden Club Banquet and Presentation to the Right Honourable Charles Pelham Villiers, M.P.* (London, 1896).
Vincent, J. (ed.), *The Diaries of Edward Henry Stanley, 15th Earl of Derby (1826–93) between 1878 and 1893* (Oxford, 2003).
Walling, R.A.J. (ed.), *The Diaries of John Bright* (New York, 1931).
Walpole, S., *The Life of Lord John Russell* (2 vols, London, 1889).
Watts, J., *The Facts of the Cotton Famine* (Manchester, 1866).
Wemyss Reid, T., *Richard Monckton Milnes, 1st Lord Houghton: Life, Letters and Friendships* (2 vols, London, 1890).
Wilson, P.W. (ed.), *The Greville Diary* (2 vols, London, 1927).

Secondary Sources

Books and Chapters in Books

Adburgham, A., *A Radical Aristocrat: Sir William Molesworth of Pencarrow and his Wife, Andalusia* (Padstow, 1990).

Adelman, P., *The Rise of the Labour Party, 1880–1945* (London, 1980).

Alison, K.J. (ed.), *Victoria County History, A History of the County of York East Riding*, vol. 1, *The City of Kingston-upon-Hull* (1969).

Anderson, G.M. and Collinson, R.D., 'Ideology, Interest Groups and the Repeal of the Corn Laws', in Cheryl Schonhardt-Bailey (ed.), *The Rise of Free Trade* (4 vols, London, 1997), IV, *Free Trade Reappraised: The New Secondary Literature*, 38–52.

Arnstein, W.L., *Protestant versus Catholic in Mid-Victorian England: Mr Newdegate and the Nuns* (Columbia, 1982).

Ashton, O. and Pickering, P., 'The Aristocrat of Chartism: William Stephen Villiers Sankey (1793–1860)' in Owen R. Ashton and Paul A. Pickering, *Friends of the People: Uneasy Radicals in the Age of the Chartists* (London, 2002), 55–80.

Ayers, G.M., *England's First State Hospitals and the Metropolitan Asylums Board and its Work, 1867–1930* (London, 1971).

Balgarnie, F., 'The Women's Suffrage Movement in the Nineteenth Century', in Brougham Villiers (ed.), *The Case for Women's Suffrage* (London, 1907).

Barnsby, G.J., *Social Conditions in the Black Country, 1800–1900* (Wolverhampton, 1980).

Bebbington, D. and Swift, R. (eds), *Gladstone Centenary Essays* (Liverpool, 2000).

Bebbington, D., 'The Union of Hearts depicted: Gladstone, Home Rule and *United Ireland*', in D. George Boyce and Alan O'Day (eds), *Gladstone and Ireland*, 186–207.

Bebbington, D.W., *Unitarian Members of Parliament in the Nineteenth Century* (Stirling, 2009).

Biagini, E.F., *Liberty, Retrenchment and Reform: Popular Liberalism in the Age of Gladstone, 1860–1880* (Cambridge, 1992).

Biagini, E.F., *Gladstone* (London, 2000).

Biagini, E.F., 'Exporting 'Western & Beneficent Institutions': Gladstone and Empire, 1880–1885', in D. Bebbington and R. Swift (eds), *Gladstone Centenary Essays*, 202–25.

Biagini, E.F., *British Democracy and Irish Nationalism, 1876–1906* (Cambridge, 2007).

Blackett, R.J.M., *Divided Hearts: Britain and the American Civil War* (Baton Rouge, 2001).

Blake, R., *Disraeli* (London, 1966).

Boyce, D.G., *The Irish Question and British Politics, 1886–1996* (London, 1998).

Boyce, D.G., 'In the Front Rank of the Nation: Gladstone and the Unionists of Ireland, 1868–93', in D. Bebbington and R. Swift (eds), *Gladstone Centenary Essays*, 184–201.

Boyce, D.G. and O'Day, A. (eds), *Gladstone and Ireland: Politics, Religion and Nationality in the Victorian Age* (London, 2010).

Briggs, A., 'John Arthur Roebuck and the Crimean War', in A. Briggs (ed.), *Victorian People* (London, 1954), 60–94.

Briggs, A., 'Robert Lowe and the Fear of Democracy', in A. Briggs (ed.), *Victorian People*, 240–71.

Briggs, A., *The Age of Improvement* (London, 1959).

Briggs, A., 'The Language of 'Class' in Early Nineteenth-Century England', in A. Briggs and J. Saville (eds), *Essays in Labour History* (London, 1967), 43–73.
Brighton, P., *Original Spin: Downing Street and the Press in Victorian Britain* (London, 2016).
Brock, M., *The Great Reform Act* (London, 1973).
Brooks, D., 'Gladstone's Fourth Administration, 1892–1894', in D. Bebbington and R. Swift (eds), *Gladstone Centenary Essays*, 223–42.
Brown, D., *Palmerston: A Biography* (Yale, 2012).
Brown, L., 'The Chartists and the Anti-Corn Law League', in Asa Briggs (ed.), *Chartist Studies* (London, 1954), 342–71.
Browne, H., *The Rise of British Trade Unions, 1825–1914* (London, 1980).
Brundage, A., *The Making of the New Poor Law: The Politics of Inquiry, Enactment and Implementation, 1832–39* (London, 1978).
Brundage, A., *The English Poor Laws, 1700–1930* (Basingstoke, 2002).
Burk, K., *Old World, New World: The Story of Britain and America* (London, 2007).
Campbell, D., *English Public Opinion and the American Civil War* (Woodbridge, 2003).
Cannadine, D., *The Decline and Fall of the British Aristocracy* (London, 1992).
Cannadine, D., *Class in Britain* (London, 1998).
Carnegie, A., *The Autobiography of Andrew Carnegie* (London, 1920).
Cash, B., *John Bright: Statesman, Orator, Agitator* (London, 2012).
Cawood, I., *The Liberal Unionist Party: A History* (London, 2012).
Chaloner, W.H., 'The Agitation against the Corn Laws', in J.T. Ward (ed.), *Popular Movements, c.1830–1850* (London, 1970), 135–51.
Chamberlain, M.E., *British Foreign Policy in the Age of Palmerston* (London, 1980).
Churchill, W.S., *Lord Randolph Churchill* (London, 1907).
Clark, C., *The Sleepwalkers: How Europe went to War in 1914* (London, 2013).
Coohill, J., *Ideas of the Liberal Party: Perceptions, Agendas and Liberal Politics in the House of Commons, 1832–52* (Chichester, 2011).
Cook, Sir Edward, *The Life of Florence Nightingale* (2 vols, London, 1913).
Crosby, T.L., *Joseph Chamberlain: A Most Radical Imperialist* (London and New York, 2011), 76.
Daly, M.E. and Hoppen, K.T. (eds), *Gladstone: Ireland and Beyond* (Dublin, 2011).
David, S., *Victoria's Wars: The Rise of Empire* (London, 2006).
Davidoff, L., *The Best Circles: Society Etiquette and the Season* (London, 1973).
Dunbabin, J.P.D., 'Electoral Reforms and their Outcome in the United Kingdom, 1865–1900', in T.R. Gourvish and Alan O'Day (eds), *Later Victorian Britain, 1867–1900* (London, 1988).
Dunkley, P., *The Crisis of the Old Poor Law in England, 1795–1834* (London, 1982).
Edsall, N.C., *Richard Cobden: Independent Radical* (Cambridge, MA, and London, 1986).
Englander, D. and O' Day, R., *Retrieved Riches: Social Investigation in Britain, 1840–1914* (Aldershot, 1995).
Englander, D., *Poverty and Poor Law Reform in Nineteenth-Century Britain, 1834–1914: From Chadwick to Booth* (Abingdon, 1998).
Escott, M., 'Liverpool Borough', in D.R. Fisher (ed.), *The History of Parliament: The House of Commons, 1820–1832* (Cambridge, 2009).
Evans, E., *The Forging of the Modern State: Early Industrial Britain, 1783–1870* (1983).
Evans, E., *The Great Reform Act of 1832* (London, 1983).

Evans, E., 'The Strict Line of Political Succession? Gladstone's relationship with Peel: An Apt Pupil?', in D. Bebbington and R. Swift (eds), *Gladstone Centenary Essays*, 29–56.
Finer, S.E., 'The transmission of Benthamite ideas, 1820–50', in G. Sutherland (ed.), *Studies in the Growth of Nineteenth Century Government* (1972), 11–32.
Fisher, D.R., 'Villiers, Thomas Hyde (1801–1832)', in D.R. Fisher (ed.), *The History of Parliament: the House of Commons, 1820–1832* (Cambridge, 2009).
Fraser, D., 'The Agitation for Parliamentary Reform', in J.T. Ward (ed.), *Popular Movements c.1830–1850* (London, 1970), 31–53.
Garrard, J., 'Parties, Members and Voters after 1867', in T.R. Gourvish and Alan O'Day (eds), *Later Victorian Britain*, 127–50.
Garvin, J.L., *The Life of Joseph Chamberlain* (3 vols, London, 1933).
Gash, N., *Politics in the Age of Peel* (London, 1953).
Gash, N., *Aristocracy and People, 1815–1865* (London, 1979).
Gaunt, R., 'Gladstone and Peel's Mantle', in Roland Quinault, Roger Swift and Ruth Clayton Windscheffel (eds), *William Gladstone*, 31–50.
Ginswick, J. (ed.), *Labour and the Poor in England and Wales, 1849–1851*, (5 vols, London, 1983).
Gladstone, W., *Gladstone: A Bicentenary Portrait* (Norwich, 2009).
Goodlad, G., 'British Liberals and the Irish Home Rule Crisis: the dynamics of division', in D. George Boyce and A. O'Day (eds), *Gladstone and Ireland*, 86–109.
Grainger, J.H., *Character and Style in English Politics* (Cambridge, 1969).
Grampp, W.D., *The Manchester School of Economics* (Stanford and Oxford, 1960).
Green, D.R., *Pauper Capital: London and the Poor Law, 1790–1870* (Farnham, 2010).
Greenleaf, W.H., *The British Political Tradition* (2 vols, London, 1983).
Griffin, C.J., *The Rural War: Captain Swing and the Politics of Protest* (Manchester, 2012).
Halevy, E., *A History of the English People in the Nineteenth Century* (6 vols, London, 1927).
Hall, C., McLelland, K. and Rendall, J., *Defining the Victorian Nation: Class, Race, Gender and the British Reform Act of 1867* (Cambridge, 2000).
Hallett, C., 'Nursing, 1830–1920: Forging a Profession', in Anne Borsay and Billie Hunter (eds), *Nursing and Midwifery in Britain since 1700* (Basingstoke, 2012).
Hammond, J.L. and B., *The Town Labourer* (London, 1917).
Hammond, J.L. and B., *The Bleak Age* (London, 1934).
Hammond, J.L., *Gladstone and the Irish Nation* (London, 1938).
Harrison, B., *Drink and the Victorians: The Temperance Question in England, 1815–1872* (London, 1971).
Hawkins, A., *Victorian Political Culture: 'Habits of Heart and Mind'* (Oxford, 2015).
Heffer, S., *High Minds: The Victorians and the Birth of Modern Britain* (London, 2013).
Henderson, W.O., *The Lancashire Cotton Fame, 1861–65* (Manchester, 1934).
Henderson, W.O., *Charles Pelham Villiers and the Repeal of the Corn Laws* (Oxford, 1975).
Hewitt, O.W., *Strawberry Fair: A Biography of Frances, Countess of Waldegrave, 1821–1879* (London, 1956).
Hibbert, C., *The Destruction of Lord Raglan: A Tragedy of the Crimean War, 1854–55* (London, 1961).
Hilton, B., *The Age of Atonement: The Influence of Evangelicalism on Social and Economic Thought, 1785–1865* (Oxford, 1998).

Himmelfarb, G., *The Idea of Poverty: England in the Early Industrial Age* (London and Toronto, 1984).
Hinde, W., *Richard Cobden: A Victorian Outsider* (New Haven and London, 1987).
Hobsbawm, E.J. and Rude, G., *Captain Swing* (London, 1969).
Hobsbawm, E.J., *The Age of Empire, 1875–1914* (London, 1987).
Hollis, P. (ed.), *Pressure from Without in Early Victorian England* (London, 1974).
Horn, P., *Children's Work and Welfare, 1780–1890* (Cambridge, 1994).
Howe, A.C., *Free Trade and Liberal England* (Oxford, 1997).
Howe, A.C. and Morgan, S. (eds), *Re-thinking Nineteenth Century Liberalism* (2007).
Howkins, A., *Reshaping Rural England: A Social History, 1850–1925* (London, 1991).
Huzzey, R., 'Gladstone and the Suppression of the Slave Trade', in Roland Quinault, Roger Swift and Ruth Clayton Windscheffel (eds), *William Gladstone: New Studies and Perspectives* (Farnham, 2012), 253–66.
Jackson, P., *Harcourt and Son: A Political Biography of Sir William Harcourt, 1827–1904* (New Jersey, 2004).
Jenkins, R., *Gladstone* (London, 1995).
Jenkins, T.A., *Gladstone, Whiggery and the Liberal Party, 1874–1886* (Oxford, 1988).
Jenkins, T.A., *Parliament, Party and Politics in Victorian Britain* (Manchester, 1996).
Jones, W.H., *The Story of the Municipal Life of Wolverhampton* (London, 1903).
Jones, G.W., *Borough Politics: A Study of the Wolverhampton Town Council, 1888–1960* (London, 1969).
Jordan, D. and Pratt, E., *Europe and the American Civil War* (Oxford, 1931).
Jordan, J., 'The English Delilah: Katharine O'Shea and Irish Politics, 1880–1891', in Roger Swift and Christine Kinealy (eds), *Politics and Power in Victorian Ireland* (Dublin, 2006), 69–83.
Kidd, A., *State, Society and the Poor in Nineteenth-Century England* (Basingstoke, 1999).
Kinealy, C., 'Peel, Rotten Potatoes and Providence: The Repeal of the Corn Laws and the Irish Famine', in A. Marrison (ed.), *Free Trade and its Reception, 1815–1960*, vol. 1, *Freedom and Trade* (London, 1989), 50–62.
Kinealy, C., 'Famine Queen or Faery?: Queen Victoria and Ireland', in Roger Swift and Christine Kinealy (eds), *Politics and Power in Victorian Ireland*, 21–53.
Kollar, R., *A Foreign and Wicked Institution?: The Campaign against Convents in Victorian England* (Cambridge, 2011).
Lamont-Brown, R., *Carnegie: The Richest Man in the World* (Stroud, 2005).
Lawrence, J., *Speaking for the People: Party, Language and Popular Politics in England, 1867–1914* (Cambridge, 1998), Part II, 'A Local Study: Wolverhampton, c.1860–1914', 73–162.
Lawrence, J., 'Popular Politics and the Limitations of Party: Wolverhampton, 1867–1900', in Eugenio Biagini and Alastair Reid (eds), *Currents of Radicalism: Popular radicalism, organised labour and party politics in Britain, 1850–1914* (Cambridge, 1991), 65–85.
Linehan, P., *St. John's College, Cambridge: A History* (Woodbridge, 2011).
Longmate, N., *The Workhouse* (London 1974).
Longmate, N., *The Breadstealers: The Fight against the Corn Laws, 1838–1846* (Hounslow, 1984).
Loughlin, J. (ed.), *Gladstone, Home Rule and the Ulster Question, 1882–93* (Dublin, 1986).
Lovett, D., *The Grove Story* (Watford, 1984).
Lubenow, W.C., *The Politics of Government Growth: Early Victorian Attitudes Toward State Intervention, 1833–1848* (Newton Abbot, 1971).

Lubenow, W.C., *Parliamentary Politics and the Home Rule Crisis: the British House of Commons in 1886* (Oxford, 1988).
Lucas, F., *Lord Glenesk and the Morning Post* (London, 1910).
Magnus, P., *Gladstone* (London, 1954).
Mander, G.P., *History of Wolverhampton* (Wolverhampton, 1960).
Martin, G., *The Cambridge Union and Ireland, 1815–1914* (Cambridge, 2000).
Mason, F., *The Book of Wolverhampton* (Wolverhampton, 1979).
Matthew, H.G.C., *Gladstone* (Oxford, 1997).
McCord, N., *The Anti-Corn Law League 1838–1846* (1958).
Mackay, T., *A History of the English Poor Law* (London, 1904).
MacRaild, D.M., *The Irish Diaspora in Britain, 1750–1939* (Basingstoke, 2011).
Maccoby, S., *English Radicalism, 1832–1852* (London, 1935).
Mandler, P., *Aristocratic Government in the Age of Reform: Whigs and Liberals, 1832–1852* (Oxford, 1990).
Milne-Smith, A., *London Clubland: A Cultural History of Gender and Class in Late-Victorian Britain* (London, 2011).
Moore, T., 'Anti-Gladstonianism and the pre-1886 Liberal Secession', in D. George Boyce and A. O'Day (eds), *Gladstone and Ireland*, 65–85.
Moore, J.R., *The Transformation of Urban Liberalism: Party Politics and Urban Governance in Late Nineteenth Century England* (Aldershot, 2006), 264–5.
Nardinelli, C., *Child Labour and the Industrial Revolution* (Bloomington, 1990).
Neal, F., 'The Famine Irish in England and Wales', in P. O'Sullivan (ed.), *The Irish World Wide*, vol. 6, *The Meaning of the Famine* (London, 1997).
Neal, F., 'The English Poor Law, the Irish migrant and the laws of settlement and removal, 1819–1879', in D. George Boyce and Roger Swift (eds), *Problems and Perspectives in Irish History since 1800* (Dublin, 2004), 95–116.
Nicholls, Sir G., *A History of the English Poor Law in Connection with the State of the Country and the Condition of the People* (London, 1904).
Norman, E.R., *Anti-Catholicism in Victorian England* (London, 1968).
O'Day, A., 'Gladstone and Irish Nationalism: Achievement and Reputation', in D. Bebbington and R. Swift (eds), *Gladstone Centenary Essays*, 163–83.
Parry, J.P., *The Rise and Fall of Liberal Government in Victorian Britain* (New Haven, 1993).
Paz, D.G., *The Politics of Working-Class Education in Britain, 1830–50* (Manchester, 1980).
Paz, D.G., *Popular Anti-Catholicism in Mid-Victorian England* (Stanford, 1992), 17–18.
Paz, D.G., 'Gladstone as Friend', in Roland Quinault, Roger Swift and Ruth Clayton Windscheffel (eds), *William Gladstone: New Studies and Perspectives* (Farnham & Burlington, VT., 2012), 129–54.
Pearce, E., *Reform!: The Fight for the 1832 Reform Act* (London, 2010).
Pickering, P.A. and Tyrell, A., *The People's Bread: A History of the Anti-Corn Law League* (London, 2000).
Political Economy Club Minutes of Proceedings, Roll of Members and Questions Discussed, 1821–1920 (London 1921).
Quinault, R., 'Joseph Chamberlain: A Reassessment', in T.R. Gourvish and Alan O'Day (eds), *Later Victorian Britain, 1867–1900* (London, 1988), 69–92.
Quinault, R., 'Democracy and the Mid-Victorians', in M. Hewitt (ed.), *An Age of Equipoise?: Reassessing Mid-Victorian Britain* (Aldershot, 2000), 109–21.
Quinault, R., 'Victorian Prime Ministers and Ireland', in Roger Swift and Christine Kinealy (eds), *Politics and Power*, 54–68.

Reynolds, K.D., 'Politics without Feminism: the Victorian Political Hostess', in C.C. Orr (ed.), *Wollstonecraft's Daughters: Womenhood in England and France, 1780–1920* (London, 1996), 94–108.

Reynolds, K.D., *Aristocratic Women and Political Society in Victorian Britain* (Oxford, 1998).

Rhodes, P., *The Loaded Hour: A History of the Express & Star* (Worcester, 1992).

Ridley, J., *Lord Palmerston* (London, 1970).

Roper, J., *Wolverhampton: The Early Town and its History* (Wolverhampton, 1966).

Rose, M.E., 'The Anti-Poor Law Agitation' in J.T. Ward (ed.), *Popular Movements, 1830–1850* (London, 1970), 78–94.

Rose, M.E., *The English Poor Law, 1780–1830* (Newton Abbot, 1971).

Rose, M.E., *The Relief of Poverty, 1834–1914* (London, 1972).

Royle, T., *Crimea: The Great Crimean War, 1854–56* (London, 1999).

Sanderson, M., *Education, Economic Change and Society in England, 1780–1870* (London, 1983).

Saunders, R., *Democracy and the Vote in British Politics, 1848–1868: The Making of the Second Reform Act* (Farnham, 2011).

Schonhardt-Bailey, C. (ed.), *Free Trade: The Repeal of the Corn Laws* (Bristol, 1996).

Schonhardt-Bailey, C., *From the Corn Laws to Free Trade: Interests, Ideas, and Institutions in Historical Perspective* (Cambridge, Ma., and London, 2006).

Shannon, R.T., 'Gladstone and Home Rule, 1886', in *Ireland after the Union* (Oxford, 1989), 45–59.

Shannon, R.T., *Gladstone: Heroic Minister, 1865–1898* (London, 1999).

Small, R.F., 'Free Trade Radicals, Education and Moral Improvement in Early Victorian England', in M. Shirley and T. Larson (eds), *Splendidly Victorian: Essays in Nineteenth and Twentieth Century British History* (London, 2001), 69–90.

Steele, E.D., *Palmerston and Liberalism, 1855–1865* (Cambridge, 1991).

Steinfeld, R.J., *Coercion, Contract and Free Labour in the Nineteenth Century* (Cambridge, 2001).

Swift, R., *Irish Migrants in Britain, 1815–1914: A Documentary History* (Cork, 2002).

Sykes, A., *The Rise and Fall of British Liberalism, 1776–1988* (London, 1997).

Taylor, M., *The Decline of British Radicalism, 1847–1860* (Oxford, 1995).

Temperley, H., 'Anti-Slavery' in P. Hollis (ed.), *Pressure from Without*, 27–51.

Thomas, H., *The Slave Trade: The Story of the Atlantic Slave Trade, 1440–1870* (London and New York, 1997).

Thomas, W., 'The Philosophic Radicals', in P. Hollis (ed.), *Pressure from Without*, 52–79.

Thompson, D., *Queen Victoria: The Woman, The Monarchy, and the People* (New York, 1990).

Thompson, D., 'Who were 'the People' in 1842?', in M. Chase and I. Dyck (eds), *Living and Learning: Essays in Honour of J.F.C. Harrison* (Aldershot, 1996), 118–32.

Thompson, D., 'The Languages of Class', in S. Roberts (ed.), *The Dignity of Chartism: Essays by Dorothy Thompson* (London, 2015), 13–20.

Thompson, E.P., *The Making of the English Working Class* (London, 1963).

Thorne, R.G., 'Villiers, Hon. George (1759–1827)', in R.G. Thorne (ed.), *The History of Parliament: the House of Commons, 1790–1820* (London, 1986).

Upton, C., *A History of Wolverhampton* (Wolverhampton, 2007).

Villiers, G., *A Vanished Victorian: Being the Life of George Villiers, Fourth Earl of Clarendon, 1800–1870* (London, 1938).

Webb, S. and B., *English Poor Law Policy* (London, 1910).
Webb, S. and B., *The History of Trade Unionism, 1666–1920* (London, 1920).
Wood, P., *Poverty and the Workhouse* (Stroud, 1991).
Woodham Smith, C., *Florence Nightingale,1820–1910* (London, 1950).
Woodham Smith, C., *The Reason Why* (London, 1957).

Journal Articles

Cox, D., '"The Wolves let loose at Wolverhampton": A Study of the South Staffordshire Election Riots, May 1835', *Law, Crime and History*, 2 (2011), 1–31.
Feheney, J.M., 'Towards Religious Equality for Catholic Paper Children, 1861–68', *British Journal of Educational Studies*, 31, 2 (1983), 141–53.
Foot, M.R.D., 'The Hawarden Kite', *Journal of Liberal Democrat History*, 20 (1998), 26–32.
Hamer, D.A., 'The Irish Question and Liberal Politics, 1886–1894', *Historical Journal*, 12 (1969), 511–32.
Henderson, W.O., 'Charles Pelham Villiers', *History*, 37 (1952), 25–39.
Heyck, T.W., 'Home Rule, Radicalism and the Liberal Party, 1886–95', *Journal of British Studies*, 13 (1974), 66–91.
Lawrence, J., 'The Complexities of English Progressivism: Wolverhampton Politics in the Early Twentieth Century', *Midland History*, 24 (1999), 147–66.
Lubenow, W.C., 'Irish Home Rule and the Great Separation of the Liberal Party in 1886: the Dimensions of Parliamentary Liberalism', *Victorian Studies*, 26 (1983), 161–80.
McDonald, L., 'Florence Nightingale A Hundred Years On: Who She Was and Who She Was Not', *Women's History Review*, 19, 5 (November, 2010), 721–40.
McDonald, L., 'Florence Nightingale as a Social Reformer', *History Today*, 56,1 (2006).
Mandler, P., 'The Making of the New Poor Law Redivivus', *Past and Present*, 117 (1987), 131–57.
Morgan, S., 'The Anti-Corn Law League and British Anti-Slavery in Transatlantic Perspective, 1838–1846', *The Historical Journal*, 52 (2009), 87–107.
Munden, A.F., 'The First Palmerston Bishop: Henry Montagu Villiers, Bishop of Carlisle, 1856–1860, and Bishop of Durham, 1860–61', *Northern History*, 26/1 (1990), 186–206.
Quinault, R., 'John Bright and Joseph Chamberlain', *The Historical Journal*, 28 (1985), 639–45.
Quinault, R., '1848 and Parliamentary Reform', *The Historical Journal*, 31, 4 (1988), 831–51.
Quinault, R., 'Gladstone and Disraeli: A Reappraisal of their Relationship', *History*, 91, 304 (2006), 557–76.
Quinault, R., 'Gladstone and Slavery', *The Historical Journal*, 52, 2 (2009), 363–83.
Swift, R., '"Another Stafford Street Row": Law, Order and the Irish Presence in Mid-Victorian Wolverhampton', *Immigrants & Minorities*, 3,1 (March 1984), 5–29.
West, J., 'Gladstone and Laura Thistlethwayte, 1865–1875', *Historical Research*, 80, 209 (2007), 368–92.
Woods, D.C., 'The Operation of the Master and Servant Act in the Black Country, *Midland History*, 7,1 (1982), 93–115.

***Online*: Oxford Dictionary of National Biography.** *http://www.oxforddnb.com.*

Baker, A., 'Hickman, Sir Alfred, first baronet (1830–1910), *ODNB*, 48625 (2004).
Beaver, S.A., 'Roebuck, John Arthur (1802–1864)', *ODNB*, 23945 (2004).
Brown, A., 'Lytton, Edward George Earle Lytton Bulwer, first Baron Lytton (1803–1873), *ODNB*, 17314 (2004).
Burroughs, P., 'Molesworth, Sir William, eighth baronet (1810–1855)', *ODNB*, 18902 (January 2008).
Cocks, R.C.J., 'Bethell, Richard, first Baron Westbury (1800–1873), *ODNB*, 2305 (May 2009).
Deane, P., 'McCulloch, John Ramsay (1789–1864)', *ODNB*, 17413 (2004).
Grimsditch, H.B. and Matthew, C., 'Lucy, Sir Henry William (1843–1924), Journalist', *ODNB*, 34626 (September 2004).
Hamburger, J., 'Alexander Somerville (1811–1885)', *ODNB*, 26016 (September 2004).
Hamburger, J., 'Grote, George (1794–1871)', *ODNB*, 11677 (May 2008).
Hamilton, G., 'Delane, John Thadeus (1817–1879)', *ODNB*, 7440 (September 2013).
Harris, J., 'Mill, John Stuart (1806–1873)', *ODNB*, 18711 (January 2012).
Harling, P., 'Hayward, Abraham (1801–1884)', *ODNB*, 12793 (2004).
Hawkins, A., 'Stanley, Edward George Geoffrey Smith, fourteenth Earl of Derby (1799–1869), prime minister', *ODNB*, 26265 (May 2009).
Howe, A.C., 'Villiers, Charles Pelham (1802–1898), Politician', *ODNB*, 28286 (October 2006).
Howe, A.C., 'Anti-Corn Law League (1839–1846)', *ODNB*, 42282 (May 2011).
Jenkins, R., 'Dilke, Sir Charles Wentworth, second baronet (1843–1911), writer and politician', *ODNB*, 32824 (2008).
Larsen, T., 'Fowler, Henry Hartley, first Viscount Wolverhampton (1830–1911)', *ODNB*, 33224 (May 2006).
Lee, S., 'Leader, John Temple (1810–1903)', rev. H.C.G. Matthew, *ODNB*, 34453 (January 2009).
Mandler, P., 'Lamb, William, second Viscount Melbourne (1779–1848)', *ODNB*, 15920 (January 2008).
Marsh, P., 'Chamberlain, Joseph (1836–1914)', *ODNB*, 32350 (September 2013).
Matthew, H.C.G., 'Gladstone, William Ewart (1809–1898)', *ODNB*, 10787 (May 2011).
Munden, A.F., 'Villiers, Henry Montagu (1813–1861)', *ODNB*, 28298 (2004).
Parry, J., 'Disraeli, Benjamin, Earl of Beaconsfield (1804–1881)', *ODNB*, 7689 (May 2011).
Potter, J., 'Hume, Joseph (1767–1844)', *ODNB*, 14147 (January 2008).
Prest, J., 'Peel, Sir Robert, second Baronet (1788–1850), prime minister', *ODNB*, 21764 (May 2009).
Prest, J., 'Russell, John [formerly Lord John Russell], first Earl Russell (1792–1878)', *ODNB*, 24325 (May 2009).
Pullen, J.M., 'Malthus, (Thomas) Robert (1766–1834)', *ODNB*, 17902 (May 2008).
Reger, M., Taylor, Sir Henry (1800–1886)', *ODNB*, 27030 (2004).
Smith, D.A., 'Lewis, Lady (Maria) Theresa (1803–1865), *ODNB*, 16595 (October 2006).
Smith, P., 'Cecil, Robert Arthur Talbot Gascoyne, third Marquess of Salisbury (1830–1903)', *ODNB*, 32339 (January 2011).
Spencer, H.J., 'Buller, Charles (1806–1848)', *ODNB*, 3913 (January 2008).

Steele, D., 'Temple, Henry John, third Viscount Palmerston (1784–1865), prime minister', *ODNB*, 27112 (May 2009).
Taylor, M., 'Cobden, Richard (1804–1865)', *ODNB*, 5741 (May 2009).
Taylor, M., 'Bright, John (1811–1889)', *ODNB*, 3421 (September 2013).
Turner, M., 'Thompson, Thomas Perronet (1783–1869), *ODNB*, 27280 (May 2009).
Tweedale, G., 'Carnegie, Andrew (1835–1919)', *ODNB*, 32296 (May 2012).

Theses

Cawood, I.J., 'The Lost Party: Liberal Unionism, 1886–1895', PhD thesis, University of Leicester (2009).
Ferris, W., 'The Liberal Unionist Party, 1886–1912', PhD thesis, McMaster University, Ontario (2008).
Hobbs, A., 'The Irish of Caribee Island: Wolverhampton's Irish District', MPhil thesis, University of Wolverhampton (2003).
Hook, A.J., 'Charles Pelham Villiers and the Anti-Corn Law League in the Black Country, 1836–1846', MA dissertation, Wolverhampton Polytechnic (1985).
Huffer, D.B.M., 'The Economic Development of Wolverhampton, 1750–1850', M.A. thesis, University of London (1957).
Lawrence, J., 'Party Politics and the People: Continuity and Change in the Political History of Wolverhampton, 1815–1914', PhD thesis, University of Cambridge (1989).
Levin, J., 'Much ado About Nothing: British Non-Intervention During the American Civil War', MA thesis, Department of History, University of Sydney (2000).
Smith, R., 'The Governance of Wolverhampton, 1848–1888', PhD thesis, University of Leicester (2001).
Swift, R.E., 'Crime, Law and Order in two English Towns during the early Nineteenth Century: The Experience of Exeter and Wolverhampton, 1815–1856', PhD thesis, University of Birmingham (1981).
Taylor, E., 'The Working Class Movement in the Black Country, 1863–1914', PhD thesis, University of Keele (1974).
Wright, R.A., 'Liberal Party Organisation and Politics in Birmingham, Coventry and Wolverhampton, 1886–1914, with particular reference to the development of Independent Labour Representation', PhD thesis, University of Birmingham (1977).

Index

Aberdeen, Lord 129
Addington, Henry 8
Adullamites 179, 180, 193
'Advanced Liberalism' 6, 158, 177, 236, 299
agriculture, depression in 272–3
Allowance system for the poor 18
Almond, Thomas 123
American Civil War 162
Anglican Church and the Established Church Bill 60
Anglo-French Commercial Treaty of 1860 191
Anglo-Russian Entente of 1907 274
Anson, George 37
Anti-Corn Law Association 80
Anti-Corn Law League 1, 4, 67, 70, 79, 191, 294, 295; not recognizing Charles Pelham Villiers' role 298; and repeal of Corn Laws 83–87, 90–91, 105–6
Anti-Slavery movement 61
anti-truck legislation 67–69
army being investigated during the Crimean War 135–40
Arrow (ship) captured by the Chinese 141
Asquith, Herbert 240
Association for the Improvement of the Infirmaries of London Workhouses 174

Bagehot, Walter 171
Balaclava, battle of 135, 136, 139
Balfour, Arthur 237, 286–7
Balgarnie, Florence 202
Ballot Bill 201
Barker, John 32, 42, 46, 68, 98, 119
Barker-Poutney dispute 67–68
Becker, Lydia 202
Bedchamber Crisis of May 1839 56
Benbow, John 42
Bentham, Jeremy 11

Benthamite principles 52, 54
Benthamite Radical 11, 294
Bentinck, George 125, 205
Berkeley, H. 136
Bethell, Richard 145, 179
Biagini, Eugenio 51, 232
Bissett, Andrew 98
Blackburn, Helen 202
Board of Trade 198
Boards of Guardians 23, 65, 161, 163–4, 167, 169, 173
Booth, Charles 273
Borthwick, Algernon 172
Borthwick, Peter 172
Bourke, Patrick 170
Bowring, John 141
Boyce, D. George 232
bread tax 79. *See also* Corn Laws
brewers and corruption in licensing system 130–4
Briggs, Asa 84, 121, 178
Bright, Jacob 202
Bright, John 1, 5, 98, 99, 106, 115, 129, 142, 176, 179, 203, 213, 234, 270, 297; and the Corn Laws 79, 80, 87; friendship with Charles Pelham Villiers 119, 121, 208–9; as President of the Board of Trade 198; Radical reform programme 121–3; supporting Villier's Resolutions on Free-Trade 103, 128
Brighton, Paul 171
British and Foreign Anti-Slavery Society 62–63
British and Foreign School's Society 71
Bromby, J. 13
Brooks, David 241
Brougham, Henry 10
Brown, David 141, 144
Brown, William 130

Browne, John 170
Brownlow Hill Workhouse Infirmary 172
Bulwer-Lytton, Constance Georgina (great-niece) 202
Burton, J. R. 42

Cambridge Union Society 10
Cannadine, David 271, 297
Canning, George 13, 196
Cardigan, Earl and Crimean War investigation 136, 139–40
Carlyle, Thomas 94, 104
Carnegie, Andrew 243–6, 248; friendship with William Gladstone 251–2
Caroline, queen of England 10
Catholic emancipation 4, 12, 15, 33, 105, 269
Catholicism 40, 199–203, 238, 252
Catholic Relief Act 15
Catholic Workhouse Committee 161–2
Cato Street Conspiracy of 1820 10
Cecil, Robert 194
Central Society of Education 71
Chadwick, Edwin 22, 66–67, 175
Chamberlain, Joseph 210, 231, 239, 240, 254, 269, 271, 280, 299
Charge of the Light Brigade 135, 136
Chartism 44
Chartist petitions 58–59
Chelsea Board 140
children, employment of 69–71
China capturing the *Arrow* (ship) 141
Churchill, Randolph 115, 296
Church of England 60
Church of Ireland 60–61
Clare, John 37
Clarendon, Lord 107, 117, 136, 142, 158–9, 196, 298. *See also* Villiers, George William Frederick (brother)
Clay, William 80
Coalition Ministry 129
Cobbett, William 51
Cobden, Richard 1, 4, 5, 64, 94, 96, 99, 100, 106, 107, 270, 295; on the American Civil War 162, 164; censuring China for capturing the *Arrow* (ship) 141; death of 166; and Free Trade 88–91, 103; high regard for Charles Pelham Villiers 115–17, 120; repeal of the Corn Laws 79, 80, 81, 83, 84, 87; unveiling of statue of 191–2
Complete Suffrage Union 58

conventual and monastic houses investigation 199–200
Coohill, Joseph 51
Cornewall Lewis, George 66, 67
Corn Laws 277, 281–3, 285; repeal of 2, 3, 4, 5, 19, 43, 73, 79–108, 294; 50th anniversary of its repeal 276–8
Corrupt and Illegal Practices Act 216
Coulson, George 12
Courtney, Leonard 276
Cowper, Lord 13
Cranborne, Lord 174
Crawford, Sharman 230
Crawford, William Sharman 58
Crimean War 5, 135–41
Criminal Law Amendment Act of 1871 202, 203

Daly, Timothy 172–3
Davies, Joseph 145
Delane, J. T. 172, 174, 192, 195
Derby's Ministry 126, 129
Dicey, A. V. 231
Dilke, Charles 208, 275
Disestablishment of the Irish Church 231
Disraeli, Benjamin 254; friendship with Charles Pelham Villiers 124–5; Reform Bill 145, 192–4; on Villiers' Resolutions on Free Trade 126–7
Dissenters 59–60
Dixon, George 201
Docking Union of Norfolk 169
Dual Alliance of 1894 274
Dual Parliaments proposal for Ireland and England 231, 234, 236, 239
Duke of Argyll 129

Earle, Maria Theresa (niece) 139, 202, 264
East Anglian Rising 9
Education Act of 1870 71, 201, 203
Elcho, Lord 136–7
electoral reform 176–7
employment of women and children 69–71
Entente Cordiale of 1904 274
Established Church Bill 60
Estcourt, Southeron 160
Evans, Eric 158
Express & Star (newspaper) 244–6, 249

Factory Act of 1833 69–70
Factory Act of 1844 70
factory reform 69–71

Factory Regulation Bill of 1836 70
fancy franchises 193
Farnall, H. B. 163, 173, 175
Fawcett, Millicent Garrett 54, 202
Fereday, Dudley 33, 35
Ferrand, William 66, 67, 92
First Reform Act of 1832 31
First Report of the Select Committee on Poor Relief 172
Fitzmaurice, Lord 196, 197
Fitzwilliam, Lord 83
foreign policy 141–2, 274–5
Fortesgue, Chichester 207
Foster, Charles 213
Fowler, Henry 193, 194, 210, 211, 213, 216–7, 242–3, 251, 253, 297
Fowler Reform Club 211, 246
Fox, W. J. 102
Franchise and Redistribution Bill 179
franchise reform 216
Free Trade 3–6, 40–41, 43, 52, 91, 103, 277–8, 280, 283, 294, 295
Free Traders 52, 116
Free Trade Speeches (Villiers) 2
Fryer, Richard 32, 33, 35, 44, 69, 80
Fryer, Richard Jnr. 32
Fuller, W. M. 246

George III, King 8
George IV, King 10
Gibbons, John Lloyd 286
Gibson, Milner 122
Giffard, T. W. 205
Gladstone, Herbert 231
Gladstone, William 63, 90, 99, 144, 167, 270, 296; cordial towards Charles Pelham Villiers in public 253–4; critical of Palmerston's government 141–2; defending the repeal of the Corn Laws 126–8; excluding Charles Pelham Villiers from his Cabinet 3, 195–7; friendship with Andrew Carnegie 251–2; Home Rule Bill 1, 231–2; last known correspondence with Charles Pelham Villiers 278–9; loss of support 202–3; 'New Departure' 231, 234, 235; offer to secure Charles Pelham Villiers a Grand Cross of the Bath 214–15; and the Parliamentary Reform Bill 5, 192; personal and political differences with Charles Pelham Villiers 6, 229–30; retirement of 202–3, 242; return to politics 210; sympathising with

South in the American Civil War 162; on Union Chargeability Bill 171; and universal male suffrage 177–9
Gladstone Papers 6
Gladstonism 296
Gladstonites 236, 238
Goodriche, Francis 37
Goschen, G. J. 196
Gough, R. D. 205
Gowling, Richard 276
Graham, Sir James 142; supporting Villiers' Resolutions on Free Trade 127
Graham, Thomas 243–8
Graham-Fuller campaign to replace Charles Pelham Villiers as Wolverhampton representative 246–51
Granville, Lord 196, 212–13
Great Reform Act 15
Greenleaf, W. H. 299
Greville, Charles 55, 58, 95, 103, 121; on death of Charles Pelham Villiers' mother 138–9
Grey, George 134–5, 142
Grey, Lord 103
Griffiths, Sam 179–80
Grote, George 34, 57, 71

Hammond, Barbara 182
Hammond, J. L. 9, 182
Harcourt, William Vernon 172, 182, 211, 239, 240
Hardy, Gathorne 172, 174–5
Hartington, Lord 203, 269
Hartley, John 159
Hawkins, Angus 55
Henderson, W. O. 2, 79
Herbert, Sidney 142
Hickman, Alfred 210, 217, 251
Hill, Henry 38–39
Hill, Rowland 63–64
Hill, Thomas Wright 8
Hilton, Boyd 16, 52
Hinde, Wendy 97
Hobsbawm, Eric 274
Hodgetts-Foley, Henry 193
Hogg, Gilbert 131–2
Holland, Lord 13
Home Rule Bill 1, 2, 6, 229–54, 283, 296 *See also* Irish Home Rule movement; passed by House of Commons 241–2; rejected by House of Lords 242
Home Rule crisis of 1886. *See* Home Rule Bill

Horner, Leonard 71
Howick, Lord 10
household suffrage 193, 216
House of Commons 4, 39; Charles Pelham Villiers as 'Father of the House of Commons' 263, 299; Charles Pelham Villiers speaking to 2; and the Corn Laws 80–82, 85, 87; and Irish Home Rule 231, 234–6; passing Home Rule Bill 241–2; reforming 56–58, 123, 126
House of Lords: and the Corn Laws 83, 89; and the Home Rule crisis 242; reform of 242, 271
Howe, Anthony 2, 79, 83, 118, 121, 299
Howkins, Alun 272
Huskisson's reforms 79
Huzzey, Richard 63

Imperialism 6, 217
Independent Labour Party 272
'Inquiry into the Supplies of the British Army in the Crimea' 139–40
Ireland: Charles Pelham Villiers' knowledge of and sympathy for 229–31; and the Home Rule Bill 229–54, 296; not benefiting from Home Rule 233–4
Irish Home Rule movement 1, 2, 6, 229–54, 296. *See also* Home Rule Bill
Irish paupers being removed from England to Ireland 169–71
Irish Universities Bill 202–3
Irremovable Poor Bill of 1861 167–8, 170
Issue of Exchequer Bill of May 1838 60–61

James, Henry 240
Jenkins, Roy 199
Jewish Disabilities Bill 124

Kay-Shuttleworth, James 212
Kingston-upon-Hull 11–12

labourers 15–16, 65–66, 161, 216; and the Corn Laws 83, 87, 92, 96; Irish 169–70; and the Poor Laws 18–21, 273
Lambert, Agnes 2, 115, 230
Lambert, John 177
Lancashire 'Cotton Famine' 2, 5, 163, 282
Land Act 238; of 1870 and 1881 231
Landsdowne, Lord 13
law reform 41
Lawrence, Jon 32, 46, 179, 202, 242

Laws of Settlement 22
Laws of Settlement and Removal 168
Leach, John 14
Leng, John 286–7
Lewis, Frankland 67
Lewis, George Cornewall 141, 160, 182, 230
Liberalism 53–54, 201, 242–7, 296
Liberal Party 5, 6; and parliamentary reform 177–8; split over the Home Rule Bill 229, 231, 235–9, 296
Liberals 51–52, 294; contesting Parliamentary Reform Bill 192; enmity between Liberal Unionists and 238–40; loss of support 203; and parliamentary reform 194–5; victory of 1880 210–11; in Wolverhampton 179–80
Liberal Toryism 4, 12, 23, 33; and the Corn Laws 79
Liberal Unionists 1, 6, 229, 236–7, 239, 250–2, 269, 294; enmity between Liberals and 238–40
Licensing Act of 1872 203
Licensing Bills 203
licensing system for public houses and beershops 130–4
Linney, Joseph 193
'Little Charter' 123
Local Government Bill 239
local government reform 59
London Statistical Society 11
Lowe, Robert 178; as Chancellor of the Exchequer 198
Lucan, Earl and Crimean War investigation 136–41
Lucas, Reginald 268
Lucy, Henry 241, 279, 286
Luddism 9

Macaulay, Thomas Babington 10
Maccoby, S. 122
MacGregor, John 86
Mackintosh, James 9
Major, J. C. 212
Malthus, Thomas 9
Manchester Anti-Corn Law Association 80, 82
Manchester Society for Women's Suffrage 202
Mandler, Peter 51
Manners, John 125
Martineau, Harriet 52, 83, 174
Mason, Frank 204

Mason, James 162
Master and Servant Act of 1867 202
Matthew, Colin 197, 231, 251
McBean, Alexander 284
McCarthy, Justin 215, 296
McCord, Norman 88
McCulloch, J. R. 10
McDonald, Lynn 175, 176
McIlwraith, William 2, 6, 211, 229–53, 265–75, 280–1
McNeil, John 139
Melbourne, Lord 53, 55, 56, 83, 85
Mellish, Catherine 4, 6, 13–14, 209–10
Mellish, John 13–14
Metropolitan Asylums Board 176
Metropolitan Common Poor Fund 176
Metropolitan Poor Law Act of 1867 172, 174–6
Militia Bill 126
Mill, James 11
Mill, John Stuart 10, 202
Milne-Smith, Amy 207
Miners' Federation of Great Britain's strike 272
Mines and Collieries Bill of 1842 70
Mingchin, Yeh 141
'Moderates' in Wolverhampton 32
Molesworth, Sir William 54, 71, 80, 129, 142
Molesworth, Lady Andalusia 207, 264
Morley, John 247
Morris, John 204
Municipal Corporations Act of 1835 59
municipal reform 41–42

National Liberal Federation 296
National Reform League 180
National Society 71
Newcastle Programme of 1891 273–4
Newdegate, Charles 199–200
New Poor Law 16, 65–66, 92, 160–1, 167, 295
'New Unionism' 272
Nicholls, George 66, 167–8
Nicholson, John 33, 35, 42
Nightingale, Florence 5, 135, 172–6, 212
Nonconformists 71, 201, 203
nursing, reforms in 172–4

O'Connell, Daniel 15, 61, 230
Old Poor Law 15–23
O'Neill, Christopher 12

Open Vestries 21
Outdoor Relief Regulation Order of 1852 163

Pakington, John 134
Palmerston, Lord 5, 128, 160, 166, 177; Amendment in favour of Free Trade 128; being criticised for his foreign policy 141–2; commissioning 'Inquiry into the Supplies of the British Army in the Crimea' 139–40; favoring neutrality during the American Civil War 162; forming second administration 147, 158; as Prime Minister 136; and public houses and beershops' licensing 135
Palmerstonian Centrism 158
Parish Councils Act of 1894 273
Parish Councils Bill 266
Parker, John (grandfather) 8
Parker, Theresa (mother). See Villiers, Theresa (mother)
Parkes, John 115–16
Parkes, William 180, 193
Parliamentary and Financial Reform Association 122
parliamentary reform 5, 57–59, 123, 176–81, 192–5, 216
Parliamentary Reform Bill 192–4
Parnell, Charles Stewart 231, 232, 233, 235
Parry, Jon 51
pauperism: reduction in 160; removal of Irish paupers from England to Ireland 169–71
Paz, Denis 200
Peel, Robert 56, 82, 87, 90, 99, 277; and the Corn Laws 103–7, 127
Peelites favoring duty on corn 126–9
Pender, John 209, 264
Pentrich Rising 9
Perpetual Crimes (Coercion) Bill 237–8
Peterloo massacre 9
Philips, Mark 95
Philosophic Radicals 4, 52–55
Pickering, Paul 83
Plowden, Margaret 248
Plowden, William 242
Political Economy Club 11
Political Memoir (Villiers) 2
Political Pensions Act 198–9
poor. *See also* poverty: aiding and providing relief to 15–18; irremovability of 167, 169; treatment of the sick 172–3

Poor Law Amendment Act of 1834
  22–23; repealing provision of the cost
  of poor relief 168
Poor Law Board 1, 5, 67, 160–2, 181–2,
  196, 212, 282
Poor Law Commissioners 66
Poor Law Reforms 1, 3
Poor Law Union fund 167
Poor Law Unions 23, 168
Poor Relief Act 1601. *See* Old Poor Law
postal duty 63–64
Post Office Reform 64
Potter, John 84
Pottinger, Henry 118
Poulett Thompson, Charles 34
Poutney, Humphrey 67–69
poverty 19–21, 65–66, 160, 169–70, 178
  See also poor; metropolitan/urban 5,
  15–16, 172, 273
Prentice, Archibald 80
Protectionists 101, 104–5; favoring duty
  on corn 126–8; and the repeal of the
  Corn Laws 85–86
Protestantism 40
public houses and beershops' licensing
  corruption 130–4
Public Works (Manufacturing Districts)
  Bill 165, 166

Queen Caroline affair of 1820 10
Quinault, Roland 63, 176, 254, 297

Radicals 51, 52–55; in Palmerston's
  cabinet 158; in Wolverhampton 32
Raglan, Lord and Crimean War
  investigation 136–8
Rathbone, William 172
Rawlinson, Robert 164–5, 166, 167
Reciprocity of Duties Act of 1823 79
Redistribution of Seats Act of 1885 216
Reeve, Henry 107
Reform Act of 1832 51, 55, 56, 57
Reform Act of 1867 193–4
Reform Bill 5, 58, 145, 179–80
Reform Club 54, 55
Reformers 51, 52
Reform League of 1865 177
Reform Union 177
Refreshment Houses and Wine Licenses
  Bill 135
Reid, Stuart J. 129
religious liberty 59–61
religious teaching in schools 201

Representation of the People Act of
  1884 216
Reynolds, Karen 207
Rhodes, Cecil 275
Richard, Henry 61
Richardson, George 86
Ridley, Jasper 168
Robbins, Keith 121
Roe, Frederick 37
Roebuck, John Arthur 52, 55, 63, 66,
  122, 136
Romilly, John 34
Rose, Michael 176
Rosebery, Lord 275
Rothschild, Lionel Nathan de 124, 207–8
Russell, G. W. 13, 268
Russell, Lord John 15, 37, 63, 71,
  82, 115–17, 142, 144; and the
  Corn Laws 83, 87, 102; as Foreign
  Secretary 158–9; Irish reforms 230;
  parliamentary reform 55, 58–60,
  176–80; resignation of 180; supporting
  Villiers' Resolutions on Free Trade
  127; and universal male suffrage 177
Russell, William Howard 135

Sale of Beer (Sunday) Act 134
Salisbury, Lord 275
Salomons, David 124
Saunders, Robert 123, 124
Schnadhorst, Francis 247
Schonhardt-Bailey, Cheryl 79, 84, 105
Sebastopol Russian naval base 135, 138
secret ballot 57–58, 201
Select Committee of the House of
  Commons on Public Houses 130–5
Select Committee on Conventual and
  Monastic Institutions 6, 199–200
Select Committee on Poor Relief 161–2
Select Committee on the Employment of
  Children in Mines and Manufactories 70
Select Committee on the Irremovable
  Poor of 1860 167
Select Vestries 21
Senior, Nassau 15, 16, 22
Shannon, Richard 196, 296
Shaw, Charles 247–8, 251
Six Acts (1820) 9
Six Points on parliamentary reform 58
Slavery Abolition Act of 1833 61
Slavery Abolition Amendment Bill 61
slavery and efforts to abolish 61–63
Slidell, John 162

Sliding Scale 87, 90, 99, 103
Smith, Edward 174
Smith, J. B. 80, 83, 85
socialism, rise of 6, 272–4
social reform 65–73
Somerville, Alexander 14, 72, 73, 106
Spa Field Riots 9
Staffordshire County by-election disorders 37–38
stamp duties 63
Stamp Duties and Excise Bill 63
Stanhope, Philip 247
Steele, E. D. 176
Storey, Samuel 243
Strutt, Edward 34
Sturge, Joseph 58, 61–62, 82
suffrage: household 193, 216; manhood 216; universal 58–59, 123, 177–9; women's 202
Sugar Duties Bill 63
sugar import from slave countries 62–63
Sunday closing of public houses 60, 132, 133–4
Sunday Observance 60
Swing Riots of 1830–1, 16
Sykes, Alan 158
Sykes, D. 12

Taylor, Henry 11, 264
Taylor, Miles 52
temperance movement 130
'Ten Hours' Act of 1847 70
Test and Corporation Acts repeal 15
'The Academics' 10
'The Ministry of All the Talents' 129
Thistlethwayte, Laura 253
Thomas, William 55
Thompson, Dorothy 298
Thompson, Poulett 70
Thorne, George 286
Thornely, John as Charles Pelham Villiers' Private Secretary 159–60
Thornely, Thomas 2, 32, 35, 36, 38, 82, 99, 117–18, 142, 160, 297; dealing with Richard Fryer 44; on death of Charles Pelham Villiers' mother 138; and General Election of 1837 42; re-elected to represent Wolverhampton 143, 147; on the repeal of the Corn Laws 84; retirement of 144–5
Throckmorton, Nicholas 32, 39
tommy-shop system 67–68

Tories 9, 43, 195; contesting Wolverhampton South Division 33, 249, 250, 251; and the Corn Laws 79; dislike for 52–53; and Irish Home Rule 231, 237; the Parliamentary Reform Bill 192
Torrens, William 165
Tory Protectionists 104–5, 125–6
Trade Union Act of 1871 202
trade union legislation 201–2
Trainor, Richard 204
Trelawny, John 159, 171
Tremenhere, Seymour 71
Trent affair 162
Trevelyan, Charles 139
Trevelyan, G. M. 88, 121
Triple Alliance of 1882 274
Truck Act 1831 69
truck system 67–68
Tufnell, E. Carlton 71
Tulloch, Alexander 139
Tyrrell, Alex 83
Tyrrell, John 96, 101

Ulster Liberals 232, 252
Ulster Protestants 232
Union Assessment Committee Act of 1862 168
Union Chargeability Act of 1865 168
Union Chargeability Bill 170–2
union fund 169
Union Relief Aid Act of 1862 164
United Kingdom Alliance 130
universal suffrage 58–59, 177

Victoria, Queen 55–56, 81, 83, 129, 158, 195, 279–80; on the Crimean War 139; visit to Wolverhampton 204
Victorian Liberalism 4, 51–3
Villiers, Augustus Algernon (brother) 8, 97
Villiers, Charles Pelham: absence from Wolverhampton after 1874 205–6; accused of being a Tory 33–35; accused of involving tommy-shop 67–68; acting as Assistant Commissioner for the Poor Law Inquiry 15–23; and the American Civil War crisis 162–3; Anti-Corn League role 1, 4; asked to sit for South Lancashire 118–20; associated with Benthamite school of philosophic radicals 11, 52–55; attempt to enter Parliament in 1826 11–12; attending social and

political events in London 206–9; awarded pension for political office 198–9; as a brilliant conversationalist 268–9; British foreign policy 274–5; campaign by Andrew Carnegie and Thomas Graham to replace Villiers as Wolverhampton representative 244–51; Catherine Mellish and friendship with 13–14, 209–10; chairman of the Select Committee of the House of Commons on Public Houses 130–5; chairman of the Select Committee on Conventual and Monastic Institutions 6, 199–200; childhood and youth of 8–10; civil and religious liberty 59–61, 124; considered as Governor of Bombay 117–18; contribution to radical causes 71–73; Corn Laws repeal 2, 3, 4, 5, 19, 43, 73, 79–108, 115–17, 125–8; Corn Laws repeal 50th anniversary 276–8; Crimean War army investigation 135–41; critical of Gladstone's Ministry 201–2; critical of trade union legislation 201–2; death of 281; death of brother (George) 199; death of mother 138; death of Richard Cobden 166; deaths of family members 182; declining post of American Ambassador 142; declining post of Secretary of State for Ireland 142; defending Poor Law Commissioners 66; defending the Free-Traders 126–9; on depression in agriculture 272–3; early political convictions 23–24; education of 10–11; establishing Select Committee on Poor Relief 161–2; eulogies for 212–14; as Examiner of Witnesses 14–15; as 'Father of the House of Commons' 263, 299; final speech on parliamentary reform 216; and Florence Nightingale to improve the sick poor 172–6; on free trade 3, 4, 5, 6, 40–41, 43, 52, 277–8, 280; Free Trade Resolutions 126–8; *Free Trade Speeches* 2; friendship with Benjamin Disraeli 124–5; friendship with John Bright 119, 121, 208–9; and General Election of 1837 42–43; during his old age 263–87; Home Rule for Ireland opposition 1, 2, 6, 231–54; illustrations of 155–7; Irremovable Poor Bill of 1861 167–8, 170; as Judge-Advocate-General 5, 129; knowledge of and sympathy for Ireland 230; and the Lancashire 'Cotton Famine' 2, 5, 163–5; law reform 41; Laws of Settlement and recommending its repeal 22; as a Liberal 5–6; as a Liberal Unionist 1, 6; Metropolitan Poor Law Act of 1867 172; Metropolitan Poor Law Bill 174–6; municipal reform 41–42; negative opinion of Andrew Carnegie 244–5; neglected by historians 1–3; New Poor Law support 65–66, 167; offered the honour of CB [Companion of the Most Honourable Order of the Bath], 166–7, 214–15; offered Vice-Presidentship of the Board of Trade 116; offers of Governorships 118; opinion on foreign affairs and war 145–6; opinion on modern-day House of Commons 270–1; opposed to exploitation of workers 67–73; parliamentary career: outset 56–73; overview 1; review 294–300; parliamentary reform 5, 57–59, 176–81; Parliamentary Reform Bill 192–4; paternalism of 297–8; paying tribute to Richard Cobden 191–2; *Political Memoir* 2; politics as chief topic of conversation 269–71; Poor Law Board profile 160–1; and Poor Law Reforms 1, 3; post office reform 63–64; as President of the Cambridge Union Society 10; as President of the Poor Law Board 1, 5, 158–82; press and manipulating it 171–2; public accolades 211–15; and the Public Works (Manufacturing Districts) Bill 165, 166; as a Radical Reformer 2, 23; re-elected in 1857 143; re-elected in 1868 194–5; re-elected in 1874 203–4; re-elected in 1885 216–17; re-elected in 1892 251; re-elected in 1895 269; rejected as Secretary of State for the Colonies 142; rejecting a Peerage 214–15; on the Select Committee on the Irremovable Poor of 1860 167; socialism and its rise 272–4; social reform 65–73; speech after winning parliamentrary borough of Wolverhampton 39–42; statue erected in his honor 211–12; supporting the disestablishment of the Irish Church 194; supporting elimination of slavery 61–62; supporting parliamentary

reform 123; supporting local government reform 59; supporting Palmerston's record in government 143; supporting secret ballot 57–58, 123, 201; supporting suffrage 123, 177–9, 202, 216; supporting union between Great Britain and Ireland 231; sympathetic to the working classes 297; and 'The Academics' 10; Thomas Thornely and relationship with 42–46; tributes after his death 281–5; Union Chargeability Act of 1865 168; Union Chargeability Bill 170–2; welcoming accession of Queen Victoria 55–56; William Gladstone and relationship with 5, 195–7, 229–30, 253–4, 278–9; and Wolverhampton constituency 1, 2, 3, 4, 6, 31–46, 118–20, 204–5, 210–11; as a young Parliamentarian 51–73
Villiers, Edith (great-niece) 264, 269
Villiers, Edward Ernest (brother) 8, 97–98
Villiers, Ernest (nephew) 286
Villiers, George (father) 8
Villiers, George (great-nephew) 299
Villiers, George William Frederick (brother) 3, 8, 14, 36, 53, 55, 57, 63, 136, 195, 230. *See also* Clarendon, Lord
Villiers, Henry (nephew) 286
Villiers, Henry Montagu (brother) 8, 36, 182
Villiers, Hyde 8, 11, 13, 15, 16, 22
Villiers, Maria Theresa (sister) 8, 9, 172, 182
Villiers, Theresa (mother) 8, 9, 13, 138
Villiers, Thomas (uncle) 8
Villiers Reform Club 211, 229

Wakley, Thomas 55
Waldergrave, Countess Frances 203, 207, 264
Walker, William 100
Walsh, Maria 263, 286, 287
Weguelin, Thomas 179–80, 194, 201, 203, 297
Weinstein, Benjamin 13
'Westminster Bubble' 207
Whigs 15, 51–52, 54, 56–57, 79, 83, 85, 103, 117, 122
'Whitewashing Board' 140

Whitmore, William 32
Wilhelm II, Kaiser of Germany 274
Willenhall Exhibition of Fine Art, Models and Manufacturers 146
William IV, King 54
Williams, Walter 203
Wilmot, Eardley 61
Wilson, George 80, 83, 97, 103, 118, 119, 192
Wilson, James 91
Wolverhampton 31; campaign by Andrew Carnegie and Thomas Graham to replace Villiers as representative 244–51; constituency 1, 2, 3, 4, 6; divided into three parliamentary constituencies 216–17; Liberalism in 242–7; Liberals in 179–80; 'Moderates' in 32; Parliamentary Borough of 31–32; Radicals in 32; receiving Charter of Incorporation 59; represented by Charles Pelham Villiers 1, 2, 3, 4, 6, 31–46, 118–20, 204–5, 210–11; Tories contesting South Division 33, 249, 250, 251
Wolverhampton Chronicle 38, 39, 44–45, 284–85
Wolverhampton Liberal Association 210
Wolverhampton Liberal Club 211
Wolverhampton Liberals 5, 46
Wolverhampton Political Union 44
Wolverhampton Races 205
Wolverhampton Reform Association 201
Wolverhampton Trades Council 180
women, employment of 69–71
Women's Disability Bills 202
Women's Social and Political Union 202
women's suffrage 202
Women's Suffrage Bill of 1889 202
Wood, Peter 160
Woottton Bassett 15
workhouses 17, 18, 21, 22–23; improving their infirmaries 172–6
working class: exploitation of 67–73; linked with drunkenness and crime 130–4; support of the repeal of the Corn Laws 85
Working Men's Liberal Association 180
Working Men's Reform Committee 180